SUBTLE MOMENTS

SUBTLE MOMENTS

Scenes on a Life's Journey

BRUCE GRANT

MONASH University
Publishing

Monash University Publishing
Matheson Library and Information Services Building
40 Exhibition Walk
Monash University
Clayton, Victoria 3800, Australia
www.publishing.monash.edu

Monash University Publishing brings to the world publications which advance the best traditions of humane and enlightened thought.

Monash University Publishing titles pass through a rigorous process of independent peer review.

www.publishing.monash.edu/books/sm-9781925495355.html

Series: Biography

Design: Les Thomas

Cover image: *The Bulletin*, 1980.

National Library of Australia Cataloguing-in-Publication entry:

Creator:	Grant, Bruce, 1925- author.
Title:	Subtle moments : scenes on a life's journey / Bruce Grant.
ISBN:	9781925495355 (paperback)
Subjects:	Grant, Bruce, 1925-
	Foreign correspondents--Australia--Biography.
	Journalists--Australia--Biography.
	Diplomats--Australia--Biography.
	Authors--Australia--Biography.
Dewey Number:	070.433092

Printed in Australia by Griffin Press an Accredited ISO AS/NZS 14001:2004 Environmental Management System printer.

The paper this book is printed on is certified against the Forest Stewardship Council ® Standards. Griffin Press holds FSC chain of custody certification SGS-COC-005088. FSC promotes environmentally responsible, socially beneficial and economically viable management of the world's forests.

At that subtle moment when man glances backward over his life, Sisyphus returning to his rock, in that slight pivoting, he contemplates that series of unrelated actions which become his fate, created by him, combined under his memory's eye and soon sealed by his death. Thus, convinced of the wholly human origin of all that is human, a blind man eager to see, who knows that the night has no end, he is still on the go. The rock is still rolling.

Albert Camus, *The Myth of Sisyphus*

CONTENTS

BRUCE GRANT *Louis Kahan*

Louis Kahan, *Meanjin Quarterly*, Vol. 27 No. 3 (1968), 260.

INTRODUCTION

A word of explanation about the foreword … As a student at university I had learned of the existentialists on the Seine, including Albert Camus, but I did not read *The Myth of Sisyphus* until later. I did not share his view of the world as absurd and meaningless but I was drawn to his vivid sense of life and his passion that humanity was more important than religion or ideology. Like him, I was not able during the Cold War to justify the cruelty of communist regimes simply because they were on side with an imagined history. As he had sought in Algeria a continuing presence for France, I was always on the lookout in Asia for settlements that would accommodate Australia. I came across the foreword when I was writing these memoirs. It explained a lifetime of trying to get Australians involved in the world as I saw it, and they so often did not, and I decided to use it.

"At that subtle moment when man glances backward over his life …" It is, truly, a subtle moment. At times, even though one tries to be concise and truthful, the reality one is trying to catch remains elusive, a subtle moment in itself. I wanted to avoid the sequential assumption of autobiography and defer to events over which I had no control. I came to realise that there was another subject of these memoirs … Australia … and, as the prime subject aged, distilling his experience, the other subject remained adolescent, on the lookout for whatever might turn up. The reader will need to persist to the end to discover how, or whether, this is resolved.

Undertaking these memoirs has meant discovering the person who took the journey. Writing about yourself is harder than writing about others, real or imaginary. I found I have been neither privileged nor neglected or abused. My life, rather, has been part of an evolving human story from the certainties of what might be called small history, with its national heroes and racial and religious myths, to the uncertainties of big history, with its invitation to contemplate a common humanity and global governance.

The challenge is not the famous blank sheet of paper but how to select from an overflowing basket. I can see a certain shape in my life. I learned as a child to be self-reliant, but not solitary, independent but not rebellious. A tension between individual and group remained. It helps to explain why I never joined a political party, why, although I protected my independence, I also acknowledged a duty as a responsible citizen. I never became part of the counter culture. My social mobility was outward, not upward, and, although in awe at times at the grandeur and brilliance elsewhere, I always assumed that I could accommodate whatever it was that existed in other realms. This became a core of confidence, sometimes helpful, sometimes misleading, in my assessment of what Australia could achieve.

My indebtedness to others is apparent in each of the fourteen scenes in this book and need not be repeated here. One difficulty from having delayed writing these memoirs is that many of the people in them have died, so that I have not been able to check whether my recollection of encounters with them is accurate. I did not regularly keep a journal and my recollection is often dependent on memory, haphazard notes and what I was writing at the time or have written since.

1

A COUNTRY BOY

I am running up a hill, waving in one hand a piece of paper that tells the world I have won a scholarship to Perth Modern School. My excitement would be shared a few minutes later by my mother's parents, who had accepted the task of caring for a country boy, lacking in urban graces, not to mention street smartness. They were too old and set in their ways to teach me new tricks, so they needed a good school that would channel energy and ambition and keep me out of trouble. Perth Modern School was a school for bright children, or at least those good at examinations, and it was also welcome because it solved a problem confronting my parents, like almost everyone in the years of the Great Depression: it was free.

That piece of paper marked the end of my life as a country boy and the beginning of the rest of my life. I had two sisters, one older, one younger, and it was assumed, in the convention of male primogeniture, that I would take over the running of the property as my father aged. But the boy waving that piece of paper never looked back. I was not there when my father's health collapsed and he was forced to abandon the farm. I was out in the wide world, busy with nations and states, government and business, class and power, war and peace. The pleasures of memory now come with twinges of guilt. When I paid a nostalgic visit half a century later, nothing remained of our house, the men's quarters, the buildings and stables that had sheltered machinery and animals. Only the dam, and occasionally, like the Great War battlefields of Belgium, a piece of rusted machinery, marked the spot.

Our community was probably typical of the wheat and sheep country of Western Australia and my upbringing was probably also typical. We were pioneers, soldier settlers, battlers, cockies, whip-stick gimlets (after a local hardwood, with a tight, twisted trunk), worn down by the immensity of our mission, yet resilient and defiant, with high opinions of ourselves. Our names, Treasure, Reid, Medcalf, Cottle, Biglin, Repacholi, Retallack, Mouritz, Lovering, Want, Lucas, de Grucy and de Largie identified us, some from Europe, especially England, most from the city, Perth, or from regional centres, drawn to land in what was called the Eastern Wheatbelt, surveyed by John Septimus Roe in 1848 but not opened up for settlement until the 1920s and 1930s, particularly by soldiers from World War One. Our eastern boundary was the Rabbit Proof Fence; beyond it were miners and pastoralists, sandalwooders and Aborigines. Our towns were Kondinin, Kulin, Karlgarin (mine) and Hyden. We were made memorable later by Albert Facey in *A Fortunate Life*.

Children do not know they are typical. My memory of childhood is that it was astonishing, full of excitement and adventure. I imagined myself as richly resourceful. Walking to school, for example, three kilometres there, three kilometres back, rain or shine, sometimes with my older sister, sometimes with a boy from an adjourning farm, usually alone. No one thought it was too arduous for a small boy, or that I might get lost or kidnapped or bitten by a snake, although I imagined all of these and how I would deal with them.

I divided the journey into stages. On the first stage, the flat land of our property, I shaped the head of a stick I had selected from roadside brush, pushing it through sand and gravel, like the figure-head of a galleon engaging pirates in the Spanish Main or Cook discovering Australia or an engine pulling carriages across the Nullarbor Plain. Or I would toe my way on the railway line, on and off the rails, until the second stage, the red hill, a short, sharp incline of gravel, when my stick became the trusted aide of an explorer, breasting a mountain range in search of pastures beyond. At the third stage, the white hill, a longer slope of shining sand, I leaned on my stick to survey the landscape, so flat and scrubby that it was not evident, until you stood on a mild rise, how flat and scrubby it was. It was wide, as far as one could see, and so spacious that it swallowed people like flies, their existence apparent only from smoke or the dust of a harvester, or a figure on a horse, blurred by heat waves into a centaur. Then, the last stage, the triumphant descent to the one-room, one-teacher school (the stick secreted in a bush for the return journey) my head filled with impressions and ideas, a quandong or two in my schoolbag, its sour red skin to be eaten with the egg or meat and beetroot sandwiches my mother had made for my lunch. Occasionally I was given a ride to school, but rarely. At that time of the morning everyone was busy.

Childhood prepared me for a lifetime of walking and wondering. What was hidden in the landscape as it unfolded? Many years later I read Robert Menzies on imperial nostalgia: "To me the British Empire means (and here you will find a curious jumble in both time and place) a cottage in the wheat lands of the north west of the state of Victoria, with the Bible and Henry Drummond and Jerome K. Jerome and The Scottish Chiefs and Burns on the shelves.

It means the cool, green waters of the Coln as they glide past the church at Fairford, the long sweep of the Wye valley above Tintern with a Wordsworth in my pocket, looking north across the dim Northumbrian moors from the Roman Wall, with the rowan trees on the slope before me, and two thousand years of history behind; old colour and light and soaring stone in York Minster …" I did not share his imperial instincts but agreed with his approach. Walking is the right height and pace to keep one both curious and humble. I still sometimes find myself walking as if the world around me is revealing itself for the first time.

Because people were few, and lost in the distance, they stood out when near at hand. The road that ran past our property brought men looking for work, including a Spanish sailor with curly hair and a ring in one ear, two pale, plump young men who spoke to each other in Hebrew and a Cockney who took off his shoes at the dinner table and cut his toenails. A gnarled and toothless itinerant presented himself mournfully one Christmas, arousing my mother's pity. She inserted several silver coins into his pudding, which he swallowed without (my father's words) them touching the sides. A tall, haunted man who drank only wine (singular in our beer-drinking community) shut himself up, threatening to kill himself with a rifle he had been given to shoot rabbits. He eventually collapsed, whimpering, and was taken away by police (summoned from their base forty kilometres away).

People were valuable; you never knew when you might need their help. We developed friendly caricatures of each other. The Treasures, who were tall and stately, gave themselves airs. The Reids were serious and religious. The Medcalfs (our in-laws, my mother's sister on a visit to us having met and married an eligible neighbour) were well connected, having been educated at private schools, with friends in conservative politics. The Mundays were convinced they were irresistible, the life of the party.

You had to have a strong impression of yourself to journey into a wilderness, living in tents and huts while you cleared the land, then acquiring machinery and animals, planting, harvesting and selling the first crop, building a house. You were Jack-of-all-Trades and, if master of none, valid and substantial as explorer and innovator, farmer and agricultural scientist, stock and business manager. My father's face was etched in anguish on the telephone, deciding whether to sell his harvest or hold out for a better price. There was no Australian Wheat Board in those days.

We ate together, family and workers. The evening meal was a round table of information; not much happened that I did not know about, or so I thought. Before a post office was established in the general store, the telephone exchange was in our house, which kept us in touch with local events and crises. At the table, the workmen were scrubbed up and docile, easing into chairs too small for them, their rough, sun-burned hands grasping at the cutlery, their long vision adjusting as they assessed warily what was on their plates. My mother cooked for everyone on a wood stove, winter and summer, with a water-conducted hessian cooler for storage in the hottest months. She was an elegant woman with a troubled, perhaps discontented, face, until you noticed her warm brown eyes, and she served at table with a distant air, as if she had done her job and that was that.

Karlgarin School opened in 1932 and, aged 7, I was among its first students, twelve of us, increasing to seventeen the next year, and twenty by 1936, when I left. The building was rudimentary, unlined inside, with an unfloored porch and no fly-wire on the windows and door. There were no teaching aides and no sports equipment. Many of us walked long distances to school. Some rode horses or bicycles or arrived in what we called "sulkies", which were light, two-wheeled carriages for no more than two people, or "buggies", which were bigger and clumsier. Our school was run by young women on their first posting. They were devoted to us, a motley of dullards, bright sparks and smart alecks, but their resources were limited. The school's first teacher was Marion Wilson, who passed on to me her brothers' *Gems* and *Magnets*, from which I learned of the upper-class ways of boys in the great schools of England. How these young women taught us, all shapes and sizes in one room, stretched education theory to its limits, but I remember the experience with pleasure.

Miss Doris Ford, who was our teacher in 1935, recalls us in affectionate detail. She sent this recollection to the committee organising the school's 50th birthday celebration in 1982. "I can visualise the pupils I taught and can see them in their seats now. In the back row there was Don Read, who was much taller than I, supervised the playground activities, took the 'drill' lesson and generally was the school prefect. I have been told he became a teaching brother at a Catholic school. I know he went to Albany High School as, in my second year there, the Inspector granted him a scholarship. I felt very thrilled, as you can guess. Then there was Bruce Grant, quite a clever lad, very good at writing compositions. I have read some of his works, written in countries overseas. Very interesting articles, too. Also in the back was Mick Aggiss, a good, quiet worker, who I think would have taken over his father's farm. In the middle seat – long forms they were and no back rests in those days – was John Treasure, not as robust as he should be. I remember him as being tallish and thin, who had to drive the younger members of his family to school in a buggy. It was his job always to tie up the horse and feed it, which sometimes made him late. I remember when the Inspector came to the school in 1936, John got all his sums correct. This was such a triumph for John that the Inspector made a note of it in his Report. Then there was Daphne Bell, David Treasure and Harry Want, all in Grade 4, as it would be now. They were good workers, with average ability. Daphne had quite a good singing voice, I remember. In the front row was young Stan Cottle, Ada Pinnington, Gloria Kirkham, Johnny Ball and the Treasure twins, Marjorie and Robin, a boy. Being a one-room school, the four little ones were squashed in one corner – Billie Aggiss, Alfie Bell, ? Linto and ? Jones. I cannot remember the Christian names of the little fellows but I do know what excellent workers those young ones were. Then there was Bill Read, Don's brother, who was doing correspondence work, because of his age. Bill sat at the end of my table. I heard a few years ago that Bill had been one of those killed in the war."

When I wasn't at school, I worked on the farm. I caught bundles of hay as they were pitch-forked from the ground to the wagon and then again, later, as they were pitch- forked from the wagon to the stack. I carried the wool from the sheep's back as it was shorn by men in singlets and shorts and spread it for sorting by my father. I had for spectacle the savagery of an Australian bushfire, with the searing smell of burning eucalypt and the flying terror of parrots. I killed a sheep once. I remember its warm, trusting eyes as I slit its throat. I saw the quick mouse defeat the plunging eagle, while the lamb was carried off. I helped to trap foxes and dingoes. I watched a calf being born. I learned how to squeeze the teats of cows' udders so that the milk squirted rhythmically into a foaming pail. I sewed up the top of wheat bags after they had been dumped and pummelled into shape by stronger arms than mine. I gathered eggs and fed horses in stalls smelling of hay and urine. I carried morning and afternoon tea across paddocks harrowed for seeding, the uneven surface causing the hot pail to swing against my leg, sometimes spilling and scalding. I remember the drama of my arrival, as my mere presence was a signal to stop work, the languor of 'smoko', men in sweat-stained shirts and hats in lazy conversation, chipped enamel mugs, crunchy biscuits my mother had just baked.

Rain-watching. I copied the ritual from my father, legs apart, hands on hips, head cocked, eyes narrowed to pierce the pale blue orb of sky for a figment of hope, the shrug, the turning away, the bracing of shoulders to show that life went on. The rain never came when we watched for it. It came in the dead of night, a patter of drops on the tin roof that became a drum roll, by which time my father was in command mode, handing out shovels to channel coursing streams into our dam. Water management was a serious business in our district. Our annual rainfall was between 250 mm and 375 mm; every drop of water was precious. My mother, recalling the bountiful backyard vines of suburban Perth, tried to grow grapes near our house, but hard soil and water shortage defeated her.

The first story I wrote was called "Inheritance" and it began: "If you squinted and strained your eyes you could just make out the shelter patch, half a mile away, in a shimmering haze of heat. The Boy could see it, and his father too, for they were used to this kind of day. This kind of day!" The story ends with the thinly disguised author returning to the land with his wife, Mary. "'It's very dry – it doesn't rain here very much,' said Mary, as the dust billowed about her skirts, and the Boy started and frowned and said 'No'. And up in the sweltering sky King Hawk of the Inland circled and watched them come." I wrote later in the *New Yorker*: "I have never yet, in spite of some years spent among spring's European wonders, been able to appreciate the ecstasy of vernal poetry. Spring was not the season to which we looked forward. It meant that summer, with its heart-breaking heat, was not far behind. I loved best April, the month of my birthday … The earth lost its dust and the plough began turning the soil over, wet and shining in the sun, then still high."

Country life is believed to make you conservative and we probably were. Being dependant on things over which we had no control – the climate, of course, but also the price of wheat and wool and the exactitude of bank mortgages – made us fatalistic, but we were also self-reliant. The savage gods that ruled our lives were impersonal, unlikely to look on us with favour or disfavour: you had to look after yourself. So while we were conservative in that we accepted that much of what happened was outside our control, we were radical in our resilience. We were prepared to stand up for ourselves on local issues, like pressing for the construction of a railway or a road. There was a road board and a railway league, as a delegate for which my father once paid a visit to Perth to meet the Premier, to our great excitement.

We regarded ourselves as civilised, but it is striking how little we were concerned with what is now known as human rights, indeed rights of any kind. Workmen took what was on offer or moved on. If they stayed, becoming part of the community, they would be helped to get a property of their own. We were quick to pass the hat around, but we were not conscious of "rights" in a broader sense. We were not social Darwinists but we had a Darwinian sense of nature; part of the fitness of things was human beings keeping control of rabbits, foxes, dingoes and snakes. The domestic animals were different. They served us and relied on us to feed and protect them. Before he bowed reluctantly to progress by getting a tractor, my father lavished on his teams of horses more affection, we sometimes thought, than on his family.

I never saw any Aborigines. There were reputed to be "hand paintings" in caves in our miniature Uluru, known as The Humps, where we went for picnics, and at Wave Rock, later a tourist attraction, but we didn't bother to investigate. Aborigines were not on our radar. Their life style of periodically moving in the past must have brought them to the district in good rainfall years, when the rock pools were full and game and plant food were available, but there was no record of their presence and no folklore about them. Indeed, officially they were erased from the history of our region. In Roe's survey, Karlgarin was originally Carlgarin, derived from Aboriginal "carl" (meaning fire), "gar" (hill) and "in" (used at the end of a word meaning "little fella water"). Kondinin was "Condinin" and Kulin was "Coolin".

My awareness of the wider world was sharpened by imperialist culture, like the Great War and Country-Week Cricket, an event in Perth in January with which we timed our annual holiday at the seaside. My father, an elegant, left-hand batsman, was for a while captain of our local team, so we attended punctiliously, although my mother was reluctant to spend more time than was necessary with the people with whom she had already spent the year. My experience of the cricket tournament and our holiday at the sea was overwhelmed by the discovery that we were different from city people. We had a confidence that came from ownership of property, including food, animals, machines, cars and trucks, but our social skills were rudimentary. We were rugged and open-faced, socially boisterous but essentially modest; city people were private and appraising, withdrawn and shrewd. We were honest, ungainly folk; they were individuals, stylish and self-possessed. We dressed for the occasion; they, fat or thin, dressed in a manner tailored for personal effect. The great Australian sun had treated us differently. We were like pinto ponies, brown faces, white foreheads, brown fore-arms, white bodies, brown legs, white feet, while they were lightly tanned or pale all over, their skin shading imperceptibly from hatless head though filmy blouse or Hawaiian shirt to tinted finger tips, through fitted shorts to pink toes peeping from pastel sandals. I have a particularly sharp childhood memory of toes; the big toe on my left foot was almost perpetually stubbed on city asphalt, the tip hanging by a thread like a spider's trap door.

We spent Christmas with my mother's family in Perth. It was a large family with a strong sense of itself. Her father's job in a printing firm was modest and they lived in a modest suburb, but they were imbued with ambition and buoyed by prospects, supported by a high moral code. As was often the case in egalitarian Australia, a genealogical mystery was allowed to simmer, supporting the family's self-regard. My mother's grandfather, although illegitimate, had received an education before seeking his fortune in Australia, meaning that a mysterious patron had looked after him. According to family lore, a coach (with a crest on its door) had delivered him to the docks the day his ship sailed.

My father regarded all this as romantic folly, his blue eyes sparkling. I don't think my mother took it seriously. The imperatives of her family life were moral rather than social. Her father was a stalwart of the local Baptist church. Her mother was the child of two remarkable lay preachers, who, in my childhood memory, travelled the country as a kind of performing duet. I never discovered what my mother's parents or grandparents, or herself for that matter, thought or believed, doctrine being too abstract to bother her, but one thing was clear to us all: regular church attendance was as vital as paying your bills and cleaning your teeth. To that staple of civilisation, even my father bowed. His rebellious spirit emerged in his war stories, which were so anti-British that I was confused as a child about who Australia was actually fighting at Gallipoli. Poor leadership and strategic errors were faults of the British; humour, camaraderie and bravery were shared with the Turks.

I do not know how my parents voted; probably, like almost everyone else in our district, for the Country Party, progenitor of today's Nationals. My father was a Justice of the Peace and active in local affairs. I got from him a rudimentary understanding of the character of those involved, but not of the issues. "He's a good man, on the side of the people" or "He's only interested in number one" was about the level of analysis.

A visit by the Governor-General Sir Isaac Isaacs created a stir in our district. I went with the rest of our school to a regional centre, where, while waiting for His Excellency, we sang "There is a land where summer skies ... Australia! Australia!" I expected the news that he had actually spoken to me (even if, also, to every second or third child down the line) would be greeted at home with interest, but I discovered that the appointment of our first Australian and first Jewish Governor-General was not regarded with favour in our household. My father, who was a Mason, had unspecified reservations about both "Romans" and "persons of the Jewish persuasion", held, however, with such nonchalance that it was hard to know how serious he was. "Did he speak to you in English?" he asked me, with a twist of his lips. He approved of the Labor government in Canberra appointing an Australian rather than another "chinless wonder" from England, in contrast with my mother, whose reaction was a mild form of Anglomania. "I'm sure, dear, that he's a nice man and highly qualified, but we need someone from England who actually knows the King."

We were once visited by a member of the English aristocracy, whose precise status I cannot recall, who was entertained in traditional country style by local wives, including my mother. Lamingtons. Cream puffs. Custard tarts. Sponges with icing sprinkled with hundreds-and-thousands. Trifle, spiked with alcohol. The visitor returned the hospitality with tea and cucumber sandwiches (according to gossip, some sandwiches contained nasturtium leaves). Our ladies were surprised, then indignant. My mother gave a light laugh for weeks whenever the occasion was mentioned, but she was thoughtful. Was hearty country hospitality the start of a social slippery slope?

Culturally, we were a lost tribe. My idea of bliss as a child was lying on my bed with a book to read and a bowl of apples under the bed, but my reading was limited. I recall old, tattered copies of *The Illustrated London News*. The books in our house were the classics and popular novels of England and America, including those of Upton Sinclair and Georgette Heyer. My favourite books were *Treasure Island* and *The Thirty-Nine Steps*. Of Australian writers, I recall Mary Grant Bruce, Ethel Turner and Ion Idriess. We listened on the wireless to American jazz, big bands and crooners.

Occasionally, we flocked to the local hall for a screening of silent films, including the Steele Rudd stories *On Our Selection*, featuring Dad and Dave, Mum and Mabel in an unlikely (we thought) version of outback life in a location called Snake Gully. Most of the films we saw were American, usually westerns. While the impression of Britain I gained from its films was that it was introverted and, for all its pomp and circumstance, unsociable, America seemed to be action and fun. Later, when I was a film critic for a daily newspaper, I learned to be more analytical about American films and even to join the chorus of concern about Hollywood values, but I never lost my enthusiasm for fun and action.

Another symbol of America was what its creator, the Ford motor company, called a pick-up and we called a utility. It was shiny brown, or perhaps beige, with a powerful V8 engine, thick tyres, and a low-slung look that was new to us. Our cars and trucks at that time were upright, with running boards on both sides. This new, sleek vehicle was so low you could step out directly onto the ground. For a small boy, this was itself a challenge. Then there was the dashboard, with a speedometer like a clock, and glass windows that wound up securely, rather than curtains of cracked, yellow cellophane that flapped in the wind. But what I liked most of all was the space behind the seat, where I could lie and, on long journeys, sleep. The seat was wide enough to take my father, mother and older sister, as well as my younger sister on my mother's lap. I had the reputation of being able to sleep anywhere, so I was given this new space at the back of the seat. I snuggled down behind my parents' heads, which acted as a buffer when my father braked. If I turned on my other side I could look through the rear window at the stars. It was, more or less, heaven.

I was a pleasing soprano before my voice broke and sang at school concerts two songs of contrasting sentiment. The first, with Miss Daphne Bell:

Dressed in your gown of blue brocade,
A rose upon each dainty shoe,
Lady in loveliness arrayed,
I'd love to dance with you.
Soft, shining hair and gentle face
Sweet, smiling eyes of tender blue,
Lady of gentleness and grace
My heart's aflame for you.

Or (in a false Peter Dawson baritone), with corks dangling from one of my father's hats:

Comrades of mine, when my day is done,
When the last sun sets for me,
Bear me forth in an old bush cart
Till you come to a tall gum tree.
And lay me deep in its leafy shade
Where the great roots twist and twine
And leave me there for my long last sleep
Comrades, comrades of mine!

We were experts at postponing pleasure. All the advertised refinements of civilisation were in the cities, or at least in regional centres. We had voluntarily renounced them and found our own compensations, in which we all took part. One of these was The Dance.

Families came from far and wide. The local hall was decked out with streamers and the floorboards were waxed by boys and girls riding on wheat bags filled with wool, rope-hauled by young men over a dance floor strewn with candle scrapings. In an ante-room, women arranged supper. After making their presentation, each stayed to see what others had brought, so the small room was crowded. In a corner, men stood around another table at which, wreathed in tobacco smoke and tense with excitement, were the poker players; some would be there all evening. Outside, in dimly lit cars, behind bushes and glowing cigarettes, beer, not allowed in the hall, was consumed. The dance band was a pianist, a drummer and a saxophonist. The first dance, probably the Gay Gordons, possibly the Pride of Erin, was a haphazard affair, with children taking part. It was the Last Dance, a waltz to be performed only by nearest and dearest, that everyone watched, checking who was with whom. Even the poker players stumbled out to do their duty.

Children were taken on evening social visits. We had several men working on the property but no house staff; babysitting was virtually unknown because of difficulties of distance and transport. After the Ford arrived, I clamoured to be taken everywhere. I was so pleased with our new vehicle that I asked my parents why it was different from the other cars and trucks in our district. "It's from America," they said solemnly, one after the other. So my first impression of the United States of America was that it was the source of what was new and stylish. Years later, during the Cold War, when I wondered at the difference between military tanks in the United States and the Soviet Union, I remembered our Ford utility. When the Russians wanted a new tank, they simply upgraded the old one. The Americans went back to the drawing board and designed a new one, like they designed a new car. What is new and stylish is not always tasteful, of course. Revisit the 1950s (or go to Havana) and you get a glimpse of what newness without taste can look like when it becomes old, with cars that now look like tanks, or small aircraft carriers. Our Ford, however, followed the dictum that form should follow function and it always looked good.

Why my father left a good job in the city to become a pioneer in wheat and sheep farming on marginal land was a puzzle. He was a city boy from a middle-class family with a job, guaranteed by his wartime service, with Malloch Brothers, vendors of farm machinery. His father was a civil servant, with no farming background. His mother's family was comfortably off. Her sister had married Tom Cadd, founder of a customs and transport company in the port of Fremantle, which I used in the novel *The Budd Family* as a model for a family business. When my father later became ill from the effects of gas used at the Western Front and had to leave the farm, he became a manager at Cadd's.

Something had propelled him out of his comfort zone. He told the story that, returning from the war, leaning over the rail of a troopship in the Indian Ocean, a woman's face appeared on the surface of the water. When he met my mother, he recognised her as the face in the water. Was he carrying her off to a redoubt, as far away as possible from the roots and tendrils of their past lives? My mother had a certain allure. She had been denied marriage with a local boy, Fred Silverwood, Australian manhood's perfect suitor according to family lore, when he was killed in action. She had a manner of withdrawn propriety and hidden sensuality that might have appealed to my father. He was a sexually active man. His war service record contains periods in hospital for treatment of venereal complaints.

My mother might have thought at first that my father's proposal to carve out a farm from the bush hid an endearing, romantic streak. She tried, but never acclimatised. One of my cruellest memories of my father is drawing our attention, blue eyes dancing, to one of my mother's moods, whether of despondency or resistance, I do not recall. They had been arguing about something. "Watch the trembling lower lip" he clinically advised, as we waited for her to burst into tears and leave the room.

Sexuality, which seems to have afflicted so many childhoods, was not memorable in mine. The physicality of farm life was all around us. We saw horses, cows, sheep, pigs and fowls (chooks, we called them) engaged in bursts of noisy, brief, sometimes violent, coupling. Only once did I become aware of my parents having a sexual life different from the creative enterprise around me. I was sharing a hotel room with them. I awoke to a rustling of bedclothes from their direction and heard my father say something, in a peevish tone. After more rustling, my mother, in a consoling voice, with a girlish lilt she never lost, "There, that's it, isn't it?" I went back to sleep with the comfortable feeling that my parents were pleased with each other. There was gossip about some private lives in our district, which I heard but did not understand. It was not until I moved to the city that I became interested in the bodies of girls. As a country boy I was aware only of the bodies of men. Girls were soft eyes and light voices.

Perhaps my father, in choosing a farm life, was affected by the legend of Gallipoli, a moment when Australia came to "know itself", in the phrase of official historian, C.E.W. Bean. The stories my father told were of two kinds. One was his middle-class, city-boy amazement at the crude humour and dare-devil antics of his compatriots from the farms and goldfields of Western Australia. Many stories of bravery and bravado have been told about Gallipoli; in my father's telling of them, the heroes (sometimes the villains) were almost always boys from the bush. Gallipoli was for him not so much a military epic as a personal and social revelation. He discovered that the Australia he was fighting for was a more robust, diverse society than he had imagined. The 1981 Australian film *Gallipoli* touched on this issue of national identity. Under its major theme of British strategic blunders and Australian courage and innocence, a minor theme was the testing of "mateship" in the friendship of two young men from contrasting backgrounds.

My father's other kind of story revealed a surprising (for me) affection for "Johnny Turk". As mentioned earlier, I was uncertain at times as to who was the enemy, because he was unflagging in his scorn of the British and unstinting in his respect for the qualities of the men he was fighting. The remarkable physical conditions of Gallipoli provide another clue. After the early assault, the two sides were entrenched side by side, within shouting – and throwing – distance of each other. A camaraderie of shared fear and boredom developed. Compton Mackenzie, who was ecstatic in his appreciation of the Australian soldiers as Homeric heroes at Gallipoli, records a thoughtful moment from his own experience. "I wanted to argue with [the Turk gunners] about the futility of war. It seemed so maddeningly stupid that men should behave as impersonally and unreasonably as nature."

After the gallant intimacy of Gallipoli and the noise and filth of the trenches at the Western Front, my father might have longed for the peaceful solitude of the Australian bush. He was a member of the Returned Sailors and Soldiers Imperial League, as the RSL was then called, but not a fan of its social activity. In memorials to the dead and in commentary on what those who live owe to those who died, much was made of honour, duty and sacrifice, but the depravity of war remained with those who actually took part in it. My father was 19 when he enlisted and his brother Lionel was 19 when he died as a prisoner of war of the Germans. On the brink of human experience, they learned that human bodies were made neither for love nor beauty, but to be mutilated and destroyed. When I was being moved to tears at school by poems of young Englishmen dying in foreign fields that would be forever England, my father might still have been coping with memories of the muck and stench of trench warfare.

Or it might simply have been the age-old fascination of property. His father had tipped him off about the preferential release of farming blocks to ex-servicemen. Like many others, my father took advantage of the status that his survival of the war gave him. A thousand or so acres, while it proved later to be too small for modern farming, might have seemed like a lot of property. He named our farm "Inverurie", capturing in the Australian bush a territorial fragment of his ancestry.

*

These impressions a country boy carried with him when he moved to school in the city, and later to other cities in other countries. He entered life's maelstrom with a grounding in some things, and a vast ignorance in others. The tension at the heart of his story is that, while he spent his life escaping from the small community into which he was born, the more involved he became in the wider world the more he cherished the values of his country boyhood. He never lost respect for the dogged values of survival and remained wary of ideology and utopian solutions. During the Cold War, his sympathies were with those in the Third World who tried to avoid the righteous violence between the Communist and anti-Communist blocs. He was suspicious of high-sounding rhetoric, knowing that nature had its own relentless ways. He accepted religion, but as a personal comfort, not an organising principle. He never joined a political party, never accepted the division between capital and labour that governed politics in his time. The more the world became truly global, the more the Internet, the digital revolution and broadband scattered the hierarchies of class and learning, the more it seemed to him to reflect the truly local community he grew up in.

There was much to admire in the character of the vain and humble people of Karlgarin. They were persistently challenged, both by the daily tasks they set themselves and by outside circumstances over which they had no control. Their response was not imaginative, but it was tough and resilient, two qualities that have served human evolution well.

The Australian outback instilled in them respect for the great elements of sun, rain and wind, and self-respect as well. They were part of humankind's ancient endeavour to produce food from the soil, not just for themselves, but, because Australia was an exporter, for the world. Space and heat, dominating their lives, were connected. The baked earth and lack of rain meant that growth was sparse and low. The hills were worn down. Their eyes were always aware of the sky, high and usually cloudless, and of land stretching to the horizon. How marvellous it was in the afternoon when a cooling breeze sprang up. In Perth, it was called the Fremantle doctor. On our farm it was the Albany doctor, without which my family could not imagine living, or not the way we did. Without it, we would have had to adopt a different style of life, as other people did in hot climates, working early morning and late evening, resting, even sleeping, after lunch. With it, we were able to work what we thought were normal hours and to work hard, as if we inhabited a temperate zone.

We were Australian, not in the sense of having a conscious national identity, nor in the political sense of looking to Canberra rather than Perth, but in the sense of being embedded in Australian land. We were more susceptible to the great, unchangeable facts of the Australian environment than we would have been in a town or a city, which were like the towns and cities of other lands, proclaiming "civilisation". We were not conscious environmentalists. We destroyed trees with abandon to make way for land to farm, but we were sensitive to the land itself, responding to the soil with the encouragement of different seeds and fertilisers. My father set out to be a scientific farmer and won prizes in the district agricultural show. The paddock next to our house was planted with rows of experimental crops (I remember Gluyas Early and Gluyas Late), creating a spring carpet of variegated green strips.

We imitated and copied, but we knew that the land was incorrigibly Australian and we needed to keep our feet on it. This developed a strategic middle vision. On the one hand, we were not captivated by visionary ideas, like ending poverty or inequality, but neither were we seduced by a handful of dollars during election campaigns. A few dollars a week was neither here nor there to a family that lived mainly off its own produce from its own land, had assets of substantial value, was massively in debt and depended for its margin of income on forces beyond its control. This was the beginning of a kind of wisdom about the world.

Being sensitive, or in the local idiom, up yourself, was not a peculiarity of my parents. Their particular form of it was their own, but on every property in our district were men and women, and even children, who thought they were special. My mother, who was uncomfortable in her environment, found a way of ensuring that she survived, which was to be reserved in public, showing herself only to her family. She encouraged me to explore life beyond our patch of earth. "Trust your imagination," she said. She smiled with satisfaction whenever she discovered me reading in bed. My father's real world, although he opened it readily enough to me, was not so inviting.

I had no inkling then of the life I would lead. I might have gone to an agricultural college and become a wool-classer, which was the dream of mothers in our community. My understanding of nation and state, government and business, class and power, war and peace, came slowly out of personal experience, not family lore. I enjoyed stories, and liked to write them, but I was still inclined then to imagine myself as a heroic figure present in the moment, an explorer, a highwayman or a midshipman on a battleship.

One lasting impression.

A feeling that you are part of the stillness of the landscape, disturbed only by waves of heat, has stayed with me. I have felt it in the wine country of South Australia, in Morocco looking out at the desert from the ramparts of the ancient city of Fes, in a roof top restaurant in Cairo over the Nile, walking in the Alhambra garden, in India in a grove of Ashoka trees, at a restaurant in Ubud, at a carpet stall in Kabul, in a coffee shop in Tashkent, outside a mosque in Samarkand, even in suburban Melbourne one hot February day.

Emotionally, the effect is peaceful, even if the heat is palpable. It is not stimulating, like the sea or mountain snow. You do not challenge it, throwing yourself into it. You detach yourself from it, because there is nothing you can do about it; the surprise is that the act of detachment enables you to be part of it.

2

GROWING UP

My mother's parents lived in a rambling house on a double block on a hill in Bayswater, one of the suburbs strung out along the Swan River, as it found its way to the sea. I was already familiar with it, from family visits we made to Perth from the farm at Christmas. The currant grapes were always ripe then and, as a small boy, I used to ride on my grandfather's shoulders, devouring the bunches with eager hands and open mouth as they dangled over a path leading to outhouses of laundry, bathroom and lavatory. The art of eating currant grapes was to pull the stem through your closed teeth, leaving behind a mouthful of the little black fruit. My plaintive cry when my ride ended, "Any more gapes, gandpa?" became family lore.

The area was hilly and two of my mother's sisters had married and lived on hilltops, within waving distance of each other, it was said, and their watchful mother. My mother's younger sister Marion and brother Allen were still living at home, occupying in spirit a halfway house between their parents, me, and a world of busy young professionals – cars, parties and entertainment – into whose modest fringes they invited me. Aunt Marion teased me about girls and took me to movies. Uncle Allen took me to football and taught me algebra, which had been ignored (with geometry and trigonometry) in our one-teacher school.

And there was Tim. Her name was Laurel, but she was always Tim, after crippled Tiny Tim in *A Christmas Carol*. My grandfather was in awe of Charles Dickens. Our Tim had Downs Syndrome and was "Mongol" to the local kids. She was highly sexed and physically adventurous, a winner in street races and hopscotch. She talked incessantly, mostly to herself, with humour and enthusiasm but rarely in a manner you, or at least I, could understand. Her mind was a mystic wonderland to me. It was her body you noticed, a woman's body with a child's head, alert to every sound or movement. She loved food and would look around, after demolishing a plate of cakes or a bowl of cereal, with a beaming smile before giving a whoop of pleasure.

My grandmother once told me, in a rare moment of reflection, that she thought "poor little Tim" was the result of being born during the "Belgian atrocities" committed by the Germans in the First World War. But both grandparents were devoted Christians and, publicly, Tim was the cross they had been given to bear. Everyone needed a cross, or your life meandered from the path that was straight. Tim went everywhere with the family, and I learned to stare down anyone who gawked at a small, excitable girl-woman, interested in everything around her, especially young men. She had fallen in love with her cousin Lloyd Lawson, a radio announcer, and, whenever she went out, especially to the city, she expected to meet him.

Two neighbours were especially welcome at the house on the hill. One was Nurse Greenhalch, a midwife who seemed to have delivered most of the babies in the neighbourhood, including my grandmother's; the other was Mrs Nesbitt (Nessy) who could "see the future". Nessy sometimes came with my grandmother, Tim and me to the city on shopping expeditions. She was short, with jelly-like flesh that actually quivered when she laughed, and we must have looked like a troupe from a travelling circus as we waited for a train at the local station. Nessy had sharp eyes, with a habit of peering at strangers. I asked her what she did if she "saw" something. She said she would warn the persons concerned (not to go swimming that day, for example), although when I tested her understanding of the connection between cause and effect, she admitted she was never confident that what she "saw" was inevitable. My grandmother, however, was convinced that Nessy's gift was not only spiritual but useful and claimed that the family's good fortune was in some measure due to her care in following Nessy's advice. I carried this conviction with me into later life, despite the cynicism of my peers, and was delighted to learn in America of the experiments of Dr J.B. Rhine, of Duke University, who tested students for extra-sensory perception and found that a small but persistent number had a capacity for clairvoyance and precognition.

Every Sunday morning we went to church, where my grandfather occasionally preached. We usually walked, and I remember the half-hour journey as strangely convivial, grandma gossiping about the people in the houses we passed, Tiny Tim circling in a range of acrobatic manoeuvres and grandpa out in front in a light grey doubled-breasted suit and, in summer, a white pith helmet with green lining. My grandparents offered a prayer before each meal, including at the kitchen table before breakfast. One morning my grandfather surprisingly asked me "Would you lead us today?" It was more an order than a question, and while we waited, heads bowed, I struggled to find the words. "Almighty God…" It sounded blasphemous. "Our Father…" I saw my father, swinging an axe. Grandfather took over, reciting the Lord's Prayer, which I knew well enough but was too confused to summon. Later, over hot scones, my grandmother gave me advice: “Don't think about anyone else. It's just you and the Saviour, the two of you.”

My grandmother's affection shows in a letter thirty years later, written from the old address, 23 Copley Street, where she now lived alone.

My dear Bruce,

Many thanks for your wonderful book, which has arrived safely. It gave me great pleasure to receive it. I had always hoped I would be spared to see it in print, and it has been granted. How wonderful God is.

The children are all anxious to read it but I want to read it first, or it may be too late for me. My eyes at times are not too good. I hope it will sell well and be made a help and a blessing and you will be spared to write many more. How pleased Grandpa would have been to have seen you an author, and he would have been very interested. Perhaps he knows all about it.

I had the pleasure of your mother's company. It was nice to see her again. She looks much the same. She is coming again this weekend, when we will all go to church together on Sunday morning.

Of course you have heard of the passing of Tim. He doeth all things well.

The years that I put up with you! I often live them over. What happy years they were. I don't think I have forgotten anything, even you making toast in the dining room by the big fire, Sunday nights' tea and (illegible) frying up vegetables to go with it.

Much love to you all,

Grandma

My grandmother passed gossip on quickly, so the personal trials and triumphs of each year were known to us all. I recall the buzz when Uncle Allen's salary was raised to seven pounds a week and the tremors when an uncle was suspected of tampering with Tim. He had a big, sleek car, the envy of the other uncles, in which, once a week, he took grandma and Tim for a ride. Then he offered to take Tim, alone, for a ride. My grandmother sang his praises, while the other uncles squirmed. Then came the denouement. I still do not know precisely the nature of the evidence, which was whispered at family gatherings, but the big, sleek car stopped coming.

In my grandparents' house I developed a more explicit sense of ethics (as the way you behave when no one is looking) than I had brought with me from a country boyhood. My mother had been brought up according to Copley Street values, although she was not herself religious. She was romantic, and could be swept off her feet by daring and vigour. My father was not at all religious, was indeed agnostic, even probably, if he had bothered to think about it, atheist. He used to explain, in a typically light manner, that I had not been baptised because there was a water shortage that year. Actually, my parents had not bothered. Without a local church and resident clergy (religious services were sporadically conducted by touring preachers in the town hall) the demands of farm life tended to ignore formalities that were not locally organised. Neither of my sisters was baptised.

My father's sensitivities were personal and prickly rather than moral. His father, who had an engineering background but became a public servant, was from Scotland, his partly German mother had social and business connections. Neither was religious but each had a strong sense of what was right and proper, which he followed, although he was permissive as a father. He criticised me harshly only once. Men were playing kick-to-kick after a football match and I was scouting in front of one pack, which included him. Someone in the other pack kicked poorly, the ball tumbled erratically and I managed to gather it. Pleased with myself, I turned and poked out my tongue in the general direction behind me, not at anyone in particular, but he was incensed, maintaining his anger all the way home in the car, finally admonishing me before bedtime with a raised finger. "If you ever do that again, my boy, I'll do more than get angry." I had behaved badly in front of his peers. He never touched me in anger (although once, for some trifling misdemeanour I cannot recall, he chased me around a thousand-gallon water tank, but, when I looked back, he was laughing).

I had run free as a country boy; no one could know for sure where you were and what you were doing in a land without vertical boundaries under a glaring sun and immense sky. I was given plenty to do, but could still roam without supervision, especially at day's end, when the discipline of work collapsed and people became individuals, sliding off to be themselves. Harry Want (my neighbour) and I had a secret meeting place in a grove of trees (known as a "shelter patch"), where we indented mossy ground to resemble what we believed were girls' bodies and into which, with knowing glances at each other as we performed, we inserted ourselves. In the grove of trees, sighing mournfully over our heads, what we did was not so much erotic as a gesture to nature.

At Copley Street, I was introduced to precise tasks with observable outcomes, like sweeping the front verandah, extracting weeds from a side path of red brick and pumping the organ at church. I performed them conscientiously but also began to practice the fine art of ambiguity, turning the childish traits of trust and surprise into thinking for myself. It would have been hard for me to deceive my parents, had I continued to live with them. One of my sisters would tell, if it was something at school, or it would come back to my parents through other parents, informed by their children.

My grandparents were no match for me. Their lives had entered a calm that they did not want disturbed. "Why," I asked, "doesn't the King come out here if he wants to rule the country?" My grandfather explained patiently that only God ruled. I would then dazzle him with some recently acquired knowledge about social conditions in England (about which his beloved Dickens had written), and he would be forced to acknowledge that God and government were what he called "ill-wedded companions". My grandmother doted on me. I began to discover how trust, if unaccountable, can be abused, and how clever young minds can be bored by goodness.

Because of the love and care my grandparents gave me, however, I graduated from their household with respect for people of faith. They were neither narrow nor dogmatic. They observed the passing parade, including a grandson's flirtation with the sins of the flesh, with resignation, even amusement. Their religious beliefs kept their minds, and to some extent mine, on the big questions of life. But as soon as I ate from the tree of knowledge, that is, at some stage in my secondary schooling, I began to think of religion as a hindrance rather than a help in understanding why I was alive at this time and in this place and what I was supposed to do about it. The human spirit rather than the Holy Ghost became my guide. It was all very well to focus on higher things, I decided, but dealing with imponderables should not blind us to the fact that some problems near at hand needed urgent attention. My experience of adolescence was, of course, in the shadow of the Second World War. It was all very well to find evil in human beings, I declared, and the evidence was plentiful, but what about the problems of war and peace, which were created by nations and governments, not by people?

Perth Modern School opened its doors each year to fifty boys and fifty girls who had been successful in state-wide examinations. Whether we were an intellectual elite is an open question. The school produced several political leaders, including Kim Beazley (father and son), Paul Hasluck and Bob Hawke. It did not seem to nurture creative people, like artists and writers. More typical of the school's output was a stream of academics and civil servants.

I moved from the space and good humour of a rural community to a combustible world of intellectual rivalry, competitive sport and girls. I was shielded from confusion and distress by the warmth and kindness of my grandparents and the delightful comfort of an extensive family. When I look at photographs of gatherings at the old house on the hill, with its cypress hedge in front, its side lawn the size of a building block, its backyard of lemon trees and grape vines, I can count between twenty and thirty people. I would not have found it easy to move to a non-family environment in the city, like boarding school. As a child, I was prone to be easily home-sick. I recall a disastrous weekend with a family near our farm, when I had to be rescued on Sunday morning after a tearful night. Moving outside the nuclear family, but not into the vortex of peer group pressures, was like being part of the extended family of other cultures.

I was a good student, adventurous rather than competitive, content to remain in the upper regions of class lists rather than striving for primacy. My schooldays were marked as much by sporting skill as scholarship. I was the first student to become a member in my second year of the senior football team, which otherwise was filled with third, fourth and fifth year boys. I was less effective at cricket, but managed to squeeze into the first XI, having as a bowler developed to my surprise (helped by Perth's summer sea breezes) the ability to swing the ball perceptibly both ways, into the batsman and the stumps and away, into the slip field.

The school did its best to compete with the *esprit de corps* of the private schools. We had a fagging system, which allocated you on arrival to a senior student for whom you were expected to run errands and tidy up lockers and sports gear. We had our own cadet corps and a few went on to become professional soldiers. In *The Sphinx*, the school magazine written and managed by senior students and produced twice a year, was a page devoted to film titles: "Two Bright Boys – Trev and Bruce" referred to Trevor Gibson and myself. Trevor became school captain and later a professional soldier.

Boys and girls were separated, inhabiting different parts of the main building and attending different classes. We speculated about the love life of our teachers, and began to experiment with our own. In *The Sphinx* much was made of supposed romance. In one issue, Gloria Swain, an attractive young woman who I thought was irrevocably committed to Dick Lee, then school captain, was reported to have "someone in the B.A.G." (my initials), based on two social visits I had made to the Swain household. In another issue, prefect Ian Ingle was said to be a love-sick Swain and I was linked with "Tootie", described as a demure resident of the harbour city Fremantle, with a pet song "The Boys in Navy Blue" and a pet expression "I'm all for it." For the record, I still correspond with "Tootie", who married a Fremantle footballer.

I wrote love poetry. The following example survived, scribbled on tattered paper. I cannot recall for whom it might have been written, but it captures the love-sick author well enough, as well as, perhaps, the rebel in a Christian household.

I love you more than God does.
Would he, all-loving, want a heart
Bruised, to warm and wet his own?
Would he, omniscient, want a mind
So bright with fear to flash against his own
Would he, beyond flesh, want lips to make
Him dream of summer, or biting winter warmth
Or the hot body.
Would he forgive another God, with powers as his,
Who loved you once
Would he, now and everlasting,
Love you just for a lifetime
Could he, the big, lonely one, the judge
Come down and struggle with the accused.
What is this love of God's next to mine
Would he lay down his own life
Not his son's.

My emotional memory of "Mod", as we called it, is however of male intellectual rivalry and camaraderie. The jockstrap, not the bra, was our signature emblem. Girls were admired or rejected for qualities that with time have lost their salience – and to be vocally supported when they were representing the school in competition with other schools. They were not as important in the challenges of life as ourselves. The great world turned only in response to our fears and desires. What were our prospects? Would we follow our fathers or try something different? Were we (was I) capable of becoming this kind of important person or that kind of important person? In my second year, the war began. We shared thoughts and feelings about courage and skill on the playing field and bravery in the war that was looming over us.

Perth Modern School was socially mixed. Well-off families sometimes preferred it to private schools because, as a scholarship school, it had an academic reputation. It seemed to be a school of the future, representing intelligence and opportunity against privilege and inheritance. The school motto was not in Latin, popular with the founders of private schools, but in French: *Savoir c'est Pouvoir,* which, with the flair of hopeful youth, we translated as "Knowledge is Power". Like state schools and unlike private schools, we were not attached to a particular religious denomination. There was something called "Religious Instruction" but it must have been voluntary, as I cannot recall attending it. This may have been why Moral Re-Armament (MRA) made an impression.

An offshoot of the Oxford Group, founded by Dr Frank Buchman, it swept through the school like a new fashion or a catchy tune. The demand for absolute love, purity, honesty and unselfishness had an adolescent appeal, presented in Peter Howard's *Ideas Have Legs*, a racy account of the conversion of a Fleet Street journalist into a campaigner against Materialism (and its offspring Fascism and Communism). Enticing word-of-mouth marketing raised the level of excitement; word got around that MRA was interested in "leaders", on the sensible assumption that followers would follow. To be invited to one of their weekend house parties was, like the Calvinists to whom wealth was a visible sign of having been chosen (Dr Buchman was a Lutheran pastor), a sign that you were leadership potential.

Two student leaders, Jim Coulter and Gordon Wise, joined MRA and became active in it later. Leaders were assumed to be male, and the movement had a masculine bias.

The house parties gathered a reputation, because of "sharing". You were paired with another potential leader in a mutual confessional, during which you told each other the bad things you had done. A tennis coach at Perth Modern, a family man known to take boys to bed, was mentioned in the gossip that circulated among those boys who had attended house parties. It was exciting and mysterious, as were MRA's financial circumstances. Where did the money (for house parties in posh Mount Street) come from? The movement's official representative was said to live by the welfare of providence. One morning, the story went, he was sitting with his pencil and notebook, waiting for "guidance" and wondering how financially he would get through the day, when he felt impelled to go out into the street and stand on a corner. Within seconds, a man approached and gave him a substantial sum of money.

I attended a house party and marvelled at the testimonials of people who had stolen from the corner store, masturbated, contemplated sex with animals, fudged the reading of a microscope or wondered if Dr Buchman was a phoney. But I seemed to have been inoculated by some other kind of providential guidance against MRA's appeal. My sense of the workaday world was even then too complex to submit to absolute moralities. Ethical behaviour was one thing, and self-reliance another, but the idea that individuals could be "absolute" anything, in defiance of the angry gods of war, climate and the commodities market, was too fanciful for me to take seriously. In any case, after sweeping through the school in the years just before the war, MRA succumbed to the drama of real war, leaving behind a trail of unverified confessions, uneasy consciences and broken hearts.

My career as rising star of school and suburb came to an abrupt end. I look back on the following incident with a sense of wonder. I was sixteen. He was an experienced educator who had been given one of the most important appointments in the state school system. His sedate, head-masterly letter, written four years after the event (at my request, as I needed a reference to explain a gap in my education) glides over the hidden drama.

Perth Modern School,

Subiaco, W.A. 18th December 1945

Having won his place in the State-wide competitive examination, Bruce Alexander Grant entered this School in Feb., 1938; did well in the Junior Examination in Nov., 1940; and left in December, 1941, after completing four years of the course.

Capable as a student, he was successful throughout his time here, and showed above-average literary ability. A leader in sport, he was a mainstay of the 1st football XVIII and of the 1st XI; and was vice-captain of his faction. Well-mannered, and of good address, he is self-reliant, alert, competent, trustworthy and of above-average promise.

Noel E. Sampson

Head Master

The circumstances surrounding my departure a year short of the normal five-year span were a mix of economic hard times and my impulse to discover the world. I did not know the details of the financial arrangements, if any, between my parents and my grandparents, but, even without school fees, there was a cost in keeping a teenager at school, and travelling back and forth during holidays to the farm. When a wheat silo was established at our railway station, an opportunity came to earn money during the summer as a weighbridge clerk. I applied and got the job. However, I had also been chosen to be a school prefect in my final year. The headmaster we had known and liked, Joseph Parsons, had retired and his replacement was Noel Sampson, who had a sharp sense of his own authority and was a stickler for rules and regulations. He decided that next year's prefects should stay back to assist staff in cleaning up the school at the end of the year. It had not happened before; the gossip was that "Sammy" wanted to show he was in charge. I asked to be excused; I would be weighing trucks in and out of the wheat silo at that time. The word came back that Mr Sampson was adamant. I wrote him a letter in which I explained that I needed the money to help my parents pay for living in the city with my grandparents.

He called me before him. I had had two conversations with Mr Parsons, which had been conducted by him as if he were indebted to me for the pleasure of my company. The new Head looked up from the papers on his desk as if my arrival in his office was an intrusion for which I would not be forgiven. He said (leaving me standing) that I would have to choose between the weighbridge job and serving one of the state's great educational institutions (or words to that effect). Rules and regulations were not established for fun and had to be obeyed, or people might get the idea that they were only there for decoration. Moreover, it was not entirely improbable (or words to that effect), that I could be school captain the following year. This unfortunate prospect, which appeared to be beyond his control and for which he showed no enthusiasm, was presented as if, in the face of such irresistible logic and enticement, my answer was inevitable. His face was a mask of disciplined authority, providing no chink of light that might be misinterpreted as the end of the tunnel. I responded uneasily, clinging to the impregnable pillar of middle-class morality that my family needed the money. He did not answer and the silence between us became unbearable. I was bold enough to suggest that filial devotion was a worthy attribute. He remained silent. I asked whether it might be possible for him to discover a "helpful way out" in this particular case (I was careful not to suggest that he might "bend the rules"), as the arrangement with the wheat silo had been made in ignorance of the new rules for prefects. Mr Sampson shook his head and stood up, ending the interview. I left his room with the matter unresolved.

It surprises me still that he did not take the opportunity to tell my parents what was happening. I knew that if I sought advice from parents or grandparents, they would tell me to accept his terms and drop the weighbridge job. But I had become accustomed to making decisions of my own, not as important as the one I was now facing, but enough to give me confidence that I understood myself and even, perhaps, how the world worked or should work, if I were to find a place for myself in it.

When I needed time to think, I liked to sit among the reeds on the banks of the Swan River and search on its restless surface for answers to life's mysteries. All I could see now on the still waters of the Swan was Mr Sampson's mask of a face. I decided that I did not wish to be a prefect in his kind of school, let alone its captain. Extending my thoughts, I discovered that I did not wish to be in any kind of school. I was ready to explore the fascinating world outside the classroom. I had been writing snippets for a Perth afternoon newspaper, the *Daily*

News, which had attracted the attention of the chief of staff, Frank Goldsmith. By the time my parents learned of my defiance of Mr Sampson (my father later paid the headmaster a visit), I had begun work as a newspaper reporter.

The final school year was, of course, the one in which you established entitlement to tertiary education. I was defying the system. School friends commented over succeeding years that none of them would have done it, or would have been allowed by their parents to do it, although whether the implied criticism was of me or of themselves or our parents was never clear. Curiously, neither my parents nor my grandparents seemed concerned at my missed step on the educational ladder. I was a bright boy and something would turn up.

It did. The weighbridge job was only for the summer and I was soon engaged on a range of newspaper assignments around the town, including court reporting. Copley Street was impressed. Grandpa reminded everyone that the great Dickens had started his writing life as a reporter. Uncle Allen and Aunt Marion were delighted to have in the house someone who supposedly knew the "inside story" of local events. My parents accepted that, whatever I did, it was unlikely I would return to help my father run the property and, to that extent, my future was out of their hands.

We were also at war, which overshadowed everything. The world of events, the hustle and bustle of happenings that appealed to me, and the opportunity to observe them, and, even more, try to make sense of them, pressed down on us as the Japanese moved south.

Among war's fatal attractions is its totality. It is a peak experience, not only for those who risk their lives on battlefields but also for those at home. Emotions are high, everyone is bound to the great cause and hope of victory. As the nature of the end is beyond dispute, all means are justified. The state takes over, imposing a single narrative of duty and sacrifice on society's wilful rights and pleasures. Governments are given latitude because of secrecy and contingency. Families and individuals adjust their plans and expectations. Business adheres to a new political definition of the market. Blackmarketeers are traitors. The people sing to keep up their spirits: "Keep the Home Fires Burning" and "We'll Meet Again".

I put up my age to join the army, hoping to follow in my father's footsteps and explore the world. Although my parents had become used to me making my own decisions, they were concerned; they had been through the excitement of war themselves. My mother sent food parcels, as if to build up my strength for foreign travel, and my father gave me advice that was a rare distillation of his experience: "Don't drink strong spirits and don't go with women in the Middle East." Their fears were premature. I was sent to guard the coast of Western Australia, competing with mutton birds for space on an off-shore island in Jurien Bay. I transferred to the navy, knowing that at least I would be sent to the other side of the continent for training. I was despatched to HMAS *Cerberus* at Flinders, outside Melbourne. After training, I was posted to Darwin.

In the novel *The Budd Family*, I later wrote about the experience of defending Australia at the top end, observing the war from a slit trench.

> There were three kinds of planes. Very high up are the twin-engine heavy bombers, moving slowly against the sky like drowsy flies, remote and untouchable, the anti-aircraft fire bursting harmlessly beneath them. Behind them, and riding comfortably at a lower height, as if challenging the gunners on the ground to test their disposition to peel off and deliver some

unmentionable punishment from their power-packed bodies, are the single-engine dive bombers. Third, the familiar Zero fighters are buzzing in the wake. They all ride across the sky like an invincible armada, arrogant, inhuman, programmed for destruction. The puny Australians, cowering in their trenches and puffing away with their ineffectual anti-aircraft guns, can only watch helplessly. They have no way of stopping the Japanese invaders, who can do what they like … The Japanese faces in the cockpits of their aircraft … look straight ahead. But their lips are caught in a slight, superior smile. He hates them … He is not frightened. He is not curious. He is filled with a blind fury. If a Japanese soldier were in front of him now, he would have no hesitation in putting a bullet into him or running a bayonet through him. The bastards! The rotten little slit-eyed shits!

And later, in Timor.

The sound is no more than a crackle, nature turning over in its sleep. Or a foot on dry twigs? Max stops, listens. The guide is ahead, still walking. He can see in the early morning light that they are on a ridge, with a volcanic crater below. Max touches the pistol at his hip, the knife at his back, the suicide tablets in his pocket. They are the reflex actions of training. He is not actually expecting an encounter.

So he is completely taken by surprise when the body hurtles at him, as if it has swung or dropped from a tree. It carries him breathlessly to the ground. The small man on his back is grunting, clawing, what could be words erupting from his mouth, his knees gripping, his hands searching. He is trying to take Max's pistol from its case. Max throws himself to one side, twisting and turning. He is expecting a sharp jab of pain or the explosion of a bullet (would he feel it, or would it just blow him away?), but nothing happens … He can make out the man's features, under a small, peaked cap. He is Japanese. Max can see the man's teeth, his hooded eyes stretched wide, whether with anger or fear is hard to tell. He can feel the rough texture of the man's uniform. Max's right hand has taken the knife from its sheath at his back. He jerks himself up on his left elbow, which is pressed against a wriggling shoulder. He brings the knife in an arc over his head and with all his strength plunges the blade into the man's chest …

The guide is cautious, approaching the dead Japanese soldier as if he might be a booby trap. He watches the trees and the bushes for more flying assailants from the corner of his eye as he squats to examine the body. He raises his hands in disbelief, also to express emptiness … The soldier is unarmed. What impulse, what mad idea in his head had propelled him on to Max's back? … The face of the dead Japanese soldier is young. Except for wispy tufts of beard and moustache, it is pale and smooth and his lips have closed in a tender smile. The knife is still sticking out of his chest and one of his hands has come to rest lightly on the handle. Max stares at him fiercely. Kill or be killed. That is the law.

He walks away with a new appreciation of himself. He has engaged in man-to-man combat with the fabled enemy, and won. He has killed a man. He can actually feel the blood rushing through his veins as he strides from the scene of his triumph, every detail firm in his memory. The world in which he walks is quiet and still, heavy with the night air. The guide walks ahead more quickly than before, as if he wants to reach the end of this particular journey as quickly as possible.

I was spared war's peaks, suffering only at lower levels of boredom the human experience that, when a grand moral narrative is used to galvanise people for war, is undiminished, indeed increases exponentially. In the false excitement of war, men (and, I suppose, women) discover an appetite for power. Of all the armed services, the navy was organised on the most traditional lines, emphasising obedience to orders that came from the level above you. I did not fit easily into its hierarchy, which supported self-importance and bullying at higher levels.

On a small ship in the sub-tropics, where it was difficult to sleep at night in crowded conditions, I was nominated by the sailors to speak to the captain. There was plenty of space on deck, where he liked to walk for exercise. He was dumbfounded when I suggested he might like to share the space with a few bleary eyed sailors, who could sling their hammocks there at night. I thought I was being helpful, making what seemed like obvious suggestions for improvement, but, according to the Navy's bible, *King's Regulations and Admiralty Instructions*, I was guilty of insubordination. Shades of Mr Sampson.

In the following extract from *The Budd Family* it is not difficult to see the boy who listened to his father's stories of throwing bully-beef tins filled with gelignite as Christmas gifts for the Turks at Gallipoli, and devoured *All Quiet on the Western Front* on summer holidays at North Beach.

> *All Quiet on the Western Front* rang for him irresistibly and irrevocably true, as true as a cry of pain or a look of surprise. This is the human condition. This is mankind. This is me. He is Paul, the narrator, with Kat and his bent shoulders and Tjaden who wets his bed and Muller, the scholar, still carrying his textbooks, and Leer, who will only consider girls from officers' brothels. He is Paul, with the little French girl across the river, as her cool, brown hand touches his clear skin, and Paul on leave from the front, the stairs creaking under his boots, his pack, his helmet and his rifle heavy, discovering his mother lying ill with cancer in her bedroom … There is Detering, the farmer, unable to take the cries of wounded horses, which are to him 'the moaning of the world'. There is clever Kropp, who proposes that war should be turned into a festival, like a sporting event, with ministers and generals of the combatant countries in the arena fighting it out … Max has to close his eyes in wonder … The world of (these young German soldiers in the trenches) is his father's world, but their feelings are not his father's. They

> are his … When Paul falls – on the last page … on a day so lacking in action that it provides the title of the book, with an expression of calm on his face that Remarque suggests is relief that the end has come – Max sits up in bed, a half-eaten apple in his hand, the other just holding open a drooping book, and cries.

My time in the Navy was relieved by meeting David Broughton, who was the naval chaplain in Darwin. David was cheerful and contented, a man of the church without religious fervour. In the intellectually desolate circumstances of wartime Darwin, we fell upon each other like long separated brothers. I had what he called a "teleological" mind, which he, an admirer of understated English style, humour and pragmatism, regrettably lacked, he thought. He wondered if he were more suited to administration than parish work, although he was attracted to the Iona religious community on a small island in remote Scotland, which combined meditation with political activity. For my part, I was relieved to find a man of religion who was knowledgeable and worldly. We often talked late into the night and he encouraged me to test him with my barely formed ideas about Australia. He was the first person I openly asked what it meant to be an Australian.

My crude patriotism was coloured by class and national identity. The British were either snobs or weaklings. The Turks were gallant enemies. The French were pleasure-lovers. The Germans were highly organised thickheads. Only Australians embodied the virtues of both country and humanity. Yet I was also aware of a gap between admirable country and people and the government that was supposed to represent them. The cockiness of Australians who believed that they came from the most democratic country on earth was lost in the rarefied air of the councils of war, where Australia seemed not to have a voice.

I struggled to find words to describe to David the hole at the centre of what it was to be Australian. Everything made sense if we behaved as part of the British empire, but once we began to behave as if we were a distinctive nation – Australia – our prospects clouded over. We had to summon up our emotions and take part as if we shared responsibility, while knowing that resolution and decision-making rested with others. The Great Depression had begun in America with the collapse of the US stock exchange triggering off a crisis of confidence in the industrial, capitalist societies that eventually spread to Australia. We had as bad a Depression as anyone else without being able to do much more than endure it, until the source of it beyond our shores was revived. It was like waiting for rain in a drought; there was nothing you could do except participate in the drought, and wait. The same could be said of war. Australia had nothing to do with its beginning, enlisted automatically at the side of the British and would probably have nothing to do with its end, yet emotionally we were expected to participate as full-heartedly in these wars as anyone else.

I was aware of resistance to conscription in World War One and John Curtin's determination in my war, against British advice, to bring home Australian troops from the Middle East to use against the Japanese, and to turn for help to the Americans. But all I was certain of in Darwin was that Australia was not important in world affairs. We were robust, conscientious and courageous, as good as anyone on the fields of sport and battle, but we did not control our destiny, which was determined somewhere in the northern hemisphere. Whatever this condition was called, it was neither right nor fair!

David listened patiently, reminding me that the time for asking imponderable questions was not now, when we were being bombed in very practical fashion by the Japanese. Not much choice about that! All you could do was grin and bear it (like the British did at the beginning of the war, when they were bombed by the Germans). His advice was not to be upset by circumstances you could do nothing about. Also, there was a silver lining. The call to arms in Australia was nation-wide and socially inclusive. Our shipmates were from all over the continent and, if I intended to be active politically when the war was over, I might take the trouble now to find out more about my fellow Australians. He was a sensible bearer of my grandmother's dictum that it took all types to make a world, and I followed his advice. I learned that it took all types to make Australia. I made several friends in the navy, a rangy, slow Queenslander, a beach boy from Sydney and an insurance salesman from Melbourne.

With Tom, the rangy, slow Queenslander, I had a great debate about art that continued after the war, as glimpsed in extracts from one of his letters that happened to survive.

> *My first and worst suspicions have been confirmed. You are becoming conservative. (An irreverent "Bless you" escapes me) ... This is not merely a communication between friends. This is a remonstration and a castigation. I take virulent exception to the ponderously intellectual manner of your treatise upon art. If I were able to spit viscously, I would, at these two thoughts. The first is "art for art's sake" and the second "all art should be didactic".*
>
> *Have you never sat at coffee in a dimly lit tavern behind a curtain of cigarette smoke, uncomfortably avoiding partisanship in a futile discussion by an "art" enthusiast on aesthetics, appreciation and durability and a Wellsian person with a drooping, listless moustache who persists, between mouthfuls of mutton chops*

and gulps of coffee, in large quotations from Milton, Thoman Mann and our dear bard, Will, stolidly maintaining that art is meritorious by the extent and length of its popularity … A thousand things, words, signs, symbols, run through my mind … Lawrence Olivier's "Henry V", "Bells Across the Meadows", Beethoven's Fourth Concerto, Wagner's prelude to "Lohengrin". Australianically, I lean against my mental telegraph pole … and, deliberately … spit.

I believe that we are living in a dangerous age, Bruce, when, for want of better language, we are becoming Platonistic … And we have a new school of aesthetes, delightful people, developing a new, monosyllabic language of Ugh, Caw, Soul, too barbarically ugly and so on. At the same time, I have not noticed any chronic aversion to conventional amenities; some, it is rumoured, even find sexual intercourse not distasteful, when between kindred souls.

And so on, for several pages. I have no record of my reply or of additional correspondence. By this time, I had knuckled down to the discipline of a late education.

3

A LATE EDUCATION

It was like living in a state of sublime content, those few weeks in that first summer in Melbourne after the war. The water was sparkling green and the beach sparkling white. At the hottest time of the day, water and sand collided in a shimmering glaze, like ancient pottery. Everything seemed light and airy. I went down to the beach almost every day and made friends recklessly. I had nothing to do and much to think about, a potent combination.

An elderly medical doctor practised theosophy on the beach, holding up his hand so that a spectrum of light was created in the space between two fingers, through which he claimed to be able to see people's astral bodies, including mine. He took me home to show me what he thought could be (he was cautious, but also gleeful at the possibility) a snap photograph of the astral body leaving the physical body of a patient who had died. It was a blip, like an indistinct star. A young soldier, returning to journalism, told me how scared he had been in New Guinea, more by the jungle, the rugged terrain and the local inhabitants than by the enemy, which he never encountered. A Scottish nationalist, who was planning to bring the poet Hugh MacDiarmid to Australia as part of a campaign to secede from the United Kingdom, sought my support. A golden-skinned girl with long legs, known as Bunny, sauntered about the beach and allowed me to walk her home. I became friends with all of them, but only for that summer. We understood somehow that what happened then was not to be connected with the real world.

My head was full of plans; I knew exactly what I wanted. The world that had beckoned when I defied the logic and authority of Mr Sampson had collapsed and the future belonged to those who could understand what had gone wrong and were equipped to build a different world. I was keen now to experience the excitement of learning. I wanted to discover all I could about the human condition as quickly as possible, and the beliefs, institutions and organisations that shaped it. I would later grapple with Martin Luther King's phrase "the bigotry of low expectations"; I was now at the other end of the spectrum, the enchantment of high expectations. The ride into town from Brighton Beach on the old, red trains was a journey of exploration; the unfamiliar names of stations and glimpses of comfortable suburban houses invited a sense of civilisation. Every embarking passenger was a person of dramatic interest. Indeed, some turned out to be. Melbourne itself, with its arcades and lanes and occasionally splendid buildings, was a stroller's delight. My writing took a sudden ascent. I wrote short stories, radio dramas and even poetry.

I was enrolled at the University of Melbourne, with an ex-serviceman's allowance that was enough to live on, frugally, and the prospect in a few weeks of throwing myself into studies that the symbiotic states of war, boredom and danger, had made highly desirable. In the meantime, I savoured the pleasures of peace – the taste of ice cream, the smell of cut grass and hot paint on railway carriages and the sight of Bunny's red fingernails in the sand.

I had chosen the University of Melbourne, after a successful aptitude test for higher learning, rather than the University of Western Australia, because it offered a diploma course in journalism that could be combined with an arts degree. Also, my friend from the Navy, David Broughton, was from Melbourne and arranged for me to board with his mother. She was a cultured semi-invalid who was looked after by her sister, Miss Marion Seymour, who had been a nurse. They lived simple, self-contained lives and I did, too. We met occasionally in the back garden where I was allowed to pick fruit. An apple, chosen in the morning but still full of yesterday's sun, was, that summer in Mrs Broughton's backyard in Gordon Street, Brighton, a cultural gift. I abandoned a recently acquired opinion that the greatest fruit on earth was the mango.

The fine-tuning of Mrs Broughton's language caught my attention. She spoke of "my doctor", "my dressmaker" and "my greengrocer". As a child with my parents, a schoolboy with my grandparents and in the ranks of the armed services, I had heard only of "the" doctor – and, impersonally, of all the other personnel and services that Mrs Broughton and I were now likely to encounter. With this small, decisive difference, an elderly and fragile lady stamped her social authority.

The Australian education system then had a British view of the world, but the war in the Pacific had brought the United States to our notice; it was the Americans who kept the Japanese at bay. In one of my classes were two American ex-servicemen, Mike Bray and Vincent Terracino, who had married Australian war-brides, and a Canadian, Kathryn Purnell, who had married an Australian scientist now working for the United Nations Educational Scientific and Cultural Organisation (UNESCO). Like them, I was a stranger in Melbourne, unversed in its code language of schools, religion and politics. Kath entertained us with stories of existentialist bickering on the banks of the Seine. Terry, who had married a girl from Ballarat and experienced its cold weather, enthralled us with tales of American central heating. Mike had been posted to an airfield in the Pacific and told us that the United States was already preparing for war with its communist wartime allies. We did not believe him.

As our own men and women returned from prisoners-of-war camps, we learned about the cruelty of Japanese warrior culture. We absorbed the implications of Hitler's policy of ridding Germany of its Jewish people, many of whom had come to Melbourne. And we were only beginning to appreciate the implications of a particular form of cruelty on our side, a new kind of bomb that had been dropped on Hiroshima and Nagasaki.

Emotions were simple in that post-war period. The wicked had lost the war and would be punished with righteous anger. Countries ravaged by war would be rebuilt. Service men and women would be restored to society with privileges to assist their rehabilitation. After centuries of prejudice in Western Christendom, the Jewish people would be given land of their own, a "homeland". The United Nations would be established to remove forever the scourge of war. Swords would be turned into ploughshares. The split atom, creating an horrendous weapon of mass destruction, would be turned into a cheap and clean form of energy. And the Great Depression of the 1930's would never be repeated. In its own extravagant way, the war had solved the problem of a depressed economy, but now arose the regenerative idea of reconstructing society on a sustainable basis of equity and justice.

Melbourne University was at that time the only university in Victoria and there was a concentration of talent in both staff and students. The returning servicemen (I cannot recall any women) added colour and substance. They had brushed with death, some wore ragged uniforms and their skin still had a yellow tinge from the use of Atabrine, an anti-malaria tablet. We weren't simply moving from mastering exams at secondary level to mastering exams at tertiary level, rivals for examination marks and glittering prizes, intent on gaining professional status or a meal ticket, although Melbourne University was known as The Shop. We wanted to change the world. Our minds had been lying fallow. Now was the time to plant the seed of knowledge. It was a heady moment and we were carried away by it. We were alive at a turning point of history. We were cohorts and comrades in the great adventure of building a better world.

The appeal of Melbourne University at that time was also the appeal of Melbourne itself, a combination of Italian food and red wine. For a boy from the wheat belt, where drinking wine suggested an effeminate disposition, or worse, who had grown up with grandparents for whom the demon drink was a source of human misery, and who had spent time in the beer-swilling warrior culture, Melbourne's café society was exotic. Melbourne University was in Carlton, which had a strong Italian flavour and was often the first stop of Jewish refugees from Europe before they moved to suburban homes in Elwood and Caulfield. This was when hotels closed at 6 p.m., so, if you wanted to continue drinking, the restaurant was the place. They were predominantly Italian and Chinese; for reasons that I cannot recall, my friends and I avoided Chinatown and were committed to Italian food and red wine.

I remember my teachers with pleasure and affection. There was unusual rapport between students and staff; they, too, relished the idealism of the time and the confidence that something could be done. In particular, I came under the influence of two teachers of unusual distinction at a time when they were testing in their own minds ideas that later became their public signatures. In my elevated mood at the time, it was as if they were there to answer my questions about the hole in the middle of Australia that had bothered me in Darwin. Manning Clark was in early pursuit of the "fatal flaw" in his story of Australia as a contest between Catholicism, Protestantism and the Enlightenment. Macmahon Ball was encouraging Australian engagement in Asia as part of his theme that we should be a "party principal" in international diplomacy. My good fortune was not just that I had the benefit of their teaching. Both became friends, so the great themes were discussed in many conversations over time.

Before he renounced the demon drink, Manning had a tendency to take off occasionally into the night with a group of acolytes. We are on the No.8 Toorak tram heading for an election rally at which, as I recall, one of us, Peter Ryan, is standing as an independent. Manning was living in Croydon and rode a bicycle to the railway station. Over his shoulder, he had slung a Malvern Star bag in which are sandwiches his wife Dymphna had prepared for his lunch and he had neglected. Now he walks up and down the tram with beetroot-stained offerings for sedate and startled passengers: "You look like a victim of the class struggle. Have one of my wife's sandwiches." On another occasion he and I attended a party in South Yarra. He prepared me with wisps of information about our hostess, to the effect that she was embedded in the high society he disdained yet could not quite resist. He was cornered by a bevy of young women seeking his advice on "affairs of the heart". He said they should speak to his brother, who was "a man of the cloth". They protested that men of religion had no understanding of their predicament. Manning said his brother also "had a great thrust from the loins". In giggling disarray, the bevy disbanded, carrying to all corners of the party the professor's latest indiscretion.

Manning could not help himself. He loved showing off. He was always fun to be with, always revealing something unexpected about himself, always warm and affectionate about other human beings, even when they were his rivals, opponents and enemies. He has been seen by some as a profoundly torn and anguished man, which he sometimes convinced himself he was, but in my experience he was also a lover of life, as interested as Tolstoy was in the way Anna Karenina's hair curled at her neck as in the moral consequence of her infidelity.

My first sight of Mac Ball was at a lunch-time discussion in the public lecture theatre. The topic was post-war Germany and the other speaker was a professor with a European background who was knowledgeable on detail, personally involved in some of the issues for discussion and spoke first, quickly and intensely. Mac was dressed in a tropical suit, his face tanned and his attitude languid. "As I came here," he began, "on such a lovely, sunny day, with young people relaxing on the lawns, I asked myself 'Why bother with such a trying problem as Germany, when life is so full of pleasant and interesting things to do'?" Anyone who has engaged in public debate will recognise the technique, but it also enabled him to establish the ground for his presentation, which was that Australia's problems lay elsewhere – in China, Japan and Indonesia, particularly. At his best, he had the gift of direct and lucid speech and writing that made him a popular commentator, but he was also serious, engaging his audience by understanding and penetrating complex events.

The intellectual fashion of the period was caught in the journal *Meanjin*, created and edited by Clem Christesen, nationalist in sentiment and internationalist by conviction. Both tendencies, especially the latter, got him into trouble during the Cold War. Stephen Murray-Smith, a leading student politician and a member of the Australian Communist Party, established a more left-wing journal, *Overland.* Marxists dominated the intellectual discourse at Melbourne University, but there were others. The existentialists were vogue heroes, preaching a new kind of personal freedom that was somehow compatible with the determinism of Marxism. Several students who later became leading figures in the Liberal Party formed the Centre Party; to be more to the right than centre was to be beyond the pale.

We were all believers in progress, as an expression of the goodness and creativity of humankind. We would go on a Sunday afternoon to the Yarra Bank, from where John Curtin, a respected wartime Prime Minister, had once castigated the silvertails on the other side of the river Yarra, and from whose podiums now spruiked communists, anarchists and other harbingers of global revolution. It was in Curtin's time, and still in mine, although showing signs of nostalgia, the place where men (women were rare) spoke freely of what they passionately believed.

The gloss of my childhood admiration of the United States received its first dent at university. My small boy view of America had become more sophisticated, but remained essentially unchanged. The Americans had saved us from the Japanese. American servicemen in Australia all looked shiny and stylish, like our Ford; making war, for all its boredom and terror, seem like fun and action. It hadn't bothered me that the Americans in our midst were highly paid and highly sexed and were getting all the girls. When I discovered that they were, the war was almost over and we were grateful they had been around to repel the enemy.

But Mike Bray turned out to be right. The Second World War had been fought between fascists on one side (Germany, Italy and Japan) and democrats and communists on the other (Britain, France, America, China, Russia). There was a certain intellectual satisfaction in this. Fascism relied on mythology and sensation, creating an ecstasy of violence, including war, while communism and democracy were avowedly rational, believing people to be naturally inclined to be peaceful. The ideological equation changed when the United States took over the political leadership of the West. Our wartime ally ("What about Uncle Joe?" was shouted at movies when the credits rolled over pictures of Churchill and Roosevelt) was now improbably portrayed as just as tyrannical as the fascists we had been fighting. Democrats were now opposed to communists, who were barely distinguishable from fascists. A distinction was later made between totalitarian (left-wing) regimes, which were regarded as incorrigible, and authoritarian (right-wing) regimes, which were thought to be redeemable, but essentially the Cold War opposed the American version of democracy and its indispensable ally, capitalism, against the Russian version of communism and its essential ally, the state.

Complicating this new symmetry was decolonisation, the end of European rule over millions of Asians, Africans and Arabs. During the time that the island continent of Australia had been colonised by the British and developed by people calling themselves Australians, the West had held undisputed sway over the world. Since 1683, when the Turks were turned back at Vienna, the world's major conflicts had been within the Western family. Quarrels over imperial spoils, schisms and splits over religion and ideology, dynastic rivalries, the evolution of capitalism, the emergence of communism, the nation state as the expression of sovereignty of the people – all these had been within the West until the rise of Japan. Japan's naval victory over the Russians in 1905 and its aggression against China in the 1930s were warnings to the West; its attack on the United States in 1941 and its early rout of Western power in Asia were a threat not just of an enemy but also of another civilisation. Even by losing the war, Japan had ended European dominance in the Asia-Pacific region. Australian fears of an alien "threat from the north" had proved to be realistic. Japan had been turned back but Indians, Chinese, Indonesians and others barely known were rising in their place.

We knew little of Asia then, and by "we" I mean the whole University, staff as well as students: indeed the whole country, which is why Macmahon Ball was exceptional. Returned soldiers knew something, some of them having fought in Asia, but they knew only fragments of the big picture. Knowledge came, not from our own resources, whether within the University or newspapers and journals, from parliament or government, but from abroad and from the ideological combatants. The Marxists seemed to know everything those days; they had an explanation at their fingertips, whether it was for the Indonesian nationalists' revolt against the Dutch, the Marshall Plan in Europe, or the latest jazz or Hollywood movie.

Some of us wondered (with *Meanjin* and *Overland)* whether Australia itself had anything to offer the world. Founded as a gaol, our self-esteem could have been strangled at birth, but we had refused to be daunted, asserting ourselves, not in declarations of the rights of man but in tough, practical measures that protected our livelihood, like trade deals, immigration laws that kept out cheap labour, social and economic policies that supported the worker against the boss and an arbitration court to resolve industrial disputes. We liked the idea of democracy and worked at it, giving women the vote (New Zealand was the only place ahead of us) making voting compulsory (so that money and influence could not get out the vote on polling day) and, to reflect the sentiment of the electorate more accurately, introducing preferential and proportional voting (as against, in racing parlance, first-past-the-post). We were inventive in practical ways (the stump-jump plough) and in sport (the Australian crawl in swimming and Australian rules in football). Australian nationalism and the improvement of humankind seemed to be moving in tandem.

I kept my notes from lectures and tutorials in a wide range of subjects – English literature, French language, Philosophy, Law Affecting Journalism, Modern History, Australian History and Political Science. A notable omission was Economics, which was absorbed in history and politics. It was exciting to demolish the pessimists; for a brief moment you were the equal of some of the great thinkers. I recall especially the pleasure in despatching the views of Friedrich von Hayek, whose book *The Road to Serfdom* was required reading. Hayek's ideas, picked up by Milton Friedman, not only survived but later became influential on the conservative side of politics. But in the first post-war flush of eradicating war and depression and establishing in their place a planned society reflecting humanist values and cooperative behaviour, we would have none of him.

From the evidence of notebooks and underlined passages in annotated books, I was drawn to the Metaphysical poets, especially John Donne, not because of his religious struggle to convert from Catholicism to the Church of England, I suspect, but because of his sharp language and arresting thoughts. For example, *Twicknam Garden*:

Blasted with sighs, and surrounded with teares,
Hither I come to seeke the spring,
...
And that this place may thoroughly be thought
True Paradise, I have the serpent brought.

In *Song*, he scoffed at the ideas of an "honest minde" and a "woman true, and faire."

If thou findst one, let mee know
Such a Pilgrimage were sweet;
Yet doe not, I would not goe,
Though at next door wee might meet,
Though shee were true, when you met her,
And last, till you write your letter,
Yet shee
Will bee
False, ere I come, to two, or three.

In politics and history, I discovered for the first time teachers and books that took seriously the vague unease I had revealed to David Broughton late at night in Darwin. As even the most confident learn, it is reassuring to find that one's melancholy is not entirely due to temperament. The discovery that Australia had its own history, with its own heroes and villains, and its own moral and intellectual issues, was the most exciting experience of my life – the shock, not of the new but of the ordinary. The everyday experience of my country boyhood had become a subject of learning. Manning Clark told a story to illustrate the Australian trade-mark "faq" (fair average quality). Two men are digging fence holes and they line up the posts. "How is she?" asks one. "Pretty bloody" says the other, squinting along the line. "How bloody?" "Oh, about average bloody" "She'll do," was the summation. The improvising and deflating Australian character I knew well was for the first time intellectually shaped and dramatised into a national identity, with a style and a purpose. I learned in an Australian history class of D.H. Lawrence's insight into the absence of an Australian soul – and the response of his wife, Frieda, that it was the reason she wanted to live here. I was able to understand Michels' "iron law of oligarchy" more clearly, not from the clash of communism and fascism in Europe, but from our study in Australian history of the formation of the Australian Labor Party.

The sardonic, mocking, fatalistic message of Australian history, which accounted for convict origins, a physically harsh continent and unheroic colonial rule, did not entirely fill the hole in the middle. It said little about women, nor of the love of men and women for each other, nor of what was in the minds of the original inhabitants when they greeted the invader. Its nationalism lacked the grace and grandeur of liberation. What it said about other races and other religions was crude and often vicious. And even its engaging, self-deprecating humour could seem at times to be the whine of the perpetual underdog. So my moment of national regard, while exciting, was circumspect, although it distracted me from both the lure of Marxism and the habits and dogmas of conservatism. A country upbringing helped: I was suspicious of utopias that did not take account of the sun and the rain.

*

Political Science Department April 4, 1949

TO WHOM IT MAY CONCERN

Mr Bruce Grant in the last three years has completed most successfully the three main subjects offered by the Political Science Department, University of Melbourne:

Political Science A (Australian and English government), Political Science B (American, German and Russian government) and Political Science C (contemporary social and political theories) – as part of his work for the degree of Bachelor of Arts.

The quality of his work from the outset clearly set him apart from the run-of-the-mill, industrious pass-man, and gave evidence of exceptional intellectual clarity, maturity and detachment.

In his Final Year (when I obtained my closest view of his abilities) he was prominent in an excellent class for a developed analytical facility, and a broad range of interests and sympathy and his performance at the 1948 examinations in Political Science C set a new standard of attainment for this subject.

From my experience of Mr Grant's work in this Department, I am convinced that he possesses in uncommon conjunction the prime qualities both of the potential social science researcher and of the responsible administrator.

(ALAN DAVIES)

Lecturer in Political Science

This came as a surprise to me. I had never thought of myself as a researcher in the social sciences or an administrator. Alan Davies, who later succeeded Macmahon Ball as professor, probably intended his commendation to keep me at the University or induce me to offer myself to the Commonwealth public service, the preferred option at that time. The private sector was not then considered an interesting area of employment for young men with brains, ambition or imagination. It had been overshadowed during the war and was still subdued, despite the agitated profile of the banks. In addition, of course, it had failed during the Great Depression. The more entrepreneurial of my friends were prepared to consider the professions but none, so far as I can recall, went into business. I was the only one to consider journalism.

I took a job on *The Age* newspaper. The drama of life and the unpredictable transit of events still appealed to me, but my decision also owed something to chance. David Broughton's mother introduced me to a neighbour, Matthew Macfarlane, an elderly gentleman who was a leader writer on *The Age*. I showed him some things I had written and he recommended me to the editor, Sir Harold Campbell. While still at university, I reviewed books for the newspaper. I recall two reviews in particular. *The Reach of the Mind* by J.B. Rhine, of Duke University in the United States, elevated my boyhood experiences with Nessy into the realms of science. Dr Rhine, in a series of experiments, showed that "extrasensory perception" existed to a surprising degree in the student body of his university. He concluded that the mind was capable of conquering space (clairvoyance) and time (precognition). The other book was George Orwell's *1984*, which I did not like. I opened my review with a quote from the book: "The old civilisations claimed they were founded on love or justice. Ours is founded on hatred. In our world there will be no emotions except fear, rage, triumph and self-abasement … If you want a picture of the future, imagine a boot stamping on a human face – for ever." I thought the book was heavy-handed, lacking the social satire of his earlier *Animal Farm*. I wasn't impressed by his use of "doublethink" which provided governments with reversible slogans like War is Peace, Freedom is Slavery, Ignorance is Strength. I thought his view of human society was overly influenced by the experience of Nazi Germany, which had been defeated, and I offered, as a corrective to his view of the world, not the promise of Australian egalitarianism but a mild version of English social democracy. I had to accept that the book had a "brutal, compulsive vulgarity about it, which commands attention, and the subject is one that will excite the mind of the most incurious ..." Today, I accept that Orwell knew more then about the heart of human darkness than I did.

I was an experiment for *The Age* – the only university graduate on the reporting staff, with an opportunity to write for the Literary Supplement on Saturday. The Literary Supplement was the most prestigious newspaper publication in Melbourne at that time and it had the additional advantage of discreetly recognising authors by the publication of their initials. By-lines were not yet in use, but in the Literary Supplement your initials revealed your identity to the world. Sometimes, as in a special edition to mark the centenary of *The Age* on 16 October 1954, even the author's full name was revealed.

The Age was then not as influential as it became. The newspaper of influence was the oldest and most conservative morning daily, *The Argus*, which was later acquired by the London tabloid, the *Daily Mirror*, changed dramatically, indeed traumatically, and, when it failed, closed down. *The Age*, established in 1854, was a writer's paper with a radical tradition in politics. We inhabited a four-storey building at 233 Collins Street in what might amiably be called austere conditions. Elderly gentlemen (one still wearing a winged collar) sat in rooms in what was called "the corridor" – the centre of editorial power. The rest of us wrote, standing at high benches like Dickensian clerks, or sitting on several copies of Lloyds Registers to provide height, if we were fortunate enough to find a chair. Some ancient fire problem had necessitated setting aside, on the other side of the building, a "smoke room", in which you could smoke but were not supposed to work. In practice, this was the room, with a cluster of partitioned cubicles around it, where the senior reporters (the men, anyway) did work, out of sight of the Chief of Staff, who was inclined to despatch visible reporters on urgent assignments, and of the even more predatory Chief Sub-Editor, whose hatred of late copy burned in him as the night wore on.

Gossip in the smoke room was about "the story", the mythical entity that in one form or another became the "news" that the newspaper printed. Most stories had their origins in the outside world of public events, but, in the secret world of the smoke room, they were subjected to the ingenuity and imagination of the reporters who were now telling the tale. Their stories were shaped by skill and serendipity – being in the right place at the right time, finding the "angle" that would satisfy the sub-editors, writing the story "up" so that it became more important than it was, putting two stories together to make a third that was more interesting than either of the original pair. Nor was it beyond the wit of the really imaginative reporter to invent the story. Two old hands exhumed, for my benefit, the shark story. When they were youngsters, employed at weekends as casuals and paid according to the number of words published, one, covering the St Kilda-Elwood beaches would invent a shark-sighting and his mate, covering the Brighton-Sandringham area, would, after a suitable lapse of time, confirm the sighting off his beaches. They chortled at the sheer effrontery of their victory over the wielders of blue pencil morality on the sub-editorial desk. I listened, unable to respond because I believed that the role of journalism was to uncover the "truth". If I had been courageous enough to say so, I imagine they would have smothered me with advice to the effect that if I carried my sentiment with me into the real world I would soon find myself without a job.

I was later given a desk, not always with a chair, in a shared cubicle near the smoke room. The ability to write fast, in the middle of the night, surrounded by clamour, which is often demanded of journalists, was not my *forte.* I preferred writing in the morning, on pieces of paper of notebook size. In those days, each sentence was written on small, separate sheets, so that the sub-editor could quickly throw out or re-write sentences, or just shuffle the pack. On one celebrated occasion, the logic of this method was remarkably demonstrated. An article, on thirty-two slips of paper, was printed entirely backwards by mistake, and read surprisingly well.

When Erle Cox died in November 1950, having for many years reviewed films for *The Age* as "The Chiel", I had the opportunity to write about films and eventually to succeed him, which introduced me to a lively section of Melbourne cultural society. Film, like sport, was the domain of everyman – and woman. Everyone went to the cinema and, in addition, a small group of addicts believed that cinema was a new art form, to be treated with the same respect and intense scrutiny given to old art forms. The Chiel, with his leisurely, humorous essays, in the manner of Walter Murdoch, had managed to please everyone.

The black hole in my new firmament was that there were no Australian films. There was almost no Australian theatre and Australian literature was thin on the ground, but the absence of Australian films was made more dramatic by the popularity of the medium. The cinemas in Melbourne then were almost all owned by two companies, 20th Century Fox and Greater Union, the first distributing American films, especially its own, and the second British films, especially those from the studios of J. Arthur Rank. I had a difficult time sustaining a dogged faith in Australian culture while reviewing only British and American films. I learned one lesson about Australian political society at that time – you could get away with criticism of America if you were pro-British, or vice-versa, but if you took on both you were regarded with suspicion.

The best films those days were English comedies, gently promoting eccentricity, and American social dramas, exposing crime and corruption. Because the cinema was popular, especially with young people, it was possible for a film critic to become something of a public philosopher. It was a relatively natural progression to become a critic at large, pronouncing on life's passing parade, not just advising people what to see by explaining what it was they were seeing but also pointing out what they were not seeing, what had been left out. Inevitably, conflict developed between a young critic using the medium of film and a largely captive readership to reveal what was wrong with the world, and the film distributors and cinema managers who advertised, at great expense, in *The Age*. The industry was, however, not united. Some cinema managers found that sharp criticism attracted an audience, who came to see if the film was as bad as it was said to be, and were even satisfied when it was, and other cinema managers were pleasurably surprised by an unexpected influx of long-haired enthusiasts who came to see B-grade supporting features that had somehow acquired cult status. But there was a sterner view, which was that films were shown for entertainment and newspaper advertising was designed to attract readers to be entertained; a critic who persisted in seeing moral, political and social implications in what was meant to entertain was in the wrong business. After all, the editor wouldn't think of sending a wowser to report horse and dog races. And (the unkindest cut of all) as the films had already amply demonstrated their capacity to entertain abroad, what weight could be given to the judgement of a callow local?

The editor firmly rejected all suggestions that I should be found something else to do, which was in the best tradition of *Age* editors. I was helped, however, by the fact that the local film industry was not much more than the distributors, who were influential about the town like any other branch of commerce but were not connected with the political and social families of Melbourne, and were not backed by stars and their satellites or investors and their retinues, as they were in countries with a thriving film industry.

The theatre was more complicated, as I discovered when I was asked to review plays. It was, so far as Australian content was concerned, very little different from film. I cannot recall, during this early period, an Australian play. The Melbourne theatre showed West End and Broadway successes brought out to Australia with leads from America or Britain, and backup support from an Australian cast. The two interesting theatre developments at that time were at Melbourne University, where the student union theatre, under the direction of an Englishman, John Sumner, began to do contemporary plays, and left-wing theatre at the New Theatre in Flinders Street.

Sumner nurtured the Union Theatre into a professional repertory company that became the Melbourne Theatre Company and was responsible for the great leap forward in Australian theatre with the staging of Ray Lawler's play *The Summer of the Seventeenth Doll.* The New Theatre flourished for a while with Australian satirical reviews, where I first saw Barry Humphries. Most of the Australian drama at that time was on radio, before television began in 1956, and most of it on the ABC Radio kept alive a sense of Australian history and culture with poetry readings, serials and full-length dramas.

The difference between film and theatre criticism was chalk and cheese. I slipped into cinemas unnoticed (and usually in daylight), writing up a couple of days' viewing at leisure later. The theatre had Opening Nights. You attended sometimes in black tie, as these were social occasions. Even if the play were not Australian the director might be, the cast, excepting leads, probably were and the stage staff and management certainly would be. These were all real people and they were aware of you and what you wrote. The anonymity of the film reviewer in a dark cinema gave scope for detachment. The struggle to find words to match the virtual reality of the screen was a test of skill and ingenuity. The theatre critic, throwing down the last glass of champagne and rushing back to the office that night (with possibly less than an hour to write a review) was inclined to reflect the atmosphere of the evening. It may have been a form of protection for both the newspaper and the critic, that my film writing was done under my own name while the reviews of plays were written by "*The Age* theatre critic". No reason was ever given for this and as the arrangement suited me I made no enquiries. What it meant was that I had more control over and more responsibility for what I wrote about films, whereas my theatre reviews, written hurriedly late at night, could be cut and rewritten by sub-editors to the newspaper's satisfaction and with less anguish on my part.

I wrote later about the Australian theatre:

> The most important pressure on the Australian theatre today is that of ordinary Australians who want to see themselves on

> the stage. We have finally moved from the tradition begun by convicts quaintly performing Drury Lane successes a century ago and perpetuated by 19th and 20th century theatrical businessmen and classicists alike – the tradition that romance and drama suitable for the stage occurred only in the lives of people who lived overseas. The Russian peasant and the mid-West sharefarmer lived profoundly, but the Australian cocky was allowed on stage only as an unrecognisable buffoon. Other soldiers died heroically; the Australian Digger got drunk and seduced foreigners' wives. Indoor Australian life was particularly dull; interesting things happened only in Surrey drawing rooms or in New York penthouses or tenements in Dublin ... This has changed, or is changing so quickly that the end is in sight. The Australian playwright has forced his way into the limelight, and he is shouting something that his compatriots have heard only faintly and intermittently before. He is saying that their lives are fascinating, that everything they do is significant. He is holding up the mirror and they are seeing themselves for the first time.

I meant it, but I was ahead of my time.

Those early years with *The Age* were an introduction to Marvellous Melbourne, the city that had been built with money from the goldfields. The office was in Collins Street between Elizabeth and Swanston; opposite were the Town Hall, the Manchester Unity building, the Block, with the Hopetoun Tea Rooms, and several elegant multi-storeyed buildings that are still there today. Melbourne was then a socially conservative city. No Jews were admitted to the Melbourne Club, no Jew had a seat on the stock exchange. There was a desperate, at times pathetic, social scramble to be acceptable to the occupants of the large, white, Italianate building adjacent to the Royal Botanic Gardens, copied from Queen Victoria's residence on the Isle of Wight.

A certain Governor wished to announce the engagement of his daughter. He called in the editors of the newspapers to give them the news. It was agreed that, on the day the announcement would be made, those entrusted with actually receiving the news and bringing it to the outside world would not be normal reporters, but news editors. The social charade went ahead as planned, performed by mature men who believed they were carrying out their civic duty in a dignified manner. Was it the distant gleam of the sword on the shoulder that propelled them? The Australian correspondent of *The Times*, London, kept his nerve. When informed of the impending event, he advised Government House of his paper's rates for engagement advertisements.

The British connection was strong in the universities, the churches, the clubs (men's and women's) the professions, the courts of law, the arts, in trade, industry and architecture. The wave of mainly Jewish refugees from Nazi Germany had just begun to make its presence felt; the post-war million or so of assisted migrants not yet at all. The American influence was slight, still largely a lingering reflection of the wartime alliance. The Melbourne establishment looked to a revived Britain to regain leadership of the Western world, and shared British distaste for the vulgar populism and crude commercialism of America.

I was an outsider, having arrived unheralded from the far West, without any of the identity tags that Melbourne liked to bestow (school, family, suburb), so I was allowed to bloom in my own way. I was given interesting reporting assignments, such as the Royal Commission into Communism, established in May 1949 following a series of articles in *The Herald* newspaper by a prominent Communist, Cecil Sharpley, alleging rigging of union elections and espionage. I became involved in an exchange of views in *The Herald* newspaper with Dr Lloyd Ross, who was its writer on labour and the unions. Ross had written an article on the "Commi-But" (a person who was not a Communist, but agreed vaguely with their stance) to which I took exception in a letter to the editor.

I wrote: "All that the article by Lloyd Ross on the 'Commi-but' does is to point the bone at anyone who stands with the Communists on certain issues. Is one a 'Commi-but' when he accepts Communist policy on housing and not their foreign policy? Or if he accepts Marx's theory of history as a fruitful guide to the explanation of past events without accepting dialectical materialism?" I went on, in a lengthy letter exhibiting my new intellectual enthusiasms, to put the case against "enforced and narrow loyalties" and for those who were not concerned with the struggle against Communism but were concerned with the "struggle against ignorance, lies, prejudice and injustice."

Lloyd Ross responded carefully, defending himself against any suspicion that he wanted to restrict the freedom of Australians, but ending reasonably with some advice from his own experience dealing with Communists. "The way out of the problem for Mr Grant and others is to pursue their ideas in ways that do not strengthen the views of people opposed to such ideas. But he will not come to this conclusion so long as he fails to see that the struggle against Communism is involved in his 'struggle against lies etc.'"

If I had gathered a reputation as a radical by aligning myself with "Commi-buts" and as a film critic taking up the case for an Australian film industry against the established British and American studios, I now engaged in the greatest promotion of imperial ties that Australia had ever seen. I was given the job of reporting the 1954 Royal Tour.

I travelled to New Zealand, meeting the new young Queen and the Duke of Edinburgh, as well as some well-known names in British journalism. This was the first visit by a reigning Monarch. When today I read what I wrote on 4 February 1954, when the Royals arrived in Australia (the lead story on the front page and the main article on the editorial page), I am reminded how I had struggled to give expression to the event itself, without allowing republican sentiment to get in the way. Journalism is a useful antidote to day-dreaming. The Queen and the Duke of Edinburgh liked my front page, I was told, because of the words "cool and blue" to describe the dawning of their first day in Australia (imagine how an English couple would have felt if it had been overcast, hot and sultry) and because of the emphasis given to the "armada of mischief" – the local craft that disobeyed instructions and came swarming up the harbour to greet the stately Royal yacht. In my editorial page article I sublimated Australian nationalism in a hymn to youth.

> They are young and – the one gentle, slender and dignified, the other adventurous, strong and self-possessed – so much in their thoughts and actions part of the traffic of the modern world that their stay in this country is unlikely to be attended by that imperious aspect of monarchy which Australians traditionally hold in dread.

I had no social connections, no political patrons. I had married Enid Walters, a school sweetheart, who had followed me from Perth to Melbourne, and we had three young children. I used my low-interest rate wartime service loan to begin the process of achieving the great Australian dream of home ownership. We lived in a weatherboard cottage at 33 Torbay Street, McLeod, a semi-rural outer suburb away from the high life of the city. I travelled to work by train. At weekends Enid and I created a garden and painted the house, inside and out. And yet, because of an ability to write, in particular to write without fear or favour, I became known to a wide circle of influential people, including political leaders like the Prime Minister and Lord Casey. I met the Prime Minister a couple of times for brief, formal chats and Casey more frequently and informally, sometimes in his house in East Melbourne.

The conservative forces in Australia had regrouped and regained office in 1949. In later years, Menzies, the dominant political figure, became known for grand illusions about imperial Britain, but, when I first encountered him, the life he envisaged for Australians reflected middle-class virtues – a good education and owning your own house. During the Menzies era Australian home ownership rates became the highest in the world and – in a surprising act of centralism – funding for tertiary education was taken over by Canberra. Labor's desire to nationalise the banks was doused and Curtin's hint of an independent strategic outlook was ignored, but the Australian tradition of a major role for government and public utilities in social and economic development continued, with the Commonwealth Bank, the Commonwealth Scientific and Industrial Research Organisation, Qantas and Trans Australia Airlines, the State Electricity Commission in Victoria, the Snowy Mountains Authority, public transport systems, the Australian Broadcasting Commission.

I had a warm personal relationship with Sir Harold Campbell, editor of *The Age*. We relaxed in each other's company: I liked his kindness and respected his experience, he accepted my ambition and liked my writing. He was a widower, living in a serviced apartment and dining usually at the Melbourne Club or as a guest of another pillar of the establishment at another of Melbourne's males-only clubs. All this made me wary of him, yet I was also, grudgingly at first but later, with more confidence, an admirer. Despite all the political pressures on him and the daily compromises inevitable in bringing out a newspaper, he clung to liberal, humanist values. At the newspaper, he was famous for his ascetic private life and incorruptibility. Even the restrictions on smoking and drinking in the office, while a source of grumbling, bore the stamp of his integrity. He worked hard to shield himself from any distractions that might prevent him from making the daily judgement of the public interest that he had decided years ago was his duty. So, while accepting a knighthood and a politically conservative view of the world, he kept the paper open to other views, ensuring that, as the Cold War intensified, the intellectually adventurous of Melbourne continued to buy it.

One issue of the time was censorship. The political turmoil of the 1930s, when almost all radical writing, including the Communist Manifesto, was banned, and strict wartime controls, had left a powerful censorship structure in Australia. Reflecting our cultural dependence, this was mainly a function of Customs, affecting especially the entry of books and films. The censorship issue touched a raw nerve of Australian nationalism, for it could not be denied that Australia, like any other nation, such as Ireland or South Africa or communist or developing (especially Islamic) countries, to mention only the more notorious of the censors, had the right to prevent material from entering. But cultural nationalists in Australia adopted the enlightened stand that what was good enough for the people of Britain, Europe and America was good enough for the people of Australia. Not for the first time in Australian history, nor the last, were the sophisticated standards of advanced Western countries contrasted with our more primitive standards; the "cultural cringe" was enlisted to bring greater freedom to artists and audiences in Australia. Similar arguments were used against the Menzies government's attempt to ban the communist party, as they were later used to oppose the wars in Vietnam and in Iraq. The cultural values of Western civilisation provided a standard against which an Australian civilisation should be measured.

Campbell sometimes invited me into his room for a chat at the end of a long day-night. His book shelves were untidy with ready-reference books and galley proofs were strewn over the floor. I remember two occasions. We pored together over the pages of J.D. Salinger's *The Catcher in the Rye*, the editor's face a mixture of wonder and dismay. The book had been banished from the shelves of the State library (of which he was a trustee) because it was considered to be "lewd". We went through every sexual reference and blasphemous nuance, an intimate experience for any two people. I sat doggedly at his elbow, explaining the jargon, contesting, scorning, each accusation. Eventually I got my way. "Alright," said the editor, "write it your way." That night, because the deadline for the editorial page had already passed, I wrote what must have been the fastest "leader", as they were called, in the paper's history – fourteen minutes from the time I sat at his desk and slipped the triple-layered slip of self-copying paper into my typewriter. I was happy, not just because I was publicly brushing away some cobwebs, but because the older man, who was my father's generation, had treated me as an equal and, in the tussle between us over the meaning of one layer of human experience, had conceded to me.

On the other occasion, in the middle of an account I was giving of a book on the actor Oscar Asche, he dreamily interrupted: "Ah, the long, white arms of Lily Brayton." I hesitated, not knowing what might follow. "I once saw them in Othello," he explained. His tired eyes glimmered with what might have been pleasure. Was this unexpected glimpse of the editor's inner life a sign that he might share personal confidences that he was not known to share with any other members of the staff? Nothing more was said, but I took away a fresh appreciation of my ageing companion. I convinced myself that the editor had not only referred to Lily Brayton's long white arms but had expressed a hidden longing for them, and perhaps therefore (as he presumably gave himself little chance of becoming acquainted with her) for any long, white arms, or for any white arms, long or short, or even perhaps for any arms, long or short, white, black, brown or brindle. My glimpse of a vulnerable man would have surprised my colleagues if I had revealed it, which I did not.

But these were small disturbances compared with the intrusion of his son. The editor asked casually one day if I had met his son and, when I said I hadn't, suggested that the omission should be rectified. I did not ask why. However, when the son rang to make the appointment, I sensed an ominous motive. The arrangements were elaborate. We were to meet not for morning coffee or a late afternoon drink, the usual manner of disposing of social obligations, but at night in a vacant lot on the other side of Princes Bridge from the Flinders Street railway station. It was not literally vacant, but its occupation by the Trocadero Dance Palais and a deserted circus ring gave it a temporary, desolate appearance. The son was seated in a station wagon. He was in the espionage business, more precisely a member of the Australian Security Intelligence Organisation (ASIO). We had a long, desultory conversation in which he invited me to keep in touch with him. I cannot recall exactly how I managed to decline the invitation, but I did.

Campbell trusted my instincts as an honest writer and never tried to restrict me to a line that was favourable either to *The Age* or to the Menzies government. He was a conservative man in almost all respects, but he also had a broad understanding of public life and of political culture, and enough confidence in his own judgment, to know that a young man who was an honest writer would find his own checks and balances without the additional prods of a nervous editor.

I was now about to leave the backwaters of the Cold War in Australia and enter the mainstream. But before that happened, I had to deal with a personal tragedy. My father was seriously ill. His lungs, weakened from the use of gas on the western front, had succumbed to tuberculosis. I arranged with *The Age* to spend several months working on the *West Australian* newspaper in Perth. It was a gesture by the editors and management of both newspapers that belied the maxim of hard-nosed journalism; neither gained anything from it. But it gave emotional support to my mother and, although I was back in Melbourne when he actually died, on 22 May 1952, aged 57, I think my father was pleased to see the return of his prodigal son.

4

EXPLORING THE WORLD (1)

I lived mainly outside Australia for ten years from 1954, first as correspondent for *The Age* in London, then as a Nieman Fellow at Harvard University, then as correspondent in Asia, based in Singapore, for *The Age, Sydney Morning Herald,* and occasionally other newspapers, including *The Observer*, London, and the *Washington Post*, and, finally, for *The Age* in Washington. During this period I developed ideas about the world and Australia's place in it that have remained with me.

On my first flight out of Australia to London, I stopped in Johannesburg, officially to see *apartheid* at first hand, but also to meet Nadine Gordimer. I had read her stories in the *New Yorker* magazine, then her first novel. Something about the way she wrote (the way she thought) was thrilling. Someone who could write like that, with such energy and precision, noticing everything, yet in the end poised, as if nothing unusual was happening, must be unusually wise.

She wrote about blacks and whites in South Africa as if they were normal people. They were divided from each other by prejudice, and also by law, yet they reached out to each other through and under the law, defying the rules not to eat and drink with each other, dance with each other, touch, tease, tempt each other. They even made love to each other. They did all these things without heroism, without telling the reader that the system was reprehensible or tragic or inhuman, although it was all these. She never hinted that the people in her stories were actors on the world stage, agents of history or even especially self-aware. They just lived their lives the way they did because they were human. They knew they were breaking the law and the thrill of lawlessness added tension, but they sought each other as if it were natural to ignore the absurdity of the law. Human beings need each other, they, she, seemed to be saying, and must be able to find each other if they are to remain human. It was a bold statement in the context of what even uninformed readers like myself knew of the complexity and danger of race relations in South Africa, and yet was delicately, although firmly, stated, as if the writer had no wish to disturb the authorities.

Nadine Gordimer responded with surprise and caution to my telephone call, reasonably enough, as I had given her no warning and South Africa was a police state, but she asked me to come to her house. We had a cup of tea in the kitchen and continued our conversation in the back garden. She took me that night to a party, where I met several Africans who became prominent in the struggle against apartheid and a British journalist, Anthony Sampson, who had come to South Africa to edit *Drum* magazine and later became known for his book *Anatomy of Britain* and a biography of Nelson Mandela.

Later, I used our meeting for a fictional encounter of Max Budd, an Australian journalist, with Tessa Judt, a South African writer, which, although fiction, is a true account as I remember it now.

> She answered the doorbell herself. He saw a slender woman in her early thirties with an alert face, which she preferred to keep

in profile, and a charming, nervous manner. She was wearing an apron, holding aloft hands of flour-covered fingers. Kitchen smells hovered behind her.

"I'm cooking scones in honour of your visit. Come into the kitchen. I don't want them to burn." She bustled down a passage and through a doorway. "Will it hurt them if I open the oven?" she asked, as she opened it. "I can't see through the glass. It's all smoky. Oh, I think they're right, don't you?" She explained as she placed a tray of nicely browned scones on the kitchen table that she was learning to cook. "I'm trying to do without servants. It's a dilemma, of course, like everything else in this country. They need the work, but the pay is pitiful, and you're not allowed to treat them like human beings."

The house opened up inside as you moved through it, homely kitchen, small, wall-papered rooms, dark wooden furniture, the warm domestic colours becoming larger and lighter, until you walked through an enclosed, sunlit verandah into a perfumed garden.

"The berries aren't falling yet," she said, indicating a relatively unstained, brown earth. "Anyway, we need the shade. The sun gets awfully strong about this time of the day." A quick smile. "But I suppose you're used to the sun." She pointed to a bush laden with small blue, white and pink fluted petals. "The perfume comes from there. We call it yesterday-today-tomorrow, because it seems to flower all year. I don't know its real name."

Max wondered if her nervousness was her own, or a form of courtesy to strangers. Or because he had said almost nothing since he arrived. She chattered so charmingly that he did not want to interrupt her. He was happy just to be here. He had set eyes on her, as his father would have said. He was here, sitting in her garden, which was even the more remarkable because he hadn't telephoned or cabled or even written ahead. She might have been away. His mind was so full of the idea of meeting her that he had not considered the possibility that she might not have been at home in Johannesburg when he happened to arrive there. He often did that. Living in his head, Lilli called it.

She was sitting up straight in her chair, against a blue sky, with flowers trembling around her, a Chilean jasmine, single white roses. It was a moment he did not want to end. If he were a painter, he could fix this moment on canvas, forever. She would stay like this, becalmed, the flowers over her shoulder and the air around her, still and silent.

She observed him carefully, as if she were calculating how far, or at what depth, she should continue the conversation.

"I live here. I have no choice. I have to be hopeful."

"I envy you," said Max. "You have one big problem, which you can't escape. It's your own, home-grown. You've got to take sides."

"And you have lots of little problems, like the rest of the world. Lucky you." She was leaning back in her chair, observing him calmly, appraising him. "You don't have to live under phoney laws, official bigotry, pseudo science, pseudo sociology, petty fundamentalism, the technicalities that are solemnly presented as the essence of civilisation ..."

Her voice faltered. Her eyes were clouded and anxious. A little smile quivered on the edge of bitterness.

"But you're at the heart of things," he encouraged. "You've got your own centre. We have to go looking for it. Or we're marginal."

"We've only got one body," she said. "You have to live somewhere ... You can't live globally. I mean, properly. And, once you live somewhere, the rest follows."

... As he stood up, preparing to leave, she added quickly: "They waited until fascism was defeated to announce themselves. Crazy, they're fascists. No, shrewd. They're hoping they'll be saved by the Cold War. They're hoping that the West will prefer a white racist South Africa to a black communist South Africa."

He continued his reluctant departure in the doorway. "What can outsiders do?"

"Should you be hopeful, too?" She seemed to be considering the possibility, then answered herself. "No. Leave hope to us. Be as nasty as you can. Outlaw them. Ban them. Banish them.

Make them feel awful. For a while they will think they are martyrs. They believe in the healing properties of punishment. They will bond more closely to keep up their spirits. They will blame the world for failing to understand. But in the end, they will crack. They are an outpost on the southern tip of Africa, no use to anyone, nowhere to go. Isolate them. Let the world pass them by. The world will win. It always does."

She was flushed with the effort of a speech with the loftiness of prophecy.

"You understand, don't you? From one southern outpost to another …"

*

England had been an image in my head all my life, the voice of authority, a corner of a foreign field, a pale, stubborn, blue-capped adversary on the cricket field, "Home" for homesick English in Australia. How, for reasons of state, the rotting hulks transported their human cargo to Botany Bay. How men and women pleaded to be hung rather than sent to the end of the earth. How mistaken British military strategy was corrected by Australian valour at Gallipoli; and not corrected at Singapore. How, during the Great Depression, the Bank of England sold Australia down the river. How, in the war against fascism, with France crippled, sturdy John Bull stood firm across the Channel.

Now, the old country was recharged with confidence. London seemed to be brimming with hope and vigour. No hole in the middle here, no daydreams and doldrums. A nation-state in which action and conviction reinforced each other, a tightly-knit society of dash and cunning, of high policy and low politics, each somehow contributing to a sense of being British, a sense so strong that each interest and social group had an allocated role, which, when performed according to script, was applauded even by opposing players. The disparate components of society cohered, which is what angered the angries, the young men, among them John Osborne (*Look Back in Anger)* and John Braine (*Room at the Top*), who thought that glaring differences of class and opportunity should divide society.

Tweedy coats and scarves, scruffy clustering in pubs, fog, musty and windy underground stations and steep, crowded escalators. Cold air on the tip of the nose, vapour in your breath. The sudden warmth and intimacy of shops. You lost yourself in swirling masses at Piccadilly Circus and in credulous audiences around East End buskers. Cab-drivers, threading their way through heavy traffic, were oral historians. Street names tingled with history. Great calcined edifices that had survived fires and plagues and bombings reminded the world that this was the hub of a global empire. I stood in wonder at the sweep of Regent Street. Five-storey buildings, no more, a spacious quadrant that curved elegantly away. The proportions were precise, so precise that you looked for the architectural trick, like the upward lift of St. Bride's wedding cake steeple, each tier not only a little narrower but also a little longer than the one below it. Genius! I examined the height and width of the buildings, their porticos and cornices, the breadth of the street, its swirls and plazas, all the way down to the Duke of York's column.

The lights came on in the middle of the afternoon, creating a mellow effect, sharp to the eye. In Australia, strong light diffused outlines. Out of sorts in a sunlit country, flushed in the heat, their handsome worsteds and tweeds adding to their confusion, the English had got it right here at home in their own climate. They loomed up in the softness of a winter's afternoon like figures from legend, striding into their weather with caps and mufflers, stamping their feet, breathing briskly.

I am stalking in the fog, pretending to the children to be Sherlock Holmes. "Not fog, smog," Enid says. "Britain is well-known for its dirtiness." She muses over my delight at the good humour of the British. "They are enjoying themselves after the war." A quick note of admiration in her voice: "They are entitled to do so. They saved the world."

At weekends, we visit the stately homes of England, buildings of such size and grandeur that they are forts and castles rather than houses. I bought an old and suitably stately Jaguar car, which transported us to imposing edifices up and down country lanes, as if it were a sniffer dog trained to the task. England's great houses were visible evidence of a great civilisation. Cathedrals also. You did not have to be religious to appreciate that the design of the great Gothic cathedrals was sublime and the workmanship impeccable.

Secular humanists from the antipodes, we allowed ourselves some reservations. The cathedrals, while physically splendid, were dedicated to an illusion, which is that the God they try to reach with their spires created humankind, and the great houses, with their turrets and libraries and servants' quarters and immense grounds, were now unmanageable and could only survive as museums. They were relics of an era that, while prosperous and productive, was based on the subjection of slaves and colonial people. As architecture, they were flawed because their function was limited.

English literature and English life were closer than I had imagined. The characters in Dickens were not caricatures, but dramatised versions of the real thing. They were all over London, red-cheeked and boisterous, sallow and saturnine, short and tubby, tall and lugubrious, ragged, judgemental, on the make, all part of the surging mass that make up that mysterious entity, the English. We stood together in front of Dr Samuel Johnson's house off Fleet Street. "The dominating literary figure of his age" I say solemnly. "Ponderous," says Enid. We gaze upon William Shakespeare, pampered face, high forehead, pursed lips, soft, reticent eyes. "A man for all seasons," say I. "He looks like an English country gentleman," she says.

On Sunday mornings we lolled in bed with *The Observer* and *The Sunday Times* interleaved with tumbling children. Every now and then we muttered, "God, that's good." Or "Absolutely brilliant!" Or "Who or what is the Imam of Oman?" Or "Makes our Sunday papers look like suburban shopping guides." Wit and brilliance were all around us. My weekly column "A Window in London" seemed dull and heavy, weighed down with well-meaning words about public events and hopeful phrases about humanity. I drew on my interest in film and theatre to spice it up and inserted lighter items – debutante balls, buskers and the ancient art of hunting – but I could not match the irreverent cleverness of London journalism.

The first stirring in spring of fauna and flora, archly reported in the quality press. Quaint and humorous and even delightful at a distance, it could be suffocating as the only topic of conversation. The desire of English males to walk in step. If none of the usual excuses (like a resurgent war wound or an urgent appointment elsewhere) worked, I would skip a step to break the beat. My companion would notice immediately and, without comment, as if correcting a moral weakness, skip a step to get back in tandem. Their love of uniforms, civilian as well as military. You could tell a solicitor, a stock-broker, a doctor, a store floorwalker, a salesman or a plumber from their clothes. Brought up to be accepted, or not, on personal merit,

I wondered at this brandishing of what, not who, you were. The delicate matter of picking up the bill. Bankrupt from the war, they were struggling to make ends meet, so they discussed endlessly who should pay for meals, or even for cups of coffee (with a choice of one biscuit) or tea (no choice of biscuit). They did it with such an air of *noblesse oblige* and yet with such an obvious preference not to pay at all that I become as boorish as Americans in demanding instantly that I should pay the bill.

The upper-class accent; the distinction between those who have it and those who don't. The resentment and inverted snobbery of those without it and the inability of those who possess it to complete sentences. The English upper-class voice became for me a caricature of itself, a symptom of inarticulate haughtiness, a national aversion to anything clear and explicit, a jigsaw mind overloaded with pieces that never matched. I found myself sympathising with the French and even the Germans, both of whom liked to think clearly and to get to the point. The notion of "muddling through", which I had regarded with affection, became instead a telling description of a nation incapable of making up its mind, tolerant simply because it was baffled by irrelevant detail. No eye for distance. Then I remembered Britain's heroic resistance to Hitler's Germany after France had fallen in nervous disarray, and was ashamed of myself.

In Australia, you noticed bodies. Here you noticed what covered the bodies. The tweeds and the worsteds were made for solid frames outdoors in bracing weather, but the finer clothes of England showed a sensuous interest in comfort and pleasure. Was this civilisation? Did style take centuries to develop, testing human taste through years of trial and error so that good taste became known and accepted? Or was it simply a matter of money, the rich acquiring what was most expensive and establishing it as desirable because its cost placed it beyond the reach of ordinary people?

You begin to believe that the inhabitants of this green island off the continent of Europe might have found the secret of how to live. They love nature; not conquering it or taming it or worshipping it, just letting it have its way, within reason. That was the secret. Liberty, but also order. The informality of an English garden is the essence of Englishness, a natural balance between freedom and constraint. Hedges and borders, but, in between, the delicate rose and the bushy hawthorn, the blue larkspur and the prickly bramble. Living, mingling, flowering together.

British sexuality was puzzling, combining raunchiness and foppery. The men were surprisingly self-conscious. How could they possibly have won the war, I wondered, listening to their cocky pub chatter and lilting laughter, watching them strut and twirl their umbrellas, observing their hour-glass figures, their velvet collars, the myriad angles on which their bowlers perched on flaunted heads of hair? I met a man whose journalism had been an inspiration when I was battling the killjoys of Melbourne over censorship. His work had the grandeur and resonance of a great novel, emotion held in check with such tension and yet with such grace that you felt the writer must be a person not only of great sensitivity but of deep understanding. I was astonished to meet a youthful dandy, who insisted on doing a pub crawl during which he introduced me in simpering and suggestive fashion to a succession of barmen he obviously knew well. "My fwiend from Orstralia". Then he tried unsuccessfully to climb light poles on the Embankment and was eventually told to be a good boy and go home by one of those unflappable policemen who somehow both served and managed the English upper class.

One morning, I began reading in *The Times* a solemnly authoritative article on "The Changing Commonwealth" by a "Special Correspondent". The phrases seemed familiar ... "the historical genius of our race"... "our inductive intellectual tradition", the notion of allegiance to the Crown as "a rod of steel". Then the author revealed himself. "The Crown was and, I am happy to say, is an essential ingredient in Australian government and life. Our acts of parliament are made by the Queen's Most Excellent Majesty, the Senate and the House of Representatives of the Commonwealth of Australia, the Governor-General is the Queen's personal representative; the Queen's writs issue from our courts; I am her Prime Minister of Australia; Dr. Evatt is the leader of her Majesty's Opposition."

Alfred Deakin reported anonymously and ambiguously for a British newspaper during the time he was Prime Minister of Australia, but that was before the Statute of Westminster, Gallipoli, the Second World War and, in any case, before I was born. That *The Times* could reduce the Prime Minister of Australia to an anonymous correspondent seemed to me to be taking admiration for constitutional formality too far, and I was able to say so, but my view was not widely shared in Melbourne. The article, I was told by my editor, was an important attempt to influence British thinking on Commonwealth affairs, and the fact that it adhered to *Times* style made it acceptable in the right circles, whereas a statement by the Prime Minister of Australia would be seen as a statement of public policy. Well, perhaps, but I nevertheless could not think of another prime minister in the world, except perhaps New Zealand, who would have submitted his copy in such a deferential manner.

To London flocked Africans and Asians who were using it as a base for political causes, including independence, in their own countries, Poles, Czechs and Hungarians who were fighting communism, central Europeans from aristocratic families awaiting the return of their monarchy, Latin American emigres fighting authoritarian military governments backed by the United States. Also dissidents of a different order – Australians, who lived in Earl's Court, called each other mate and lolled about complaining of the weather and telling tales of Spain and the Greek islands. They groaned and scowled when an Australian took a knighthood or when there was speculation about someone being "elevated" to the House of Lords. New Zealanders and Indians were inclined to imitate the English. Americans and Canadians preferred their own clothes and their own accent. Was it the insidious cultural imperialism of cricket? But South Africans remained upright, in their unappealing fashion. Some Australians, especially if they needed to be accepted for professional reasons, quickly smoothed out their distinctive accent, even fell into step when walking in the street. Still, I never saw an Australian wear a bowler hat.

A strained voice on the telephone. Manning Clark was in London and wanted me to meet him immediately at the British Museum. I took a taxi from Fleet Street and discovered him standing on the museum steps in pouring rain, looking pale and intense under his big Australian hat. I ran up the steps. "What's wrong?" He asked if I had counted the steps. I complied. "Eleven." He told me that it was on the eleventh step of the sacred staircase that Luther had his first doubts. A lengthy discussion followed (inside the museum) about the current doubts of M. Clark.

It was a thrill to be in London when Ray Lawler's play *The Summer of the Seventeenth Doll* opened at the New Theatre, St Martin's Lane. The reviews were universally positive but, before they arrived,

I stood with John Sumner outside the theatre, leaning backwards and sideways to hear what the issuing audience was saying. Sumner, expert at foyer intelligence, tilted casually this way and that like one of those grinning dolls that are weighted never to fall over. Did all theatre audiences look like this when they came out into the world – shiny-eyed, chattering, happy with each other? I had watched cinema audiences blinking in the sunlight or loping off into the night and had never witnessed such gaiety before. Sumner, still swaying for information, was trying not to smile outright, perhaps not to burst into song. It must be very good. I caught some words … "Extraordinarily interesting" and "A breath of fresh air." Sumner, satisfied, waved me over. "It's a hit," he said, "Let's have a coffee." As we turned the corner, we stopped to look at the faces of Lawler, Jago, Ryan and Warren framed on the wall. "It's true!" said Sumner, "It's really on!" We then went on to convince ourselves over coffee that it did not really matter whether English audiences liked the play. If they didn't, so much the worse for them. Australians had liked it.

In Australia, I might have walked past an oddity like Arthur Hickman. The intimacy of English weather made people more human, more companionable. You were drawn to people, tempted to become closer. Arthur looked as if he had just emerged from a minor accident. But it was his face, shining with pleasure at his escape, that made him different. It was large and fleshy, slightly unstable, with a perpetual half-smile that gave it, even when withdrawn, a genial goodwill.

When we met, Arthur was 54. He was short, plump, stooped and unquestionably shabby. He wore shapeless, greyish clothes, flannel trousers noticeably hitched by a belt, nondescript sweaters and jackets, whitish shirts and darkish ties, a grey raincoat incorrectly buttoned.

His head shook slightly and he was unsteady on his feet (his eyesight was damaged during the bombing), although he walked quickly and skilfully dodged traffic until the day of his death. Usually he carried a case of brown, pressed cardboard, of the kind children used to carry their school lunch and books, in which were several magazines, including at least one *Times Literary Supplement* and one *Times Educational Supplement* and probably a packet of jubes.

He worked in the art department of *The Times*; one of those victims of British society who was, however, accorded a role in it and, despite opportunities, could never bring himself to leave it. Belonging to *The Times* was for Arthur like being a member of a large and celebrated family. Within minutes of our meeting, he told this story: a senior person on *The Times* had in his desk drawer a piece of the skin of the Abominable Snowman. The opening line caught everyone's attention. Then came the background, in his slow, rich voice, sibilant because some teeth were missing. *The Times* had sponsored the successful assault on Everest by Edmund Hillary and the skin specimen was an unexpected by-product. But no-one in authority at *The Times* knew how it had found its way into the drawer of the senior person. No-one Arthur knew was aware of any other person at England's greatest newspaper who thought it was authentic. Yet, in the presence of important visitors, a small box was ceremoniously produced and the skin unwrapped from layers of tissue. Most visitors thought at first it was a joke, like the Chinaman's finger through a hole in the bottom of a tobacco tin, but the senior person would solemnly disabuse them.

It was this – a grandee of *The Times* patiently explaining to unsuspecting, hard-headed visitors on official business his belief in the existence of the Abominable Snowman – that Arthur would make the high point, the *coup de theatre*, of his story. No witty punch line to bring down the house. No memorable dialogue. Just an even-tempered unravelling of an absurd situation. He was so temperate he could even allow that the Abominable Snowman might exist, without detracting from the senior person's absurdity. He had a deliciously slow sense of humour.

He had friends from everywhere, drawn to his transparent lack of guile, his humour, his interest in almost anything, his scepticism of the political establishment and the power game, fame and money, his love of Britain, his country and his people, alongside his irrepressible desire to make fun of them. Also, his possession of second-night theatre tickets. On my first second-night, I sat next to Anthea Fairfax-Ross, who was in the lady-in-waiting business at Buckingham Palace. I later met a diverse group of Londoners – socialites and professionals, soldiers and hat-makers, a Scotland Yard detective and a charlady from Peckham.

Arthur had received a letter from friends in Canada which began: "We are very concerned about China." He was vastly amused that anyone could be concerned about so huge and unmanageable a matter as China, more particularly that they should write to him about it. He reminded us of the three tailors who had warned the Czar not to go too far. He chuckled over the inescapable enormity of China and the incorrigible sincerity of his Canadian friends all the way to coffee at a Lyons Corner House.

He walked hurriedly, never strolling, even when his mind was idling. When he attended an exhibition at the Royal Academy he moved quickly between paintings, as if worried that someone would get in his way. He had a tranquil personality, as was evident when he read a book. He could sit for long periods, motionless except for the turning of the pages. The mystery of his hurried manner when upright was that one eye was almost blind. He walked sideways in order to see where he was going, and seemed always on the verge of overbalancing.

But his secret life was an astonishing *oeuvre* of patient ambition. For thirty years he had been writing everything down. In rooms of supreme untidiness at Tiverton Mansions, Gray's Inn Road, the black-covered exercise books occupied row upon row in a section of floor-to-ceiling shelves. More than ninety black books. Millions of words.

On the inside of each cover were pasted selected newspaper cuttings dealing with the people mentioned in this particular volume. Then an annotated index, meticulous, no erasures or corrections, page number against each item. Then the text. Page after page in immaculate, upright, full-bodied, old-fashioned handwriting. Dates and cross-headings underlined with the use of a ruler. Page numbers in sequence. The page numbers reached into the thousands. Each page number was formed with a calligrapher's care. Not a word was altered.

Arthur explained. Everything was jotted down first in shorthand while his memory was fresh, then typed up and edited as time permitted. Finally each entry was handwritten into the notebooks with copperplate certainty. I was torn between admiration and doubt. Would all this note-taking amount to anything or was it just another example of English trivia?

Arthur took me to the "lower depths". We stood away from the light by a bookstall near an underground toilet at Piccadilly Circus. A male figure emerged from the steps and handed back a magazine to the stall keeper. They touched hands, exchanged money. Arthur raised a finger, signalling me to wait. Another figure approached the stall keeper, touched his hand, was given a magazine and disappeared downstairs.

"They pay two shillings for the magazine and get one shilling back if they return it," said Arthur as we walked away. "It's only twopence to lock themselves in a toilet. So it's much cheaper that paying the tarts. And safer."

He took me to Marble Arch, not to see the gallows where criminals were once publicly hanged or Orators' Corner where free speech was still celebrated on Sunday, but at midnight to observe the young men, some of them in their teens, lounging watchfully in the shadows. Older, well-dressed men stroll past, hesitate, exchange some words with the lounging figures, sometimes walk away with one of them.

"I happened to be passing Marble Arch and fell into conversation with …" says Arthur, as if giving evidence in court or making an entry in his journal. "They're mostly country boys from the north, or sailors. Most of them have been sexually abused as children. They dress up in leather and metal. They like wrestling and whipping. They do it for a good feed and a warm bed."

He took me to Curzon Street, not to see the old mansions or the genteel cottages and coach houses, or even the boutique hotels, clubs, townhouses and secluded blocks of smart new flats, but to observe the tarts, an old phenomenon in a new form. Dozens of women are lined up, only a few paces apart, along a wall. "The really expensive ones make their arrangements by phone," he explains, "But these are the top of the street walkers."

Some from Asia and Africa are dark-skinned and brightly dressed, some have a jaunty European or Mediterranean style, but the majority are pink-cheeked young English women, demure in dress and manner, promoting, it seems, the attractions of modesty.

"Most are from Ireland, actually. The pimps hang around the railway stations and try to pick up any likely-lookers. You've read *Fanny Hill*? Nothing's changed."

"Is that good or bad?"

"You're always asking imponderable questions. Why don't you ask something ponderable for a change?"

"Like what?"

"Like where's the best place to have coffee."

Over coffee, we considered the imponderable issue of equity. Was it fair that people who sold themselves for sex were social outcasts, and even in some countries outlaws, while those who paid for it were merely having a night out? Gender was one reason. Those who paid were men, who had social and economic power, while women, who sold themselves, were socially and economically dependent.

"Only sellers obey the rules," said Arthur. "Buyers make their own rules. You colonials will have to learn the first law of society – always protect those who have at the expense of those who have not."

He took an unorthodox view of paedophilia. "Men and women who prey on children have a heightened sense of beauty. They are not interested in what most normal persons are interested in, namely flesh, especially, if they are men, bosoms. They are interested in matchstick girls and boys like deer. They may be despicable, but their aesthetic sense is shared by the fashion industry. People are drawn towards purity and innocence, especially if it is knowing and self-conscious. The perversion is not in wanting to possess innocence, but in wanting to destroy it."

He thought Vladimir Nabokov's book *Lolita* was a masterpiece, whatever its morals. "No matter how innocent Nabokov makes little Dolly seem, she takes the initiative as much as Humbert does. He lusts after her, but she entices him – and others. Who is to blame – the nymphet or the male pervert. She is only twelve years old, the critics say, as if that resolves the dilemma. Child labour! But Dante's Beatrice was only eight or nine when she guided him to Paradise."

My mother stayed with us in London for six months in 1955–56 and quickly fell under Arthur's spell. In letters home to my sister Audrey, she felt it necessary, after lavish praise of his rich voice, detailed knowledge of London and engaging possession of second-night theatre tickets, to assure them that they were "just friends" and that "nothing was happening." The letters were kept by Audrey and, after her death, her daughter Cathy gave them to me.

My marriage to Enid was a projection of schooldays, sharpened by the emotional pressure of wartime. I had noticed her at Perth Modern School because of her athletic poise and speed. She could run like a breeze, seemingly without effort, and her attitude to life was to keep moving, ignoring obstacles. We were part of a stream of events, carried along by forces outside our control; marriage was part of the post-war world of relief and rejoicing, approved by everyone, accepted by each of us as the next step in the direction of our lives. At the beginning we were too busy to discover our differences, or to notice them, moving to Melbourne, finding accommodation, having a family. By the time I was due to leave for work in London, however, our differences had become serious.

She was a practical person, with an eye for business, while I was on a steep learning curve on the affairs of the world. She wanted, however, the benefit for herself of the experience of living in London and I was unhappy with the prospect of not seeing the children for long periods. Our meeting point was that the children would benefit if we made the move as a family, even though it was contrived. It was a sensible decision. For three years we were involved with new experiences, which took our minds off personal difficulties and reminded us of our ability to live amiably together. The busyness of my work in London gave us some purpose and direction and Enid was a good manager of what was in effect a small business. I was often away and she liked to explore London for herself, leaving my mother to look after the children, apparently without success. My mother's letters are a mother-in-law's lament at the noisy, rude behaviour of the three children and Enid's inability to do anything about it. But intimacy and understanding did not improve and after we returned to Australia and the opportunity to take a year at Harvard came up, we agreed that I should go alone, establishing the necessary period of separation as grounds for divorce.

*

At a conference in Geneva of the so-called Big Four (the United States, the Soviet Union, the United Kingdom and France) I encountered a Russian spy, Boris, who pretended to be a first secretary at the Soviet embassy in London. He survived the rigours of the Cold War by being suave and enigmatic, twirling in his fingers a glass of pink champagne at fashionable restaurants. After Geneva, I pressed him for a visa to visit the Soviet Union.

"Why on earth would man of world from Melbourne, Australia want to go to poor old Moscow, still suffering deprivation from great patriotic war – no restaurants like this, no elegant clothes, no cars. No beautiful women! Why, I ask myself, why?"

"Moscow is the capital of the communist world, which is engaged with the capitalist world in a life-and-death struggle called the Cold War. I am a foreign correspondent. No more explanation necessary."

"You are Cold War correspondent? I am sorry to hear. War correspondent reports only one side. I thought you were objective journalist, capable of seeing both sides of struggle." "Struggle" did not seem the right word to come from his pleasured lips at that moment and he quickly entered a correction. "Peaceful coexistence."

He was keen to convince me that Stalinism was over and this was a new era. The Soviet Union was undertaking massive development. The last thing it wanted was another war.

"Point taken. War mongering is out. But is there any point in continuing to apply for a visa?"

"Of course!" His eyes twinkled as he leaned closer and whispered. "Gives them something to do at embassy. Keeps them on toes!"

We had discussions like this each time we met. Then, one day, he leaned across the table even more conspiratorially than usual and said, in a tense voice: "I need your help." I waited, watchful. "My wife, the engineer, must be properly attired." He ran his hands down the shape of his body. "She is being given important award. I must buy dress."

His wife the engineer lived in Moscow with their two children. She was large, if his indications of her size were in any way accurate. "She is not *petite*," he said thoughtfully. "She has commanding presence." We went to Oxford Street to find a suitable dress. I acted as a model, he affected a mincing manner, eyeing me off.

"Mauve – or is it a pink – brings out sallow look." A pout. "Makes you Slavonic." He made a Slavonic complexion sound like sex appeal. And: "Not your height, exactly, but chest measurement probably accurate. Russian men babes in arms of real Russian women." He gave an impression of exhausted pleasure.

A few days before a Tory party conference in Bournemouth, he rang to advise that he would be driving down from London and offered me a ride. He chuckled. "Car is red colour. You don't mind?"

A brown envelope arrived at our house in Barnes. When opened, another sealed envelope, also brown, was revealed, marked "Personal and In Confidence", which, when opened, disclosed a letter from the Ministry of Defence, asking me to telephone a certain official at a certain number, who told me that MOD believed I was "in possession of information that might be of interest to Her Majesty's Government."

I sat facing a brigadier across a small table in a windowless room. The table was bare except for a single, unmarked folder. I reminded myself that this was Britain, home of the Magna Carta. But it became obvious that my lunches with Boris (Zaitsev, I was now informed), our escapade in Oxford Street, our telephone conversations and our little trip to Bournemouth were all now safely recorded in MOD. I felt more weary than affronted. The Cold War again. The brigadier said that MOD would be most grateful if, after one of our lunches, I would let them know what we had talked about. I declined, just as I had rebuffed the editor's son. The brigadier turned to Plan B. Of course, if I wished I could continue having lunches, discussing world politics and pursuing a visa, but I should be aware that Zaitsev was a spy and that, as inevitably as night followed day, he would make an improper proposal. If he did, would I be kind enough to inform the brigadier? I said I would, thinking it unlikely.

However, Zaitsev did make a proposal, which I later recorded from memory in fictional form.

"Max," said Boris, leaning across the table in the conspiratorial manner he adopted whenever he was about to say what he had arranged a luncheon to provide him with the opportunity of saying, "I have small offer to make." He immediately corrected himself with a flurry of disclaimers. "Not small offer. Little request."

He smiled at Max as if he were on the brink of declaring an emotional bond. "You have interesting point of view. In Soviet Union, interesting point of view hard to find. People busy building country destroyed in great patriotic war. No time for interesting point of view."

Max could see a hazy outline, and awaited the detail.

"We have Moscow journal publishes articles with interesting point of view. Would Mr Budd enjoy contributing such article?"

Max was surprised at the directness of the offer, but assembled a conventional response.

"What kind of article did you have in mind?"

"Of course, your interesting point of view. You are travelling around, meeting other people with interesting point of view, chatting about world affairs. That kind of thing."

"What kind of journal is it?"

This was difficult for Boris. Not only in the West were there journals with different opinions from the government! But in the Soviet Union, where the people were busy building peace, these journals did not have many readers.

"Not big journal, but influential. Important Soviet people read it."

"What is it called?"

This also was difficult. Max would not have heard of it. Its name was hard to translate into English, because it wasn't a simple name like *Times* or *Foreign Affairs.*

"Perhaps it can be called Journal of Interesting Points of View?" Boris, open hands inviting, subsided in speculation.

"Is it owned by the government?"

"Of course." Boris had no difficulty with that. "In Soviet Union, everything is owned by Soviet people."

"Well, who controls it, edits it?"

"Answer is, scholars and intellectuals, officials, journalists with knowledge of foreign affairs, and so on and so forth. Just like journals on international affairs in the United States."

After a dutiful pause, Boris added smugly, "Pay is very good."

"What is good?"

"Ah," said Boris, rolling his eyes. "People say contributors highly paid."

He waved a wrist vaguely between them, either to indicate that the actual figure was not known or that it was of such magnitude it could not even be guessed at by lesser mortals like himself. When Boris thrust out his lower lip, full and wet and disgruntled, Max decided it was the latter.

"In roubles?"

"Of course." A low, grumbling voice was Boris' defence against an unfair world. "Rouble is official Russian currency."

He suddenly brightened, sat up straight. "You can get visa, go to Moscow, be big spender!"

"On what?"

"Caviar. Vodka. Russian champagne. Pink." He beamed at the prospect. "Salmon. Things like that."

"Is it possible to be paid in dollars?" Max asked, trembling at his audacity.

"May be possible," said Boris quietly, eyes downcast. Was he disappointed in Max because he was taking the lure. Or in himself because, despite all the talk about remaking the world, this was his real job? Or just because US dollars were so much more attractive than Soviet roubles in the world as yet unmade?

"I would prefer dollars," said Max, as if a deal had been made.

"As you wish." Primly. "I will inquire."

It ended in a whimper, Max used to say afterwards. Both men parted without eye contact. Why did he go along with Boris' silly idea? Why did he not brush it aside with a mocking laugh? Why afterwards, when Boris came back with the offer of American dollars, did he not tell him the whole thing was a joke and take him to lunch? Why, instead, did he creep back to the dreary brigadier, informing him that Boris had made an improper proposal?

On 26 July 1956 the President of Egypt, Gamal Abdel Nasser, nationalised the Compagnie Universelle du Canal Maritime de Suez, the company that operated the Suez Canal. A shipping canal 171 kilometres long, connecting the Mediterranean with the Red Sea, it had been built by a former French diplomat Ferdinand de Lesseps during 1859–69 and operated by an international company in which the British Government, at Disraeli's instigation, had acquired a majority shareholding. Essentially a commercial enterprise, it operated under an international convention of 1888 that guaranteed passage through it of ships of all flags.

The responses to Nasser's bold decision brought into play all the forces that had been simmering beneath post-war politics. I went to Cairo to report on Menzies' mission on behalf of the canal users, and saw his brilliance pegged back, his inability to understand Egypt's national pride or Nasser's ambitions, made clear.

My first sight of the bulky, white-haired Australian prime minister in his dark, double-breasted suit, wiping his pink brow in the heat, moved me unreasonably. My father had been here on his way to Gallipoli and I wondered how he had coped with this ancient city. Menzies was representing a hastily organised body of countries that depended on the Suez Canal for trade (most of Europe's oil, two-thirds of Australia's imports and exports). His job ostensibly was to get assurances from the Egyptian president that use of the canal would not be affected by his decision to nationalise it. His subliminal message, on which I had been briefed at the Foreign Office before leaving London, was that international control of the canal was essential to its survival as a global highway and, if Nasser did not acknowledge this, he was in dire, if as yet unspecified, trouble. As the talks progressed, it seemed that Nasser had not got either message. If

Menzies had thought he was negotiating from a position of strength (as veiled threats from London and Paris and the movement of French troops to Cyprus at the time implied), President Eisenhower dispelled the illusion with an announcement that Washington would not be party to the use of force to settle the dispute. The smile on the face of the Egyptian leader could be seen all over the world.

The Australian delegation was not only attached to a singularly London point of view but was floundering in a complex international gathering. The officials Menzies had brought from Canberra lacked the skills and the professional poise to manage the event, especially to brief the large, cosmopolitan press corps. The world that was pressing on Cairo at this historic moment was remote and exotic to the Canberra caravanserai. Its members may have served the prime minister's purpose admirably at home, with deflationary humour, confident Aussie values and an indefatigable breasting of the bar, but here they were out of their depth. The international press corps swirled dangerously around them, fretful and gleeful Third World correspondents, arrogant and anxious Europeans, serious and watchful Russians and Americans. Mixed together, they were a volatile brew, knowledgeable, suspicious, influential. They were as unfamiliar with the language and customs of the Canberra contingent as it was with theirs.

"Excusez-moi, monsieur, mais … who was *present*?"

"Well, there was the Australian prime minister, the honourable R.G. Menzies. Nasser, of course …" A pause and an ingratiating grin. "I'm not sure I got their names."

Some modest, understanding laughter, and then, "Was Monsieur … (a long name, rapidly pronounced) … present?"

"He might have been." Covering embarrassment, "Sounds like Billy the Blackfeller."

Or: "Excusez-moi, monsieur, if negotiations do not succeed ..."

"We don't answer hypotheticals in Australia." A pause for humour. "If your auntie had balls, she'd be your uncle."

I lowered my eyes and scribbled, as the clown-courtiers entertained a puzzled, increasingly irritable, international press. Later, some British correspondents approached with a plea to do something – and, by chance, we encountered Menzies in the lobby of the Semiramis Hotel.

"Ah, my favourite newspaper," said the Prime Minister. I mentioned that the international correspondents were concerned about the briefings. The Prime Minister was in a buoyant mood, seemingly undisturbed by the news.

"I am compassed about with a great cloud of witnesses," he said genially. "Hebrews 12:1."

A British correspondent, trying to find a word that did not plumb the depths of Canberra insularity, said the briefings were "repetitious".

"That's the wise thrush," said Menzies. "He sings each song twice over, lest you should think he never could recapture, the first fine careless rapture!" He paused. "Browning."

We thought we had wasted our time. But the next day, the briefings were given by Noel Deschamps, a multi-lingual, middle-ranking Australian diplomat, hurriedly despatched from the embassy in Paris. Threatened, the boys from Canberra hung on. While the sophisticate from Paris (apologising in fluent French for his absent Arabic) amused and informed the press, they sat in stern silence, with lowered faces, like counsel in the presence of an unreliable witness.

They employed a renowned Australian tactic, the king hit. When the official summary of the talks was released, Deschamps provided a background briefing. So did Hugh Dash, Menzies' press secretary, in an adjoining room. The result was that two conflicting accounts emerged. The official version was that, while much work remained to be done, substantial agreement had been reached. The men from Canberra said the talks had failed.

"See what international diplomacy can do for you," joked the man from *The Observer*. "A few days in Cairo and you've become sophisticated."

In London shortly afterwards, a man in a trench coat, a portable typewriter in one hand and a satchel under his other arm, burst into my Fleet Street office. He was an Australian novelist, Eric Lambert, a member of the Australian Communist Party.

"Do you want a sensational, world class story?"

He was so agitated, so fierce and determined, that he was barely coherent. He had apparently just returned from the uprising in Hungary, had seen what happened with his own eyes and wanted to write an article, probably two, denouncing the Russians. The details of his journey were so dense that I could not at first follow them. He had gone to Vienna and somehow got himself across the Austrian border into Hungary, where he had seen Russian trucks heading north with "the flower of Hungarian youth" on board and Russian tanks heading south, driven by "Mongolians". He was investigated at a Russian roadblock. He took a bedraggled, miniature Australian flag from his pocket and waved it. It was seized and shredded by a Russian guard. He was searched and a scar discovered on his body, for which they wanted an explanation (why he did not know but he gave it to them – from fighting the Japanese in Malaya). All of this tumbled from him without form or direction. It crossed my mind that he was making it up, that he was so upset at Moscow's repression that he wanted any excuse to hit back.

"Did you get to Budapest?"

"No, I didn't. After the roadblock I had to get back to Austria, or they would have shot me."

Really? Why would they shoot him? Because they were murderous brutes, shooting anyone who stood in their way. Was he standing in their way? Well, if they knew even half of what was in his mind, which he suspected they did, they would know that he was standing in their way politically, totally. Now, however, in my room in Fleet Street, not having reached Budapest made him anxious to establish his credentials.

"I was where I said I was, don't worry. I can give you the names of the towns. I saw what I said I saw. I can give you the markings on the trucks." He sagged in the chair, tired, dispirited. "God, those bastards. I'll never forget them, riding off in those trucks with those young Hungarians." He ground his teeth. "They were like the Nazis, arrogant, ruthless." He closed his eyes. "And the youngsters, crushed but still defiant. You should have seen their faces. Handsome, heroic. And cheerful! Like gods." He sagged again, crushed. "Bound for some slave labour camp. If they're lucky."

I decided that Eric was telling the truth. I sent off a supporting cable to the editor and we arranged to meet the following day to discuss details. A cool response arrived overnight. The editor was not interested. The writer was not regarded as a substantial authority, nor perhaps a reliable witness.

"Never mind, I'll give it to your opposition," Eric said, which he did.

The overnight telegram also asked me to contact a well-known British historian, an enthusiastic supporter of the British government throughout the Suez crisis, to see if he could contribute an article, giving his own thoughts on "dramatic developments so far". It was unclear whether the article should refer to Hungary, which was not mentioned. The office was still in the grip of the Suez crisis. Its desperate plea for an acceptable explanation of the chaos from someone it could trust was a vote of no confidence in me, but the crisis had reached a stage where personal feelings were insignificant. I arranged for the article from the historian, which was, as I expected, limp and ambiguous.

As crisis descended into farce, the overnight telegrams from Melbourne became more pained and abstract, especially after the bizarre climax, when the United States turned against its NATO allies Britain and France, and its protégé, Israel. Even before his re-election, President Eisenhower had been critical of the Anglo-French-Israeli military venture to recover the Canal. Now, shocked by what had happened in Hungary, the US hammered home its point – that, in the struggle for the hearts and minds of the people of the world, especially the developing world, it was not aligned with the old imperial European powers, or even with Israel, the admired new nation in the Middle East.

According to Arthur Hickman, the "view upstairs" was that Anthony Eden, the long-awaited successor to Churchill as Prime Minister, had made a tragic mistake in getting involved with France and Israel. The king-makers were now intent on finding a replacement for Eden, the quicker the better. Britain had been isolated at the United Nations (with Australia) and forced to withdraw from the Canal Zone. From this moment on, British influence in the Middle East sank. Israel was forced under US pressure also to withdraw, but she was in the Middle East to stay – and fight another day. The French? Oh, well, the French. It was just another disaster for them. It had been happening regularly since Waterloo. They would now return to what they did best, as Albert Camus would remark, fornicating and reading the newspapers.

Eden had himself negotiated with Egypt two years earlier the withdrawal of the last British forces from the Canal Zone. He may even have believed, as he said, that Nasser was another Hitler, although that seems improbable. More likely he hoped to draw attention to his record in opposing Hitler, when he had resigned from Neville Chamberlain's government in 1938. Eden's hostility was shared by a socialist government in Paris. The difference was that the French acted alone, while the British were required to work with what Menzies called the "Crown Commonwealth" and their wartime ally the United States. The Suez crisis became the turning point in the Cold War, with the Americans rudely wrenching the baton of Western leadership from the British. The French – and the Israelis – were secretive and unilateralist, but the British were forced to lie to their closest partners, with whom an intelligence sharing arrangement had developed during the Second World War. Eden was unable to manage this humiliating spectacle, played out at the United Nations in one embarrassing vote of no confidence after another, until his health collapsed and he resigned early in 1957.

In 1956, Menzies was at the height of his powers. He would remain as prime minister for another decade before stepping down at a time of his own choosing. His political opponents were divided among themselves and his authority within his own ranks was undisputed. His Suez failure stemmed from a personal attachment to Britain and a belief that Australia's interests were served by Britain remaining strong.

The Suez and Hungary crises brought to a head misgivings about Australia I was beginning to formulate. My sympathies were with the Hungarians against the Russians and the Egyptians against the British and the French. These two acts of force against small countries were evidence that social and economic and political change would not be allowed if it threatened the stability of the military balance in Europe. What I wrote about the Hungarian revolt was eagerly printed in Australia while my despatches on Suez were either emasculated or not printed at all. I found that many of my colleagues writing for British or American or European newspapers and journals did not have the same difficulty. They were able to reflect and comment critically on the Suez crisis, as well as the controversy over Hungary.

I complained to Sir Harold Campbell, who defended the paper's editing on the grounds that "In moments of real crisis it would be confusing to our readers to take one line in the leaders and print in the same day comments and conclusions by you putting the opposite side of the general argument, because you and *The Age* cannot be separated in the minds of the readers." I replied that in the *New York Herald Tribune* people like Walter Lippmann, the Allsop brothers and Roscoe Drummond at various times expressed political opinions different from those in the editorial columns. "My own feeling is that this makes for lively and informative reading and enables the newspaper when there is a deep division of opinion to reflect it honestly."

Campbell responded:

> *It is natural for any intelligent writer to have strong and positive views on big issues but a newspaper is not a medium for the expression of those views. Your task is to reflect and interpret the London scene, not to assume editorial functions in matters of policy which have to be dealt with here. We have always given you greater licence than most newspapers do in this matter but that does not*

> *exclude your copy from editorial or sub-editorial attention. Your letter refers to Lippmann and others. They are specialised foreign affairs commentators of long experience who do nothing else and whose work is syndicated. No doubt they are subject to editorial supervision; Lippmann certainly is in* The Age. *I do not want you to specialise in this way (although naturally foreign affairs will dominate your articles). A wide and diversified cover from London, with interpretative (as distinct from personal) comment is what we need ... You mentioned cuts in your articles and your dissatisfaction that you have no control over your material here. That is the normal state of affairs. Your responsibility ends when you file the copy.*

Back and forth, we argued about editorial direction and personal responsibility.

A wise man, Campbell decided that the best way to deal with this young fellow who took himself so seriously was to bring him back to Melbourne to write the paper's editorials, where he could keep an eye on him. I do not know what my future at *The Age* would have been if the Anglo-French-Israeli intervention had been successful, but I was saved from being branded a collaborator of Colonel Nasser by the Americans. On my return to Australia I was greeted by Kathleen Syme, from the family that owned *The Age*, with the question: "Did you meet that dreadful Dulles man?"

I took my responsibilities as "leader writer" seriously. I have written elsewhere describing the thoughts of a fictional journalist writing an editorial on the death of Stalin.

> Yet, when he sat down to write, he felt the whole world was watching over his shoulder, as if every word he wrote would be scrutinised by people who had a profound understanding of Stalin, who knew everything he had done or not done, who had

> calculated precisely his place in history and ideology, communist and anti-communist. Even now ... they would be scanning editorials like his for mistakes, misunderstandings, errors of judgment, and, above all, predisposition. Every fact would be checked. Being predisposed was a weakness. Once you revealed yourself, you lost the argument. Every adjective would be weighed, every verb ideologically tested to see on which side the anonymous author actually, perhaps naturally (or "objectively"), resided. He chastises himself for solipsism. But he knows that he cannot think in any other way when he sits down to write. Or, if he does manage to think otherwise, he just dries up. He has to believe that, at the moment thoughts form in his head, at the very moment he organises these thoughts into words, what he thinks and what he writes are crucial. If he doesn't believe, his mind becomes a blank.

Intellectually, it was a game between the proprietors, the editor and myself, finding ideas, policies and words that suited each of us, but there was more to it. One was trying to find sentiments that reflected the feeling of the whole country, that united rather than divided, moved thinking about the issue under discussion forward, rather than just taking a side or scoring a point. I can recall occasions when the editor and I disagreed over what was a "discussible" subject, but I cannot recall any when I was asked to adopt an opinion I did not hold. The *Age* style was collegiate and the result was a balanced and reasoned opinion that lacked thrust and sparkle, but was conservative in the best sense.

Family life resumed at a new and larger house at 3 Hawthorn Grove, with the children, Susan, James and Johanna, at nearby Preshil School. Enid took a part-time secretarial job in a company selling cars. I had met fashion model Bambi Shmith, now divorced from photographer Athol Shmith and preferring her actual name

Patricia Tuckwell and reviving her long-held interest in music. We had memorable family outings with my three children and her son Michael in the botanical gardens and on several beaches, especially Red Bluff.

5

EXPLORING THE WORLD (2)

It was in Asia that my perception of Australia changed profoundly. Suddenly, you see something familiar in a different setting and it is barely recognisable. I saw Australia for the first time, not as an outpost of European colonialism nor as a strategic adjunct of the United States, but as a large landmass between the Indian and Pacific oceans, looking out at a neighbourhood of largely unknown nations and cultures. I was not a geographical determinist, but Australia's continental size and island security gave me confidence and I set out to discover what was in the hearts and minds of our new neighbours.

Cold War geopolitics were more open in Asia. In Europe, the two sides were locked in confrontation. In the Americas, the United States was dominant. In Asia, the situation was fluid. Japan was tied to the US but was testing itself as a new economic power, having failed as warrior nation. China was communist, but anxious to distinguish itself from the Soviet Union. India and Indonesia were non-aligned. The South-east Asia Treaty Organisation (SEATO) was a mere shadow of NATO. Small states had some prospect of remaining independent. I knew little of Asia when I first went there, but instinctively felt that it offered Australia room to move, despite the ascendancy of Cold War politics in Australia at the time and the decision to commit Australian forces to the war in Vietnam. This was the time of Menzies' mistaken view that Hanoi's plan to take over South Vietnam "must be seen as part of a thrust by Communist China between the Indian and Pacific Oceans".

There was no cultural connection between Australia and its neighbours. The links with Britain and the United States, so fundamental in Australia, were a mixed blessing for us in Asia. Sometimes it was more advantageous to present oneself as different from either or both. The margins of difference between Australia and Britain or Australia and the United States, suddenly expanded to become empty pages, waiting to be filled.

Asia tested your patience. Impressing on attendants at cable offices the urgent nature of communication with Melbourne was like dealing with children. They smiled and placed your cable in a neat pile with all the others, in the exact order in which it had been received, your pleas for expedition disregarded with charmingly vacant faces. Or they waved pencils in the air and marched out with the precious cable held high, returning without it and with a calmly accomplished look, which might mean that it had been sent but could also mean that it had been placed in another pile. Or thrown out a window.

You learned to wait in dark corridors of old colonial buildings, now occupied by bureaucrats of the new emerging forces, or at ramshackle airports, where brisk young women with figures like schoolgirls and pieces of chalk in their hands did or did not, for reasons undisclosed, clear you through customs. The river of life accommodated all living creatures, including you, your people, your government; you must float on it, like everyone else. Go with the flow. If you try to direct its course you create havoc. Survival, with its pleasant accessories, such as courtesy and cooperation, rather than striving, with its unpleasant extras, like rivalry and tension, was the core of civilisation. And you learned to sweat. My country boyhood came to my rescue.

The work was different, more difficult and also more satisfying. The vast filter of opinion and commentary that was available in western Europe and the United States – the media, universities, think-tanks and individual voices of dissent – were not generally available in Asia. You had to deal more directly with political leaders and government officials, as well as your own government's, or friendly, secret intelligences services. Opposition was more often than not hidden, sometimes underground, and dealing with it was dangerous.

In London and Washington, you rarely met personally the politicians you wrote about, except at formal press conferences, but you read excellent accounts in excellent newspapers of those who did. You finished up with a full view, but it was a view from an observation tower. In Asia, the politicians sought you out, eager to convince you and your readers of their point of view. The local newspapers were part of local politics, often owned and edited by the same person, without competent professional staff, or still run by foreigners who were easily intimidated by a new political elite. The material you gathered was raw and had to be sifted and shaped. No-one who edited my articles in Melbourne had any knowledge of Asian politics, so I had to make sure that what I wrote was clear and internally self-evident.

Australian diplomats were well-informed and helpful and a useful exchange of information often developed. Australia was beginning to count for something. Canberra's view on issues was thought relevant, even at times influential. The Indian prime minister, Jawaharlal Nehru, told me that when other members of the Commonwealth came to him asking him to do something about Papua New Guinea, he said it was Australia's business (just as he expected in return that when Australian political leaders were asked about Kashmir they would say it was India's business).

Menzies wrote to our ambassadors in Asia, a sample of which, to Sir Alan Watt in Tokyo, follows:

> *My dear Watt,*
>
> *Bruce Grant of the Melbourne "Age" is going abroad for them to Asia to make a special series of reports. Mr. Grant is a most talented writer and, as you know, the Melbourne "Age" is a highly intelligent and responsible newspaper.*
>
> *I am writing to you in a direct sense because I would not have you believe that Bruce Grant is merely a routine reporter. He is a man of considerable talent and I believe the reports he sends back can prove to be of very great educational value in Australia. I would, therefore, be glad if you would give him some special personal assistance and open a few doors for him. He is to be completely trusted and will, I am sure, not involve you in any embarrassment.*
>
> *With kind regards,*
>
> *Yours sincerely,*
>
> *R.G. MENZIES*

The letter was the same to each, with a slightly different personal tone in each case. Dear Forsyth (in Laos) and Dear Ridley (Hong Kong) were all formally addressed, but not to the degree of Critchley in Malaya (Dear Mr Critchley) while McIntyre in Indonesia, got "My dear Mac" and McNicol in Singapore "My dear David".

I wondered how Menzies, after our stand-off during the Suez crisis, could now be confident that I would not write anything that would embarrass either an Australian diplomatic mission or the government. Of course, he could rely on Campbell's hand on the tiller at *The Age*. But it is also possible he accepted that the challenge of what to make of our location in Asia was a test for all of us. He liked the look of Lee Kuan Yew in Singapore and tried to be open-minded about other new political leaders. He was possibly genuinely interested in what I would make of it all, and thus offered a helping hand. I was taken into the confidence of Australian officials, even the inner sanctums of intelligence agencies. In a public lecture later, I noted that it was sometimes necessary to "declassify in your head" information you had been given in confidence. I was taken to task by the writer Frank Moorhouse, who pointed to the danger of the writer being used by governments. It was a fair point, but I found that Menzies' letter was helpful to me in doing my job, which was to get to the core of what governments were actually doing.

I was given no such letters to carry in Europe or the United States. Lord Casey gave me a letter of introduction to Dean Acheson in Washington, but our conversation had been entirely about Asian affairs. I chafed him about a telegram the Indonesian foreign minister (Dr Subandrio) had shown me from President Kennedy to President Sukarno, in which Kennedy said he proposed to take a "new initiative" on West Irian, which the Dutch were withholding from Indonesia, and he suggested to the Indonesian president that it would help if he would "maintain tranquillity" in the region. The implication was that the United States was supporting Indonesia, not Australia, which was supporting the Dutch. In the droll manner that the former US Secretary of State liked to adopt, his answer went something like this.

"Have you ever been to The Hague?" I had not. "A very boring place. I was appearing before the International Court of Justice in a case about a disputed temple between Thailand and Cambodia." He paused to allow the incongruity of the event to sink in. "To break the monotony, I asked a few friends from the Dutch cabinet to have dinner. Did they really want this … West Irian?" He waved a dismissive hand. "No, they didn't. No-one wanted it except Luns, the foreign minister. Well, if I could get the Australians to take it, was that alright? It sure was, and the sooner the better." Having established his honourable credentials, Acheson settled back in his chair. "So when I got back to Washington I asked Jack (President Kennedy) if I could offer it to the Australians. Go ahead, he said. So I rang that fat fraud, Bob Menzies." (My introduction to Acheson being from Casey, whose disagreements with Menzies on several foreign policy issues was well known, Acheson probably assumed I was no friend of the Australian prime minister. Both he and Casey were lean, aristocratic types.) "Menzies probably thought 'Beware Acheson bearing gifts.' Anyway, he declined, saying. 'We've got enough trouble with our own half of New Guinea.' So you see, West Irian only went to Indonesia after you wouldn't have it."

Allowing for Acheson's magisterial manner (he called his memoirs "Present at the Creation"), his account contained a core of truth. West Irian was finessed through a barely authentic "act of choice" supervised by the United Nations, but essentially Indonesia got it because neither the Netherlands nor Australia wanted it and because the United States needed Sukarno as an ally in the Cold War. Of course, according to Indonesian history, the new state struggled politically and militarily for West Irian and was finally rewarded.

Editorially, *The Age* resisted my view that the United States was sympathetic to Indonesia. After several articles from me were not published, I asked for an explanation from acting editor Keith

Sinclair, who expressed the opinion that Denis Warner and I were considered "appeasers" on the West Irian issue, having been persuaded by Pat Shaw, then Australian ambassador in Jakarta, whose position was not widely supported in Canberra, either in Shaw's department or amongst intelligence sources. I explained to Sinclair that Shaw's judgment was backed by President Kennedy's telegram Subandrio had shown me and described the circumstances in detail: Subandrio had only revealed the telegram's source when I had told him that I could not accept his word for it and needed to assess the wording myself. Subandrio also asked that, in quoting the content of the telegram, I did not mention that he had shown it to me. Eventually, *The Age* accepted I had not been duped and published the articles.

Most Western correspondents were based in Hong Kong, from where they had covered the Korean War. Although the Korean War was seen later as the first conflict of the Cold War, the circumstances were complex: the Soviet Union was absent from the Security Council, in protest against the non-seating of Communist China, when the United Nations decided to commit forces against North Korea. The military engagement was at first a "police action" which became a "civil war" and then a "limited war", when the Chinese became involved in support of North Korea and President Truman decided not to extend the war, sacking General Douglas MacArthur. The war ended in a draw, leaving Korea divided.

I worked from Singapore, which was part of the post-colonial ferment of South-east Asia. In Asia generally, the Cold War was territorially more open and intellectually more fluid than in Europe and living in Singapore, with its Chinese, Indian and Malay communities, and a pragmatic political leadership that distrusted ideology, the fluidity was tangible. It seemed possible that the openness of the situation in Asia gave small and medium-size states, especially one as singularly placed as Australia, a chance to take stock and begin to operate outside the power blocs, even to discover something unique in itself in responding to these ancient and powerful civilisations. There was just a chance, I thought, that Asia could be the challenge needed to wake Australia up, get its act together, fill the hole in the middle.

Then I would be reminded of the intractable nature of what was still called in those days "race". Singapore was a good place to observe the tensions of ethnicity and culture, with its three main communities, but it was an incident within the European community that made me think again about Australia's prospects. The British had established a swimming club, with fine facilities and "whites only" membership, which had survived the political turmoil of independence and was still in pristine condition when I arrived in the early 1960s. With three young children on visits from school in Australia, I found the club's facilities invaluable. Then an internal crisis erupted. Should the management committee include non-British members? At first I thought the club was about to take the inevitable step and let locals in. But it was non-British Europeans who were thought to be a threat to the club's management and identity. Family values were at stake; some of the Europeans, especially the women, had an itinerant, rakish style. I cannot now recall how the club resolved its crisis, but I do recall that Australians tended to side with the British.

The war in Vietnam, however, was the big story. I reported it with a heavy heart, accepting in principle the use of American power in Asia, but concerned by a mistaken strategy. I did not think that the triumph of communism was inevitable in Asia. Asian nationalists, whether a Nehru, Sukarno or Lee Kuan Yew, would resist it and they should be encouraged and supported. But how? Introducing overwhelming power into such a small country could only succeed if it brought quick results. To anyone with a grasp of the nationalist feeling in Vietnam against the French and now the Americans this was unlikely. While the Vietnamese refused to "surrender" and "victory" remained elusive, the commitment became open-ended. To sustain such a major military effort without victory would require political conviction and popular support in the United States and, for that matter, Australia, which was not there, especially after the assassination of President Kennedy. A long-haul, low-grade strategy, which had shown itself in Malaysia to be effective was a possible response, but it did not suit the American style.

I wrote in *The Crisis of Loyalty* (1972):

> I could not share the early view that the Vietnam war was, in some particular way, immoral. All war, in my view, is immoral, but that does not make it any the less necessary at times. The Vietnam commitment became, however, insane when a great power like the United States became committed to the escalation of an unrewardable effort by the decision in early 1965 to bomb North Vietnam and send American combat forces to the South. The war then became America's, not South Vietnam's. The means lost all rational relationship to the end, as the interests of the United States were much greater than the survival of an independent South Vietnam. Yet the war had to be fought as if the survival of the United States, not to mention democracy and the world itself, were at stake. The Vietnam war became a gross crusade, justifying the use of three times the tonnage of bombs dropped on Germany, Italy and Japan during World War Two and crimes against the ordinary men, women and children of Indo-China.

I am tempted to judge places according to whether I have written well there, and what I have written. I don't find it surprising that it was in America that I wrote about my boyhood and the ambiguities of detaching myself from my parents, nor that in Asia I was prompted to write my first book, *Indonesia*. It was written partly because I became absorbed with that country and partly to reflect Australia's role in its struggle for independence. In a rhetorical flourish in the introduction to the first edition, I wrote: "I first went to Indonesia expecting to contemplate Scott Fitzgerald's 'fresh, green breast of the new world'. When I found that the lovely land had been pawed for centuries, I became absorbed in the political corrective to this sordid affair: nationalism as a form of idealism, nationalism as rebirth."

In a short story called "A Bicycle Ride", published in *Meanjin*, I imagined that Angkor Wat was in the hands of the communists (not such wild imagining, it turned out) and that the question before the Americans was whether they would bomb a thousand years of civilisation. I was able to write that story from an Australian viewpoint (which I did by putting an innocent Australian couple at the centre of the drama), because when I visited Angkor I was surprised that the "jungle" turned out to be sparse-leafed, white-stemmed trees which reminded me of eucalypts. Asia and Australia met in the extraordinary, slow-motion struggle between nature and civilisation in those ruins. I stood for hours in front of the Bayon, one of the temples at Angkor Wat, hoping to witness some noise or movement that was part of what my eyes told me was happening – the takeover of the temple by the jungle. Not a movement. Not a sound. Yet the evidence was there. The head of a girl in a mosaic had moved several centimetres from her body. A root like an elephant's trunk was wrapped around a pillar. So slowly it was imperceptible, the temple was being destroyed by nature.

A novel, *Cherry Bloom*, set in Singapore, was an attempt to place the imported urbanity of Melbourne in the eponymous heroine and her English, diplomat husband against the raw poverty and ancient Chinese wisdom of the island colony, asserting itself in the turbulence of communist revolution and anti-colonialism in Asia.

I also began to think that I should put my shoulder to the wheel of Australia's mission in Asia. Friends in the Department of External Affairs (as it then was) arranged a meeting with the Minister, Sir Garfield Barwick, who arranged a meeting with Sir Arthur Tange, who was head of the department. The result was an offer to join the department at a level which I understood to be that of First Secretary in an embassy. My friendly departmental advisers were adamant I should only accept at a higher level, that of Counsellor, and nothing came of it.

My last posting as a foreign correspondent was to Washington. It is worth noting that I was the first full-time Australian correspondent in Washington. All Australian correspondents had been based in New York, on the assumption that readers were more interested in the financial affairs and entertainment of America than its politics. I had previously spent a year as a Nieman Fellow at Harvard University. For convenience I will treat the two periods in the United States as one, although they were different in an important respect. In the first, Kennedy was preparing his run for the presidency. In the second, Lyndon Johnson was in office, and the New Frontier, suggesting adventurous rigour, had been replaced by the Great Society, representing power and bounty now. Kennedy was a man of taste, Johnson a man of appetite. Each reflected aspects of the American experience.

In the United States, I did not have the feeling of returning to the source as I did in Britain. Although America was familiar, especially through the cinema, it was also a foreign country, a beautiful, powerful and exciting country that didn't have the finely tuned instincts of the British, but sprawled rather, dominating the land, a federal system dedicated to checking and balancing power yet obsessed with unity and with leadership. The people had swarmed over a bounteous continent, not clinging to coastal settlements looking hopefully out to sea, and they were believers, even if mostly in making money. They spent money as if in Marx's classless paradise, believing that if you spent according to your ability, the system would respond according to your needs. They talked about the market as Australians and Britons talked about the weather. They discussed money matters openly, asking how much you earned and how much you paid for your house or apartment. I had to re-examine words like "liberal" and "republic" to locate a position on the political spectrum. Homely verities like compulsory voting and the Australian Broadcasting Corporation had to be defended against libertarian enthusiasts, who saw them as the thin edge of the socialist wedge.

Harvard was Kennedy's intellectual base and I met him on a couple of occasions in small, friendly groups and sat in the classes of Ken Galbraith and Arthur Schlesinger Jnr., both of whom later served in his administration. So much has been written about Kennedy and his brief tenancy of the White House that it seems perverse now to recall that what I remember was none of the things for which he became known. Not charm nor charisma, rather a canniness, or caginess, that left me with the feeling that he would be a careful and even cautious president.

When I needed to engage with the US on questions of foreign policy, I was influenced by that first impression. The charm, which was a kind of humorous candour, was there, but it was on a leash. You could tell at a glance, or at least I thought I could, that Kennedy did not expect to transform the country, much less the world. Here was someone who liked to trim and tuck, not sail with the wind, who knew that progress in government was two steps forward (perhaps the second slightly to one side) and one step back (perhaps slightly longer than either of the forward steps), and who relished adversity as much as popularity. There was more of the New England particularism of Robert Frost ("I never dared be radical when young / For fear it would make me conservative when old") in Kennedy than the panoramic democracy of Walt Whitman. It was no surprise to me when Frost was chosen to read his poetry at Kennedy's inauguration.

I read *Profiles in Courage* after our first meeting, confirming my impression. This was not courage of the stand-and-deliver kind. John Quincy Adams, Sam Houston, Thomas Hart Benson, Daniel Webster and the others were not lustrous heroes but complex, even enigmatic, American politicians, protecting their backs, groping for a niche of self-interest, yet drawn irresistibly to serve the interests of the nation. What Kennedy said about them could be said about him. "However clear the effect of his courage, the cause is shadowed by a veil which cannot be torn away", he wrote in summary of his subjects. He said he shared the feeling expressed by Prime Minister Melbourne (of Britain), who, when irritated by the criticism of the then youthful historian Thomas Babington Macaulay, remarked that he would "like to be as sure of anything as Macaulay seemed to be of everything."

On my reading of Kennedy, I made sense of the Bay of Pigs (an inheritance he had to accept), the Berlin airlift (a warning line in the sand) and the Cuban missile crisis (patient, precise consideration of his opponent's interests). As for Vietnam, his assassination, a few weeks after Ngo Dinh Diem's, froze his presidency in a romantic capsule. We can still believe that the political turmoil in Saigon after Diem's removal would have been handled more adroitly by the US if Kennedy had still been president. We can conjecture that he would have been able to manage the larger crisis of Vietnam without threatening the stability of relations between the US and the USSR or China, and without tearing the American nation apart at home. But we do not know. What we do know is that the difference between a twilight struggle and a full-blown war became clear when Lyndon Johnson took over. People like myself, sympathetic to the US but unable to stay silent while the Vietnamese were bombed into submission in a replay of the Second World War, turned against the war.

Kennedy's leadership bid was based on the need for change domestically, where the years of "private affluence and public squalor", in Galbraith's phrase, had created an opportunity for the state to act, especially in support of the black population, which was not sharing in the spread of affluence and was now making political, as well as moral, demands. Internationally, the US had to take account of the fact that the Soviet Union had acquired a thermonuclear bomb; the Dulles-Eisenhower rhetoric of rolling-back communism was outdated and even containment was in doubt. All this seemed very evident in Harvard. Nevertheless, Kennedy only won (against Nixon) by a whisker.

At Harvard, I wrote a short story with autobiographical bearings called "Outpost of Christendom" which the *New Yorker* published. It began: "I noticed not long ago that it is twenty-two years since I gave my heart to Christ … The date and the circumstance are noted on the flyleaf of a Bible. The Bible is a legacy of my uncle, who was killed in World War One, and, on the flyleaf, the date of his transformation is also inscribed … Perhaps when he died in France, as a prisoner of war of the Germans, his heart was still in Christ's hands, but although I followed him exactly, becoming involved in war at the same age a generation later, I doubt whether, had I been killed, my heart would have been anywhere except in my own painful breast." I ended the story, having traversed pretty well everything I could think of about the juxtaposition of my family and the odd geopolitical identity of Australia, with a supposed nephew of mine pondering the future. "He would not be able to avoid noticing the irony that, at a high point of awareness of Christianity in Australia, some advanced thinkers among his countrymen were insisting that the future lay with Asia. He would certainly have to cope with Zen Buddhism, sooner or later." My last words were quixotic. "But I still have the Bible, and what I am going to do with it, is undoubtedly a nice question."

My encounter with the *New Yorker* was a lesson in editing. I was encouraged to build up a section by a couple of thousand words, although I had thought the story was already long. Then came the galley proofs, filled with explanations of editorial changes and suggested addendums and queries: "We have checked with the Australian embassy, and they have no record of this song" about a mildly ribald song my father used to sing; "Please check your figures for population of Perth in 1938"; and "What is the antecedent of 'it'?"

And the commas! There was someone on staff known as the 'comma king', whose job it was to ensure that all copy followed *New Yorker* style, scanning it like blank verse, breaking the flow with commas to produce a precise and upright effect. Ken Tynan, who was then the magazine's theatre critic, told me that he had been sent a cable in Havana requesting a grammatical change. He grumbled about the magazine being in a "comatose" state, but I liked the distinctive style, and submitted myself to it willingly. In David Remnick's obituary of the staff grammarian Miss Eleanor Gould we were given a glimpse behind the scenes. "Transparent, precise and muscular" was Miss Gould's policy. I was grateful for the magazine at the height of the Cold War for its relentless scrutiny of Mutually Assured Destruction (MAD), an acronym that embodied an opposing style, opaque, abstract and quiescent.

I wrote a story about madness in the Australian outback, "The Bride in the Creek", which was also published in the *New Yorker*, and a glimpse of politics and gentility in a one-horse town, "The Cocktail Party", published in *The Reporter*. In England, I had written some sketches of Australian life for the *Guardian* newspaper, but the cleverness of the English acted as a stopper on the literary and intellectual ambitions of a boy from the bush. In the United States and in Asia, on the contrary, I felt they wanted to know about this strange land in which I had been born.

I responded more readily to American politics than I had to British politics. There was an element of raw, pragmatic horse-trading about it that I found familiar, coupled with the rhetoric of what critics like Jacques Barzun called the "burdensome morality of good intentions". Although much of America was familiar, especially through the cinema, it was also a powerful, violent country which did not have the finely tuned national instincts of the British but sprawled, dominating the land, indeed the western hemisphere.

Missing was the world of variety, ambiguity, mystery and contingency that one found in Europe and Asia. I wrote: "Lack of surprise is what others might see as lack of charm. There is a harshness about the United States which is an amalgam of several things – a belief in good and evil, in facts and literal meanings, in efficiency and outcomes, in the power of numbers ... Americans can seem overbearing at times, as if the world in which they live is controlled and predictable and they know only too well how it works."

With time to investigate the archival resources of Harvard, I discovered a little known naval officer, Alfred Thayer Mahan, whose book, *The Influence of Sea Power upon History 1660–1783*, changed the outlook of official America in the decade that followed its publication in 1890. Mahan linked the desirable expansion of American commerce world-wide, which most Americans supported, with the need for a strong navy with fuelling posts and bases around the world, from which it could police those markets. His thinking captured a restless American mood and the attention of Theodore Roosevelt before he became president, when he was Secretary of the Navy in the Polk administration.

Some significant foreign events in United States diplomatic history foreshadowed Mahan. When Commodore Matthew Perry arrived offshore in Japanese waters in 1853, he may have been just looking for ports and supplies for American whalers, but he precipitated a defining moment for Japan, which for two centuries had been closed to trade with the outside world (except for the Dutch, who were allowed access through a quarantined island off Nagasaki). The "open door" policy on China at the time of the Boxer Rebellion in 1900 was another signpost to Americans of an active foreign policy, again not in Europe.

The war with Spain over the independence of Cuba brought this activism to another level. This was not just an expression of interest by an expanding nation; this was the American state in action. President McKinley, the last Civil War veteran to occupy the White House, was originally opposed to acquiring the Philippines, for all the right anti-colonial reasons. He then changed his mind, leaving a record of one of the most remarkable changes of heart in statecraft, after pacing the floors of the White House one night:

> It came to me … that (1) we could not give them back to Spain. That would be cowardly and dishonourable; (2) that we could not turn them over to France or Germany – our commercial rivals in the Orient. That would be bad business and discreditable; (3) that we could not leave them to themselves. They were unfit for self-government – and they would soon have anarchy and misrule over there worse than Spain's was; and (4) there was nothing left for us to do but to take them all, and to educate the Filipinos, and uplift and civilise and Christianise them, and by God's grace do the very best we could by them, as our fellow men for whom Christ also died. And then I went to sleep and slept soundly.

This early connection between commercial opportunity and military power, backed by moral authority, stayed in institutional memory, taking over as the guiding principle of American foreign policy during the 20th century. Some critics have said that it made the United States no different from the European colonial powers. McKinley's late-night monologue made the United States a colonial power in the Pacific: the Philippines did not regain its independence until after the Second World War. The essence of the "open door" policy was to demand equality of opportunity with the Europeans, who were carving up China between themselves.

Walter Lippmann argued during his lifetime (and with particular force during the Vietnam War) that the extension of American authority into the Pacific was a mistake. From the end of the War of 1812 with Britain until the war with Spain in 1898, United States foreign policy was, according to Lippmann, solvent. It met his requirement that: "a nation must maintain its objectives and its power in equilibrium, its purposes within its means and its means equal to its purposes, its commitments related to its resources and its resources adequate to its commitments ..." This elegant equilibrium was more easily attained in thought than in practice, but Lippmann shared with many others the view that after the war with Spain, the United States became overly interventionist outside Europe, especially in the Pacific, straining its resources, entangling its policy lines and confusing the American public.

During the 20th century, George Washington stood in American mythology for nationalism, as Woodrow Wilson stood for internationalism, and the comparison was almost always in Washington's favour. He was a hero, being leader of the revolutionary army and the new nation's first president, while Wilson was an idealist, believing in collective security. Until the Second World War, American "isolationism" contained elements of both Washington's distrust and Wilson's idealism.

Washington had warned Americans about Europe's "entangling alliances". The US reluctantly entered the First World War. President Woodrow Wilson drew attention to the secret diplomacy of the Europeans, which had both precipitated and been unable to prevent the war. He had a point. In 1914, the French Assembly was unaware of the secret clauses of the France–Russia alliance, which its diplomats had negotiated and which committed the two countries to each other's support. Sir Edward Grey, Britain's Foreign Secretary, had concealed from his own Cabinet the exact nature of the military arrangements reached between the French and British general staffs. Wilson advocated "open covenants, openly arrived at" and promoted the self-determination of nations rather than the stability of imperial power as a basis for a peaceful world. His high moral tone was reflected in American diplomacy of the period. Secretary of State Henry Stimson closed down the American code-breaking service with a remark that has passed into diplomatic history – "gentlemen do not read each other's mail".

By the time I lived in the United States, however, isolationism had become a form of solitary interventionism (in Central and South America, in Asia and the Middle East) and the doctrine of "exceptionalism" was emerging. It had not yet become the organising principle of state policy, but its self-regard, coupled with unilateral intervention, presented the world with a national belief that Americans had produced the greatest society of all time.

America shifted my perception of Australia. Most Australians assumed that the US welcomed a loyal and dependable ally. I found this not to be the case. Of course, it was hard to rebuff an excruciatingly loyal ally, and Americans were not slow to look after their own interests. But, outside official circles, a common American sentiment was, "You've got a great little country down there. Get it together. Do your own thing." And the comment of a senior foreign affairs and intelligence official has remained with me. "When your diplomats get in to see us, they always want to know what we think. They never tell us what they think." My time in the United States confirmed my view that our problems with the US were largely of our own making.

American journalism was impressive. The English – and the Europeans – were more brilliant writers, but Americans valued research. The columnists, the daily opinion-formers, were then at their height, before the new journalism of Tom Wolfe and the even newer journalism, or faction, of Norman Mailer. A great newspaper, like the *New York Times*, took itself seriously, printing each day for the public record during a long delivery strike, accepting no paid trips, requiring its foreign correspondents to use a local dateline only if the actual copy was sent from that place on that day. Rural and regional newspapers were also impressive, the *Baltimore Sun*, the *St Louis Post-Despatch*, the *Atlanta Constitution*, covering local news in detail with a good cover also of national and international news and background. The old American tradition of exposing corruption, or "muckraking" had been refined into stylish investigative journalism and would reach a peak with the Vietnam War and the Watergate scandal.

Occasionally, when I returned to Australia, I wrote articles for the *Washington Post*. As an example of the care and attention to detail that surprised and impressed me about the best of American journalism, consider this letter from the managing editor Philip Foisie. Australian editors tended to be sharp and unforgiving and British editors were not inclined to be solicitous about what Australians were thinking or doing.

Dear Mr Grant,

I recently mailed you a tearsheet of your column, as it appeared in the prestigious Outlook *section of our Sunday paper. You should* *also have received a check for $75 by now. Please let me know if the money fails to arrive.*

The column was well-received, and was in fact the first thoughtful piece we've carried on the Australian political scene for more than a year. At least a dozen of your acquaintances in Washington (you seem to have almost as many here as I do) have remarked to me about your column and you appearing in The Post.

One of them was Denis Warner, who was here to reorder his life following the demise of The Reporter. He did rather well, I gather. He left for home today, so you will probably soon hear first hand how he fared. It's possible that some of his valued reports from Southeast Asia will now appear in The Post.

I hope you'll try another "Letter from Australia" in a month or so, and I'm arranging a credit cable card for you as you suggest, so that when you must refurbish a mailer, as you had to in the first one, you can do so with greater despatch.

I have these suggestions:

None of us wishes you to "write down". We have an informed readership in Washington, for whom columns like yours are primarily intended. But even this readership, while informed, is out of touch with Australia and need a little help in two ways.

First, though you must not feel inhibited from referring to any person, party, event or whatever, your allusions should not be too abrupt for American readers. For instance, it would have helped the forgetful though informed reader, who has seen precious little from Australia in recent years, if you had been a bit more explicit about the fact that Menzies and Holt had been the only prime ministers since Menzies came to power, and I would have added the word "opposition" to the first reference to the Labor party (we're so accustomed to thinking in terms of British Labor); and I would have recalled that Holt had drowned, for while that event of course was the lead story in The Post on that day, we have short memories and the reminder would help.

This is mere detail, of course. It's only a matter of a word or a phrase here and there, and we could put them in on the desk, but it's always better when we don't have to touch copy.

The other matter is one of approach, and I enclose a copy of a recent "Letter from Ottawa" to make my point. Your lead laid it right on the line in a no-nonsense way, which is normally preferred, but in the "Letter" format you can afford to relax a bit – write it more like a real letter. Also, Eastabrook's "Letter" – which was not a whit more informative than yours – nevertheless covered a bit more ground. I realise you were dealing with a difficult topic, since Gorton had not yet come into focus (has he yet?). But perhaps in the next "Letter" you can touch on a number of subjects of interest, letting one lead into the next, as Bob [Eastabrook] did.

Perhaps you could even allude to a piece of current Australian life or gossip, squeeze it into your "Letter", merely by your choice of metaphor. A phrase here and there might serve both as a simile to support the point you're trying to make and, at the same time, tell us what the weather is like, how Australians feel about open tennis, how the stock market is going (very well, I hear) or what Australians are reading about in the papers or hearing about on television.

This, I think, would make your "Letters" more fun to read and give a more life-like picture of Australia, without crudifying or distorting in the least the important and serious points you wish to make.

I write this in the certain knowledge that you write much better than I do. All I have to offer is a better knowledge of how our readers react to material.

We will always be interested, of course, in how Australia reacts to American policy and action, and in Australia's policies in Southeast Asia, especially Vietnam and Indonesia, and toward Japan and China. Also, how Australians view our domestic problems – what view they get of them as well. We would welcome more information on major internal Australian developments and trends – the growth of your mining industry, for example, and even whatever you deem worthy of note in what we call the "back of the book" field – art, drama, literature, religion, anything not wholly political or economic. But I would guess it would be better for you to merely allude to events in this category rather than to dwell on them, unless the event is of international note, or can be related more or less directly to things American, or is extraordinary per se – like the Sydney opera house.

Could you tell me, by the way, if you are available to do a spot story should the need arise? And whom would you recommend as a standby, in the event that you are not, or are away travelling? We occasionally use the Newsweek man in Sydney. Do you know him?

I'd also like to know when you do travel, and where. Could we pick up your material from The Age *in that case and, if so, under what conditions. I'd have loved to have used your tourism piece from Ulan Bator.*

Best regards

I had met Walter Lippmann in London. We strolled from Clarendon's hotel, where he was staying, to the Foreign Office, where he had an appointment. I had always been affected by his writing; the common criticism that it was too intellectual, or, as some said, cerebral, for journalism, seemed to me merely to point to its distinction. It had a quality lacking in most journalism; it was critical of those responsible for public policy, without resorting to verbal or logical trickery, and it made an effort to understand the context in which people exercised power. The spark that kept him alive for at least one reader was, however, something simple and personal – a sense of drama that touched his writing with emotion. He was not just an observer but a participant as well, moving among political leaders and nations as someone who clarified what they were doing. He was sought by statesmen all over the world not only because they hoped to convince him of their cause, but because he might help them to understand what they were doing, what their cause was, and what chance it had of success.

I discovered, as we walked in London, that he had an enviable confidence in the authenticity of his own life. He made appointments well in advance, sometimes a year ahead, and kept them, no matter how unwelcome or irrelevant current events made them seem. He was interested in exploring my impression of the British. We stopped at the Horse Guards. "Yes," he said, admiringly. "They do know how to dress up."

He later in Washington gave me some valuable advice about writing a column. First, he said, keep it short. The people who were interested in serious thinking on what he called heavyweight topics were busy. Also (with a twinkle that rarely showed in his writing) you can be syndicated in the tabloids. Second, no "straw men". Give your opponents a fair hearing. Set out their position clearly, even better than they do themselves, then demolish them. "Your position will be all the stronger for having overcome theirs," he concluded sagely, with a glance in my direction that showed he knew he was taking the high road. The view was better from the high road and, at the end of the journey, the satisfaction was greater. This was the intellectual speaking, the liberal, rational man who, in his search for the proper use of power in the everyday world of politics, where giving your opponent a fair hearing was a sign of weakness, clung to the belief that truth had its own value. His last advice was to get a research assistant. If academics needed help on research, why not newspaper columnists, who were just as vulnerable if they got the facts wrong? People who were not capable of contesting your argument would be quick to undermine it by citing inaccuracy. I recalled his advice when, later, I was asked by *The Age* to write a political column.

The life of a foreign correspondent then was more leisurely and romantic than today. We did not have to contend with the 24-hour news cycle and were able to immerse ourselves on the fringes of normal life. The insouciance of Sir Wilmot Lewis, when he was correspondent of the London *Times* in Washington, was legendary. His office door was jammed by a cascade of letters and cables from London that he refused to answer. "Remember," he told his successor. "Whatever happens, you are right and London is wrong."

In a lecture in 1966, I mentioned some correspondents I had known. "How does one compare the professional equipment of a great reporter like Patrick O'Donovan, who perhaps more than any foreign correspondent alive can write of nations as if they, too, were alive, but who may have difficulty reporting accurately the essential politics in, say, a discussion between two heads of state or government, with a great reporter like Abe Rosenthal, who built his brilliant despatches from Poland on primary sources, especially secret ones, or with, say, Henry Brandon, who has no great flair, I would suggest, for conveying the tone and quality of American life, but who is knowledgeable about the inner politics of Washington? Or Dennis Bloodworth, with his immense knowledge of Asia, especially China, his laborious cross-documentation of a story and his love of puns, covering Vietnam like a trembling Doberman, with David Halberstam, immensely serious and dedicated, covering Vietnam like a bloodhound with a scent? Or Bob Trumbull, according the day's events no more and no less than – from his great experience – he estimated them to be worth, with Bernie Kalb, who would launch himself on each day as if it contained the final reckoning? Or two Indian correspondents, T.V. Parasuram, who covered everything in shorthand, and filed a good deal of it, with Ajit Battarcharghea, who wryly bestirred himself occasionally in order to send a piece that would delight his readers for months? Or Dick Hughes, who is perhaps incomparable, one of the world's great amateurs, with a skilled and courageous professional like Denis Warner?"

Those mentioned were all men. Today, there are probably as many women in the field, especially in television. I also touched in the lecture on something that, in fiction, had troubled Joseph Conrad, Somerset Maugham and Graham Greene – how to live other than passively among people who are not your own. "You can be active professionally. You may be involved intimately in all kinds of human affairs – indeed, the romantic picture of the foreign correspondent is that he is, most of the time. But you have no rights, and in a civic sense you are passive. In their own countries, journalists at least have the rights of citizens, but a foreign correspondent had neither civil rights nor the immunity of the diplomat as compensation for the deprivation."

6

192 DAYS AND NIGHTS

Ms Joan Pennell wore black stockings, wrote poetry, played the guitar, spoke French fluently, lived alone in a Federation apartment at 6 Grove Court in Greenwich Village and worked at *Radio Free Europe*, 2 Park Avenue. For me, she was quintessential New York ... intellectual, sophisticated, worldly. But she was also a dutiful Jewish daughter, thoughtful and considerate, and she was seemingly interested in me.

Her father was a doctor with a Brooklyn practice. Her friends, including former boyfriends, were active in politics. William vanden Heuvel became US Deputy Ambassador to the United Nations and Chairman of the Roosevelt Foundation. Ulric Haynes became US Ambassador to Algeria.

We met through Evelyn Maxwell, wife of Neville, a friend from Melbourne who had become a Washington correspondent for *The Times*; Evelyn and Joan had shared an apartment in New York.

I was something of a curiosity to her family and friends. They looked east, to Europe, not west, and Australia had not occurred to them as worthy of notice. Asked by my presence to think about it, they decided it was a frontier society like the United States had been before their families arrived – and civilised it. Still, I was at Harvard, which must mean that, at least, I was capable of intelligent thought.

Joan arranged a lunch with several of her girlfriends, which made me uneasy, so, to mark my independence, I flirted with them. Joan won me over, however, by telling them she liked the way I thought.

One way of encouraging a friendship is to explore new territory together. We took to the road to discover America's heart of darkness, the South, especially Birmingham, where the Ku Klux Klan was active and racial rioting was more intense than anywhere in the United States, and New Orleans, the home of jazz. The everyday humiliation of segregation (not just the suburbs but public transport and churches) shocked us both, affecting Joan perhaps even more than it did me. I had glimpsed the banality of apartheid in South Africa, was more widely travelled, and this was not my country. But on that journey we forged a bond against racial discrimination that has remained throughout our lives.

It was 1959 and the Cold War was ascending, but neither at Harvard nor among Joan's circle at Radio Free Europe (funded partly by the Central Intelligence Agency) was there the sense of urgency or concern about a global communist threat that developed in the 1960s with the Vietnam War. The US had been on the winning side in the Second World War and that generation was now in positions of power and influence. The Korean War had ended in a kind of draw. George Kennan's moderate response to the Soviet Union – contain it, not attack it – was conventional wisdom; the idea that communism should be "rolled back" by military force was a fringe obsession. There was a sense that, as Henry Luce had predicted, the 20th century was still America's, to be shaped and determined by the intrinsic superiority of American values and American know-how. The failure of the great American melting pot to absorb the African slaves who were still without civil rights was a troublesome shortcoming for thoughtful Americans but not a threat to the United States.

When I visited New York from Cambridge, Massachusetts, I stayed at the Hotel Van Rensselaer. Joan received from the manager a hand-written letter, which can be recorded as among the most delicately seductive invitations of its kind.

Dear Miss Pennell,

It has been brought to our notice that occasionally you have stayed overnight here, apparently in room 201, which, according to our records, is occupied by a Mr Grant, of 233 Collins Street, Melbourne Australia. We are also aware that you made the booking for Mr Grant. We would like you to know that, if you have any other gentlemen friends who might be induced to stay here, presumably on the understanding that you are their guest from time to time, we would be most considerate in finding a suitable room, paying due attention to the likely requirement that another means of entry and exit used by the aforesaid Mr Grant would be desirable.

We also have a number of single men in residence here who would, we feel sure, welcome the opportunity to make your acquaintance.

Your servant,

The Manager

Joan was convinced that the letter was a spoof compiled by her friend, the writer Alfred Grossman, now deceased.

Joan's father died suddenly of a heart attack shortly after we met and this tragedy hung over our romance. Her sister, a talented pianist, was undergoing expensive medical supervision, which, after the death of their father, became unsustainable. Her mother had adored her father and was dependent on him. Joan seemed set to become the breadwinner and manager of an unhappy little family.

Our early relationship is glimpsed in selections from the many letters we wrote to each other, beginning soon after we met in 1958, when I was at Harvard and Joan took a holiday with her mother in Florida, staying at the Hotel Roncy Plaza at Miami Beach. It continued until she came to live with me the following year in Singapore, where my children visited on school holidays, and where, in 1962, we were married. I have calculated our time apart in this subtle moment as "192 days and nights" from the dates of the letters.

126 Hancock Street, Cambridge 39, Massachusetts (undated)

The mail, with infuriating impartiality, delivered to me two letters from you today – one written last Friday and stamped 11.30 that night and the other written on Sunday and stamped 10.30 the next morning, which is only yesterday. I was reminded of a conversation I had here a few months ago with a mailman who sat next to me in a coffee shop ... I complained about the mail service: he listened with that kind of emergent smile which suggests that the reply to what you are saying is already well formed in his mind. I went on, referring to specific cases. Ah, yes, he said, broadening his smile, but no letters ever get lost. No matter how long it may be delayed, it is certain to turn up ... one day. What if the mailman drops a letter from his bag and the wind blows it down a drain? It happens, he said, it happens. But it will turn up, sodden perhaps, so that no-one can read it, but the address can be deciphered and the letter will be delivered to the right person ... some months later. But what's the good of mail that takes four days to come from New York, I asked. That's exceptional, he said, but even if a bag may get put aside and forgotten for a day or so, you can be sure the letter will always turn up. They always do. Yours did, didn't it?

You will recall the two letters, the Friday one about icy tree fingers and honesty, the Sunday night one, exclamatory and excited (your tipsy evening) about men and vanity. I am beginning to see you in the round … One of the reasons I am not a scholar is that I don't believe that politics is the play of social and economic forces. I think it is men and women in action. I do not believe that history is determined … I'm with Pasternak, with free personality and moral responsibility … I don't like working within a definition of what I can do, which means that I make lots of mistakes. What a life you will have with me, fashion-show-cocktail party-and dance girl … You will have to learn to be deep and steady and true, to keep me from bruising and braining myself. You have a sustaining effect on me, a confidence which grows from the sense of you as someone who can be trusted, loved deeply without self-consciousness, and with whom the ideas of honour and respect can be shared in experience. Flippancy is something I do not always object to in other people … sometimes it is charming … but it comes in me with a mixture of vanity and dishonesty and it always leaves me feeling annoyed with myself.

***The Age*, Melbourne 30 August 1959**

Enid and the children went to see a friend who lives in the country and met, by chance, another family with children at the same school as ours. And they had HORSES! Sue is practically incoherent on horses; she loves them as other children love cats and dogs. She knows all about short-rein riding, short-stirrup mounting and talks excitedy about their manes and tails and the sensitivity of their mouths to the 'bit' … Enid and I had a long talk about the Bambi [Shmith] gossip. She said she intended to take no notice, that she would remain Bambi's friend and have her to the house as before, that it would be alright for her to go to Singapore with the children to visit me if it suited her ... generally she was awfully good. The gossip now is that Bambi was not actually in England while she was away, but in America and that she has come back here to marry me ... Bambi is self-conscious about it ... Enid is sure it will die down, but it isn't easy to handle because of the grain of truth in it ...

Vincent Buckley, a Catholic poet I lunched with the other day, thought Dr Zhivago was the best statement of Christian values that he had read. We didn't have time to go into it, but I keep thinking about it ... I think it's more a statement in favour of "life" than Christian values ... Today, coming in to work on the train, looking at the houses, the trees, the sky, people, I had that feeling of excitement in the particularity of life that is essentially poetic ... somehow a woman turning in a lane to look over her shoulder (at what?) becomes universal ... Bear with me. Now that my article on David Riesman for Esquire is finished, I will write a long, steady letter on these interminable thoughts about life, work and you.

In August 1959 Joan wrote to me at 1A Cairo Flats, 98 Nicholson Street, Melbourne, with a detailed account of her many calls on newspapers and magazines for possible work in Singapore. "It is an awful feeling walking into places you don't know and, as it were, offering yourself ... And my feet hurt!"

The Age, Melbourne 4 September 1959

Two busy useful interesting days in Canberra, with officials and collecting visas ... and two nights in long conversations with Manning about his new book, which is superb. He also spent half an hour on an ecstatic description of a river near Canberra which is full of fish and strange insects and comes to life at dusk. He is still under the influence of his trip to Russia and his encounter with "Soviet Man". What seems to have moved him is the boundless optimism and faith in 'good works', and yet the feeling underneath (Russian, he says, rather than Communist) that this will never achieve … well, what? … the 'answer' (which has a lot to do with Manning's sense of inevitable tragedy). I had an hour with the Prime Minister (Mr Menzies) and an hour with the Leader of the Opposition (Dr Evatt). The PM was affable ("Have a cigar, old boy – the last time I saw you was on television") and has written, or is writing, personal letters to all our ambassadors in Asia and "other important people", advising them of my new job. Dr Evatt was more interesting – a humane, intelligent man, broken by the unscrupulous tactics of opponents, bad luck and perhaps a large dose of ambition … The Clarks are in fine shape and James and I have been incorporated into the household without any noticeable effect. There are six Clark children (aged 3–20). Only four are here but they have a cousin staying with them, which makes a household of nine.

We're flying over snow-capped mountains (yes, we do have them in Australia) and James is as pleased as Punch, because we didn't see much when we flew up at night. He had the time of his life at the Clarks, playing table tennis, shuttlecock, football, watching Manning and me making fools of ourselves "flying" for high marks. I am more than ever aware, after these few days, that we should marry and live in Australia. I love the force of life in Manning and his sense of this country, not in a nationalistic sense, but as a home for humanity. Also, I found Canberra attractive. We must come here. The air is clear, the flowers smell, there are birds everywhere, the mountains are near, the sky changelessly blue. It's full of small official snobbery, but the Clarks accept that as part of life. Important, I was able to see people and do things, without having to change anything in myself.

The Age, Melbourne 7 September 1959

I'm very interested in your comments on War and Peace … your fascination with the book's "wholeness". This is what the psychological novel has destroyed. It was inevitable, but it seems to me now that with all the knowledge that Freud et al have given us of ourselves we ought to be able to get back (with added depth) to the whole-of-life novel … Alfred (Grossman) said in Acrobat Admits, "I'm not going to over-simplify. I'm going to make it more difficult." I admire that, just as one admires Freud (and the whole inquisitive, scientific tradition) but I don't think you can explain the "life-ache" you talk about by "total cognition". What's more, the detailed, scientific approach just doesn't make for good writing.

The Age, Melbourne 9 September 1959

I'm sleepy this morning. I didn't get to bed until 2 a.m., as I saw Bambi after work to discuss Ray Lawler's play The Summer of the 17th Doll. We are both so busy that after 10pm or before 9 am (her starting time) are the only times available … Bambi talked a lot about you. She says that when she first met you she thought you were particularly important to me. ("Now there's a girl you ought to marry."), that you were a rare kind of human being ("the only one in captivity?" I ask) and that you have even more integrity than I have (was this a compliment?). Most of all, you are not at all like an American … Your poor Americans … You are all so alike, haircuts, clothes, so that people can talk about Americans as if they all come out of a machine (or the melting pot?)

I am now booked to leave for Singapore on 29 September. Sue asked me today whether there would be any of my friends in Singapore. She had first asked "Why don't you marry Bambi. I think she's nice." I said a lady called Joan would help me in Singapore to look after her and the twins. "Is she nice?" "Yes." "I hope she's not bossy," said Sue. "Oh, no, not bossy," I said, "very nice and funny." (The children like Bambi because she is funny). "Will she play with us?" I said I was sure you would and that you played the guitar and sang the kind of songs I had brought on records back from America. "That's good," said Sue. "Is she white?" What a wonderfully simple approach. If I had said you were black, I doubt it would have made any difference. But you can see the stereotype, the black guitarist.

The Age, Melbourne 16 September 1959

I had an encounter today with a man from one of the intelligence agencies. Very hush-hush. We met in a street, went to a car, drove off and talked in the car (wired I'm sure) while he suggested to me that I might like to report back to them any matters I thought might be of interest. More precisely, if I were approached by Russian or Chinese representatives and any suggestion made (such as writing for them etc etc), they would like me to report this to spy headquarters in Melbourne. The interview did not go well. I left without any commitment, except a vague promise that I would get in touch if I thought it necessary. I reported all this to the editor Keith Sinclair, although my spy friend asked me not to. I think I mentioned to you that I had had spy problems in London. It seems to me we have a new kind of McCarthyism. It is not enough not to be a communist, not to "associate" with them or take their side on issues: you have to prove you are loyal by working with our spies.

3 Hawthorn Grove, Melbourne, 18 September 1959

Sue has a stomach ache and has stayed home from school, so I have come over to let Enid go to work. I am sitting in my old room at 3 Hawthorn Grove, looking through the bay windows at the rose bushes, the trees in the street beginning to sprout green, the big, two-storied house opposite that I had always thought I would like to have. The room is a little different. The big Australian oil painting still hangs over the fireplace, but a Monet print has been moved to another wall, an oil by a friend, Ian Bow, has been moved to a different position on the wall, the two leather arm chairs need repair, one bookshelf is now empty (because of my packing of books for Singapore in recent days) and there are now book shelves on each side of the fireplace. The pretty, apricot ceiling and white, elaborately lace-work cornices are the same and the plain green drops remain. The old-fashioned tiles in the fireplace grate are still there.

The Age, Melbourne 23 September 1959

Much cabling and telephoning London has produced the information that Harewood is leaving his wife, or says so, and Bambi is supposed to leave immediately for London and live with him. I can't see her surviving the scandal. She's not a Callas or an Elizabeth Taylor, nor is she a Duchess of Windsor. I think she's concerned about leaving her son Michael, who is the same age as Sue. I'm trying to persuade her that she should tell him that she will come to London, but later … I would like her to come with the children to Singapore, stay for two or three months, just to separate Harewood's leaving from her arrival. Bambi says he worries about the possibility that we might resume our relationship. Well, he'll have to worry.

Raffles Hotel, Singapore, undated

I'll be glad to leave Raffles, although it is a splendid relic of the days of the Raj. It's now an American tourist attraction and I never thought I could grow so tired of American voices. I think of you and tell myself that your voice is, essentially, the same. So what is it? It's the situation, essentially. These delicate, soft-spoken Chinese men and women rushing attendance on a lot of hot and bothered people with loud voices.

I have a curious relationship with the liftman, a young Malay who told me that he is a Roman Catholic and has trouble resisting women on his one day off a week. He has an aching back this week. He does not want to marry, but is bothered by the conflict between his religion and his appetite for sex. I wondered if there were a conflict, which led him to question me about my religious faith. His face fell when I said that, while I had no doubt that Jesus had lived an extraordinary life, I didn't believe that he was the son of God - and I wasn't even sure about God. No longer a bemused, thoughtful conspirator, hoping perhaps for guidance, he became a stern propagandist for what he believed was Christianity's largest following. I made matters worse by saying there were more Buddhists and Muslims in the world than Roman Catholics. I am now greeted in the lift each day with lofty disdain.

Cockpit Hotel, 6–7 Oxley Rise, Singapore, after a meeting with a colonel from the British army, undated

He is one of those people who presents such a comic opera view of the world that I cannot stop myself becoming seriously social-democratic … 'Great people, the Thais. They have the art of corruption under finest control … shows they are a superior civilisation, what!' A this point I say something like 'But corruption destroys dignity … We back corrupt high-class officials and then wonder why the communists get popular support'. I also disliked the colonel's attitude to Americans. 'They are decent enough. I've got some good friends who are American … but they won't do anything much with their power in the world until they have a civilisation at least equal to those they have power over … You know, I've met lots of Americans working in Indo-China who can't speak French!'

The (Lee Kuan Yew) government here has an impossible task. It is trying to make a social-welfare, even socialist, state out of an intensely capitalist, commercial centre. Singapore has no production … so it wants to link up with Malaya, which has rich resources of rubber and tin … but the Malays think that, with federation, Chinese would outnumber Malays … I miss you, but do not worry about me … my emotional life is secure and happy in spite of parting from the children and being away from you. There is plenty to do … I relish the chance to get away working on my own … My suspicion is that I won't want to work in this part of the world for more than the two years I expect to be on this assignment. I think it is valuable, but only as a small part of the total commitment. You know as much, or as little, as I do of what the 'total" is … but it can be sensed in Melbourne or New York as much as here … I don't have the feeling that I used to have … that I should 'become' a writer. Perhaps one just is a writer, wherever one happens to be. You, dear, are responsible for this, you are for me proof that certain things you want can receive recognition … I have to make a living. So drive carefully!

Cockpit Hotel, undated

Dear Field of a Thousand Blooms, Four letters from you! Dear Sea of a Million Caresses, I am sending you a tooth of the Buddha to preserve your life and beauty for ever, even after death. There are as many teeth and bones of Buddha in these parts as there are teeth and bones of Jesus Christ in Italy … I got another flip of the spirit last night reading the manifesto of the Singapore government, marvellous old 19th-century stuff … they believe that if social conditions are improved, people will be better. Prostitution? Do away with unemployment and it will cease … Racial conflict? Release the "human resources" of Malays, Chinese, Indians and English and they will form themselves voluntarily into a nation.

Racial conflict is an expression of economic uncertainty. Marvellous stuff! What a lot of rubbish is said about this "communist" government. It is about as communist as the Australian Labor Party … I'm almost sick of houses … from old places with huge gardens to lawned bungalows and high-rise flats, there's always something wrong, too expensive to keep up or to furnish, not enough bedrooms … I'll stick at house-hunting this week and then I'll have to make a decision … When you and the children are here, I am planning a trip one long week end to Malacca. We will drive to the mountains. Mountains in the tropics are like going to another country.

Cockpit Hotel, undated

The flat is fourth floor, with a lift. You walk into a large, living-dining room, perhaps a little wider and about the same length as the main downstairs room at your mother's. There is a balcony, which looks over trees, houses, lawns etc … not a panoramic view, but a pleasant one. Standing at the balcony and looking back into the room, you have right at the end and to the left the kitchen, which is largish, although a little dark because its end-on to the light, and a big pantry, which leads off the kitchen. On the right, leading from the main room at one central point (it has a semi-porch effect) you have three bedrooms. Two of them have large, built-in cupboards. One, which is in an ideal position for a study-office, is bare. There are, although I cannot remember exactly how they fit, three bathrooms, two with long baths, each with shower and toilet. Each bedroom has a lot of window, because the flat is on a corner, running the full depth of the building. It is tastefully (I think) decorated; the walls are grey-blue, the floors are parqueted in a fine, variegated tile. The effect generally is clean and airy, which is what attracted me to it. Everything is so damp here … the smell of rotting wood is everywhere. I'm sure you'll like it. The address is: 7B Wilmer Court, Leonie Hill Road, Singapore 9.

It's four pounds above the eighteen pounds the office is allowing me, but worth it. And now I have to find out how much to have fans installed and air conditioning put in.

7B Wilmer Court, 9 October 1959

I'm suffering this morning from one of those inexplicable failures of spirit. It's the first since I left you more than three months ago. I think it's connected with the film on China (The Chinese Wall, which I had seen with Denis and Peggy Warner). I remember thinking at the time that China was so beautiful, so huge and full, that I could never report it if I were there. I could only scratch the surface and this I would rather not do. The alternative? To live and study in Hongkong to become a China specialist? But I don't want that either. What I'm learning on this assignment I want to take back with me to the West, if one must look at it in political terms. I went to sleep with a heavy load of dreams concerning you and the children and people I love … an exhausting tussle with the emotions of engagement against a background of massive physical indifference, huge, endless mountains.

I want to write to you about this because it's part of our relationship … I liken the feeling to the failure of spirit that killed Andre in War and Peace. The wound was nothing: you remember how Tolstoy keeps hinting that it should have healed. What happened to Andre was that he lost ambition, the only thing that had kept him moving, kept him interested. I think that what I have been trying to do in the past few years is to replace the drive of ambition … of showing off at writing, at being successful with women (can it be traced to a mother's hopes?) with something more lasting, more impersonal. It cannot be religion. Work, genuine, self-respecting hard work has helped. (I kept thinking, watching the old Chinese scholars at work in the film, of the flashy brilliance of Ken Tynan, his superb ego, and wondering what they would think of him). I don't have the ups and downs as much. When I feel empty, as this morning, I can get through it without a lot of false activity, which used to make me feel emptier. Perhaps, if there's some mail from you today, I'll feel better quickly!

7B Wilmer Court October 10, 1959

Your last letter recounted your exploits with SANE and the dinner with Al, the MGM publicity man, at Nina's. I'm afraid I share your disapproval, both of the hostessing aspect of SANE and of the conversation. That kind of talk ("I promise I won't lay you tonight") is the kind I heard a lot in America and makes me wish the person would leave the room, or that I would. The arrogance – not even the modesty of I won't (try) to ... I suppose you are used to it, but I don't understand why you do not leave, or move to another part of the room, simply on the grounds of discomfort ... You should really do more reading and writing. Half the six months is gone. I know you're tied up with your mother in lots of ways but, unless you've been working without telling me about it, I have the impression you haven't been settling down to the solid work you need to do. Do I sound crabby? No, I'm just reminding you ... To return to the point of discomfort. People are embarrassed by that kind of talk but don't do anything about it in fear of being thought old-fashioned or "square". To hell with that. I don't see why a fashion, set by people who are obsessed with the subject (be it sex, clothes, cars or whatever) should ride over normal human respect and courtesy.

The book on Nehru gets a tremendous review in the TLS (London). My own review was equally full of praise ... I was personally surprised that on every public or private issue discussed in the book, I agreed with Nehru. I would have done exactly the same. Yet I have no idea why I would have made this decision or that, just as I'm sure Nehru doesn't know why he did. It's something to do with the balances of life.

7B Wilmer Court, 15 October 1959

A big mail today, letters from you, my mother, Nettie Palmer (Vance's widow), the London Observer (with a cheque for an article) and two issues of The Age newspaper (I get the first four news pages and editorial page airmailed daily).

Nettie's letter had been forwarded ... It was slightly pathetic, inviting me to "drop in one day for a talk." She is trying to keep up Vance's practice. He loved people dropping in for "a talk"; you would then stay for a meal, which he would cook (Nettie beaming at him). She doesn't seem to realise that I'm away from Australia. She's 75 and perhaps is slipping. I've written a cheerful note, saying I'll drop in next year.

Yesterday's session of Parliament was fascinating. The Socialist government of Lee Kuan Yew took a strong anti-communist line, saying that its social and economic reforms would "remove the need" for a communist party in Singapore. On security, it argued that subversion not only came from the Left (Russia and China) but from the Right (sponsored by the West). Lee, aged 36, is handsome, arrogant and brilliant, with double first degrees from Cambridge and a voice like Laurence Olivier's. His party is self-consciously plebian – no ties or coats (except for Lee, who was wearing, like a sports coat over cricketing flannels, a sharply cut, hacking-style jacket.

7B Wilmer Court, November 1959

It's 149 days tomorrow since I left New York. It is 56 days to the end of December, 9 weeks to January 4 ... I hope the packing is on its way. The children will be here in 7 weeks. Somehow, I feel now that it is all happening – that in fact you will all be here before I have had time to do all I have to do! I shall get very excited in December, I'm afraid.

Choi has just brought me a cup of coffee … it is 10.30; I've had a couple of interruptions. I have been thinking again about getting accreditation for you. You shouldn't be shy about presenting yourself. After all, it is a good arrangement for a newspaper or magazine. You are paying your own fare and have your own accommodation.

7B Wilmer Court December 14, 1959

All those pills! I don't think they'll care if you bring them with you. Bring a letter from Dr. Press saying you need them … I'm told by the wife of the Associated Press man that lipstick is expensive here, so bring your own brand (Somehow I can't imagine you have your own brand of lipstick) … I sent a Christmas card to your mother, writing something to the effect that I hoped next year would be a good year "for all of us", which seemed to me to cover an awkward differentiation.

I think I am putting on weight. I ate a lot on the Menzies tour of Indonesia; we were always sitting down to huge meals and the long hours meant I was often hungry. Perhaps you get fatter in the tropics, with all that moisture around.

7B Wilmer Court, 15 December 1959

We both have family problems (my children, your mother and Margot). Each can help the other. I think it is necessary for you to break with your mother – that is, live away from her – but I'm sure I would be very unhappy if I felt you wanted to break with your family for good. People who talk about loving "the whole world" are often escaping from the responsibility of loving anyone in particular. Your strong feelings about your family and my strong feelings for mine do not worry me. They make me happy, because they show that we do not want to start life "afresh". People who want to start life afresh are always starting it afresh.

I am re-reading Chekhov in bits and pieces. I come back to him time and time again. He always makes me feel happy – you know the thrill when you find something that you know is true.

7B Wilmer Court, 20 December 1959

I bought a carpet, very cheaply – 22 US dollars. It's Indian style, nine feet by six feet, large enough to make the room look less bare, made in Belgium, for heaven's sake. You find the strangest things in this busy port. The other furniture has arrived – the two beds are now awaiting occupants in the second bedroom. I had to buy sheets and blankets, pillows and slips … and stock up with food.

A letter from Enid with details of plans for the children's visit. Bambi was driving them all to the airport and she and Bambi would explain that Bambi would be joining them in Singapore later … leaving it too late for the children to be able "to spread the word around." Bambi was concerned that Michael would be upset and that the gossip about me would be revived. Enid would accompany them to Sydney, where she will have a holiday for a week or so. She seemed cheerful and I suspect she appreciates the chance to have a break.

I have joined the Swimming Club. It's a lovely spot, with a large pool and ideal for the children. It is a recreational centre, not a social club, and the cost was about half of the others, which was also a factor.

7B Wilmer Court, 21 December 1959

Well, they've been here a day. The trip up was fine, although they all pronounced it "boring". We sorted out the bed situation and they were asleep by 10.30pm. I have made return bookings for them on February 6. Many children come up for the school holidays and it is wise to book return flights early. We went to the Swimming Club this morning, then into town for Xmas shopping. On the way from the club, James said quietly, "I didn't see any black people there." So I had to explain the "Europeans only" club rule. (Actually, a furious debate is under way over the club's management committee, which is not only exclusively British, not just European, but I didn't go into that). "I like black people," said Sue," they look marvellous". She wants to meet the Indian girl downstairs, who unfortunately is away. A letter from Bambi today said she would arrive on schedule in two days' time, but would only be able to stay until 29 December, as she is meeting Harewood in Milan on 1 January. That's a pity. I was hoping that I could get her to stay longer, perhaps overlap with you. It also means two weeks between her leaving and your arrival and (for purely practical, child-minding contingencies, such as me having to rush off to Ceylon or Laos or somewhere) I had wanted to keep that gap as narrow as possible. Bambi wrote that she had a letter from you and it seemed to please her very much. The children chose Xmas gifts for her today, Chinese slippers (James), a little Buddha (Jo) and a silk Indian scarf (Sue). I'm giving her a piece of cloth I brought back from Indonesia.

I had an illegible letter today from Manning, saying something like my articles showed "a man, a rounded man, with his illusions, hopes, fears and aspirations for the highest, as well as his hope that that there may be that precious metal in the dust" … I cannot work out whether this is meant to describe me, or Asia, or humanity. I wish Manning could write clearly. His letters are so interesting, it is infuriating not to be sure what he is saying. He seems to be in low spirits. He has one concluding sentence. "I have seen lately in the distance (with "in the distance" underlined) what it is like not to be involved". This apparently refers to a kind of horror, but because the previous sentences are unintelligible, I do not know what his vision was about.

7B Wilmer Court 26 December 1959

I am still full of turkey and pudding, which we went through in traditional style. We went swimming, then to a party, where Bambi got into a long conversation with Rajaratnam, the foreign minister, about music ... he's the man I wrote about concerning Riesman and he's also the man who's withholding approval for my visa, so I'm pleased she made a good impression on him. I gave Sue a watch, Jo a camera and James an electric car. All very mechanical. We will need some books soon. Sue is reading Katharine Mansfield, who she admits is a bit "old" for her.

7B Wilmer Court December 29, 1959

Bambi has gone and we are all a bit sad. She sang songs with the children all the way to the airport. She left behind a pair of sandals, a moo-moo (a kind of smock from Honolulu), a pair of shoes, a dress, a bathing suit and cap. The girls have decided you can have first pick! Bambi gave me some Faulkner short stories for Xmas. How involved his sentences are. Han Suyin has come back from China with a lot to say in favour of the communes.

I sent off a letter to Enid today – I posted it, the children wrote it. It was quite a business; there was an argument about who should go first and an argument about who should tell what. I was quite exhausted by it all. I can understand why Enid doesn't get them to write to me more often. So far, I've managed to get three letters from them in two weeks. It will get harder as the novelty of Singapore wears off.

One day, I hope I will be able to tell you adequately how much the knowledge of you has filled my time during these past months.

7B Wilmer Court, 31 December 1959

It's two minutes past 6pm and the old year is running out. I've just come back from taking part in a radio programme in which four of us discussed the "most important events" of 1959. I kept wanting to say that the most important event of 1959 was arranging for you to get to Singapore but, fortunately, I droned on about foreign affairs. Radio Singapore is not a gay institution, even on New Year's Eve. This is one of the last letters I will write. I will have to stop writing by Sunday to make sure I catch you before you leave. If you don't get a letter saying it is the final one before you leave, you could ask your mother to forward any mail from me to you here.

I took the girls out this afternoon and bought them new "party" shoes. They are now locked in the bathroom, tending to their beautification. I doubt Enid will indulge them as much as I do. Bambi was very fond of them and made even their failings seem interesting. Their emotions are very near the surface and that appealed to her. She is that way herself. I find them very attractive – they are so easily excited, so quickly downcast – but they are a "handful" and I can't promise you a restful two weeks (it will be nearly three) after you arrive. They are already planning a "surprise" for you, but I've no idea what it is.

7B Wilmer Court, 2 January 1960

This is the last letter I will be writing to you. Good news today – my visa came through. It's for one year, renewable for another year. I must say I feel one year is enough. It might be convenient to move somewhere for the second year – perhaps Hong Kong. But, at least, I'm safe. Now, what about you?

I've just heard the news that Khrushchev will be visiting Indonesia in February, which will occupy me for a while. You might like to come with me to Indonesia? Also there's been a military coup in Laos. If I have to leave for Laos before you arrive, I'll leave the children in the care of Helen Griffin (the AP correspondent's wife, who has a flat in this building). If I'm not at the airport to meet you, take a taxi here. Incidentally, Choi is able to take over things much more than earlier. She has sorted out the children's likes and dislikes and takes the initiative in buying food.

The children have been playing around the flats all day. There is quite a group, and they get along well enough. There's the Griffin pair, a fair, pretty English girl of about nine, two Chinese. I notice a little Italian girl, with a sharp nose and sharp voice, isn't in the group. "She's bossy," says Sue. We went with the Griffins to the botanical gardens and fed the monkeys. Then we went to the post office to send off my articles, stopped at a bookshop to buy Treasure Island (which I've promised to read in bed-time instalments) … then we went to the palace of the Yang di-Pertuan Negara who, I'm sure you don't know, is Singapore's head of state. It was formerly the residence of the British Governor, but he left finally about a month ago and a local man – a former journalist – was installed. For the first time, the grounds were open to the public today. The place was swarming with curious people, all being careful about litter and behaving themselves.

178 days gone, 14 to go! I'll be thinking of you all the time. I have your itinerary at hand, and a time-adaptor. Don't forget to ring Arthur Hickman at the London Times office on Monday morning. Give my love to the sweep of Regent's Park. Don't buy anything, unless it's small. Don't go with strange men in the Middle East. Don't forget my telephone number (29472) and my cable address (GRANTAGE SINGAPORE).

From King's Hotel, Bangkok, January 1960

I'm enjoying Bangkok. After Hollandia – a beautiful bay, but chaos at the moment – it seems civilised. There were 54 foreign correspondents in Hollandia, no transport at all. I had to buy two motor scooters (one for my cameraman) and learn to ride one (which I did without mishap – a great sensation, except in teeming rain). Before I see you in a week's time, I have to cover three countries. Isn't it ridiculous?

7

PUBLIC INTELLECTUAL

On 11 December 1964 I received in Washington a letter from the University of Melbourne which began: "Please regard this as an unofficial letter from a usually reliable source." It offered me a three-year appointment to fill a position vacated by Creighton Burns, who had left to join *The Age* in my old job in South-east Asia. Creighton later wrote me an amusing letter in which he noted cases of exchanged houses, even wives, but never before of jobs.

Ten years abroad had tired me of living in other people's countries. It was fun, minding everyone else's business, but I was ready to pay attention to my own. In Washington, my readiness was tested by unexpected disagreements with the editor, Keith Sinclair, about how to do my job. For example, the time differences between Melbourne and Washington meant that I sometimes received cables and telephone calls at awkward times. I had a teleprinter installed in the house so that I could save time and trouble responding. For reasons never explained, I was ordered to remove the teleprinter, although it did not cost the office a cent. This was only one of several inexplicable differences with Keith, who seem determined to show that he, not I, ran the Washington office. I resigned, and in a letter to the managing editor of *The Age,* Ranald Macdonald, who had written to me on December 9 expressing his concern, I explained why. I told him, to scotch any gossip that I had made a convenience of *The Age*, I had not received offers from American newspapers, or anyone else. "Although we have no plans at the moment," I wrote, "in all probability we will return to Australia when this is over, paying our own way."

The letter from a usually reliable source was from Professor Macmahon Ball, head of the department of political science. It was unofficial because he had just heard of my resignation from *The Age* and was yet to get the approval of the University for the appointment he was offering me, but this was the era of the God-Professor and I received official approval by cable shortly afterwards, followed by a letter telling me what he wanted me to do. I was to be responsible for a new undergraduate subject on international relations in the Pacific and East and South-east Asia, taking thirty-four of the formal weekly lectures. He would take the first eight lectures, which would give me time to settle in. He would also "be glad" if I did eight lectures on American domestic politics and "took over" an honours course in "underdevelopment", as well as "lend a hand" in an honours seminar in political sociology. I took a mental step or two backwards. Could I do all this? What exactly was political sociology?

I trusted, however, Mac Ball's judgment. I was not needed at the University until March, which would give *The Age* time to find a replacement. Son James, who had been living with us in Washington, had already returned to Melbourne and another son, David, had been born in Washington on 12 October. Joan was an American citizen, but Australia was not new to her. She had come with me to Melbourne in between appointments in South-east Asia and Washington and had helped me on the book *Indonesia*, which had originally been published by Melbourne University Press (and by Penguin, later).

We had to find somewhere to live in Melbourne. Enid was intending to remarry and live in Sydney, and our three children were at school in Melbourne, so we were looking for accommodation for an extended family. Robin Boyd recommended a terrace house at 83 Grey Street, East Melbourne. "The front door looks mean," he said, with his usual sensitivity, "but there's space at the back for extension." We squeezed into it for a decade.

I picked up the loose ends of the private lives of people we had known before in Melbourne, including the end of the affair that had momentarily shaken British Royalty. Patricia Tuckwell, known in Melbourne as model Bambi Shmith (after her marriage to photographer Athol Shmith) had met Lord Harewood by chance. In his memoirs *The Tongs and the Bones,* Harewood wrote: "In early January 1959, I was sitting rather disconsolately at about lunchtime in the Air France terminal in Milan, eating a bar of chocolate. My mission over the past day or two – to persuade Maria Callas to sing a second opera in London that summer – had not been a success … When the flight was called I offered to carry the violin of the only other occupant of the waiting room, and was allowed instead to pick up the less precious bag she had in the other hand. She told me she was an Australian, Barry Tuckwell's sister, and on her first visit to Europe …"

Patricia had been on her way to Paris and London, then to spend time with me at Harvard. Harewood continued: "I told Marion about my chance meeting with Barry's sister, and Patricia came several times to opera or plays with us. A photograph even appeared of Patricia and me dancing together at the annual Opera Ball in March … [S]oon after the Ball, my feelings for her had become too strong to conceal any longer and I felt obliged to tell Marion about them." The affair went on for six years. During this time Joan and I kept in touch with them.

Now a letter came from Patricia expressing relief that at last they were married.

> I still cannot quite believe that life is normal, and am astonished at the difference being married to George makes. It was I who was always saying that it wasn't worth worrying about and that, as we had managed for so many years without, we could go on perfectly well as we were. But, now that my name is Harewood and (more important) Mark's is Lascelles, that we can live in our own house, that we have nothing to hide and the three of us can appear together in public, and that we need only one room in hotels, and many, many other little things that I shall never take for granted, I feel ten years younger and as if tons have been lifted from my shoulders ... We had to go through an absurd cops and robbers act to get married undetected, and were, in fact, spotted by the press in Connecticut when we went to apply for the licence. We managed to do a deal with the paper by saying that if they kept it to themselves we would arrange for them to be brought to take a picture after the wedding, otherwise we would tell them nothing. This worked and they behaved very well. Apart from that, a huge mob of them at London airport and eighteen carloads of them the day after we arrived here, they now leave us alone as we are now very dull and respectable!

The political science department at Melbourne University was at the centre of a political storm. It had a leftish reputation, due to Mac Ball's critical public stance on US policy and his retention on the staff of a member of the Communist Party, Lloyd Churchward, but it was actually eclectic, as you would expect from someone as experienced and tolerant as its head. Two of the teaching staff, Tony Staley and David Kemp, became active in the Liberal Party. I was something of a curiosity, well known in a public sense but, as I had lately lived mainly outside Australia, I was untested on the domestic political issues that had emerged as the Cold War gathered pace. I was not a member of any political party, which enabled me to think in an independent way about issues, drawing on my own experience and impressions.

As far as the University was concerned, my particular value was experience in the Asian region, but, living abroad, I had gained a fresh perception of Australia intellectually and culturally, especially in foreign policy, and I was glad of the opportunity to begin a course of lectures on international relations that would give me a chance to get my thoughts together. I tacked on to the end of the new international relations subject a few lectures on Australian foreign policy. This developed into a major part of the subject because our foreign and defence policies were being tested in a dramatic way by the war in Vietnam.

I remember vividly my first lecture. I was not new to public speaking, but had never been responsible for a full university course. The subject had proved to be popular and the lecture room was crowded. The hourly lectures were about fifty minutes, allowing five minutes at both ends for students to get to and from other lectures. About half way through I noticed a familiar face in the audience. It was Peter Ryan, then director of Melbourne University Press. He was a friend of Ball's and would no doubt report to him on the quality of the new lecturer. He did, as Mac frankly admitted when I confronted him later. "Don't worry, he gave you a good mark," he said, "but try to be more pedagogical." When Mac Ball used a word like "pedagogical", he would hold back his head, distancing himself from its implications, but, at the time, seeing Peter in an otherwise sea of unknown faces, put me off balance and I hurried, until I realised, with mounting trepidation, that I would be some fifteen minutes short. Fortunately, I had in the folder some notes for my second lecture and managed to project some ideas, bridging the gap. As a footnote, when I hurried from the city to give my last lecture three years later, I brought the wrong folder and had to give the lecture without any notes at all. It was easy.

The eight lectures on American domestic politics were given in the shadow of President Kennedy's assassination. My reading of him politically was of someone cautious and withdrawn, wary and competitive, rather than the confident and glamorous leader that, in the popular imagination, he became, but his presidency had lifted the United States from the Cold War doldrums of the Eisenhower and "that dreadful man, Dulles" period, and offered a contrast with the homely, pungent politics of his successor Lyndon Johnson. I paid respect to Kennedy's sober, clever handling of the Cuban missile crisis, but could not resist reminding Anglo-Melburnians (or their children) that Jack Kennedy was proof that, in three generations in America, a poor Irish immigrant family could produce a handsome fellow, able to mix with the finest in the world. The White House became an alternative in popular imagination to the luxury models of modern America, whether the film star palaces of California, the ranches of the West or the penthouses of New York. Jacqueline Kennedy had flair and taste. She gave small dinner parties, with gifted and artistic guests. Jack's rocking chair and model sailing ships were blended with pale blue drapes and finely modelled furniture. Pablo Casals came to play. Never before in the memory of living Americans had the White House been such an elegant place. Also, the American people were pleased with the way the Kennedys represented them abroad – not only the huge crowds, but the wit and grace. "I am the man," he informed the French, "who accompanied Mrs Jacqueline Kennedy to Paris."

You could hold out hope in this way for the United States, as Americans themselves did, after the assassination of its president. Three years later, the killing of his brother Robert, while campaigning for the presidency, and of Martin Luther King, had a different effect. These killings signified upheaval; neither tragedy nor catharsis but the grind and jolt of a society coming to a halt. Whereas John Kennedy's death saddened and inspired, the 1968 murders frightened and intimidated. They were the beginning of the end of public support for social reform in the United States. The public reacted to the social turmoil of the 1960s and became deeply conservative, buoyed by American technology's success in landing a man on the moon in 1969.

Bartholomew Augustine (Bob) Santamaria was a force in the anti-Communist movement that split the Australian Labor Party. He took me to dinner at the Latin Café. He had read "Outpost of Christendom" in *The New Yorker* and wanted to know whether it was entirely fiction or whether my aunt, as in the story, had become a Catholic. He also wanted to test my knowledge of guerrilla warfare and its objectives in South-east Asia, which he believed were a threat to Australia. He was cheerfully frank and I enjoyed his company. I must have passed muster, as I was later enlisted by the journal *Quadrant* and the Congress of Cultural Freedom to attend a Conference on "Democracy and Development in Southeast Asia" at the University of Malaya in Kuala Lumpur, where I shared the Australian perspective with Sydney-siders like Donald Horne, Peter Coleman, Douglas McCallum, James McAuley, Owen Harries and Brian Beddie. I have kept as a souvenir an invitation to attend the conference opening by the Deputy Prime Minister of Malaysia, Tun Abdul Razak, on which the name B.A. Santamaria has been crossed out and my name substituted. To be standing in for Australia's most celebrated anti-Communist was the height of irony.

The confusion was understandable. I was not anti-American and supported the alliance with the United States. I was not an advocate of the Scandinavian model of "neutrality" for Australia, which had gained momentum in Australia on the political left. I shared with Santamaria and others a perception that Australia needed to develop a more self-reliant defence capability. I was in favour not of Australia withdrawing from Asia, but of becoming more involved, including regional defence arrangements. I wanted Australia to stay militarily in Malaysia and Singapore when the British left, while at the same time negotiating with Indonesia about becoming a member of the Association of South-East Asian Nations (ASEAN). The democratic imperfections of these two states was viewed with disdain in Australia (just as, I was at pains to point out, Britons, superior in the parliamentary arts, looked down on Australia's performance). I was also in favour of independence for Papua New Guinea. My position was too audacious for either of the major parties in Australia. It was a view more common in South-east Asia among intellectuals and politicians who wanted the West to remain influential in the region without imposing itself militarily, as great powers had traditionally done.

In the West the word "Vietnam" had become a metaphor with mixed meanings – the impotence of imperial power (and, from the other side, the potency of nationalism); the frustration of political restraints on military operations; the first television war; social division at home. And also for something more elusive, as, later, in the film *Apocalypse Now*: a metaphor for horror, the evil at the centre of man's soul. The war divided Australians as it did Americans and Europeans, just as Hungary and Suez had done, but more deeply, because of uneasiness about being involved in an anti-colonial war that had been transformed into a Cold War conflict.

At universities, opposition to the war became part of the counter-culture, or what Andre Malraux called "an immense lyrical illusion", prompted by youthful energy, drugs, a sense of the futility of war and an instinctive resistance to pressures to conform and consume. Unlike the Cultural Revolution in China, which was promoted from the top, this came from the bottom, or at least from the middle. It was a revolt against an affluent society, yet it was at the same time subsidised by the affluence of the middle class.

It had an unsettling effect at universities. Years spent on mastery of a subject had to compete with instant wisdom from youthful gurus. One major source of opposition to the war, especially among the young, was conscription; I was not opposed in principle to conscription for military service, even if I did not support in this case the commitment for which conscription was thought necessary. For a more self-reliant, independent Australia, we needed, I thought, public support for a system of national defence, including a period of national service by young Australians.

I drew up a chart at this time using White Australia and Forward Defence as litmus tests of Australian attitudes. If you were against White Australia and in favour of Forward Defence, you were liberal, anti-communist and internationalist. In favour of both White Australia and Forward Defence made you conservative, anti-communist and nationalist. In favour of White Australia and against Forward Defence made you nationalist and isolationist. If you were against White Australia and against Forward Defence you were liberal, internationalist and probably pacifist. The two last groups, incompatible with each other, combined to offer the major opposition to the Vietnam War.

There was little understanding in Australia at the time of the unique nature of Vietnam's political culture. The debate over the war was conducted politically in terms of the value of the alliance with the United States and at a popular level as part of the counter-cultural offensive. But Vietnam was the only state in South-east Asia where the communists, not the nationalists, won independence from the colonial power, which gave Hanoi status and authority in the eyes of the Vietnamese people. During the Second World War, the anti-colonial organisation Viet Minh had launched a guerrilla war against both the French colonial power and the Japanese occupying power. It received arms and training from the US Office of Strategic Services, a forerunner of the Central Intelligence Agency. When the war ended, the guerrilla leader Ho Chi Minh declared Vietnam's independence, using the words of the US Declaration of Independence, such as "All men are created equal" and declaring as inviolable the "right to life, the right to be free and the right to achieve happiness." Now the US was engaged in a war against communism, backing a weak, artificial government in the south against the heroes of independence in the north. The Americans thought their military power, especially their naval and air power, would make up for their lack of credibility on the ground, and in the hearts and minds of Vietnamese, but it didn't.

As it became increasingly clear that the war was being lost, the political enthusiasm for it in Australia declined. In the 1966 election, the Holt Government made the war a major issue. By 1969, after the Tet offensive the year before, the Gorton Government was hedging its bets. In his policy speech in 1972, Prime Minister McMahon never mentioned the war.

In *The Crisis of Loyalty* (1972) I characterised the Vietnam War as another example of Australia's tendency to resort to arms to prove its loyalty to a protector. But the war was also a turning point for Australia. As a Whitlam-led Labor Party became an alternative to the floundering commitment in Vietnam, two lines of advice to Whitlam developed. One was that it was mismanagement of the alliance, not the alliance itself, which got us into Vietnam. The other was that, in withdrawing from the military commitment to Vietnam, Australia should not withdraw from Asia. Whitlam remained firm on these undertakings, although he had to deal with the less-than-congenial combination of Nixon and Kissinger in Washington and an adventurous left wing in Australia. Popular opposition to the war in both America and Australia created a link between liberal-left intellectuals across the Pacific that had not existed before. On the other side of politics, several right-wing publicists, including Santamaria, denounced the United States as a weak and sick society, even where, as with Santamaria, they supported the US war in Vietnam.

A celebrated case was the printing of the *Pentagon Papers* by the *New York Times* in 1971. A documentation of American involvement in Indo-China, including the Vietnam War, running to 3000 pages, was compiled by the Pentagon over a year and a half. It showed the gap between what the US government actually did, and was doing, in Vietnam, and what it told the American people. After the first instalments, the *New York Times* was taken to court by the Department of Justice on the grounds that the nation was at war and printing a top-secret document was harmful to its national security.

Justice Hugo Black's judgment in favour of the *New York Times* read, in part:

> Only a free and unrestrained press can effectively expose deception in government. And paramount among the responsibilities of a free press is the duty to prevent any part of the Government from deceiving the people and sending them off to distant lands to die of foreign fevers and foreign shot and shell. In my view, far from deserving condemnation for their courageous reporting, the *New York Times*, the *Washington Post* and other newspapers should be commended for serving the purpose that the Founding Fathers saw so clearly. In revealing the workings of government that led to the Vietnam war, the newspapers nobly did precisely that which the founders hoped and trusted they would do.

Walter Lippmann argued for a withdrawal of American forces from South-east Asia to Australia and New Zealand, which he described as "continental islands inhabited by Western white men". His argument was heavily affected by his opposition to Washington's Vietnam policy. He wanted to get Americans off the Asian mainland – "the era of ordering natives around is over". An American base in Australia would be "easier, cheaper and more secure" than one "could ever be in Indo-China".

I wrote in response: "I am a long-time admirer of Mr Lippmann's ability to get to the point and I suspect in this case, having heard so much in Washington of Australia's need for protection and America's need to maintain a base of influence in South-East Asia, he has tried to draw a logical conclusion. As America's base in South-East Asia, Australia would certainly be invulnerable to any of the threats we see at the moment ... But equally certain, it would make us politically impotent. It is hard to see how we could exercise influence except as an American proxy."

Creating a course on Australian foreign policy, I had to answer the questions I had been asking myself about Australia's place in the world. Why, if I was against America's war in Vietnam, and opposed to the United States establishing a military base in Australia, was I convinced that the leadership of the United States was vital to the peace and prosperity of the world? Essentially, I was not confident that Australia could manage the challenge from Asia without the alliance with the United States. However, I was beginning to hope that the obsession of Australians with the danger of being an outpost of Western Christendom in Asia was breaking down into more manageable proportions.

I sketched a series of imaginary headlines in descending order of generality. Asiatic Hordes Will Take Over Australia, says Leader (1890s); Asia, Sleeping Giant, Awakes (1950s); Asiatic Communism a Threat to Australia (1960s); Indonesia Rattles Sabre Over West Irian, Malaysia and Singapore Split, PNG to be Non-Aligned, India and Pakistan at War, India and China Clash in Himalayas, Vietnam Invades Cambodia. The increasing precision and concreteness of the headlines made the point that whatever the "Asian threat" was, it had ceased to be directed at Australia.

I set out in lectures the "manageable proportions" as follows:

> We cannot dominate Asia, even with the Americans. We have to accept that Asia is a kind of equilibrium which hopefully will remain relatively peaceful but which contains several different planes, not a fixed dividing line as in Europe with the two superpowers America and Russia and their allies in a standoff. India is a civilisation in itself, dominant on the subcontinent, although weak economically and under social pressures. China is also a civilisation, now also a major state with nuclear arms. Japan is a world economic power, historically the great disrupter

of the peace in Asia, now looking for a role in the world as a new kind of nation-state, espousing economic independence and disavowing military conquest. Vietnam is a communist state, suspicious of China, nationalistic and disciplined. Indonesia, on our doorstep, is the most populous Muslim nation in the world, with a distinctive, nationalistic outlook. Without looking any further, it is obvious that this great variety and potency cannot be dominated by either the Americans or the Russians.

We can avoid domination by any Asian state or combination of states. This is a less certain proposition, but our physical detachment, which has caused us so much anxiety in the past, is an asset. It provides us with natural security against invasion, or invaders on the way to somewhere else. The end of the line is not a bad place to be when invaders are on the move. The US alliance, while imperfect as a stabiliser, is a guarantee against full-scale invasion. So even though our defence capability is low, the combination of the alliance and our detachment made us relatively secure.

We cannot isolate ourselves from Asia. Japan is our biggest trading partner. Southeast Asia is becoming an important market and trader. China and India, with their large populations, have a huge potential. Engagement with Asia is likely to grow. As Asians come here to settle, more will want to come. We have shown that we can control our immigration intake to suit our needs and this, with the racial bias removed, will be extended to Asia.

If we cannot dominate Asia, but can avoid being dominated, and if we cannot isolate ourselves, we will have to accommodate Asia and adapt ourselves to living in it. Is this possible? Is there, within the short span of Australia's existence as a nation-state, evidence to support the idea that we could be the laboratory of a different kind of western civilisation, not of supremacy and domination, but of shared values and interests?

I was not sure. Australia had been discovered and developed during a period of Western primacy. It was hard for us to imagine how to behave in a world without the primacy of Western power and values. Most Australians saw the alliance with the US in that light. We would need the security of the alliance while we tested our potential to be more independent. If we dispensed with the alliance now, we would be tempted to become (like Israel) militarily powerful, even adopting nuclear weapons in the hope of keeping our neighbours at bay.

Indeed, after Menzies stepped down as Prime Minister and Holt disappeared while swimming at Portsea, the new Prime Minister, John Gorton, showed an interest in developing an Australian nuclear military capability, supported by the head of the Australian Atomic Energy Commission, Philip Baxter, an Englishman whose passion for nuclear energy had been thwarted at home. After the Chinese tested in 1964, domestic pressure for an Australian bomb increased, although only one political party, the Democratic Labor Party, openly advocated it. Early in 1968, Gorton had to decide whether to support the Non-Proliferation Treaty (NPT) which was to become the standard bearer of international nuclear arms control. It was a moment of truth for Australia. On the one hand, in favour of the NPT, were the traditionalists, like Australia's senior diplomat, James Plimsoll and his minister, Paul Hasluck. On the other were Gorton, his departmental head C.L.S. Hewitt and Baxter. The British High Commissioner Charles Johnston reported to London that Gorton privately told him Australia would not sign, or if it had to (having its arm twisted by London and Washington), it would not ratify the treaty. As Gorton thought it was "silly" to sign a treaty you had no intention of ratifying, he personally preferred not to sign. Eventually he accepted the compromise and Australia became one of the last countries to sign in 1970 before the treaty came into force.

These thoughts prompted the ideas behind *The Crisis of Loyalty*, which was an attempt to extract Australian foreign policy from the endless divisions and distractions of the Cold War, especially the issue of Vietnam. I wrote in the introduction, "my intention is to try to get down in a readable form the outline of a foreign policy which all Australians ought to be able to support. For it is quite clear that … policies which divide Australians are unlikely to survive, and that one of the problems today in producing a national policy is that the divisions of the past have become fixed positions which few in political life seem prepared to abandon." I turned in desperation to literature. "My guiding philosopher in this essay is no statesman, strategist, soldier or historian, but the Russian writer Anton Chekhov, who paid little attention to international affairs but who knew a great deal about people. He said: 'You will not become a saint through other people's sins.' No-one writing about Australian foreign policy gains any authority from simply pointing out the mistakes of others, so I have prescribed policies, wherever possible within the rather general purpose of the book, and have tried to remain aware of the particular problem of Australian policy-makers."

These words read now as little more than an author's mantle of humility, but at the time they were written in the knowledge that the book was unlikely to satisfy any of the major contenders for power and influence, including government, in Australia.

*

While teaching at the University, I occasionally wrote commentaries for *The Age*. In 1966 the newspaper underwent editorial changes and I was asked if I would return to write a regular column. This meant making a choice between the University and the newspaper, a choice I had already made twice before, once in favour of the newspaper and once in favour of the University. I was busy and happy at the University. Why then did I return to journalism? There were two reasons. I did not think of myself as a scholar. I thought of myself as someone engaged in public life, using the sanity and security of the university as a sanctuary to get my thoughts in order. I was more interested in the world of events, and having an influence in that world, than in stepping back from it and making up rules and laws about its behaviour. The other reason was concern about the particular state of Australian politics, which had reached an awkward stalemate.

The conservatives had been in power since 1949. An unhealthy situation had developed from the split in the Labor Party over communism and the Cold War, creating the Democratic Labor Party, which was keeping the conservative Coalition in office, although they had little in common except anti-communism. The result was a distortion of Australian politics. The conservatives were increasingly aggressive in foreign policy and Labor was increasingly pacifist. I had worked out intellectually an Australian way forward between these two extremes, which I now wanted to put to a wider public.

Journalism is a rough-and-tumble profession. It has neither the status of the established professions like law or medicine nor the celebrity appeal of entertainment, like theatre, film and television. It has certain rules, like getting the facts right, but it is under pressure to reach quick conclusions, because of the nature of news and deadlines. The result is by no means an accurate reflection of a society. So much happens that journalism does not touch. So much that it touches is hurriedly recorded. So much is tainted by commercial or personal bias. Yet, even with this disability, journalism is a vital part of public life, because it is the medium which informs the public what governments and its agents are doing. In small or primitive communities, it was still possible for everyone to know, by visible evidence and word of mouth, what was being done by community leaders but, in the modern nation-state, complex social and economic conditions make this impossible. Most people were aware of only a miniscule part of their society; for information about the rest they relied on the media. The gap was even greater when "community" or "society" was extended beyond national borders.

Unlike most Australians, who settled in their state or city for life, I had had a rapid transition from a small rural community to an international arena, absorbing and distilling knowledge and feelings about Australia and the world. As a university teacher, I had had the opportunity to test some hypotheses. I felt that Australia was at a critical stage, in danger of being overwhelmed by the divisions brought by Vietnam and the public uncertainty over the transition from Britain to the United States in the role of "protector", while my own view was that Australia should be finding a way for itself and its future in the region.

Contemplating a return to journalism, I was reminded of Walter Lippmann's advice, as we strolled from his London hotel. I was aware of the pressures on editors from their boards of directors, political parties, community groups, the big end of town, government and its agencies. Sir Harold Campbell had died and there had been a succession of editors. I wanted to be in a position to make up my own mind on the issues of the day and to express them freely. So I asked for a written agreement that my column would be independent of the paper's editorial opinion and that *The Age* would publicly acknowledge this. I asked also that my copy could only be altered by sub-editors after consultation with the editor and/or myself. Also, I asked for a research assistant, hired by me and paid for by the paper. All these conditions were met.

After three years, I left Melbourne University with regret. Teaching is a great profession, from which you take more than you give. Some of my students became, and have remained, friends. The intellectual freedom of university life was precious. There was also then still a "whole of knowledge" feeling in university life that has not remained so strongly, as professional and corporate interests have become stronger and the role of the university as a provider of useful skills and knowledge has evolved.

I had also got to know Macmahon Ball better. I had encountered him as a student and later as a public figure, especially as a commentator on the ABC. As the Cold War intensified, he became controversial because he persisted in putting a point of view about national and international politics that satisfied none of the cheerleaders on either side, yet one that his students and the public sensed was based on sensitivity to interests that were more profound and sustainable than political or ideological fortunes. These were basically the interests of peace and the social and economic welfare of ordinary people. His early training had been in psychology and philosophy and he retained a strong sense of individual responsibility and was wary of authority. I was reassured to find someone who, after an active life as teacher, commentator and government consultant and adviser, had had the kind of experience that I was beginning to envisage for myself. His experience in government was of particular interest. He valued specialised knowledge and expertise, but was less interested in them, whether of theory or practice, than he was in good government and wise policy. His priority was in guiding an Australian democracy towards a peaceful and productive place in Asia and, therefore, in the world.

We discussed the offer from *The Age*. He was meticulous in assuring me that the decision was mine, which meant that it should be made with both my own long term interests and the public interest in mind. My departure would be inconvenient for him, as I had built up International Relations B as an integral part of the department's menu, but he had a keen sense of the value of journalism in the task of informing the public in a democracy. Also – which appealed to me – he had a strong belief in personal commitment, as much as professional standing and qualifications.

He sent me a typically warm and generous letter.

> *This is a very personal letter and still a letter from me as head of the department. You have been working for us for two years full-time, and the best part of this year part-time, long enough for me to know what you are like to work with.*
>
> *You have been impeccable in your work and style of work, both as an academic and human being. But to say that is not enough for it might suggest that you have been merely conscientious and correct, though I suppose these are hard enough things to be. You have been much more than that, ready to go far beyond the line of duty to give generous understanding and help to your various students, and, for that matter, your various colleagues.*
>
> *I am specially grateful to you for having carried on the lectures in International Relations B from March to now. It must have been a lot of work and a lot of nuisance, trekking up here in the traffic peak at 5.15. And it was near enough to an honorary job.*

Writing a regular opinion column was more rigorous in one respect than teaching. Real life is messy and resists being compressed into a few hundred well-chosen words. I was often tempted to erect the straw men Lippmann had warned against. It is not difficult to have an opinion, nor to express it with anger or indignation, but to subject it to critical cross-examination is a step in self-denial that only martyrs and lawyers might enjoy. I came across Albert Camus' definition of an intellectual – "someone whose mind watches itself" – and was reminded how right he was. Demonising creates energy, I told myself; self-scrutiny can be stultifying. Journalism favours opinions that are sharp, confident and controversial. The devil on my shoulder whispered, as I laid out the opposing case. "Leave a hole you can wriggle through." But I hung on to Lippmann's riding instructions and they helped me to stay the distance, avoiding easy wins and dramatic falls.

There was some overlap with the new column and university teaching during 1966–67. The first column appeared on 16 November 1966, in which I opposed the war in Vietnam, pleasing the Labor Party and displeasing the Coalition and the DLP. "We have committed ourselves in Vietnam with old-fashioned ideas of victory and its rewards. So bitter debate threatens our credibility as a nation at the very time that we need to represent ourselves in Asia as something more than a provincial outpost of Western civilisation." But I was in favour of a stronger Australian defence, and conscription (or compulsory national service, as I preferred) if needed, displeasing the Labor Party and pleasing the Coalition Government and the DLP. I argued that "in an affluent society and without the psychology of total war, voluntary enlistment is unlikely to meet the requirements of Australian security." Our strategy in Vietnam should be long term and low key, a politically-based, counter-insurgency program as in the rest of South-east Asia.

Lippmann's advice on a research assistant was valuable. I recruited from graduates at Melbourne University; several assistants went on to careers of their own. One, Pera Wells, joined the Department of Foreign Affairs and then, after a couple of postings, the United Nations in New York. Their research was valuable both in checking and verifying information that was at issue in the public domain, and with which my column was expected to deal, but also in keeping abreast of what was under discussion in government, non-government and academic circles.

I became involved generally in public life. I joined the council of the Victorian branch of the Australian Institute of International Affairs and was joint convenor with Professor Jamie Mackie of a study group on Australian foreign policy. I was also active in immigration reform, which essentially meant getting rid of the White Australian Policy. I debated Dr Jim Cairns and Sir Wilfrid Kent Hughes at the Melbourne Junior Chamber of Commerce on the subject "Australia in Vietnam – Right or Wrong?" On 11 August 1965 I addressed the 547th meeting of BOOBOOKS in the private dining room at Melbourne University Union. I spoke at a meeting of the Erasmus Society. I was a member of the Australian Committee for a New China Policy. In 1966 I spoke at a conference of the Australian Fabian Society. I was invited to conferences in Wellington of the New Zealand council for foreign affairs, of the Ditchley Foundation in England, the Airlie Institute for International Studies in the United States, and to Japan for the World Journalist Symposium for Peace of East Asia, organised by the Japan Culture Congress. I appeared on behalf of the Australian Journalists Association in 1967 in the Metropolitan Daily Newspapers case for higher pay, and received a note of thanks from the general secretary (Syd Crosland) and a cheque for $100 to cover my expenses. I gave the 1969 Roy Milne Memorial Lecture at Sydney on "Foreign Affairs and the Australian Press." I wrote for other publications, for example "Towards a New Balance in Asia: An Australian View" in *Foreign Affairs* (New York) July 1969 and "Australia at the Crossroads" in *The Pacific Community* (Tokyo) April 1970.

My column "Public Affairs" attracted interest abroad. I was described by American scholars as Australia's Walter Lippmann, which I accepted as a compliment, but which was not accurate. Lippmann's mind ploughed more deeply and narrowly than mine. He was an American who saw global politics through the prism of European and American experience, of which the Middle East was a vital part. I was an Australian who saw global politics through the prism of Australia and Asia's potential. Asia did not rate highly with Lippmann; he regarded the extension of American power across the Pacific as mistaken, because it weakened American resolve to deal with Europe and the Middle East. In addition, of course, Lippmann wrote from the citadel of a superpower. I wrote from an outpost of empire, where views on global politics tended to disappear in the thin air of distance. We saw power differently. Lippmann was concerned with what he called "solvency", when a nation's interests and commitments were in some kind of balance. No such possibility existed for Australia. My own conception of power for Australia was less quantifiable, persuasive rather than coercive, more interested in getting common action on common goals.

Nor did I have Lippmann's Olympian confidence. I never felt, as I am sure he did, that what he thought was important, not only to his readers, but to the world at large, especially those political leaders whose decisions made the world what it was. I was confident that my readers understood and appreciated what I was saying, and I had influence within Australia's political culture, but an Australian voice in the world, even the region, could be overlooked.

My confidence was more assertive than assured. For example, the opening remarks of my paper at the Airlie conference … "I used to be upset that the view from 'Down Under' was different from any other kind of view, as if Australians were not only outside the strategic map but also somehow beyond human reason – the effect, perhaps, of walking on their heads. Today, I find the assumption encouraging: there is comfort in being *sui generis* when grand designs are faltering."

In a lecture to the Fabian Society I noted that some now saw dissent as a way of engaging in politics. "To move from dissent to assent will not be easy," I suggested, in one of the understatements of the decade, and added: "Dissent can be as sterile as the apathy it deplores … (when) it refuses to grapple with the complexity of issues and is contemptuous of those who try … I would hope … that, with a change of government, some dissenters will provide the precious energy and conviction that is needed to make the system work."

In the Roy Milne Memorial Lecture I noted the importance of the arrival five years earlier of *The Australian,* which had stimulated the Australian press to take a more serious interest in foreign news. I took issue with a journalistic obsession of exposing government, ending the lecture with an argument for a proactive role at a time when, mainly as a result of the conflict in Vietnam, there had been a collapse of the conventional wisdom governing discussion of foreign affairs in Australia. "The role of the press in these circumstances is not to feed on the discomfiture of officialdom, but to take part in the forging of new policies. Just as it is no longer sufficient for Australian governments to consider diplomacy as the art of being consulted before rather than after the event, so it's not sufficient for the Australian press to complain after policy has been decided. It must be informed and alert about developments in foreign policy before they reach the point of decision. This takes money. It also takes knowledge, for dialogue cannot be carried out when the expertise is on one side. It also takes moral energy, a sense of commitment to the continuing interests of the Australian people."

The article in *Foreign Affairs* opens with the determined view that what happens in Australia is important: "Australia's decision to keep forces in Malaysia and Singapore after Britain leaves in 1971 was taken in an election year, after the most searching public debate on defence and foreign policy in Australia's history and after a substantial official review. It represents, therefore, one country's practical assessment of South-east Asia 'after Vietnam'. The decision had significance outside Australia, for the light it throws on the development of Australian thinking, for the contribution it is intended to make to the security of the immediate neighbourhood and for the assumptions it appears to make about the broader question of stability in Asia, especially the role of the United States."

The article took issue with "the crude but central core" of the Australian policy of "forward defence", which was to keep the United States engaged in Asia, especially South-east Asia, at all costs. I pointed to an emerging "isolationism" on both the right and left of the Australian political spectrum because of the setback in Vietnam, and argued for a new form of bipartisan "involvement" in Asia, quoting the new Leader of the Opposition, E.G. Whitlam's pronouncement that "an isolationist Australia would be rich, selfish, greedy, racialist and reactionary. Beyond doubt, we would be supporting this sort of society with the nuclear bomb."

In September–October 1970 I attended in Vina del Mar, Chile, the Conference of the Pacific, the president of which was Claudio Veliz, then director of the Institute of International Studies at the University of Chile. The secretary-general of the conference was Maria Isabel Talavera, who later married the president. They later moved to Melbourne, where Claudio established the Boston, Melbourne, Oxford Conversazione on Culture and Society, which continues. The conference went for seven days, with speakers from Japan, China, Singapore, Malaysia, Colombia, Mexico, Peru, Fiji, New Zealand, Hong Kong, Canada, the United States and Australia, as well, of course, as Chile. My memory of it is vivid, as if we were all meeting each other for the first time, although we had sometimes met frequently before. For example, I had met Han Suyin, the writer, and Sinnathamby Rajaratnam, Singapore's Foreign Minister, during my time as a foreign correspondent in South-east Asia, and I had since encountered some of the other speakers at conferences around the world. But these conversations about the fate and future of the Asia-Pacific region had taken place against a shared background of the Second World War, the end of European colonialism and the Cold War. From Chile, the Pacific looked different – more spacious, and more open ideologically. The Europeans were being expelled from Asia and although the Cold War was as present in Latin America as anywhere else, the European influence there was still strong, sometimes expressed in guarded form as criticism of the United States.

For Australian speakers, it was something of a novelty to include Latin America in our thinking about the Pacific. The withdrawal of a British military presence east of Suez, the rivalry of nationalists and communists to fill the vacant colonial spaces and the uncertain behaviour of the United States kept our minds fixed on our north. I stayed during the conference with Australia's ambassador to Chile, Noel Deschamps, who had a soft spot for small countries trying to find their way in the world (like Cambodia, his favourite) and he observed that the conference was an opportunity for an alert thinker like Claudio Veliz to create links across the Pacific for Chile. Like the Andean Pact with Peru, Bolivia, Colombia and Ecuador, from which Chile later withdrew, the "opening to the Pacific" for Latin America, especially Chile, was the dominant theme of the conference.

Occasionally, my activities were noted by the new editor of *The Age,* Graham Perkin, as when an article on the editorial page of the *Washington Post* described me as "associate editor of The Age." "Will you tell the *Washington Post* – or will I?" Graham scrawled in a note to me on an advisory cable from *The Age*'s correspondent in Washington, who had concluded: "President Nixon does not read the *Washington Post* or any other newspaper, but Mr. Grant's views will probably be brought to his attention in a daily news summary prepared by White House staff."

Relations between editor and independent columnist were agreeable. We were not close, but we were not rivals, recognising that we had different roles. As Graham steered *The Age* closer to endorsing Labor for the 1972 elections, he sometimes sought my opinion on particular policy issues. He showed me a draft of a statement why *The Age* should support Labor, which he intended to present to the board. It was a thoughtful, well-researched and argued- paper of six pages, giving as reasons the paper's independent tradition and reformist history, competition from *The Australian* for "well-informed" readers, the need for a healthy two-party political system, the stagnation of the Canberra bureaucracy after twenty-three years of one party in government, the revitalisation of the Labor Party, the need for *The Age* to show independence from its conservative Fairfax partner, the *Sydney Morning Herald*, and, contrary to the evidence of the last twenty years, when support for Labor could mean lost advertising, commerce and business were sanguine about a Labor victory.

He asked for a comment, which I provided, with a cover note: "Some brief, simple notes on the concept of an Australian nation." It began: "Australia is self-evident: an island continent, one language, ethnic unity. We didn't have to fight the British for independence, as the Americans did. We didn't push ourselves across the continent in search of manifest destiny, as the Americans did, nor fight a civil war to unify the nation. We haven't had to build a nation from disparate elements. We got it, piece by piece, from a courteous Britain ... We developed a sense of the land (led by poets and painters) and a sense of ourselves as a people (mateship, sport, military courage) but no sense of a nation." I went on to develop the idea that Australia would only become a nation by "chancing its arm" in Asia and being as independent as we could be within the alliance with the United States. Whitlam seemed the only political leader capable of convincing the Australian people that this was realistic. I wrote that, in the past, *The Age* had been critical of Coalition governments until election day, then had supported them as "generally sound", with the added advice that Labor, split by the issue of communism, was not ready for office. Since Menzies' retirement and Holt's disappearance at sea, rivalry for Liberal leadership between Gorton and McMahon, coupled with the collapse of the "forward defence" strategy in Vietnam, made the prospect of Coalition government unappealing. I concluded with the observation that for the first time since the Second World War, no member of the leader-writing staff, including the editor and assistant editor, wanted to write editorials supporting the McMahon government. "Surely this in itself is significant," I wrote, with a straight face.

Although mostly confined to analysis and argument and concerned with public policy, my column occasionally attracted national and international attention by relying on staples of traditional journalism, networking and human intelligence. I can recall two examples.

I received the following letter from Ross Terrill in the United States.

> *Here is a piece of information for you, which you can use if you are able to attribute it vaguely to 'Canberra sources'. On Tuesday, October 19, Wilfred Burchett had breakfast with Henry Kissinger in Kissinger's offices at Washington. This was all very furtive, for obvious reasons. One reason not so obvious is that Burchett was in New York to visit the UN, and was not permitted by US authorities outside a 25-mile range. I had known from talks with Kissinger that he was rather interested in Burchett's writings, and that he regarded Burchett as a highly intelligent and well-informed man. So when Burchett came over to New York from his base in Paris early in October, I wrote to Kissinger asking whether he would be interested in a talk with Burchett. He was, and his staff contacted Burchett in New York and the meeting took place. They had a long and detailed talk. (When Burchett explained about his 25-mile limit, Kissinger's office said 'Just forget it'.) Henry later rang me. He found his talk with W.B. highly interesting. At my suggestion, W.B. sent Gough Whitlam notes from the talk. (Gough received them today. Dick Hall rang me). A few days later, at a diplomatic reception in New York – given by the Bulgarians – Sir Laurence McIntyre, the Australian delegate at the UN, saw Burchett and came up to him and recalled that they had lunched together in New York some 25*

years ago. Burchett could not remember that very clearly, but they had a bit of a chat. In the course of it, Burchett happened to say to McIntyre that he had breakfast the other day with Kissinger, and mentioned one or two themes from the talk: that Nixon really is ready to pull out of Vietnam totally, that the US is really concerned with the way Japan is throwing its weight around. Very soon after, McIntyre was seen to hurry from the diplomatic reception – no doubt to cable off this titbit about the Australian outlaw supping with the architect of American foreign policy. It is because McIntyre told Canberra of this that it seems to me you could speak of 'Canberra sources'. Certainly you cannot give any indication that the source was within the USA. The information must not be published in the USA either, but I think it is a piquant bit for Australians.

Perkin realised that it was a national and international story and asked me for its source. I declined to provide it, although I gave him some detail to establish its authenticity. The column was printed as I wrote it. I received afterwards a mild complaint from the *Washington Post*, for whom I occasionally wrote, that I had not told them.

The other example involved the then Australian minister for foreign affairs, William McMahon. I was dining in Canberra with Liberal minister Peter Howson when McMahon invited us to join him. He proceeded to unload a sense of personal grievance, complaining that Henry Kissinger, national security adviser to President Nixon, was "selling out" on Vietnam by having backdoor discussions with Hanoi. I assumed that McMahon had a purpose in talking so openly like this and wrote shortly afterwards an article in which I noted, in more moderate language than his, the Government's concerns. Howson explains in his memoirs *The Life of Politics* how later he had to tell McMahon that the article was his own doing.

Tuesday 24 February (Canberra)

This evening a reception by the American Ambassador, Mr Rice, and then I dined in the Lobby restaurant with Bruce Grant and Eric Halstead, a former Minister for Commerce in New Zealand. Bill McMahon asked us to join him – awkward, because I thought Bill knew Bruce Grant. He told me afterwards that he hadn't recognised him. As usual, Bill spoke rather openly, and then was rather annoyed when some of the things he mentioned tonight appeared in an article written by Bruce Grant in The Age. I told Bill afterwards that he's often spoken to Bruce on the telephone and shouldn't be surprised if Bruce expected to be known. The main comment that came out of tonight's discussion was that Bill realises that our External Affairs policy is a cross-road. He's worried that Malcolm Fraser is going to make a statement early in the life of our new Parliament and, in order to maintain the balance, he wants to make one himself.

Saturday 28 February

Bill McMahon rang this morning and we had a general review of the Premiers' Conference. I told him how unhappy I was with the result. Bill tells me that Gorton rang him to tell him how elated, almost ecstatic, he was with the results of his policy. He now feels in complete power and nothing will stop him. Altogether a terrible omen for the weeks that lie ahead.

Bill still unhappy with Bruce Grant's article this week. I explained that it's his own fault; if he didn't listen to introductions, he can't blame me for what happens.

I kept in touch with Menzies. We had in common a background as scholarship boys from the country, a liking for literature and a romantic view of leadership. On one occasion when he was in hospital

I sent him a note "I hope the wise thrush will not be silent for long". I visited Lord Casey at his home in East Melbourne and in his nearby office on the other side of the Fitzroy Gardens. On one occasion, after publicity about student dissent at Monash, he entertained me with a lengthy and detailed (he had been an engineer by profession) account of a "noise machine" he had used to quell riots when he was Governor of Bengal. "You just wind it up," he said amiably. He put his hands over his ears. "Poor little devils. They just couldn't stand it." He stopped just short of urging me to use it, as a council member at Monash University, to stop student demonstrations.

As the election of 1972 approached, Professor Hedley Bull, who was editor of an Australian Institute of International Affairs series of books in which *The Crisis of Loyalty* had appeared, suggested that we might organise a letter of non-party prominent Australians supporting a change of government. We discussed the idea with others (Walter Crocker, former diplomat who became governor of South Australia, Macfarlane Burnet, director of the Walter and Eliza Hall of Medical Research, and Rev Dr J.D. McCaughey, master of Ormond College who later became governor of Victoria) and eventually the following letter appeared in all metropolitan newspapers.

> We, the undersigned, who are not members of any political party, believe that Australia's interest will be best served by a change of government as a result of this election.
>
> Our democratic system works properly only when each of the major parties has the chance to govern. Each benefits from the responsibilities. Each gains from the freedom of opposition.
>
> Some of us think the Liberal-Country Party coalition has had a productive, as well as long, period in office. Others of us are less enthusiastic about its record, especially in recent years.

> But we all agree that today, after 23 years in office, it needs new ideas and has problems of long-term leadership which can best be worked out in opposition.
>
> Although we do not subscribe to all the Australian Labor Party's policies, we see no over-riding reason for continuing to exclude it from office.
>
> It is Australia's oldest and biggest party. It represents aspirations in our society which cannot be ignored. It has prepared itself for office and needs only a moderate swing in its favour at this election to take office.
>
> If denied office any longer, the Labor Party is in danger of disintegrating as a force in Australia's political life.
>
> We believe a change of government will benefit both the major parties, on which the vitality of our political system depends.
>
> The ultimate beneficiary will be the Australian Nation and its people.

The signatories were, in addition to Bull, Burnet, McCaughey and myself, Professor R.R. Andrew, Professor Macmahon Ball, David Campbell, Professor Manning Clark, Sir Walter Crocker, Professor R.I. Downing, Dr Frank Fenner, Leonard French, Sir Keith Hancock, Kenneth Myer, Patrick White and Judith Wright.

I drafted the letter, but, needless to say, everyone had opinions and it went through several versions. Several who were given the opportunity to sign, refused. Ken Myer was the only businessman who agreed. Sir John Vernon declined, putting a view that many who disagreed with the letter, supported. "I do not agree that in an elective system of government there should be any over-riding principle of 'your turn next'". Sir Roderick Carnegie also declined. Sir James Darling, former headmaster of Geelong Grammar School, declined in a long, complex, hand-written letter in which he agreed with most of our argument but came to a different conclusion – that Australia should abolish compulsory voting and the preferential system.

The letter was widely discussed in the final stages of the election, more because Ken Myer, a businessman from a family thought to be politically conservative, had signed it, than from the moral or intellectual weight of its other signatories. Still, it was an early example in Australia of the energy and influence of civil society.

After the election of the Whitlam Government on 2 December 1972, rumours circulated in Canberra that I would be offered a diplomatic appointment. It was reported that I was going to Hanoi. Someone in the Department of Foreign Affairs promoted the idea in the press that I should be sent to Pakistan. In another rumour, my friendly relations with Lee Kuan Yew pointed to Singapore. And, of course, Indonesia supposedly beckoned. Perkin asked me and I said I was aware of the rumours but had not been approached formally to go anywhere. Perkin rang Whitlam and afterwards informed me that a diplomatic posting was intended – but that Whitlam had not yet decided what it would be and would ring me.

The Prime Minister did ring, offering me the post of ambassador to the United Nations. He wanted someone known publicly to support his government's new positions on colonialism and racism to be in New York when they were announced as policy in Australia. Was I in a position to take up the appointment immediately? I asked for a few days' consideration with family and friends (I had Macmahon Ball especially in mind). Shortly after, however, Whitlam's office rang to inform me of a complication. Sir Keith Waller, head of the Department of Foreign Affairs, had informed Whitlam that the department had promised the incumbent ambassador, Sir Laurence McIntyre, that if he were successful in lobbying for Australia to get a seat on the Security Council, which he had been, his appointment at the UN would be extended. Also, Waller's opinion was that the UN was what he called a "pressure-post", best handled by a professional. The Prime Minister was now in an awkward position. He was not bound by a departmental undertaking, but was interested in my opinion. I contested Waller's view that the UN was a post for professionals – this was not the experience of several other countries – but I did not share the view of some young officers in the department that McIntyre had outlived his usefulness at the UN and should be retired. He was an able diplomat who, I happened to know, had good contacts at the UN. In addition, he would have no personal difficulty in promoting the new policies. In any case, the government, not the post, would be making the new policy announcements. A "voice" in New York was not essential.

An intense period of consultation with Whitlam's office followed. One possibility was a new appointment – special adviser to the prime minister on defence and foreign policy. My view (which I later discovered that Whitlam himself shared) was that such an appointment, which was popularly associated with that of Kissinger in Washington, would not work in Australia. Kissinger had the small but effective resources of the National Security Council behind him. In Australia, a solitary figure as adviser would soon be isolated by the relevant departments, not to mention the intelligence agencies. Japan was discussed. I did not think a personal appointment as ambassador to Tokyo could be justified. I had no expertise in trade and economic relations and could not speak Japanese. So it was that on 28 December 1972 the Prime Minister rang to offer me formally an appointment as High Commissioner in New Delhi.

It was a long phone call, which enabled him to embark on a survey of our relations with the United States and the Soviet Union, as well as mainland China (where he was also intending to make a personal appointment, Dr Stephen Fitzgerald, who had been a professional diplomat and had left the service in disagreement with the previous government's China policy). His reasons for making a personal appointment to India were essentially two. He felt that India, a great democracy, had been neglected by previous Australian prime ministers, because it was considered to be too close to the Soviet Union. Second, he was concerned that Australia should not be drawn into the Sino-Soviet conflict. While he was confident that our relations with Indonesia and Japan were so central to our trade, defence and foreign policy concerns that they would not be upset by our preoccupation with China, he could not be so sure of India. He hoped that a personal appointment would allay any misgivings and would underline our intention to have a broad-based and open-minded foreign policy.

He apologised for his reluctance to "take on" the bureaucracy over the UN post. It would have been the place to say to the world that Australia had risen from the divisions of Vietnam to find a new assenting voice for itself. But the India post offered its own opportunities and, in some ways, was a more practical way of underpinning the independent foreign policy that Whitlam wanted. He explained this to me at length in his typically detailed and deliberate manner. The appointment of Fitzgerald to China and my appointment to India would show that the new Australian government's more independent foreign policy applied across the full range of its relationships in Asia. However, my appointment to India involved some other high-ranking diplomatic appointments and might take some time to manage.

After twenty-three years of opposition, Labor was inclined to regard the Canberra bureaucracy as wedded to a conservative political outlook and Whitlam, who was the son of a civil servant and had a high regard for public service, was under pressure to cut the bureaucrats down to size by demonstrating that a new government was in power and "unreconstructed" officials had better watch out. I held a view similar to Whitlam's about the civil service, however, regarding it as an anchor in a period of transition. I did not want the Prime Minister to begin his period in office with an unnecessary confrontation with Canberra's top civil servants. He would need their help to implement the vast program of reform that he was promising the Australian public. But I now was in an awkward position. I could not continue writing my column, but I did not know when the appointment to New Delhi would be public.

On 29 December I wrote the following note to Perkin:

> Whitlam did ring, as you said, and offered me a most interesting appointment, which I have accepted. Waller will be getting in touch with me about details in a week or so. I am not sure at the moment whether I will be needed immediately or later in the year – and, if so, how late. In the meantime, I think I had better take my holidays. I'll get in touch with you as soon as I know the details …

On the same day I wrote to Sir Keith Waller, saying that Whitlam had offered me the Indian appointment, but was leaving arrangements to Waller to be worked out with Sir Patrick Shaw, the incumbent High Commissioner. "My immediate concern," I wrote, "is that having accepted the appointment, I can't go on happily writing commentaries for *The Age*." I also told Waller than the Prime

Minister had said he would like me to accompany him to Indonesia early in the new year.

In fact, for successive reasons over which I had no control, my appointment to India did not take place until September 1973. In the meantime, I stopped writing my column but, in a thoughtful initiative of the managing director, Ranald Macdonald, I remained on *The Age* payroll, undertaking a lecture tour of schools on the theme "Australia's new foreign policy". In a letter inviting schools to participate, Macdonald described my former association with *The Age*, noted that I had accompanied Mr Whitlam on his tour of Indonesia in February and also that I would take up a diplomatic appointment later in the year.

In the meantime, I became an unofficial adviser to the Prime Minister. He startled officials at a meeting by introducing me as his "Dr Kissinger". For a while I was unofficial post office and interlocutor between the Prime Minister's office and Alan Renouf, who was our ambassador in Paris and who became head of the department of foreign affairs. Before he took up his new position, Alan's views were sought through me on senior personnel changes and I engaged him in a discussion about the future of the Australian Secret Intelligence Service, which mainly operated from Australia's diplomatic missions in foreign countries. On Whitlam's first official visit abroad – to Indonesia and Papua New Guinea – I had a place in the official party, as I did on his first official visit to India later in the year. The visit to India took place in the middle of the monsoon, which surprised and delighted our hosts, who were used only to visitors in more humanly tolerant weather.

As my association with Whitlam became public, the terrace house in Grey Street, East Melbourne, was visited by diplomats and officials from Canberra, foreign correspondents and political journalists, as well as old faces from the intelligence agencies. One of these was Harvey Barnett, who I had known in Asia as a member of ASIS. Harvey was on a mission. He wanted me to intercede with Whitlam to get better terms and conditions for Australia's clandestine workers. For an hour he laid out, on the desk in the room I used as a study and office, the deplorable lack of material security in the spying business, the absence of superannuation, the lack of support for agents' families – all because of the need for secrecy. At that time, those who worked for ASIS were non-persons in the industrial scheme of things. It was so secret that even its existence was not acknowledged. I was not confident of my ground, but promised to do what I could.

As Harvey was leaving, a television crew arrived at the mean front door. They wanted to interview me about some lingering dissension in the Myer family over the famous letter. The look on Harvey's face, reflecting years of experience of deception, when he saw the television crew, is with me still.

8

TRUSTY AND WELL-BELOVED

The public impression of a diplomat is of high style and discretion, even deception. Popular references dog diplomacy. One is the opinion of the British diplomat, scholar and traveller Sir Henry Wotton that "an ambassador is an honest man who is sent to lie abroad for the good of his country". Another is a remark of Frederick the Great: "diplomacy without power is like an orchestra without a score". The American humourist Will Rogers described diplomacy as "the art of saying 'nice doggie' until you can find a rock."

The work of a modern diplomatic mission is a microcosm of humdrum national life, including trade and investment, defence and foreign policy, immigration and consular matters, cultural and educational exchanges. However, the diplomat is a servant of the state and, in the global society of states, self-regard has a high priority. The state is "sovereign". Imbued with the mysterious power that used to reside in monarchs and emperors, backed for some by divine right, it takes itself seriously. It has no room for weakness and little space for humour. The number of states increased rapidly as European colonialism came to an end, and the attributes of sovereignty were even more highly valued in the new states.

Because of India's importance in global politics as a leader of the group of non-aligned nations in the Cold War, New Delhi was a busy diplomatic centre. The Nehru-Gandhi dynasty was the core of an established political culture, in which bureaucracy, media, business and religion had each found a place. The Australian mission was well established, having been headed by high commissioners with standing in Canberra, such as Sir James Plimsoll and Sir Arthur Tange. Its substantial compound in the diplomatic enclave contained both offices and residential accommodation. When I arrived it had a staff of thirty Australians drawn from eight government agencies and more than double that number of locally engaged staff.

The language of diplomacy manages to be both fulsome and deferential at the same time. I wore the title Excellency uneasily, stung by the barbs of former colleagues. High Commissioner, which was reserved for ambassadors of the British Commonwealth, evoked comic opera or the management of taxes and prisons. I had a big house, with four personal servants, a cook and a driver, a well-stocked cellar of Australian wines, and two secretaries, one for general purposes and the other for social engagements. Social engagements were plentiful and regarded as useful. For newcomers, there were "calls" on colleagues. Some skipped this traditional courtesy, but I didn't and found them valuable. The order of precedence for resident diplomats is determined by time spent at the post, so the dean of the diplomatic corps has been there longer than anyone else, no matter how powerful or inconsequential the country he or she represents. This simple, democratic protocol gave some objectivity to the routine of "calls": experience is a kind of wisdom. I was able from seemingly routine conversations to form an impression of India's official outlook, especially on China.

I had prevailed upon the Prime Minister to allow me to fly with my family to New Delhi via Beijing, to give me a chance to test Chinese attitudes to India. I already had a sense of the relationship between India and the Soviet Union, but with China I was only aware of the border tensions in the 1960s. I was not as strongly identified with China as was Whitlam and his advisers. I had supported the new China policy, but the authoritarian tendency of communist rule in the Soviet Union affected my view of the prospect in China, even if one accepted that the Chinese revolution was more agrarian than industrial and the Chinese people had an ancient tradition of communal values. My visit to Beijing and Shanghai barely scratched the surface, but I was experienced in gauging official attitudes and language and I had the benefit of Joan's knowledge of Chinese language and history.

I had been warned by friends in the Department of Foreign Affairs that, entering at the top a profession known for its traditions, jealousies and closely guarded secrets, I would encounter difficulties. My experience in New Delhi was, on the contrary, relaxing. It was a relief not to have to express carefully developed and finely wrought opinions twice a week, and it was a pleasure to be working with others who had more knowledge than I had about particular aspects of the mission's work.

The constraints were mainly those of common sense. I had to watch what I said and think twice about what I did, not just to make sure I had the facts right and was not erecting a straw-man argument, but to avoid saying or doing anything that might be construed as embarrassing or controversial to the gatekeepers in Canberra. You represent, technically, the state, or more realistically the government, or even at times the nation and people. The processes of government were slow and, within official circles, inclusive. Precedent and process were more important than creativity and innovation, because the bureaucratic machine moves only in ways and at a pace that it knows how to manage. I discovered a developed system of communication, within government and with other governments, and a complex allocation of preferences and priorities that determined who sent messages and who received them. Who had the right to know what you were communicating? And who should be excluded? As head of mission, I occasionally sent directly to the Minister what was called a "despatch". Mostly these were classified "Confidential". Sometimes they were "Secret" or even "Top Secret". Sometimes, in addition, they were stamped AUSTEO, or Australian Eyes Only, or ECLIPSE, which had additional connotations. At first, I had no idea how to classify what I was writing and relied on the advice of senior staff.

Before I could begin my new life, I had to be properly accredited. This called for unexpected skills in dress, forms of speech, inspection of honour guards and other paraphernalia that the state has accumulated to protect its dignity and of which this particular representative of the new, robust Australia had no experience. Whitlam had appointed me to India as part of a major realignment of Australian foreign policy in the region. He also thought (as he said, with a quizzical look that made you wonder what was coming) that the Indians would appreciate someone with "a contemplative cast of mind". He had taken to calling me "Guru". However, neither of us paid attention to whether I had any of the formal skills or attributes of a diplomat. We assumed that any normally intelligent person could manage the formalities. One of the delights of the Whitlam era – and a possible explanation of why it was so short-lived – was that those involved in it were confident they could do anything.

Former Australian high commissioners had worn what was inexplicably described to me as "morning dress" for their accreditation ceremonies. I turned for advice not to my British or European or Asian colleagues, all of whom had fancy dress for such occasions, but to another amateur, my American colleague Patrick Moynihan, who, as a staunch upholder of democratic virtues, gave me a tip: a dark suit, with a homburg and a red, or at least pink, rose in your buttonhole will get you anywhere. The credentials ceremony in New Delhi was organised with military precision in the sandstone palace that had been the residence of the British Viceroy and was now the centrepiece of official India. I borrowed Pat's homburg, plucked a red rose from our garden and inspected honour guards and ascended palatial staircases lined with overbearing sentries armed with pikestaffs, as if I had been doing it from birth.

My letter of accreditation to the President of India was like a trumpet from a mythical past, bejewelled with extravagant claims of service to the state and issued from a mysterious sanctum called "Our Court in Canberra".

ELIZABETH THE SECOND

By the Grace of God Queen of Australia and Her other Realms and Territories, Head of the Commonwealth.

To the President of the Republic of India

Sendeth Greeting!

OUR Good Friend!

BEING desirous to maintain without interruption the representation in the Republic of India and further to promote the relations of unity and concord which so happily subsist between India and Australia, We have to that end made choice of Our Trusty and Well-beloved Bruce Alexander Grant, Esquire, to be the accredited Representative and Plenipotentiary of Australia in the Republic of India.

The personal qualities of Mr Grant and his long service of the State assure Us that he is eminently worthy of the important Mission for which he has been selected and that he will discharge the duties of his High Office in a manner that will fully meet Your approbation and esteem.

More especially, Australia and the Republic of India being free and equal members of Our Commonwealth of which We are the Head, as the symbol of the free association of its independent Member Nations, We have every confidence in commending Mr Grant to You, and in requesting that You will repose Your full and complete trust in all that he shall communicate to You in Our Name.

GIVEN at Our Court at Canberra in the Twenty Second Year of Our Reign

Your Good Friend

Elizabeth R

My address to the President was more contemporary than the Queen's. It contained the following passage: "Our two countries have long had friendly relations. Perhaps the time has come to provide a new dimension to that friendship. We live in a world that is less compelled by ideas of international cooperation and goodwill than it was when our relations began, when we were founding members of the United Nations. Although we are encouraged at times by signs of cooperation and responsibility among the world powers, we are also discovering that the ideals of social justice, economic progress and human dignity which we share are very difficult to achieve. Yet there may be benefits to be gained from the loss of illusions. Indeed, we can turn events to our advantage, for prudence in international aspirations is perhaps more likely to bring practical results. There is always a danger that grand visions will foster unattainable expectations and, even when progress is made, that people will feel disappointed. The problems of peace and progress are so pressing that we need practical outcomes. So it is timely that India and Australia should now look at ways in which additional content can be given to our relations, so that our two countries will be held together by concrete interests as well as by goodwill and mutual respect."

The President, Mr V.V. Giri, absorbed all this with the large smile that was his trademark. I adjourned with him for a private chat, in which he refrained from inquiring what I was getting at, although, as a former trade unionist and politician, he might have guessed that my words were directed as much at the high rhetoric that characterised India's conversation with the rest of the world as at the high expectation of the new Australian government.

My thoughtful hint to the president was based on my directive from the Whitlam government, which contained two key sentences, each using the word "substance". One was that, despite shared institutions like the English language, parliamentary democracy, the common law, and cricket, "our success in developing with India bilateral relations of real substance has at the best been modest." The other was that "relations of substance with India, by helping us to maintain a freedom of manoeuvre in and gain new perspectives on our relations with China, Indonesia and Japan would contribute to the Government's aim of fashioning for Australia a truly independent foreign policy."

I was also accredited to Nepal. In Kathmandu, the ceremony was quick and officious, in contrast with the gay and lively demeanour of the Nepalese people. Diplomats presented themselves in batches (usually of three), bowing three times on a long, red carpet as you approached the throne; there were no speeches and no private audience with the young King, who remained aloof. The letter I carried to King Birendra had ancient echoes even less sympathetic to the government of the robust new Australia than my letter to the Indian President. It contained some surprising intimacies. Not only was I trusty and well-beloved, I had demonstrated zeal for service not just to the state but to the Queen herself, and I would reside "near" the King (although, in fact, living in India).

> *Sir My Brother,*
>
> *BEING desirous to maintain without interruption the representation at Your Majesty's Court of the interests of Australia, I have judged it expedient to accredit to Your Majesty My Trusty and Well-beloved Bruce Alexander Grant, Esquire, to reside near You in the character of My Ambassador Extraordinary and Plenipotentiary of Australia.*
>
> *HAVING already had ample experience of Mr Grant's talents and zeal for My services, I doubt not that he will fulfil the important duties of his Embassy in such a manner as to merit Your Majesty's approbation and esteem, and to prove himself worthy of this new mark of My confidence.*
>
> *I request that You will give entire credence to all that Mr Grant shall have occasion to communicate to You in My name, more especially when he shall express to Your Majesty My cordial*

wishes for Your happiness and shall assure You of the invariable attachment and highest esteem with which I am,

Sir My Brother,

Your Majesty's Good Sister,

ELIZABETH R.

Buckingham Palace

The immediate effect of arriving in New Delhi and settling in to our new house in the diplomatic enclave was not, however, political, social, intellectual or even diplomatic, but sensual. When I later wrote about my time in India in *Gods and Politicians* (1982), I began with a description of the country's physical impact.

> The moon hung over our back garden like a huge coin. Peacocks flew heavily over our heads when we picnicked by the side of the road. The morning sounds in the mists of the Himalayan foothills were as slow and clear as bells. The heat was so fierce in mid-summer that I used to hurry the one-minute walk from house to office, as one hurries through heavy rain … Once, in Calcutta, I witnessed from my hotel window the creation of a storm. Thunder and lightning broke across the city skyline and the congested streets were violently emptied … The rain fell for several minutes as if it were trying to punish, even obliterate, life on earth. Then the clouds lifted and reared away, the rain stopped, the sun shone, and what had seemed like a rehearsal of the end of the world became within seconds a scene of resolute normality – the shouting and honking and chattering of Calcutta's streets. It was as if a trail of ants had been momentarily scattered by a spurt of water from a garden hose. Another time, in Jaipur, I walked with the crowd through a series of archways through high, old walls rising from grassy ground. Heavy doors, made of timber

> and iron, had been opened to allow the people through. I was surrounded by bright orange and dark red turbans and saris in striking primary colours. Camels and elephants were being led and cajoled and whacked, and a light dust arose. The smell of animals, the crude brilliance of clothing, the impression that the battlements were drawing us through medieval archways as if back through history, sent a thrill through me, not of fear as an isolated foreigner, but of excitement at being part of a human cavalcade.

Several of the mission staff, including the deputy high commissioner W.G.T. (Geoff) Miller and his wife Rachel, had young families like ours. My memory of the compound is of the cries of children at play, especially at the swimming pool. Heads of mission were entitled to have their own swimming pool, but I declined the invitation from Canberra to the entitlement. The pool, like our lawn, which was big enough to serve as either a field for croquet or Australian football, was a valuable community site.

I settled down to a pleasantly busy life, with occasional surprises, such as the discovery of my authority as a marriage celebrant, which I exercised on two occasions. India was a crossroads geographically and politically. A week in New Delhi rarely passed without an interesting visitor. One of these was the French writer and intellectual Andre Malraux, who came to accept the annual Jawaharlal Nehru award "for outstanding contribution to the promotion of international understanding, goodwill and friendship among people of the world." The previous recipients included Martin Luther King, Yehudi Menuhin, Kenneth Kuanda, Josip Broz Tito, Mother Theresa, Julius Nyerere and U Thant, a list that reflected India's non-aligned position in the Cold War but also Nehru's liking of people who reached out to other cultures and other countries.

Malraux was a legendary figure in India, having wanted to fight in Bangladesh in 1971 when he was 76 years of age, as he had in Spain in the civil war 1936–39 and in the French resistance 1939–45. Accepting the award, he proposed what he called an Institute of International Methods of Action, which would study ways of mobilising nations to act together against the new scourges of mankind, especially what he called "technical fall-out" from the nuclear age. Now that war, once the dynamic of global action, had become so destructive that only madmen would contemplate it, the world must find other ways of resolving differences. The auditorium buzzed with delight as he declared that India was the proper place for such a study because Gandhi's strategy of non-violence had for the first and only time in history made a revolution ethical, breaking the deadlock of revolution without ethics and ethics without revolution. In a gesture of existential bravado, he announced from the floor that the Institute already existed, because his prize money would provide the budget for its first year.

It was an evening of drama and excitement. India was the perfect venue, as anyone who has read the Bhagavad-Gita can attest, to consider the relationship between thought and action, reconciled in Hindu philosophy by disinterest, action without attachment to the result. Even in a modernising nation, there was a detached quality about action, as if, despite the hustle and bustle of politics, business and journalism, it occurred in slow motion. But the Indian state, still fresh from its release from British colonialism, was not about to surrender its authority to wage war. I was not surprised, when I inquired some time later about the fate of Malraux's institute, to find that nothing had been done.

I enjoyed what was becoming archaic as diplomacy ran to keep up with new communications technology – the occasional despatch from the head of mission in which an attempt was made to summarise the state of the world as seen from the mission's vantage point. I sent eighteen of these despatches during my time in New Delhi – on the state of relations between India and Australia, on Bhutan, Kashmir, India's nuclear test (twice), Jayaprakash Narayan's political challenge, Sir John Kerr's visit, the Indian economy (twice), India's relations with the United States and the Soviet Union, Nepal's attitude to India and China, India's incorporation of Sikkim, the influence of brilliant individuals in Indian science and technology, the dominance of the Congress party in Indian politics, Mrs Gandhi's Emergency and, my last, how the Fraser Government might maintain and develop the good relations with India established by the Whitlam Government.

I travelled extensively within India and into the Himalayas and turned with pleasure in my spare evenings and other breaks to writing – fiction, especially short stories, essays and reflections. I made an effort to show respect for Indian language and culture, arranging musical evenings at the residence, appointing the Australian film-maker, John Murray, as cultural attaché, asking all Australians at the mission to learn basic Hindi. We sent our two sons, David and Benjamin, to an Indian school, rather than the international schools popular with the diplomatic community.

Among our Australian visitors, Sir John Kerr, Governor-General, in February 1975, and Dr Jim Cairns, Deputy Prime Minister and Treasurer, in May 1975, were of particular interest.

When Kerr arrived in Nepal to attend King Birendra's coronation he greeted me at Kathmandu airport with the question "Do I call you Excellency also?" He was a strange mixture of intelligence and pomposity, impressed with protocol and precedence. There was, admittedly, a reason. I was the Queen of Australia's representative in

With my mother and father, sisters Audrey and Jocelyn and Grandma Grant, my father's mother.

With Grandpa Williams, my mother's father.

The whipstick gimlet farmer and his wife, with sister Audrey and shoeless author, with bow tie.

"As son imbibes his Father's time … when he was him." David and I retrace my walk to Karlgarin school.

Enid Walters, before we were married.

The Able Seaman who did not like King's Regulations and Admiralty Instructions.

On the way to accreditation, wearing Pat Moynihan's homburg.

The marriage celebrant.

Joan and I with the Indian President, Mr V.V. Giri.

With David, Ben and bare-footed Joan at the Raj Ghat, a memorial marking the spot where Mahatma Gandhi was cremated.

Looking thoughtful, as Sir John Kerr is introduced before speaking at a dinner with Mrs Gandhi.

Sir John Kerr arrives in Katmandu.

Clockwise from top left:

Feeding the pigeons in Trafalgar Square.

An encounter with symbolic America –
the White House and the Statue of Liberty.

The dutiful Jewish daughter who was also
quintessential New York.

Bambi with son Michael, Johanna, James and
Susan at the beach in Melbourne.

With Queen Elizabeth on tour in New Zealand.

In conversation with Prime Minister Nehru and Neville Maxwell, of *The Times*, London.

Speaking at the National Press Club, Canberra, at the launch of *The Australian Dilemma*.

Celebrating with Arts Centre personnel at the first Spoleto Festival in Melbourne.

With Ratih Hardjono and Gareth Evans.

Einstein had only one new idea. We had two.

Acclaiming the friendship of neighbours with Abdurrahman Wahid,
before he became President of Indonesia.

With Susan and her husband, Dr Peter James, at another palatial pile in Rajasthan.

A family quartet, playing, I think, at Lorne.

Johanna and Jaems dancing at a family birthday.

The Lorne house under construction.

The author in seeming retirement.

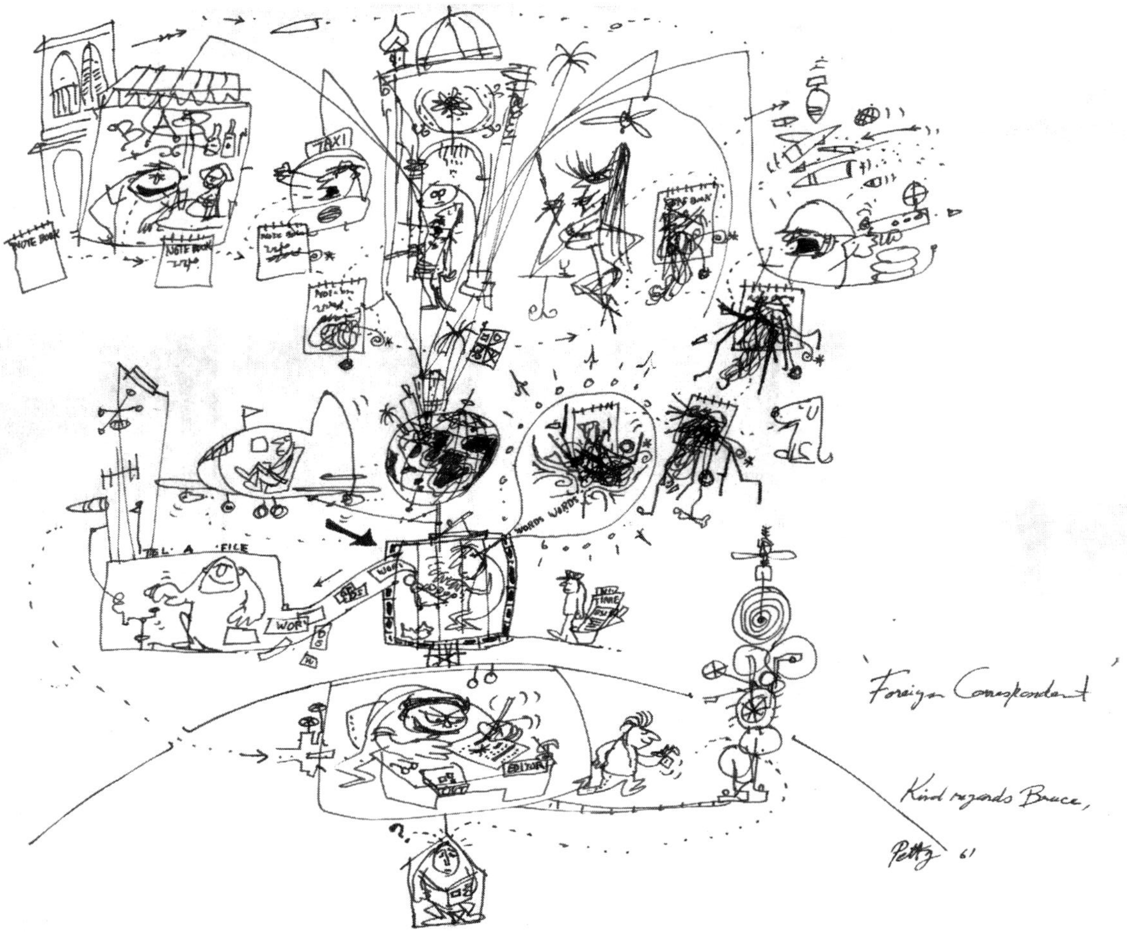

Bruce Petty gave me his version of the life of a foreign correspondent after time together on an assignment.

Cartoonist Abu Abraham captured the Indian media's welcome of the Whitlam government.

Four generations of a happy family, celebrating Christmas in the King's Domain. Photograph by Christopher Hussein-Bril.

Nepal. He was her representative in Australia, but outside Australia his status, as we both knew, had to be contrived. The delicacy of his position soon became apparent.

Because of Australia's alphabetical position, he was last of the foreign guests to enter on ceremonial occasions and the first to leave. Prince Charles was perplexed. He pointed out to me that he was representing his mother directly, while Kerr, as her representative in Australia, might outside Australia be more properly accorded a secondary rank (as I was, as ambassador). I explained that we had persuaded Nepal to treat the Governor-General as an authentic head of state, not a proconsul on tour. I pointed out that this was not a Whitlam initiative: it had been tried during the tenures of Casey and Hasluck. During this explanation, the Prince of Wales wore that long, bemused face that the world has often seen since.

Kerr was not present during this conversation but he expressed concern to me that playing the new national anthem, "Advance Australia Fair", on his arrival at the airport, could be misconstrued. I had advised the Government of Nepal that it should be played, based on Kerr's travelling status as Australia's head of state. He accepted the logic, but worried that the gesture might be interpreted in some circles as meaning that he had republican sympathies. He preferred what he called the "vice-regal salute", which contained six bars of the national anthem and eight bars of the royal anthem (or was it the other way around?). I countered with the practical difficulty of getting the Nepalese band at this late stage to learn a new arrangement, which Kerr gracefully acknowledged, but required that on his arrival later in New Delhi the vice- regal salute should be played. It was apparent during his time in Nepal and India that what had seemed to me from a distance to be an irresistible flow in Australia towards the symbols and sentiments of a new nationalism, or at least a new national style, was to him something of a problem. He was anxious not to seem part of the anti-monarchist sentiment on the Labor side of politics, nor to antagonise Labor's political opponents.

With the benefit of hindsight, my informal conversations with Kerr in New Delhi were revealing. On several occasions he stressed the importance in life of "contingency". It was necessary to plan ahead and to organise the present carefully, but the great challenge, he believed, was how to deal with unforeseen events. Kerr was a heavy man physically and when he spoke of contingency and unforeseen events he raised his voice, as if contemplating something beyond detection by logic and analysis.

A favoured topic was "power", which fascinated him. We discussed the role of Alf Conlon, who had been leader of a group of academics and analysts, including Kerr, engaged in intelligence work in Australia's neighbourhood during the Second World War. I took no notes of the conversation, but my recollection of Kerr's account is that, when the war ended, he had fallen out with Conlon. They had agreed to be demobilised together, but Conlon had double-crossed him. Before returning to civil life, Conlon had persuaded a high army authority that Kerr should be promoted from major to colonel and be posted to Duntroon to take over a school that Conlon had developed from the intelligence research unit. Kerr had wanted to go back to the bar. But he gave in. The school was important and someone had to run it. That was how Conlon worked, according to Kerr. He made decisions that were in everyone's best interests, and people accepted that he was right. He understood power. He had no power himself, but he knew how to persuade people who had power. He made himself indispensable to people. He worked out their failings and weaknesses and set out to overcome them, without the person knowing. You felt he was occupying your mind, Kerr said, and taking it over. Conlon called it "therapeutic mendacity". Kerr thought it was the end justifying the means.

Kerr was confident in his meetings with Mrs Gandhi and her ministers, showing both the benefits of experience of public life and a strong intellect. His address to the Indian Law Institute became controversial in Australia later, because he asserted that the Governor-General was not a figurehead and was bound to resist a dissolution of Parliament in mid-term if it were merely to solve the political difficulties of a Prime Minister. Much was read into this address, but it was at the time hardly surprising. Its self-important tone was an aspect of Kerr's personality that could hardly be missed. Sensitive to "power" in public life, he was anxious not to seem excluded from it. In any case, Governors-General, like High Commissioners, needed to say something of substance in their speeches to encourage the belief in their audiences that they were not mere ciphers.

Kerr's visits to Nepal and India were helpful to the mission in supporting our projection of Australia as a distinctive voice in the region, which had begun with Whitlam's visit two years earlier. In a despatch to Canberra I made some practical suggestions, such as doing away with the vice-regal salute and giving the Governor-General's speeches more policy content. I concluded, with unintentional foresight, that the institution of the Governor-General in Australia was "at an interesting and possibly creative stage of development."

Dr Cairns was travelling with both his wife and his personal assistant Junie Morosi. On his itinerary were both the erotic temples of Khajuraho and the Taj Mahal (by moonlight). Unexpectedly (at least, for me) Ms Morosi's husband, David Ditchburn, arrived, expecting to join the official party. When the Indians asked me for official approval, I declined, not having been given any advance warning of Mr Ditchburn's presence, and asked the Deputy Prime Minister if he would oblige. Cairns declined, even more mindful, no doubt, than I was about political sensitivity in Australia to passenger lists of VIP aircraft. As the unexpected visitor had already travelled on one official flight, I explained my predicament to an Indian official in the back of his car, travelling between engagements. He smiled gently, and in that smile (I wrote later) was "the wisdom of years of bending the rules to accommodate human folly." The Indian government would, on compassionate grounds, include Mr Ditchburn in the official party, as he had come all that way (he had a position with an Ethiopian airline) to be with his wife.

Cairns was in an exuberant mood. He gave the Prime Minister, Mrs Gandhi, a tutorial in 101 Economics. First, inflation was a way of redistributing wealth, within and among nations. Second, Australia talked a lot about helping the Third World, but did little. "That's not what your High Commissioner tells us," Mrs Gandhi sweetly said. I defended the Australian Government against its Deputy Prime Minister, while she beamed at both of us. Cairns later gave a vigorous and passionate speech to the National Defence College on the Vietnam War, to which I listened with admiration. Then, while we wandered by a moonlit Taj Mahal, he was enticed by Ms Morosi to chew betel nut, which resulted in a cracked tooth. He decided immediately, despite official Indian advice on the poor professional standard of dentistry in Agra in the middle of the night, to have the tooth extracted. I accompanied him to a small and basic surgery nearby, where he bore the experience with amused bravado.

Marshall Green, US ambassador to Australia, came to dinner at the residence one Sunday not long after I arrived, and we talked about Australian politics until he left at 11 p.m. We knew each other from the time when he was ambassador to Indonesia, and we quickly slipped into the easy conversational manner we had adopted then. Green mentioned an article by Peter Hastings that had apparently referred to Gough Whitlam as another Sukarno, whose foreign policy was full of image-building, and we discussed a critical article by Owen Harries in *Quadrant*. Green seemed well informed about criticism of Whitlam in Labor's ranks.

His general comment, however, was that he preferred to work with the Whitlam government than any prospective Liberal government. He liked the idea of Australia being a "robust middle power". He did not want to go back to the old "weight" of Australian dependence on the US. He said it was easier for him to work with an ally that was examining "new possibilities" rather than relying on "loyalty". Whitlam's energy and confidence in the possibility of peaceful change in Asia were welcome in Washington. President Nixon had said, after meeting Whitlam, that he was "quite a guy" (Green had passed this on to Whitlam, who was pleased). His cautionary note was that Australia was tending to down-grade South-east Asia and to speak as if Asia were Japan, China and India. He thought we should be more active in South-east Asia, "taking up the slack" as the United States withdrew. He was worried about Australia's relations with Indonesia. I dutifully conveyed his concerns to Canberra.

The search for "substance" in the bilateral relationship was elusive, but we persisted and an opportunity for cooperation presented itself when iron ore producing countries met after the oil producing countries showed how effective in raising the price of their commodity an organisation like the Organisation of Petroleum Exporting Countries (OPEC) could be. A division among iron ore producers developed between those like Sweden and Canada, who had sympathy with the major consumers, Europe, Japan and the United States, and misgivings about a producers' organisation, and Third World countries like Algeria and India, who needed every cent of export value they could get and favoured a strong organisation. As a producer, Australia fitted into the first group, especially because of our exports to Japan, but we sympathised with developing countries that needed an organisation to help them in a way that the market could not. What happened was that Australia and India took over negotiations, with India moderating the radicals and Australia moderating the conservatives and an association was established without the price-fixing authority of the OPEC model.

Cultural relations were a substantial, if diffusive, part of the work of the Australian mission. The following checklist, written as a reminder to me after a visit to Uttar Pradesh, gives an idea of the issues raised and the service provided.

1. Professor Haggi, head of the department of political science, Aligarh University, invited you to give a lecture. You suggested early November. You said you would send Haggi a good Australian political science journal. You mentioned *The Australian Quarterly* or *The Australian Political Studies Association* journal.
2. Dr Shukla, recently returned from the United Kingdom, questioned you during your address to the International Centre about advertising for immigrants. He wondered why, if Australia's policy were not discriminatory, we advertised in England but not in India. You would like to raise this with Canberra.
3. Professor Mishra asked about the possibility of giving him some books on the theory and practice of teaching.

4. The Collector, Kanpur (M. Watal) asked about the book *Wanderings of a Pilgrim*, written by Mrs Fanny Parker in the Collector's residence in the 1850s. The British Council does not have a copy. The Indian International Centre does. He will follow up the matter himself.
5. Dr Chaudhuri, of Kanpur, who produced the feature film *Atoms*, is to write to you about John Murray.
6. Mr Sanshik, Administrative Officer, Anand Bhavan, Allahabad, has translated a collection of Judith Wright's poems into Hindi. You gave him a copy of Patrick White's plays but wonder about the possibility of encouraging his interest by presenting him with a selection of books of Australian poetry.
7. Mrs Khan, Mrs Gandhi's cousin, who runs the Bal Bhavan at Allahabad, and to whom you gave *The Aunt's Story*, asked about the possibility of our sending her reading material, preferably literature.
8. You wondered if we should present something to the Allahabad High Court.
9. Professor Kamurge (History, Benares Hindu University) suggested exchanges in South-East Asian and Oriental studies, where he considered Australia to be strong, while India was relatively weak. You would like to raise this with the Australian National University.
10. A number of people at the Vice-Chancellor's dinner expressed interest in a lecture tour by Sir Donald Bradman or Jack Fingleton.
11. You thought that the Walter Burley Griffin buildings in Lucknow (the Pioneer Building and the Tagore Library at the University) would be of interest to the Griffin centenary celebrations in Australia.

Confronted with heart-breaking poverty, one marvelled at the task of democratic government in India. After a visit to Calcutta, I wrote a note to myself: "You stand one day to watch a person crawling in the gutter. His face is ulcerated, a tumour grows from his head, his eyes stare helplessly and his face is contorted with the agony of movement. People side-step around him. What can you do? Call an ambulance? How? And there are others in this street, lying on pavements under wisps of wrap, perhaps already dead. Hold him in your arms? You cannot. You wish you could, but you cannot. It would be like cradling a diseased animal. You turn away, angry. You hate yourself. You even hate him. You hate the ancient system he inhabits. You want to smash the thousand-year-old pieces at the museum, where you are heading."

Embassies and high commissions are not just foreign enclaves in other countries, but sensitive outposts of national security, protected by diplomatic immunity. They are staffed, however, by human beings who sometimes feel they have the right to do what other human beings do, like have affairs or even fall in love. This is especially the case in a country like India, with lively and attractive people who enjoy the company of foreigners, particularly those with the means to entertain.

I inherited a private secretary who was not only charming and competent, but immunised by humour against the ways of the world. She was eventually replaced by a more vulnerable young woman from Canberra who became the object of desire of an Indian man, causing commotion in the compound late one night when she locked him out. Senior residents on the compound conferred and delivered their unanimous verdict: she should be sent back to Canberra. The High Commissioner's private secretary was a vital source of information and her judgement and discretion were in question. I felt a tinge of romantic sympathy, but agreed. If she had been more impressive in her work, I might have objected.

While political and strategic interests were the responsibility of a head of mission, the mission's workload was consular, involving visiting Australians and the human and social consequences of being a foreign mission, as outlined in the following letter.

Dear Sir,

I feel compelled to report to you the following incident involving a member of your staff because it seems to me to be an unseemly performance for a member of the diplomatic corps, of any age, and because it seemed to be predicated upon the belief that any kind of behaviour is acceptable on the streets of Delhi … The writer is an older woman who has lived in this part of the world for the last twenty years.

On last Saturday morning I was driving my car and had just entered the back part of Khan Market, when I found my car blocked by an incoming car on my side of the road. The car was of light colour, had a diplomatic plate, and was driven by a young man, fair, in his late twenties or thirties, perhaps of medium build, with a young woman and daughter beside him. He was, I repeat, on the wrong side of the road, having started to pull around a car to my right, and it was at just this juncture that we arrived face to face. The blocking car, going in the same direction as myself, had pulled to the right and come to a stop, thus obstructing oncoming traffic completely, while the woman driving (a Caucasian, also in a diplomatic car) was doing her Saturday shopping from the driver's seat – shopkeepers flurrying to and from their shops with her requests. It was a lovely day, and I was really more amused than annoyed at the cavalier behaviour of the shopper, until I discerned a look of furious exercisement on the face of the driver facing me and noticed that he was verbalising very heatedly for my benefit as well. At this point, to avoid unpleasantness, I pulled off the road and parked. In driving etiquette and law, it is, I believe the obligation of the driver on the wrong side of the road to right the situation, and having parked thus at the entrance to the market my errands involved a walk of some distance. Hence it was I who made the generous gesture. Since I had thus cleared the road, the car now facing me could now pass. It did, but not before the driver leaned out of his window and shouted some exceedingly ill-sounding words. Some minutes later, on the street, I passed a young man who could be none other than this offensive young driver. I asked him forthwith exactly what he had said on the road. With his voice bristling with belligerence and nasty temper, he said, "I said 'Get your bloody car out of the way'." At which, I asked him which embassy he was with and he told me.

A young Indian woman working at the high commission came to see me. She had a European boyfriend who wanted to whisk her off to Europe. Her family was flattered, but also opposed. They wanted her to stay in India. They were not wealthy enough to travel abroad. She promised to come back to India regularly but they did not trust her boyfriend. They thought he was under the influence of drugs (which he was, she said, but only in India, where they were cheap; in Europe he would be different).

I listened and politely asked why she had come to see me about her situation. She wondered if I could speak to Mrs Gandhi about it, or at least to someone close to the prime minister. About what, I asked, unable to conceal my surprise at the suggestion. She said that if her boyfriend could be helped to travel frequently in and out of India, it would be easier for her parents to keep in touch with him and she could return with him from time to time. This would make her parents happy and they would agree to her going away with him. But how could the prime minister help her boyfriend to travel frequently in and out of India? The young woman looked at me with surprise. Was it not impossible to leave India and return without the prime minister's permission? No, of course not. But that's what people said – the prime minister controlled everything. I said she had perhaps taken gossip too literally.

She persisted. If you didn't want the customs people interfering, and "things like that", wouldn't it be good to have a letter from the prime minister? I began to discern the shape of her predicament. Was her boyfriend a drug courier? She was indignant. No, of course not. She would not have come to see me if he were. I awaited enlightenment. She said he bought and sold silver. He found the customs people "very difficult to deal with". I explained that my access to the prime minister was actually quite limited and, in any case, I didn't think she bothered herself with customs matters. The young woman withdrew courteously, thanking me for my consideration, and the matter ended.

I often wondered what urgent combination of need and opportunity brought that young lady to my office. Pressure from the boyfriend and an exaggerated sense in local staff at the Australian high commission of my influence with Mrs Gandhi were likely. But in India it was the rule rather than the exception for people to seek influence to deal with personal problems. I had a file of letters from persons unknown to me seeking redress of some wrong committed in the distant past. Human needs in India were always greater than the resources to satisfy those needs; people assumed that those who were successful had used influence (or bribery) to get what they wanted.

Immersed in India (and Nepal), I had not at first appreciated that I was responsible for Bhutan, a Himalayan mountain kingdom like Nepal, wedged between India and China and sensitive to both. In June 1974, Joan and I attended the coronation of the 18-year-old monarch, Jigme Singye Wangchuk. We took two days to get to the capital Thimpu, which lies in one of the passes to Tibet, a valley some two kilometres above sea level. We flew from Delhi to Calcutta, where we changed planes for Bagdogra, from where we drove for three hours to a border town, Puntsholing, where we stayed overnight. Next day, we took seven hours by car to cover the 180 kilometres of spectacular mountain road to Thimpu. Diplomats travelled in a cavalcade of eighteen pale blue Ford cars provided by Australia as a gift for the coronation and to be used for tourism afterwards. Heads of state travelled this last bit of the journey by helicopter. The fifty or so representatives of the media were transported by bus.

Another obstacle to entering Bhutan was political. You had to pass through what the Indians call the "inner line", for which they issued permits and in that way screened visitors to Bhutan. The influx of visitors for the coronation was a major event for the Bhutanese, who estimated that (not counting Indians) the number of foreign guests was greater than the number of foreign visitors to Bhutan in its entire history. The big news was that an official representative from China was among them, invited (the Bhutanese smilingly explained) with the other four permanent members of the United Nations Security Council.

Guests at the coronation were given a speedy introduction to the rivalry between the Dorji and Wangchuk families, the Montagues and Capulets of Bhutan. We were surprised to be informed on arrival that there had been an assassination attempt earlier in the year. According to the official version, a mistress of the King's late father, a Tibetan woman named Yangki, had conspired with a group led by the Dalai Lama's brother to assassinate the King. Thirty people had been arrested and Yangki had disappeared in India with her four children. For foreigners, cooped up in a Shangri-La interlude in their busy lives, the news was electrifying. To seasoned observers of the

Bhutan scene, however, the story of the plot was contrived. They said the Queen Mother, a Dorji, had simply used the opportunity of the coronation to get Yangki, and her bastard pretenders to the throne, out of the country.

The coronation festivities in Thimpu took three days. Bhutan's official religion is Buddhism and the monks were main players, ringing bells, banging cymbals and dancing and singing, I wrote later in a despatch to Canberra, "in a manner so hauntingly beautiful that I doubt it can ever be forgotten by those who saw and heard it." In Nepal, the singing and dancing was gay and noisy; in Bhutan it was slow and almost mournful. On this and subsequent visits I succumbed easily to the artless simplicity of Bhutan, as I did to Nepal. Perhaps I was affected by altitude, or perhaps it was a relief to escape from the hot and argumentative plains of India.

On 18 May 1974 India exploded a nuclear device in the Rajasthan desert. I was briefed by Indian officials, who described it as a peaceful experiment for economic and industrial purposes, such as the mining of low-grade copper concentrates and high viscosity oil and the excavation of dams and canals. It was technically an "implosion" not an "explosion". It was not a bomb and was not intended to be a bomb. India did not want to become a nuclear military power like the United States, Soviet Union, Britain, France and China. It wanted to start a new club for countries who wanted to use nuclear power for development.

This was not the view of the outside world, nor of influential sections of the Indian media. With the benefit of hindsight, one can assume that it was not then the view of some within the government, including the Prime Minister, Mrs Gandhi. The Indian media and strategic analysts speculated freely on the advantages to India of becoming a nuclear military power. It would remove reliance on the Soviet Union for protection. It would demonstrate that India was China's military equal. And it would show the rest of the world that India, released from colonial oppression, was not a nation of poverty and religiosity but modern and scientific. In the midst of a political struggle with a Gandhian revivalist movement, Mrs Gandhi welcomed the emerging evidence of the kind of India she and her father, Jawaharlal Nehru, had always wanted.

Politically, India had seemed to be settled under the political leadership of the Nehru family and the Congress party, committed to the immense task of grafting a parliamentary democracy onto an ancient society, which included the caste system. In fact, it was itself undergoing seismic changes, which showed in the rise of an agrarian socialist protest movement under the leadership of a former Congress figure, Jayaprakesh Narayan.

In Australia, India's nuclear test dismayed the Whitlam government. Australia had had an internal political struggle over nuclear issues, but Whitlam had been clear and purposeful. Australia ratified the Nuclear Non-Proliferation Treaty and opposed nuclear testing, especially by the French in the Pacific, securing an injunction from the International Court of Justice. With New Zealand, it introduced into the UN General Assembly a resolution for a Comprehensive Test Ban Treaty, the first of annual submissions until the CTBT was finally adopted. My advice to Canberra was to entertain a degree of scepticism about India's motives but to hold them in the meantime to the assurances they were publicly giving, and to take on board their criticism of the NPT, that it discriminated against non-nuclear states by not allowing them to experiment with nuclear energy.

I had become familiar with Mrs Gandhi's personal thinking, through official contacts that had increasingly become more personal.

Because our national days, Australia Day and Republic Day, clashed, intricate and even intimate negotiations were necessary to ensure we paid each other due respect. She came to the residence officially whenever she was invited and on two occasions Joan and I dined with her when only her family members were present. I had met her father when I was a foreign correspondent and she listened carefully to my impressions of him. She liked the fact that I represented a new kind of Australian government and was not a professional diplomat. She was worried about the security of India, convinced that China and Pakistan were a threatening combination. Like her father, she did not trust the Americans. So she regarded a friendly face from a fellow Commonwealth country like Australia as an unexpected pleasure.

I developed the view, not widely shared by my colleagues at the high commission, that she was, despite her public profile, insecure as a political leader, partly because of the heroic mould of the independence era of which her father and Mohandas Gandhi (no relation) were icons. She was faced with rising unrest due to a number of developments but especially to the crusade launched by Jayaprakesh Narayan. Like Gandhi he aroused the people and like the British Mrs Gandhi reacted by putting all the leaders and thousands of their followers in gaol. The system broke down. With her political opponents in gaol, she declared an emergency, allowing her to detain people without trial.

The emergency was at first popular because it imposed law and order. The trains ran on time, workers went back to work, students went back to their studies. But the existence of authority proved irresistible to some of Mrs. Gandhi's followers, including her son Sanjay. Shanty towns were removed. Sterilisation for males was introduced, outraging men (women had borne the brunt before of birth control), especially Muslims. Personal vendettas were settled. The houses of middle-class people were searched. Suddenly, the democratic political system that had seemed to make India strong and stable, compared with Pakistan and China, was in crisis.

*

Absorbed in India, I had detached myself from Australian politics, but in November 1974 Graham Perkin gave the Arthur Norman Smith lecture in Melbourne, in which he made some comments on my role as an independent columnist that surprised me. It was so inaccurate in detail and false in tone that I was forced to react. I sent a letter to *The Age*, which was published and to which he responded in the same issue.

He had said in the lecture that, because of my association with the so-called Myer Letter recommending a change of government in 1972, he had suspended my column on the eve of the election and "he never wrote for The Age again." This was not only untrue but bordered on fantasy. He had not said a word to me about my association with the Letter and, as earlier recorded, I continued to write through the election campaign in November and December until I took holidays at the end of the year. Thirteen of my columns appeared in *The Age* after the Letter was published on 23 November. Creighton Burns, who was deputy editor at the time, spoke to me about the Letter because, according to electoral law, the addresses of the signatories had to be provided as well as the names, before publication, but he did not say that either he or Perkin or anyone else felt "compromised", as Perkin claimed. On 29 December I wrote to Perkin (and to Sir Keith Waller, head of the then Department of

Foreign Affairs) saying that Whitlam had offered me a diplomatic appointment, that I had accepted and would not be able to continue with my column. Then, *The Age* had thoughtfully kept me on the payroll until I was able to take up the appointment. I had assumed that my relations with *The Age* were as friendly after my appointment as before.

My surprise is conveyed in letters I wrote at the time. To Clem Christesen:

> *Many thanks for your kind thoughts. I am sorry to say I am also in the dark about Perkin's strange outburst. I can only assume it has something to do with politics or, as you say, a personal vendetta, but, at the moment, I find it quite inexplicable, as I thought I had left The Age on good terms with everyone, including Perkin, and am distressed to find this small piece of history being rewritten so brutally. However, I don't propose at this moment to pursue it any further, as I have made the point (in my letter to The Age) that his statement is in fact inaccurate and I couldn't really debate with him, in public, his attitude towards me. As an old warrior in these matters, you will know that sometimes it is more eloquent to say nothing. At the same time, I am fascinated by the incident and one day will write about it in detail.*

To Andrew Farran, who had suggested that, as Perkin was in line for appointment as editor-in-chief of Fairfax newspapers, it might have something to do with the desire of the more conservative *Sydney Morning Herald* to run the policy of *The Age*: "Fortunately, I have letters to establish that he is quite wrong in all this, but whether I should use them and keep a rather trivial controversy going, when I think the point has been made, is another matter." I decided that the best course was to let the controversy die and discuss the substantive issue in quieter times personally with Perkin, when I was in Australia on leave and consultation. Unfortunately, he died unexpectedly. I happened to be in Melbourne and all I could do was attend his funeral.

When Sir John Kerr dismissed the Whitlam government on 11 November 1975 I was surprised and shocked. When the news first reached the mission in New Delhi, I thought it must be one of those wild stories that occasionally circle the world, remote from the event itself. When I was told that the House of Representatives had expressed its confidence in the Whitlam government and that the Senate had passed Supply, I even contemplated the possibility that it was a stratagem devised by Kerr and Whitlam to end the crisis that Fraser had manufactured by the stratagem of blocking Supply.

Then, as the truth dawned, surprise turned to shock. Shock is a healthy reaction. A society or individual incapable of being shocked is either decadent or has become so hardened to crimes against civility or humanity that it has lost the will to protest. I was shocked not only by the dismissal itself, but by the way it was done. Kerr had deceived Whitlam, saying nothing of what was in his mind until he sprang it on the prime minister in his study at Yarralumla.

Malcolm Fraser's crusade against "reprehensible government", backed by the intrigue of Bjelke-Petersen in Queensland, had produced a stream of events. A deceased senator was not replaced with someone from the same party. Supply bills, which twice a year came before parliament to fund government, paying the civil service and the armed forces, were blocked in the Senate. The convention that the Governor-General acted on the advice of the Prime Minister was discarded. Not only did Kerr not act on Whitlam's advice, but he concealed his own intentions, sacking the Prime Minister in secretive and unexpected circumstances. Finally, when the House of Representatives, in which the Whitlam Government still had a majority, refused to accept a Fraser Government, the Governor-General announced it was too late: he had already dissolved Parliament in preparation for an election.

I could not help contrasting the political situations in India and Australia. In both cases, prime ministers were confronted by political opponents who were using every means available to force them out of office. The difference was that Mrs Gandhi had replied in kind while Mr Whitlam relied on the system to support him. I recalled my conversations with Kerr in New Delhi. Part of my initial shock was that he had destroyed, with one arbitrary and dramatic act, the evolving role of the Governor-General as head of state that he, like Casey and Hasluck, had begun to play.

Without the backing of the public service, Whitlam needed support. For a few days, I parried inquiries at the mission and from Indian officials and friends. Then I received from Australia a telephone call on behalf of an organisation called Citizens for Democracy, which was mounting a campaign against Kerr's decision for the election. Its supporters included people I knew, such as Creighton Burns, Prue Myer, Richard McGarvie, Jean Downing, Peter Hollingworth and John Button. Would I like to join them?

I went for a walk in the Jawaharlal Nehru garden, near the mission, where I sometimes strolled at the end of the day. It had taken the place of the Swan River of my youth. I decided on my walk that I would join my friends' campaign and, after discussion with Joan, I applied immediately to Canberra for leave to take part, as a private citizen and at my own expense, in the election. It was a considered and deliberate decision, with a practical intent. I was obviously affected by the coincidence that both countries, India and Australia, were experiencing political crises that were testing their democratic systems, but the heart of the challenge to me was simple. It was an important election for Australia and I wanted to take part in it. I could not do that by remaining in New Delhi.

Andrew Peacock, who was foreign minister in the caretaker government, rang me from Canberra to ask in what capacity I intended to participate. I explained that I was not a member of the Labor Party and would not be working with the party or standing as a candidate (which public service regulations allowed) but would participate in the election like any citizen. I would take leave without pay and would travel at my own expense. My main reason was simply personal. I wished to give Whitlam any help I could, and also to encourage him back to the platform of public policy and national objectives that had been his strength.

The Department of Foreign Affairs advised Peacock against my application for leave, on the grounds that my presence in India was too valuable, but he granted it, then sought to make political capital of it, claiming that I was deserting my post in the face of a political crisis in India. During my time in India he had not visited the country, nor shown interest in it. Friends in high places advised me against the action I was taking, on the ground that the government was doomed. With worldly wisdom, they suggested that, by acting impulsively, I would cast doubt on my capacity for good judgement in the future. I was reminded of the endless discussions among scholars as to when was the "appropriate" time to have declared opposition to the military commitment in Vietnam, taking into account, of course, the prospect of success. I preferred the honesty of real contest, even if the odds were unfavourable.

My decision was warmly understood in India. Media commentary was overwhelmingly sympathetic to Whitlam and my time as High Commissioner was generally viewed in a favourable light. "Mr Grant has given a pleasant new dimension to the personality of his country's diplomatic mission in India," wrote Prem Bhatia in the *Amrita Bazar Patrika*. "He has made friends with writers, artists, musicians, architects and others who often remain outside the main stream of ambassadorial contacts ... He has made hundreds of new friends for his country in India during the two years he has been here." Sunanda K. Datta-Ray in *The Statesman* surprisingly detected "the beau ideal of the elegant, sophisticated man of the world", that he thought went down well with the Indian establishment in New Delhi, which regarded the election of the Whitlam Government as a watershed in Australian and Indo-Australian history. I called on the Foreign Secretary, Kewal Singh, who wished me well. At a meeting of Australian staff at the mission, I explained the reasoning behind my decision.

In Australia, by contrast, my decision was described by the *Sydney Morning Herald* as "the most grotesque example yet seen of political partisanship in the Public Service". *The Australian* thought my reasons for returning to take part in the elections were "pompous". My concern for stable government in Australia was "touching" but misplaced; my prime concern should have been the stability of government in India.

The public mood was sullen and irritable. The worthy sentiments of the Citizens of Democracy, based on observing conventions that had already been broken, had little impact. Low expectation has its own kind of moral torpor and bigotry. Despite the confident style of Whitlam's leadership, the Government's stocks were low. In addition to squabbling in Labor's ranks, inflation and an unorthodox foreign loan apparently being arranged by Tirath Khemlani, a Pakistani dealer, the public was uneasy about the collapse in Vietnam and uncertainty in Timor. Whitlam, however, was buoyant. I got the impression, after a meeting with him, that he welcomed the election. He was a good campaigner and he thought that Kerr had given him an issue on which to campaign. Kerr had behaved like a colonial autocrat. The Australian people would not let him get away with it. He was wrong, but his confidence allowed him to depart the scene with a flourish, maintaining the rage for future generations.

The following extract from *Gods and Politicians* reflects the mood of both the country and myself, as I saw it at the time:

> It was exhilarating to be doing something. To be out of the country, tongue-tied by regulations, was not my idea of the way to participate in this crucial election. Yet how strange Australia was during that famous campaign, a scared country on the brink of emotions it could not admit. The hostility to the Whitlam Government was intense, yet frigid. People on the left felt they had been betrayed by it because it had not refused to be dismissed from office, and had declined to flood the streets with demonstrations. People on the right thanked Kerr in their hearts for having saved the country from economic ruin, and possibly a socialist republic. There was a collective atmosphere of anxiety and exhaustion, as if no one had the strength to resists what now seemed inevitable, as in great tragedy; the fall and dishonouring of a hero in whom so much national hope had been placed. Was it simply Kerr's kinghit, the crude uppercut from nowhere, that had sent a shiver of pleasure and fear through the ringside audience? Not simply that. There was also the undercurrent of old-fashioned class war, which gave an intensity and yet also a detachment to the constitutional crisis. Just as I had noticed in Delhi that the power factors were on the side of the Emergency, the power

> factors in Australia were strongly on the side of an election and the purpose of the election was to get rid of the Whitlam Government. Once Kerr had ordered an election, Australia's political society divided on its economic interests, not on the constitutional issue … I recall saying in a television interview that, if the Senate were able to block Supply when it chose, Australia would become ungovernable. "Not if the Coalition is given a majority in both houses," said my questioner. It was a crude response, but basically true.

The gossip about Gough Whitlam was almost as vicious as the gossip in India about Indira Gandhi. Waiting for a train in Melbourne, a woman suddenly confided in me, apparently stirred by something she was reading in a newspaper, that Whitlam was trying to force Queen Elizabeth to abdicate. The medical profession was buzzing with rumours that he had gone mad. "Anything to stop the rot," an acquaintance said, justifying the dismissal. "You know, they're actually *printing their own money*!".

I returned to India just before election day with no doubt in my own mind about the result, and prepared a letter of resignation. I regretted neither taking the New Delhi appointment nor returning to Australia publicly for the elections, but, once again, my family and I were on the move. It was only then we realised how strong were the bonds that we had established with India. The diplomatic community receives and farewells its members with studied courtesy, but the Indian government, including the Prime Minister and Foreign Minister, went out of its way to express appreciation. The media was generous. Indian friends seemed genuinely sorry to see us go. Indians are emotionally demonstrative and we had difficulty responding.

The "substance" in relations between India and Australia was still elusive. The two countries were like-minded in sharing a British heritage of democracy and law (not to mention cricket) that provided a common language, but were so different that their national interests did not naturally overlap. The bureaucratic overlay in India was intimidating to Australian businesses looking to trade or invest. I had pursued a faint hope of naval cooperation in the Indian Ocean, but was resolutely blocked by Sir Arthur Tange, a former High Commissioner in India who was now Secretary of the Department of Defence. His opinion of the Indian navy was such that he joked with me about the safety of our ships in joint naval exercises. The hopes raised by the brief impact of the Whitlam government had not been in vain, however. Indians had been given a glimpse of a different Australia, not racist and irrevocably tied to Western power, and seemingly concerned as India was with problems of poverty and injustice.

For myself, the experience in India had been valuable. At a practical level, I knew more about how governments behaved. My old friends in the intelligence agencies had reappeared. As academic and public intellectual, in both roles transparently independent, they had not bothered me. Now I was again aware of the dark side of public life. I was given each week, courtesy of my British colleague and thoughtfully translated into English, the content of cables sent by the Chinese ambassador in Pakistan back home to Beijing. I wondered who had been reading my mail.

But it was the insouciance of India that I remembered most as we prepared to leave. I wrote later that I had been forced in India to think about evil, which I defined as the failure to resist the temptation to take advantage of those who are powerless to resist. Rape was evil, seduction could be charming. But, in India, Pan's laughter (or was it Krishna's?) had unsettled me, making me uncertain whether

I could detect the difference. In *Gods and Politicians,* I recalled a visit Joan and I made to Mount Abu, from where the sun sets twice. We assembled with hundreds of Indian tourists at Sunset Point in Rajasthan.

> The sun sank gradually in the west, as scheduled, first a red orb through a rim of desert dust, then more darkly over the real horizon, and disappeared. It had done what was expected of it and, to our astonishment, the Indian viewers rose to their feet and applauded, the hillside rippling with pleasure at the success of the sun's performance, as at a theatre when the audience has come with high hopes and has not been disappointed … I knew then that, even without democracy, India would remain a civilisation; I knew equally that, without democracy, Australia had no hope of becoming one.

9

WRITING LIFE

Politics, like love, is transformative. In politics, you reach beyond yourself to serve the country, the government or the party. In love, you reach within yourself to satisfy the loved one. Success in either is exhilarating, even enchanting. Failure is amplified into shame and betrayal. For the common citizen, who may be neither in politics nor in love, ordinary life is elevated when the people elect a government that does what you think needs to be done; you experience a sense of belonging, feeling at one with the nation. When the people elect a government that is committed to a course you do not like, both the power of the state and the authority of society become unfriendly, even alien. The genius of the democratic system is its lofty doctrine that, if elections are genuine, the people are always right.

We returned to live in the East Melbourne terrace house with the mean front door, grateful for small mercies, welcoming the freedom of ordinary life. Joan now had her own kitchen and there was surprising bliss, after the formality of diplomatic dining, in making a last-minute decision to get a take-away family meal. By force of circumstance, I could now do what I enjoyed most, writing. I had not intended to become a professional diplomat and I had seen enough of the life to appreciate that, while appointments like mine could serve a useful purpose at a particular time, the hard labour of diplomacy had to be done by people with the skills and patience for the long haul. It was a time for reflection. Much of what had seemed to be building in Australia with the Whitlam government had come to a jarring halt.

Our first priorities were a household income and school for the boys. My zigzag life had provided me with decent salaries, but this was before portable superannuation and our savings were modest. Enid had remarried and was living in Sydney. Daughter Susan had married and was also in Sydney, but the other two children, James and Johanna, were still living in Melbourne, in a terrace house in Fitzroy I had bought to accommodate them while I was away. An itinerant life-style had not established residential qualifications for any of the good public schools, with the result that all five children went to private schools, Preshil, then Presbyterian Ladies College for Susan and Johanna, Trinity College for James, and now, Melbourne Grammar School for David and Benjamin.

The mood in Australia was sombre, with a tinge of guilt. Two decades of steady economic growth and political conformity under the leadership of Robert Menzies had collapsed with the dramatic death of his successor Harold Holt and the subsequent rivalry of John Gorton and William McMahon. The old order was crumbling. The British were withdrawing their military forces "east of Suez". The Americans had failed in Vietnam. The Portuguese were pulling out of East Timor. Papua New Guinea wanted independence. Communist China demanded recognition. Whitlam had a vision of Australia as a confident nation engaged in its region, turning what many Australians saw as a threat into an opportunity to show our worth to the world. With his commanding presence, conventional upbringing and traditional manners, he had looked like another Menzies for another time, yet the implacable antagonism of Australian politics brought him down.

The voters had delivered a sharp rebuttal of his claim to be representing them in bringing change to Australia (confirmed in 1977 when Kerr, despite his stern words in New Delhi, gave Fraser an early election), but they were in two minds about what they had done. Fraser's determined pursuit of "reprehensible" government had created alarm and anxiety, but had not produced a useful debate about alternative policies. The republican movement had been revived, trade unions were on a warpath, feminists, whose hopes had been raised by Whitlam, were dismayed – and also vindicated by the spectacle of the nation's male political leaders playing chicken. Manning Clark, in the 1976 Boyer Lectures, said he had come to the same conclusion as the Greek tragedians, Shakespeare, and the author of the Book of Ecclesiastes: mankind suffered from a fatal flaw that stood between it and what it wanted to achieve.

"You got the bum's rush," a friend said to me. He spoke with a certain relish for the crude Australian idiom. Others were more solicitous. I received the following letter from Sir James Plimsoll, then Australia's ambassador in Moscow.

> *I have not written earlier because I have not been sure where a letter will find you.*
>
> *I am sorry that things have turned out in a way that makes you leave our service. Even under a change of government it would have been good if you had been able to remain. If I had been with you in India I would have urged caution – and I would not have been sure that the Labor Party would have used your services properly in the campaign itself. From what I have heard subsequently, the Labor Party made a number of mistakes in its*

campaigning. I suppose it was in a state of shock from the dismissal; and it also had a number of contradictions and differences within the party to conceal or paper over.

I do not know what you will do when you leave India. I doubt whether The Age is open, from what I read in it, and in any case that paper is now part of your past, not your future, and if you go back to journalism you will benefit from a different outlet.

I am probably returning to Australia for consultations in the latter part of March, but I expect by then you will have left New Delhi. If we are in Australia at the same time I shall get in touch with you so that we can have a talk. In the meantime, good luck to you all.

Some Indonesian friends got in touch with me, half-seriously suggesting exile. The Indonesian novelist Pramoedya Ananta Toer, who had endured years of confinement without trial under both Dutch and Indonesian governments and, having discovered that we were the same age, advised me of the benefit to clear thinking of exile, even gaol. I regarded as friends Buyung Nasution, one of the founders of the Indonesian Legal Aid Foundation, who had spent two years in gaol, and Goenawan Mohamad, whose magazine *Tempo* was closed down and its readers taken over by a new magazine with an indistinguishable format from *Tempo* owned by an associate of the president. The writer Mochtar Lubis wrote:

Dear Friend,

I want to thank you for your ceaseless efforts on my behalf. I want to thank you for the friendship, comradeship, sympathy, trust, which you have so generously given to me and Hally during the long years of my imprisonment. They have been, and still are, a great support to me, a great comfort, and have helped sustain me in good spirits all these past years. I am planning to publish Indonesia Raya again. More than ever, I am convinced of the great need to establish traditions of a free and responsible press in Indonesia ... With all our best wishes, and Hally sends you her very best regards and warmest greetings.

Australian writers did not face the kind of intimidation of my Indonesian friends. Their problem was not dangerous or oppressive government but a small local market in a large English-language market that did not value particular Australian experience. The voice of the writer was hard to detect in the torrent of infotainment, the drone of political discourse and the excitement of celebrity gossip and pseudo-events. The Mexican poet and diplomat Octavio Paz put it bluntly, in his acceptance speech for the Nobel Prize for Literature, in 1990: "Today literature and the arts are threatened ... not by a doctrine or political party but by a faceless, soulless and directionless economic process. The market is circular, impersonal, impartial, inflexible. Some will tell me that this is as it should be. Perhaps. But the market, blind and deaf, is not fond of literature and of risk, and it does not know how to choose. Its censorship is not ideological: it has no ideas. It knows all about prices, but nothing about values."

Academic Graham Little presented the 1975 crisis through the personalities of the main political figures. He described the tendency of Whitlam and his followers to mockery and scorn, their admiration of sophistication, cosmopolitanism, style and mastery, their dislike of secrecy, their impatience with limitations, their lack of personal intimacy, their confidence that passion and fear could be driven away by reasoned argument and clever programs, their high investment in creativity, intelligence and autonomy, their rejection of the role of threat in politics. "The enemies of their heroism are not villains, but fools."

By contrast, Cairns' followers concentrated on unselfishness, honesty and altruism. He was an example of idealism in politics. When he failed, his followers felt sorry for him. He would later be found on Saturdays and Sundays sitting at a small table at the fruit and vegetable market in Prahran, selling his books and engaging in political debate with anyone who stopped to buy one.

Kerr did not have followers in the political sense, although he had some public support for his decision to call an election as a way of resolving a political impasse. His personality was not reassuring. His strong intellect was cloaked in a manipulative manner, a desire to be noticed by the great and powerful and a tendency to be pompous. The serious work he undertook – with LawAsia, for example – was not appreciated. A caricature of him, in top hat and unsteady on his feet at the Melbourne Cup, gained currency.

Fraser's followers were suspicious of the politics of hope. Life was not meant to be easy, as he famously put it. They were relieved that he was tough and could stand up to their enemies, whether internal or external, and gratified that he was a tireless worker. But they were reluctant to admit to liking him. He was at odds with influential sections of his own party, including the "dries", who wanted economic reform to make Australia more competitive in its region and, indeed, the world. Although seemingly a Cold War warrior, he had ideas about improving relations with the Third World and was an early supporter of Nelson Mandela in South Africa, rubbing against a pro-apartheid faction on his side of politics. The public was not attracted to him and was uneasy about Kerr's behaviour, but they had voted for peace and quiet and hoped for the best.

What this analysis did not capture was the outbreak of confidence that Whitlam encouraged. There was something about his short-lived, tumultuous period in government, now embellished with the aura of martyrdom, that touched the spirit of Australians in a way that no previous government had done and no future government would, at the time of writing, be able to do.

Perhaps the Racial Discrimination Act, finally approved by Parliament just months before Kerr dissolved it, best explains the shiver of excited concern created by the moral energy of those days. Lord Casey had once described race as "the heart of our being" and Whitlam's passion on racial issues was not spread across the political spectrum. On the left, White Australia, bolstered by European migration after the Second World War, was still seen as protecting jobs and living standards. On the right, prejudice had been compromised by Cold War demands, especially in Vietnam, to compete for the hearts and minds of people who were not Caucasian, but surfaced in debate on Aboriginal land rights, non-European immigration and apartheid in South Africa. But the Racial Discrimination Act survived and remains in force, underpinning what is probably the greatest and most surprising achievement of modern Australia, the creation of a multicultural society.

A new doctrine had emerged from the crisis – that the Australian Parliament was not only the House of Representatives and the Senate but the Queen and her representative, the Governor-General, as well. The antiquated machinery of the Australian constitution seemed to back this up, if you believed in simple English and clear meanings. It reflected an outmoded autocracy, not the democratic values that the people of Australia believed was their birthright. The Governor-General was given a couple of pages. He was Commander-in-Chief of the armed forces and had mysterious "reserve powers". He appointed and dismissed Ministers and could even appoint a Minister for three months who was not yet a Member of Parliament. The Prime Minister and Cabinet, the core of executive government, were not mentioned. What were young Australians, expected to understand our system of government, to make of this?

The pulse of civil society in Australia was, however, still beating. Davis McCaughey offered an appointment as George Scott Visiting Fellow at Ormond College, University of Melbourne, which I accepted with pleasure. Hedley Bull arranged a period in London as an Associate of the International Institute for Strategic Studies (IISS). I gave lectures at the Australian Administrative Staff College in Mount Eliza to middle-management students in their mid-thirties. Editors of newspapers and magazines invited contributions, but I was keen to work at a different level than was offered by commentary on current events.

As Guest of Honour on the ABC (16 November 1976) I referred to the experiment, begun by Lord Casey and continued by Sir Paul Hasluck, to develop the office of the Governor-General into that of an Australian head of state, especially as a symbol abroad of Australian nationality. Sir John Kerr's visits to India and Nepal were essays in the new Australian diplomacy but I suggested that, by asserting the archaic powers of the Governor-General on 11 November 1975, he might have put an end to the experiment. Kerr's behaviour, concealing his intentions from the Prime Minister and seeming to believe the protocol that his office was higher in status than that of the prime minister's, would make future prime ministers reluctant to encourage future governors-general to gain status in this useful, evolving role.

One advantage of a writing life is that you can work at home, providing a constant presence for a family. Writing, however, is a solitary occupation. You are on your own. A room, a desk, a reading lamp. No committees, caucuses, seminars, actors, directors, producers, or the busy camaraderie of a diplomatic mission or a newspaper office. The danger is that, immersed in it, writers lose touch with ordinary life so throw themselves at life in short bursts between long periods of working in isolation, sustaining the tradition of romantic escapades. For people burdened with a civic conscience the excitements and exigencies of politics are a substitute for escapades.

I became active in two organisations, Change, which was not specifically republican but was devoted to reform of the Australian Constitution, and the Australian Institute of Political Science, which had a broad agenda of public accountability. Both attracted men and women from the two major political parties as well as independents like myself.

Like most Australians, I was a creature of a gradualist tradition. I had been content to see remnants of the British tradition remain, in our private schools, in the Church of England, in the remnants of British honours, and in the social world that circulated around the vice-regal palaces maintained in all the states, believing that they would in time adapt to Australian circumstances and were not a bar to social change and the development of a distinctive nation. They were even comforting, as they were evidence of a sense of excellence and even grandeur in a country of plain adornments. But I had been alerted by Kerr's action to the inadequacy of Australia's institutions, including the Constitution, and a republic seemed the best way of galvanising Australians, asking that they think of themselves as a distinctive nation in an emerging region of the world, not an outpost of empire.

Joan got publishing work with Rigby Ltd., and with McPhee Gribble. I was offered an appointment in a corporation. I did not think about it for long. The bottom line, however embellished, did not appeal to me. This was before the era of the start-up companies that suddenly appeared on the market when the Cold War ended; the big end of town seemed heavy and uninviting. Maie Casey (now the widow of Lord Casey), still resident in East Melbourne, was convinced that I should offer myself for a seat on the Melbourne City Council. I humoured her to the extent of meeting with a local furrier and real estate agent who were looking for a candidate, but could not summon enough enthusiasm for local politics.

In public lectures on foreign policy to students at Ormond College, Monash University and Swinburne College of Technology I raised directly the issue of the alliance with the United States. In the wake of the Dismissal and the suspicion among radical students that the Americans were involved, I was less sure of my support for the alliance than I had been in debates a decade earlier. But my experience in India had strengthened my view that the alliance was not an impediment to productive and peaceful relations with states in Asia that were non-aligned in the Cold War. I was also inclined to think, from what I had learned from my personal experience of the crisis, that blaming the Americans was a convenient way of shifting responsibility from ourselves.

I began a lengthy partnership with Erwin Rado, an old friend and director of Melbourne's international film festival, on a film script of the dismissal of the Whitlam government. It had several titles, until we settled, in deference to the punchy style of cinematic advertising, on *King Hit*. It was never produced, but attracted interest along the way from Phil Noyce and Paul Cox. David Williamson gave two amateur screenwriters a helping hand, although Erwin had an elevated view of what was needed, unswayed by well-meant suggestions from those with experience in the industry. His view, derived from his European background, was that the Whitlam experiment was fragile ("a feather in the wind" was his phrase) in the world of dark forces that governed affairs of state and the hearts of men. For a while, the script followed this direction, during which I tried to provide a core of human rationality and optimism. One issue between us was the role of the CIA in Whitlam's downfall.

Erwin suspected that the CIA had either managed the whole event or had manipulated those involved. There was certainly a history of tension with the CIA. The collapse of the Nugan Hand bank in Australia had fostered suspicion that it was involved with espionage or drug smuggling or both. Nugan, an Australian lawyer, was found dead in Sydney and Hand, an ex-Green Beret who fought in Vietnam and later worked for the CIA, absconded. Richard Hall's book *The Secret State* had drawn attention to the role of American intelligence agencies in Australia and Robert Lindsey in *The Falcon and the Snowman* drew on claims from a clerk, Christopher Boyce, that the traffic through Pine Gap showed that the CIA was funding anti-Labor activities.

When Whitlam took office he refused to subject his staff to a security check. His staff eventually complied voluntarily, but enough had been done to create headlines and arouse the suspicion of the security services. In the Cold War, ASIO had been keen to detect left-wing subversion, while neglecting right-wing terrorists like Croatians training in the Dandenong hills. When Attorney-General Lionel Murphy arrived unannounced at ASIO's headquarters in St Kilda Road, Melbourne, in March 1973, the press reasonably decided it was a raid. In October 1975, at the peak of the political crisis, the head of ASIS was relieved of his position and, early in November, Whitlam mentioned in a speech in the House of Representatives the name of a retired CIA officer in an attempted political smear of the then leader of the National Country Party, J.D. Anthony. The CIA indicated to the Australian embassy in Washington (on 10 November, the day before Kerr sacked Whitlam) that the CIA might break, or at least curtail, its links with Australia.

All of this was material for Erwin's case. My view, however, was that the integrity of the film depended on accepting that, whatever the CIA or even the White House might have thought of the Whitlam government, we had done it ourselves. Blaming the Americans was an easy way out (although, I had to admit, prime box office material). The dismissal of the Whitlam government may have been a king hit, but an election was different from a *coup d'état*. Joh Bjelke-Petersen, premier of Queenland, was no creation of the CIA, but it was he who had stacked the Senate against Whitlam by breaking the convention that replacements should be from the same party. Kerr had been deceitful by concealing his intentions from the Prime Minister, but he had decided that he had to be if he (and a new wife) were to remain in the big house at Yarralumla. Whitlam thought he was superior to Fraser on the hustings and might win the election, so he did not contest the dismissal notice handed to him by the Governor-General. And the three of them were trapped by Australia's archaic constitution.

Erwin listened courteously. In his well-stocked mind what I was getting at could probably be accommodated in something like Luis Bunuel's *The Discreet Charm of the Bourgeoisie*, exposing Australians as upwardly mobile, despite all the rhetoric about equality, but he did not think Australia was ready for that. He regarded himself, rightly, as a better judge of the Australian film scene than I was. We worked diligently and sometimes hopefully on several drafts but our film was never produced.

My London friend Arthur Hickman had been knocked down and killed by a truck in 1969 and the journal he had been keeping since 1923 was left in his will to me – ninety exercise books filled with fine handwriting, three-and-a-half-million words. Patricia Harewood had taken the journal from Arthur's flat and deposited it for safe-keeping in the basement of Harewood House, outside Leeds, but it was now in my house in Melbourne. Arthur had modelled himself on the great English diarists. He took the information in these journals and his judgements on its characters, many of whom were his friends, very seriously. As he had told me when we first met, he would write down in shorthand details of anything he wanted to remember, then type it up, then enter it in longhand in the journal. In thirty thousand pages of the journal nothing was changed and only one page was missing, apparently cut out with a razor blade.

Now I had the time to read the entire journal, I could see that there were two Arthur Hickmans and I could understand why the journal had been left to me and not to one of his many London literary friends, such as Arthur Crook, editor of *The Times Literary Supplement*. He examined with increasing bitterness his failure, as the son of a Luton hat-maker, to make progress at *The Times*. He had not been to Oxford or Cambridge, he had no influential friends in high places, so he was reduced to being a character, with second-night tickets for the theatre, obtained through Dirk Bogarde's father, who was art editor, as his way over the years of sustaining the youthful conceit that he was a man about town. The other Arthur was touchingly hopeful about the "white" Commonwealth – Canada, Australia and New Zealand. Based almost entirely on people he had met in London, he saw them as societies of the future, compared with England and Europe, with their feudal overhang. His attitude to the United States was essentially English – it was outlandish, great for entertainment but not to be taken seriously as civilisation. He was fond of Australians, especially one of us, Eric Muspratt, an adventurer and novelist who was a literary lion in London in the 1930s.

I extracted from the journal a memoir, *Arthur and Eric*, based on Arthur's friendship with Muspratt, It was published in 1977. Muspratt, although born in England, spent most of his early life in Australia, before embarking on a Hemingway-esque career as author-hero. He died in 1949, almost unnoticed in Australia, but remembered in London for what *The Times* obituary called "Zest for Life". His first novel, *My South Sea Island*, had received rave London reviews, comparing him with Conrad, Defoe and Jack London. Harold Nicolson wrote: "The freshness of the *Iliad*, the sheer physical arrogance of the Homeric heroes live again …"

The publishers chose for the cover of *Arthur and Eric* a nude picture of Muspratt embracing the sky, but if anyone was looking for a sexual relationship between Arthur and Eric, I could not find it in the journal. Arthur's sexuality remained a mystery. He took home young men by the dozen, wrestled with them before the fire, listened to their stories, moralised with them about life, fed and clothed them, lent them money, paid their fines and bills, spoke up in court for them. The saga of Eric Muspratt is repeated over and over again.

I wrote:

> There is no direct evidence in the Journal that Arthur had sexual relations with any of his male friends, including Eric, although it

> is hard to believe that he had not ... My own impression is that Arthur was not nearly as interested in explicit sexual experience as he was in the physical reassurance of affection, and this could be achieved with a touch, even with a glance or a tone of voice ... [H]is happiness with people depended to an extent on his ability to move quickly and without impediment among them. An entanglement with one person would have made this difficult. If only in this sense, he and Eric were alike.

Arthur devoted himself to Eric, who paid little attention to Arthur, a man whose last reference to his friend in the journal, concludes: "The sum total of his benefactions to me was two meals, three books, seven lemons – and more happiness than anyone has ever given me."

Later in the journal, Arthur makes a more self-assured assessment of his many friendships. "Whenever I have had a strong friendship it has always begun in this spontaneous way – in a flash, an instantaneous recognition, a sense of complete accord. Always the young man is healthy, virile and happy-natured. When the time comes for our friendship to recede it does so quite naturally, for I never scheme to keep a young man from his girl. There are men in all parts of the world, now happily married, who remember with kindliness the middle-aged bachelor they knew when they lived in London, and to whom they gave their youthful vitality and affection."

Eric seemed happiest when he was naked and dreaming in the Australian bush, without thinking about how to turn it into literature, but his final years, back in Australia, were not enticing. He received a Commonwealth Literary Fund grant to write a book about the Australian Navy, which was not done. Without visible means of support, he built a house for himself in Hastings, Victoria, of fibro-cement and wood from packing cases, tended chickens and worked as an axeman in the Gippsland forests. When in London, he played up to the wealthy and influential, including the newspapers, in the way they expected from a bronzed Aussie hero (with the biggest chest expansion in the southern hemisphere) but he was in awe of their cleverness, as he was of Arthur's.

He was aware in himself of a "vaguely apprehended destiny". His wife Rhonda (known in Sydney, I discovered, as "the widow Muspratt") called it "a kind of monstrous innocence". He was neither the first nor the last Antipodean to be unsettled by the artful dodgers of London, and wrote: "My own writing struggled clumsily, abortively premature … Too much to assimilate and I was only twenty-five years old … These people could be clever. They could make me feel awkward and horribly inadequate … I overheard a little, chatty conversation in one of the lavatories of a leading hotel. It dazzled me. The smooth ease of rippling wit and wisdom. It frightened and oppressed me. 'I shall never be able to do that,' I thought. 'It's beyond me. Now and forever'".

I began to get my thoughts together on Australian political culture. In 1978 I gave the keynote address at the summer school in Hobart of the Australian Council for Overseas Aid. The abstract of my remarks in the handbook reads: "The Asia/Pacific region is important to Australia as a test of our ability to build a different kind of nation from that which we inherited from our European traditions. But what kind of nation?"

My experience of government had reminded me of the value in politics of ideals and courage. The Whitlam government was accident-prone but it did many things that needed to be done and I was confident that when the events of 1975 gained perspective, it would be seen by Australians as having broken the foreign policy mould of fear and deference. I was also reminded of the high quality of Australia's public service. The complaint against cumbersome bureaucracy missed the point: bureaucrats had to manage the many interests of a competitive society, not to mention the tribal rivalry of politics, while trying also to keep their eyes on the long-term security and prosperity of the nation. Their outlook was necessarily more composed than dynamic. What troubled me most about government was the concentration of power in its hands over issues of war and peace. Even in a political society as wilful and diverse as the United States, the secret state was powerful, protected by those who served it refusing to either confirm or deny its activities. The enigma of politics was that those who were most ardent in their criticism of "big" government, the welfare state and swollen bureaucracy, were often the most vocal in their support of the authority of the secret state.

Australians were still guided in their political emotions by the examples of Britain and the United States. But while the British had centuries of experience in conflict and war to give their political system balance between democracy and authority, and the Americans had devised a constitution that deliberately created tension between executive, legislative and legal forms of government, Australians were not equipped to deal instinctively with crises, such as 1975. A practical people, we simply moved on, leaving the issues to resolve themselves, which they did not.

Thoughtful Australians were still bothered with an issue that had been nibbling at their consciences since the end of the Second World War. Were we, enriched by pastoral and mineral wealth and secured by distant, powerful friends, so fixed on material outcomes that we had become immune to the challenges that civilisation imposed on nations and peoples? Were we a second-rate people because of stubbornly-held low expectations?

At the IISS in London, discussion was about a new issue on the international agenda – human rights. The Helsinki Accords in 1975 had for the first time introduced in diplomatic negotiations the idea that human rights were as essential a responsibility of the state as agreements on trade and investment, political understandings and military undertakings. The crucial phrase in the agreement was that it acknowledged "the right of the individual to know and act upon" human rights.

Most of us at the IISS were "realists", in the tradition established since 1648, when the treaties of Westphalia brought an end to the Holy Roman Empire and established the modern, secular state. We accepted that state morality was different from the morality of individuals, who were obliged to take account of their consciences. States were not so obliged. Indeed, they were obliged not to do so. They lived in an anarchic world and their first duty to themselves and to the citizens for whom they were responsible was to survive, which meant doing whatever was necessary to protect their territory and, as their activities spread beyond their borders, what were called their "interests", some of which were considered "vital", meaning that states were prepared to go to war to protect them.

The US was initially suspicious of human rights. It was the Europeans who pressed at Helsinki for what became known as Basket Three, to distinguish it from security and economic issues in Baskets One and Two, which the Soviet Union was keen to sign. But Jimmy Carter, elected US president in 1976, was an enthusiast for human rights and used the accords to exert pressure on the Soviet Union. Scholarly research and analysis, as well as professional diplomacy, had long been under the spell of "realism" and feared now that human rights would upset the applecart, meaning the strategic balance of power of the Cold War, which, for all its faults, was at least stable. I found myself in a minority at the IISS in favour of upsetting the applecart, if that were to be the consequence of recognising the primacy of people rather than states.

Human rights was an incubus for the strategically-minded. The state, with its huge responsibilities, was being asked to accommodate the rights of individuals, who were just, well, individuals, insignificant and unpredictable, with frail bodies and uncontrollable emotions, ambitions and desires. For some, human rights was a cult of self-indulgence, encouraging narcissism and selfishness, to be contrasted with loyalty, modesty and sacrifice, attributes derived from service to the state. They predicted that the cult of the individual would become the cult of celebrity, where politicians, criminals, stars of stage, screen and video, sportsmen and their girlfriends, fortune-hunters and other attention-seekers would become indistinguishable. Looking back, one recognises the truth in this, although it did not obliterate the memory of Hungary 1956 and Czechoslovakia 1968.

In the document that emerged at Helsinki there was a familiar contradiction between principle 7, which called for "respect for human rights and fundamental freedoms, including the freedom of thought, conscience, religion or belief", and principle 6, which reaffirmed non-intervention in the internal affairs of states. The balance see-sawed over several years, as human rights issues flared up within the Soviet Union and Eastern Europe.

Arguably, Helsinki was more instrumental than military pressure in bringing the Cold War to an end. Military pressure allowed the authoritarian Soviet regime to justify itself on the grounds that its survival was threatened. Pressure on human rights pointed to incorrigible weakness in the system and, when the regime tried to respond, to brittleness. The applecart was upset, but from within. Karol Wojtyla, who became Pope John Paul II, Lech Walesa, Vaclav Havel, Andrei Sakharov, Mikhail Gorbachev and many others were catalysts for the end of the Cold War. It was arguably they, rather than Cruise missiles and nuclear warheads that brought the Soviet Union to an end. They defied the power of the Soviet Union in different ways. Wojtyla was an actor and playwright before he became a bishop, but when he made his famous declaration "Do Not Be Afraid", he spoke as a man of religion. When in 1980 Lech Walesa proclaimed Solidarity in the shipyards of Gdansk he spoke with the power of the trade union movement behind him. Havel was supported by a Czech tradition of irony and literary dissent. Sakharov was a scientist who knew both the danger of the nuclear arms race and the authority of verifiable evidence. Gorbachev was a political reformer, whose attempt to turn the cumbersome Soviet Union into a democracy and a market economy brought about the system's collapse. But each of them shared the legacy of Helsinki because, although it had no legal force, it was, as Sakharov recognised publicly later, a political document that gave legitimacy to dissent.

I was working at the Institute on a paper on security in South-east Asia, preparing a response to what had become a worst-case scenario. The United States had been humiliated in Vietnam, the weak states of South-east Asia were predicted to fall upon each other like dominoes and East Timor would become another Cuba. My paper looked to the nation-building calibre of leaders in South-east Asia, like Lee Kuan Yew in Singapore, whose strength was the authority of government, not human rights. But in Cambodia, Pol Pot's determination to return the country to a peasant economy, evacuating town populations to rural areas, was raising issues of human rights on such a scale as to invite intervention, which, in the shadow of Vietnam, was not available. I based my paper on the geo-strategic value of South-east Asia as a freeway between the Pacific and Indian oceans, available to all.

In Australia, the first "boat people" from Vietnam began arriving. Penguin approached *The Age*, suggesting a book. Michael Davie, an old friend from the London *Observer*, who had taken over as editor of *The Age*, asked me if I would "mastermind" the book, offering the newspaper's resources. So I returned to *The Age*, working with Davie, foreign editor Cameron Forbes, and foreign staff, especially Michael Richardson in South-east Asia. Penguin published *The Boat People* in 1979.

At its launch, I relied in my remarks on the people themselves, a reminder that the book was about them, not the political controversy surrounding them. "I wish it were possible for Miss Tran Hue Hue to be here, and perhaps also the young woman who escaped from Vietnam because she found communism to be boring, or Mr. Phan Van Thieu, to whom happened almost everything that can happen at sea, or Captain Healey Martin, who obeyed the old rule of the sea, which embodies the self-interest of everyone, that one should help those in distress. In their absence and the absence of many dozens of others, I can only ask you to read the book. The book is the story of the boat people and the authors have tried not to get in their way."

I contributed my two bobs' worth (as my father would have said) to the controversy, suggesting that the arrival of the boat people in Australia "marks the end of our long struggle to remain a European outpost. We are part of the region we inhabit: geography is a stepping stone of history. There is no escape from it, as there is no escape for Israel or for South Africa."

That the boat people arrived uninvited, unclassified by skilful immigration officials, did not make them more important than other refugees, but their energy and determination gave them distinction. I mentioned that one boat had travelled farther than Captain Bligh's famous voyage of 6000 kilometres when he was ejected from *The Bounty*. "You cannot erect a wall against the boat people … They are knocking on the door, not just of one's conscience or even of one's bank balance, but of one's house."

There were many ingenious proposals for resettling the boat people – camps, processing centres and uninhabited islands – but it seemed to me obvious that only the nation-state had the capacity to accommodate the likely numbers, if the 21st century continued to be as violent and disruptive as the 20th century. To do so successfully, it would need to modify its sovereignty, become less exclusive and more cooperative with other nation-states. The book, I admitted, was not optimistic, but there was a "slender hope". The boat people had exposed the bad behaviour of everyone – the ruthlessness of major powers, the selfishness of nation states, the avarice and prejudice of people. Perhaps, if for no other reason than self-protection and survival, everyone would agree to modify their savage instincts and be more cooperative. It was, indeed, a slender hope.

I turned for relief to a novel, *Cherry Bloom*, which I had begun in New Delhi. It was published in 1980, one of an early batch of Australian novels in an Asian setting. I received a warm response from Patrick McCaughey, who was on holiday in Italy, visiting Arthur Boyd at his farm house in Tuscany with Fred Williams. He didn't like the dust jacket and the "slightly too glamorous writing of the first few chapters", but was writing to "join in what must surely be a swelling chorus of congratulation on such a distinguished and moving novel." In fact, the reviews had been only mildly approving and I had been reminded of Robin Boyd's criticism of my *New Yorker* stories as tending early to pastiche, before I settled down into really serious writing. Perhaps I was too anxious to capture the reader's attention. But Patrick was reassuring.

> You do 'the Australian problem' with so much freshness and irony ... I really felt that I had missed out on something by not coming to a consciousness of self and country through Asia. And that is surely quite a new theme to see so fully realised in our fiction, although so often speculated about in the journals ... I also like the Forsterian theme – 'only connect' (and she does) – and I thought there was the added excitement that your own writing seems to grow and flourish as Cherry comes alive to the world. ... What I found most moving in the overall sphere of the novel was the way a distinctively Australian innocence – healthy, extrovert, tennis-playing, taking things as they come, warm and appealing – could become experience of the great world without exactly tarnishing or seeing that innocence corrupted. Indeed, as Cherry becomes more aware of moral complexity, she becomes more complex and interesting herself.

In 1981–82, as writer-in-residence at Monash University, I completed *Gods and Politicians*, the account of my time in India. When this was published I received a nice note from Phillip Adams, from his home in Kildare Street, East Hawthorn.

> *I read "Gods and Politicians" sitting by what we rather pretentiously call "the lake" at home. It's really a very large fish pond in which a huge, cast-iron fountain that once graced a Dublin park splashes in mild infringement of the water restrictions. However at one end we've erected the façade from a small, 18th century Indian building. And across the lily pads, there's an*

> *Indian soothsayer's cart – wonderfully elaborate with a sort of wicker-work dome.*
>
> *All in all, a suitable setting for what turned out to be a remarkable piece of work. A marvellous piece of writing, full of ravishing descriptions and rivetting ideas.*
>
> *You are, as I've observed before, an unusual and enigmatic man. But after "Gods and Politicians" I feel I know you a lot, lot better.*
>
> *I admire the book more than I can say. Thank you for sending it to me. I can think of no better preparation for a visit to India.*

At Monash I also completed *The Australian Dilemma*, which was published the following year, in 1983.

I had become familiar with the notion of defence "resilience" when writing *Indonesia*, and while I did not apply it directly to Australia it lingered in the back of my mind. In *The Crisis of Loyalty* I noted that we had transferred our loyalty from Britain to the United States without breaking the lockstep of dependence. Now, in *The Australian Dilemma*, I tried to juggle the benefits of the American military alliance and Australian resilience with a kind of double-jointed strategy (which I accepted was difficult for politicians to distinguish from being two-faced). I sympathised with the denialist tendency that began to appear in the thinking of some defence strategists, rejecting the doctrine of "forward defence" that had enticed us into Vietnam, but it had intimations of fortress Australia. The trouble with the fortress model was that it would lead irresistibly to a nuclear-armed Australia. I preferred to seek security in a more active involvement in our region, independent of the Americans.

What I was seeking was consistency between domestic and foreign policies. The dislocation between values at home and abroad seemed to me to be holding us back from discovering what kind of country we were, or wanted to become. What bothered me was the often undeclared conviction that what Australia needed, in order to discover its real values, was a show-down, preferably military, with Indonesia.

I began to think about writing as an occupation, grappling with what Plato thought of writers …

> And if a poet writes of the sufferings of Niobe … or of the house of Pelops, or of the Trojan War or on any similar theme, either we must not permit him to say that these are the works of God, or if they are of God, he must devise some explanation of them such as we are seeking, he must say that God did what was just and right, and that they were the better for being punished; but that those who are punished are miserable, and that God is the author of their misery – the poet is not permitted to say; though he may say that the wicked are miserable because they require to be punished and are benefitted from receiving punishment from God; but that God being good is the author of evil to anyone is to be strenuously denied, and not to be said or sung or heard in verse or prose by anyone whether old or young, in any well ordered commonwealth.

For their part, writers have responded to the demands of the state in every imaginable way, including both defiance and obedience. They have found private benefactors and protectors, they have holed up in monasteries and universities, isolated themselves in rural redoubts, roamed the fields and the streets and escaped to other countries. In the 20th century, they became to an unusual degree fascinated with political power. Some gifted writers supported communist and fascist regimes and as these regimes passed into dust, their reputations suffered. During the Cold War, writers were especially vulnerable to intellectual pressure, because the contest was not only for strategic ground but for the hearts and minds of those who stood on it.

I found a way through this labyrinth with the help of a Chinese writer-philologist, Lin Yutang (1895–1976), who wrote about culture and wisdom and helped to Romanise the Chinese alphabet. Somehow, I had acquired a copy of his book *The Importance of Living*, published in 1937 and given by a cousin to one of my sisters as a 21st birthday gift. I had picked it up at random when moving house and it guided my pursuit of pleasure. I had been too busy to bother with drugs, Zen Bhuddism and other fashionable eastern philosophies. Lin's eccentric book reminded me of the pleasure of the senses. A writer may have a strong spiritual life, or a powerful mind, be this way or that politically, have a particular grasp of aesthetics, but essentially he or she draws for inspiration on the senses.

I found time for more short stories – "A House To Die In" (published in *Quadrant*), "The Girls of East Melbourne" (*Playboy*), "The Day the Crows Came" (*The Bulletin*), "Head Down in East Melbourne" (*Cleo*), "Incident at Mussoorie" (*Meanjin*), "The Man from Telecom" (*Overland*). These stories touched life lightly. In my private thoughts I grappled with a question. Was fiction to be taken seriously? Was it important, like journalism, politics and diplomacy, or, for that matter, law or medicine, or sport and business, or was it merely fun, playing with life? Or was it more important than them all?

The mind and the spirit tend to detach us from the living world, establish dominion and supremacy for us, whether political, cultural or religious. Political allegiances divide us even when we have mutual interests. The beliefs and practises of one religion often exclude us from the embrace of other religions. The patriotism of the nation-state sets us against other nation-states. The senses, by contrast, involve us, connect us, implicate us with the rest of human kind, whatever the culture, religion, political or economic system. The arts don't tell us how to live, but they can tell us what it is like to be alive.

10

ARTS CITY

On 25 April 1982 a leader writer on *The Age* cleared his or her mind of other discussible subjects and dutifully wrote the following, which was published the next day as the newspaper's opinion:

> There will be some within the Victorian Ministry for the Arts who will look on the appointment of Mr Bruce Grant as special adviser to the Arts Minister Mr Mathews with some misgivings. After all, the Ministry already has a hard-working and imaginative director in Mr Paul Clarkson, as well as its own team of advisers. What is not clear is how the two groups will relate to each other and whose advice will carry more weight with Mr Mathews. Obviously there is some potential for conflict. By the same token the Ministry could benefit from an injection of new ideas. Much of the advice given to it is partisan, coming as it does from groups or individuals interested in pushing their own particular barrow. There is nothing surprising or sinister in that. Nonetheless, there is a need for someone of Mr Grant's calibre who can stand back from the day to day scrabbling for funds and calmly and objectively analyse the problem areas and suggest ways in which they might best be tackled.

And so on. *The Age* listed the problem areas – the dispute between the Australian Opera and the Victorian State Opera, the best use of the theatres in the new Arts Centre, and – a complaint that one was to hear from almost anyone who had a public opinion on the arts –

how to wrest from Sydney the crown of cultural capital of Australia, which rightfully belonged to Melbourne.

But the notion that you could "stand back from the day to day scrabbling for funds" and "calmly and objectively" analyse problems and suggest solutions could only have occurred to someone in the lofty domain of leader-writing. Even in the arts, a relatively benign area of government responsibility, with broad, if shallow, support across the political spectrum, the rivalry within the arts community was intense and their stalwarts in the political community ardent and determined.

My job with Race Mathews was the public projection of a friendship begun when I was a film critic and we met at a protest against the banning in Australia of the Chinese film *The White Haired Girl.* Now, thirty years later, he knocked on our door one weekend with the news that he was Minister for the Arts (and Police) in the new State government led by John Cain, and would be pleased if I could extract myself from whatever it was I was doing and help him with the arts portfolio. I probably seemed unresponsive at first. I was in the final stages of *The Australian Dilemma*, unable to think of anything else. I had not paid attention to State politics and was not sure what the job on offer required.

But I trusted the new minister, and the prospect of a regular income was appealing. We shared tastes in film and theatre, agreed to disagree on science fiction and political biography, and generally shared each other's instincts on the value of the arts in society. We were probably more honest and open with each other than if we had been political colleagues. In Labor circles, as in Australian society generally, the arts were seen as the voice of dissent against convention and conformity. Race, however, had a more positive view of the arts as part of the public domain. We shared a view of the arts as a force for social cohesion that was later well expressed by Paul Grabowsky:

> In our public discourse, our nation building, our projection of ourselves as an entity, the idea that art might be a builder of social cohesion is not often tabled. We have preferred to look for sporting metaphors to understand ourselves, to see the progression from football field to battle field as an aspirational arc, and to applaud competition, sacrifice and mateship. It's part of a forward compulsion driven by politics and markets. The artist's world of interior narratives, requiring empathy and compassion to communicate its messages, sits uncomfortably within the land of dust and dollars. And yet the combination of ingenuity and humanity that leads us to pursue dreams not necessarily designed to make us wealthy, but certainly collectively richer, should be at the heart of the story of a nation still very much in process of becoming.

What I did not appreciate at the time was that this was a pivotal moment for the arts in Melbourne, indeed for the city itself. My friendships with Ken Myer, Robin Boyd and John Sumner had alerted me to plans for a new national gallery and arts centre, but I had not appreciated that work going back to the governments of Henry Bolte and Rupert Hamer had culminated in a major impact on the arts, and the city, that would now have to be managed by the newly elected Cain government. David Yencken, who was working with the Planning Minister, Evan Walker, brought me up to date with the challenge facing the government.

Whatever was argued about the obligation of governments to fund the arts, there was no doubt in Australia that governments should provide the buildings in which the arts could present themselves to the public. All over Australia "art centres" were springing up. Libraries and galleries had always been a public responsibility but, in the performing arts, entrepreneurs had provided the buildings. In Melbourne, these buildings remained, handsome and ornate on prime locations in the central business district, catering mainly for successful plays and musicals from abroad. Now, on the other side of the Yarra, rose the new Arts Centre, comprising an auditorium for opera, several theatres and, in a separate building, what was grandly called Victoria's "national" gallery of the visual arts.

It was a turning point in Melbourne's development as the vibrant city it has become. Once the city broke from its confinement and moved to the other side of the river, an entirely new perspective opened, with the prospect of new urban development in the city's west. New hotels, restaurants, the *Herald and Weekly Times* and the Casino, turned Southbank into Docklands, with vast exhibition spaces and apartment buildings, which blended with Harbour City's marina of sleek boats and giant observation wheel. In addition, the Victorian government now seized the thorny issue of providing more space for the State library on the other side of town, so a new location needed to be found for the State museum.

Who would gain and who would lose from this renaissance of the arts? A premonition surfaced, glimpsed in gloomy faces at some traditional city venues and occasionally in letters and telephone calls to the minister's office: the new arts centre would act like a huge vacuum cleaner, sucking up all the activity that had been previously spread in healthy variety throughout the city. Also, some new activities, like community arts, were concerned that public funding would be drained by the demands of the new monolith on the south bank of the Yarra.

The Australia Council had estimated in 1980–81 that, of a total of $1969 million revenue for the arts, $377 million was public funding and $1592 million was from private sources, including $1567 million from earned income. The argument, especially from new sections of the arts community, was that funding in Australia had stabilised or, as some preferred, stagnated. Funding bodies preferred giving to established companies and individuals, as did corporations, which meant that newcomers had to fend for themselves. From both the need of governments for accountability of public funds and of corporations for public visibility, innovation, which was the lifeblood of art, had lost its appeal.

The arts, like human rights, raise issues for governments that are yet to be satisfactorily resolved. When human rights were introduced for the first time into the practicalities of diplomacy in the Helsinki Accords, diplomats, used to dealing with trade, military security, political one-upmanship and other quantifiable commodities, were at a loss to know how to value them. Similarly, the arts were both invaluable and unnecessary. On the one hand, spending on the arts might seem for governments optional compared with spending on health and education, or roads and police. On the other hand, the arts tantalised politicians with a sense of purposes beyond politics and the added value of beauty, glamour and entertainment. Experience in New Delhi had given me a taste of cultural diplomacy. While more serious and even sophisticated than Barry Humphries would have us believe, we were still unsure what Australia, the robust newcomer punching above its weight, should be offering the world. I later wrote:

> While the Indians were very clear about what they wished to send abroad, we were not. If we had responded to popular demand, we would have relied on male cricketers and female strippers, as these were our best-known exports. What Canberra offered, however, was a string quintet, singers of medieval ballads, a display of Aboriginal artefacts, a Sydney rock-and-roll group, puppets, or an exhibition of paintings ... In pursuit of

> our elusive national identity, we puzzled and sweated over our selection. Was a recital by Musica Viva of works of European composers who had died unaware of the existence of Australia more appropriate to our purpose in India than a performance by an Australian band playing contemporary music whose mainly American composers were equally oblivious of the great southland? Was modern dance or traditional ballet the more appropriate export for a robust middle power?

But the excitement now in Melbourne was palpable, swamping fear and envy. It was not just an idea, it was actually happening. Across the bridge, the neglected ugly duckling of Melbourne's south bank was already attracting buskers, tourists and, on Sundays, strolling families.

Melbourne has had several incarnations. It was "Marvellous Melbourne", its ornate buildings and intimate arcades created from the wealth of the goldfields in the middle of the 19th century. It was Australia's sporting capital, the home of Australia's distinctive football code, the Melbourne Cricket Ground, accommodating crowds envied by other cities, not only in Australia, the horse-racing capital of Australia, with the "race that stopped the nation", the Melbourne Cup. It was the nation's premier city of parks and gardens and the manufacturing centre of Australia, making it the headquarters of industrial corporations and the Australian Council of Trade Unions. It was the home of the self-reliant Protestant ethic, built without the benefit of cheap convict labour. It was the centre of fashion and food, the habitat of the Heidelberg school of painters and the first home of the literary magazines – *Meanjin*, *Overland* and, at one time, *Quadrant*. But, for reasons Melburnians could not understand, Sydney was considered Australia's cultural capital. It had a dishevelled past and a shady present, but it also had beaches, the Harbour, the Bridge and a commercial outlook like that of the world's new superpower of popular culture, the United States.

Melburnians fretted over the indisputable reality that Sydney was the nation's media centre, had an opera house with a scalloped roof irresistible to television and was attracting the head offices of new industries, like air transport. They worried about presenting their city more attractively. Two ideas were endlessly recycled. One was whether the railway yards leading to Flinders Street station from the east could be covered, providing a space for urban development. The other was where to locate a city square that would give the people of Melbourne a place to stroll and chat and play draughts and chess in a civilised manner, like the Europeans. Sometimes, the two ideas collapsed into one.

Then Melbourne discovered the south bank of the Yarra, a meagre stream that had nevertheless confined the city to its north. Except for Wirth's Circus and the Trocadero Dance Palais, the river's south bank had been a neglected region of warehouses, factories and a large, informal car park for city workers. Now it was the home of the new Arts Centre, which had a vision of itself as the heart of a precinct, nurturing the National Gallery of Victoria, the Victorian College of the Arts, the Australian Ballet, the Melbourne Theatre Company, the Malthouse Theatre and anyone else who wanted to be part of a renaissance of the arts.

John Cain, son of a former Labor premier, had been raised in a political home and was not known for an interest in the arts. He graciously allowed former premier Sir Rupert (Dick) Hamer to preside at the opening of the Arts Centre. Cain was not a fan of opera and ballet, but he had a soft spot for writers, believing, as he said in his address at the 1986 Premier's literary awards, that language was the way ideas were communicated, in politics as well as literature, and was therefore "the art by which we know ourselves". In the same speech he gave the Australia Council a blast for being Sydney-centric. Four of the seven members of the literature board came from New South Wales and the board had awarded fifty grants to writers from New South Wales and only eighteen to Victorians. He turned this anomaly into a tribute to the fierce independence of Victorians. "We have never been fond of the Government stroke. We are more resourceful: both more willing and more able to live off our wits." He then delivered a passionate protest against national flagships, declaring that "Australia will truly have found its cultural footing when every city, every community, is singing in its own voice." This became, as expected, an argument for the Commonwealth to devolve arts funding to the states.

Cain's strength was a clear sense of who he was. He is one of the few public figures I have known whose identity did not change with circumstance. Wherever and whenever you met, he was the same – whether in his office, around Parliament, in the street, at a rally, even (where he was least comfortable) at opening night of an opera. He seemed at times to be a provincial Victorian, but he could turn that into an asset, attributing to the typical Victorian attributes that were universally admired, such as prudence, tolerance and progressive reform. He was particularly watchful of expense accounts. On one occasion, I filled in for Race Mathews at a lunch with the Chief Commissioner of Police. When I later reported to Cain, his first question was: "Who paid for the lunch?"

My impression of Australian politics had been that the doctrine of the sovereign state, in contrast with the artificial nature of the national government in Canberra, was a mantra of Liberal, not Labor, politicians, but Cain was an ardent Victorian. That he was castigating a Labor government in Canberra made no difference. I sensed then, and appreciated many years later, listening to him speaking at the funeral service for John Button, the core of commonsense in being local. Local meant ordinary lives and practical things. National meant constructed aspirations.

The community arts movement was strong in Melbourne and had support in the Labor party. One example of this was the Italian arts festival, which had established itself around the retailers of Lygon Street, Carlton, and was the unexpected source of what eventually became Melbourne's international arts festival. The Spoleto arts festival came to the government's attention when Luciano Bini, president of the Italian arts festival, came to see me with the suggestion that a link could be made with the international festival established by Gian Carlo Menotti, based in Spoleto, Italy, but performed also in the United States at Charleston, South Carolina, known as the Festival of Two Worlds. Why not extend it to Melbourne as the Festival of Three Worlds? The idea appealed to Race Mathews. Paul Clarkson, head of the arts ministry, conducted a preliminary study, ministerial colleagues were persuaded, government money was found, Melbourne City Council came on board, private sponsors were rounded up. An international arts festival, like the construction of an arts centre, was not, of course, universally popular. Local companies felt neglected. Those with an interest in fostering Australian culture were critical of money spent on an imported product, even if it was not the usual import from London or New York. So it was important that the first festival should be acceptable to a broad base of the arts community.

When Marc Besen, a leading Melbourne businessman and sponsor, was forced by business pressures to step down, I became president of the board of directors of the Spoleto Melbourne Foundation, which had the task of ensuring that the first Festival of Three Worlds was a success. The sixteen-member board was a mix of people with experience running the Italian arts festival, from both sides of politics, media, trade unions and philanthropy. There was also a "general committee", which had almost everyone you could think of on it. Davis McCaughey, who had become Governor of Victoria, and John Cain were patrons. It was now up to Menotti and general manager Colin Sturm, who had a small (seven), almost entirely female, staff, to meet our expectations. They did. The first festival, in 1986, was a model for what followed – a couple of blockbusters (Ken Russell's ideological version of Madam Butterfly and Spain's Royal National Ballet) and three weeks of mixed foreign and local theatre, dance, music, opera, visual arts, circus and literary readings.

The early Spoleto festivals were successful because we were given sufficient start-up funding by the government and Menotti had readily available a menu of first class acts from which we could pick and choose. There were legal concerns in transporting hundreds of performers and their equipment, but the big challenge was the financial fact that the Australian dollar was worth not much more than sixty American cents, which meant that buying in shows from abroad was expensive. When the Australian government decided to float the Australian dollar, importing international acts became not only expensive but unpredictable. The festival had to establish a budget then take out insurance against the dollar falling below its budget value.

Sustaining the festival as an annual event required diplomacy. Menotti, who was artistic director of the three festivals, was devoted to chamber music and not fond of jazz. Indeed, he explicitly excluded jazz from the Spoleto and Charleston festivals. But jazz had a following in Melbourne, including the Premier and several of his ministers. As the government was being asked to fund the festival, the exclusion of jazz became an issue, especially as it was believed to be better at getting "bums on seats" than chamber music. Another issue was membership of the Spoleto board. The Italian community was especially interested in the festival, but was not as resourceful in providing patronage as, say, the Jewish community.

I was fortunate as president in having as general manager Colin Sturm, who was wise in the ways of cultural diplomacy and had useful connections in the arts world outside the Menotti circle (as with Lord Harewood, artistic director of the Edinburgh festival, who assisted us with connections and came to Melbourne himself as a contributor to the festival). Colin and I had a genial relationship with the "elderly gentleman", as he called Menotti. He was not hard to please. One night, after a performance at St Martin's Youth Centre, Joan and I took him through back lanes of South Yarra to our place. "How exciting!" the elderly gentleman exclaimed, brushing away branches of over-hanging trees and stumbling on narrow, broken paths. He wanted to talk that night about Australian culture (did it exist and, if so, where was it?).

When Colin Sturm unexpectedly died, Robert Ginn, a more orthodox arts administrator, found the high politics of the festival difficult to deal with and I was forced to rely more on placating the old gentleman. The answer was to move the festival away from its Spoleto foundations, with a more cosmopolitan board and artistic directors other than Menotti. This was done without rancour, and continuity of performance was maintained, establishing what became Melbourne's international festival of the arts.

*

I was ushered into a small room that seemed to be occupied entirely by filing cabinets. A few desks and chairs were scattered about, but the inmates of the bluestone building were all busy at the cabinets, languidly flicking the files back and forth in a familiar fashion. It is a scene from Kafka; one knows instinctively that nothing good can come of it. I recognise one of them, a classmate at university more than thirty years earlier. "What are you doing here?" I ask, with fatuous good humour. He smiles evasively and continues playing the files. I am in the infamous, secretive "special branch" of the Victorian police department, on assignment from the Premier, who is pledged to abolish it.

In Melbourne, the challenges of local politics were different but no less formidable than those of foreign policy. The Cold War was a reality in local politics as much as it was in international politics. I had been asked by Race Mathews to assist him in his arts portfolio, but he was also responsible for police. He and the Premier thought it was a good idea for me to investigate the special branch.

The special branch was controversial because of its role as a partner with the Australian Security Intelligence Organisation (ASIO) in detecting and combatting communist subversion. It was housed in old bluestone rooms at the back of the Fitzroy Town Hall. I thumbed through its voluminous files, and had meetings with senior police officers, including the Chief Commissioner, Sinclair Imrie (Mick) Miller. The extent of the files was an issue itself. In the 1960s they had numbered between 200,000 and 250,000, but were now down to 10,000, having been culled, or purged, depending on your perception. There was a reference in the files to "wholesale destruction" in the 1970s, but some in the Labor Party believed many files had been destroyed recently, following the party's election promise to abolish the branch. The officer in charge of the branch denied this, claiming that only properly authorised files were destroyed (they were taken to the APM factory in Fairfield and mulched). I could not get the figures to match but did not have the resources to be sure. In general I was not impressed by either the competence of the special branch or its integrity.

I was surprised how small it was and how ordinary its equipment. There was no telex. The staff seemed unable to answer simple questions, perhaps because they were seeking hidden meanings. They had been working for so long in confined circumstances dealing with a kind of political underworld that they had lost touch with normal human responses and responsibilities. But experience had satisfied me of the need for security measures, even if they were at times abused. The Victorian police force needed a capacity to deal with acts of violence that were not criminally motivated, even if only for the protection of official visitors. I recommended that, to minimise political interference in the operation of the branch, it should be placed under the supervision of an all-party committee of Parliament. But Cain, under pressure to honour his election promise, and judging that my proposal would be cumbersome to implement, preferred to abolish the branch, which he did, leaving the bureaucrats to sort out the consequences, like the ninety-nine year lease that the police department had on the premises in the Fitzroy Town Hall, how legitimate intelligence activities could be absorbed within the existing police force, what would happen to the staff of a dozen or so, who would decide on the files to be mulched at Fairfield, and whether ASIO could be invoiced for information provided.

I had other duties. There was a social dimension, in addition to the policy work involved generally in the arts portfolio. Opening nights, book launches and gallery events invited attendance. I had learned during my stint in diplomacy how to pace myself socially, but the pressure in Melbourne had an added intensity because this was my own community. Fortunately, Joan was an arts lover and shared the burden. "Two for the price of one," said the Premier, approvingly, who was himself pleased to be relieved of obligations to attend opening nights.

I had always been interested in film, theatre, literature and contemporary dance. I now extended my interest to music, opera, painting and classical ballet, and several hybrid forms in between. On 22 March 1983 I launched a gift of Indian and Asian art to the National Gallery of Victoria by Sir James Plimsoll, who was now Governor of Tasmania. On 6 June 1983 I spoke at a dinner at the gallery in honour of retiring trustees, against a background of envious grumbling in the local arts community about the generous funding by the Commonwealth Government of the National Gallery and the proposed National Museum in Canberra. I was firmly parochial: "Canberra may have more money, but it doesn't have the sense of a city, a large population, the energy of business and industry, the controversy of arts politics that only living artists at work in a city can give."

Sometimes I stood in for the Minister, as in launching the 1983 catalogue of the Australian Film Institute. I took the view that the Australian film renaissance had begun in Melbourne because a film culture had been developed. The key to success in the future was "not to try to outdo Hollywood, but to encourage the production of quality films on small and medium budgets that also have popular appeal". Reading the speech today, the high hopes for a distinctive Australian film industry read eerily similar to high hopes I held for a distinctive Australian foreign policy.

On 9 May 1984 I was student union guest speaker at Melbourne University. I spoke against a background of increased involvement of government in the arts, via the Whitlam government federally and, in Victoria, the Hamer government, which had established the first ministry of the arts in 1972. I adopted a provocative manner. If the arts were as important to the spiritual health of a community as we believed them to be, should they be free of government influence, as was religion? The public was entitled to hold governments accountable for money spent on the arts, like anything else, but how could governments be accountable, while leaving the arts free to express themselves. "It is no fun for a minister to have to stand up in Parliament week after week and defend the activities of people over whom he has no control," I said, with a straight face. The response was unqualified. Governments should bear the cost, as with health and education, and wear the consequences.

On 28 August 1984 I spoke at a conference of political scientists and had some fun with the new language of academic politics, which had become more lyrical since I had left it. I noted words in a paper presented by James Walter, such as "clerisy" and "labile". I was particularly impressed with the verb to "cathect". Somehow I managed to use the diversion to answer a question raised by Barbara Tuchman in *The March of Folly*, which had just been released in Australia. She asked why governments at critical times acted contrary to their interests, examining the Siege of Troy and the incident of the Trojan Horse, the failure of the Renaissance Popes to stop the Reformation, Mao's Great Leap Forward, the loss of the American colonies by Britain, and America's Vietnam War, among other acts of folly, to suggest that lust for power coupled with mental stagnation was the cause. This led her, and the conference, to a discussion of rationality in politics, which some defined as moral courage, and the role of the bureaucracy and outside advisers as providers of it to political leaders. By 1984, Labor was back in power in Canberra, reform was again on the agenda and, as in Whitlam's time, the impact of advice from outside the public service on bureaucratic thinking had become an issue.

On 22 October 1984 I launched a book of short stories at the Italian arts festival. It was no ordinary book launch; the Italian arts festival had become known as the origin of the Spoleto festival and my remarks were intended to draw attention to the impact this might have on Australian culture. I mentioned that when I had written about sex, politics and religion in short stories, I had felt that I was writing against the grain of Anglo-Saxon culture, whereas Joe Abiuso, the author of these stories, had the great good fortune when he wrote about sex, politics and religion, which he did most of the time, to be in the mainstream of his cultural heritage. As literature, and culture generally, would not exist without sex, politics and religion, I welcomed his book as a contribution to a "multicultural" Australia.

I mentioned that the Premier's literary awards committee had discussed whether there should be an award for ethnic literature and had decided against (without a single dissenting voice):

> It was felt it would be an arbitrary distinction between those who wrote from a traditional Anglo-Saxon perspective and those who wrote from the perspective of other cultures … What is remarkable about Australia at the moment is that we are doing two things at once. We are developing our national culture, which has its roots in an Anglo-Saxon tradition, and we are encouraging those who do not come from that tradition to continue working in the tradition they know best. This is the

> essence of the multicultural idea. You may contrast it with the idea of the melting pot in America – a new culture, a blend of all, produced under great heat and pressure. In our case, the appropriate image is not melting pot, but salad bowl. Each ingredient retains its flavour yet the overall effect is of a single dish. There is no heat and no pressure. The effect is cool, the result of tolerance and patience.

This was an early expression of an emerging view of where Australia was heading, without the force-feeding of changes in defence and foreign policy.

On 1 August 1985 I spoke at a memorial for Judah Waten, saying that he took the two loves of his life, literature and politics, "entirely seriously. I do not mean that he was without humour in either. On the contrary, he was able to speak and argue with wit and style about these two great passions of his life. But he took them seriously in the sense that these two powerful passions in his life enabled him to avoid fashion. He stayed committed to what he understood to be primary, realism in art and left-wing causes in politics." But my lasting memory of Judah was as a migrant who loved Australia. He wrote of his mother in his book *Alien Son:* "Ever since we had come to this country she had lived with her bags packed. This was no country for us. She saw nothing but sorrow ahead. We should lose everything we possessed; our customs, our traditions, we would be swallowed up in this strange, foreign land." Judah saw the writer in the vanguard of social change to a more just and peaceful world, and was generous to a fault in his regard for Australian literature, which he regarded as the creative force of a new kind of society.

The following year I wrote an introduction to *The Whitlam Phenomenon*, which contained papers delivered at a Fabian Society conference the year before. I took the somewhat unusual view that

Whitlam's most enduring impact had been in the arts, which he valued as an end in themselves. He gave the arts a role in Australia's development as a nation that they had not had before but, more than that, he was at his best, because eloquent and searching, whenever he spoke of the arts as a public good. As Victoria's representative on the board of the Australian Bicentennial Authority I was reminded again of Australia's difficulty in defining itself. The staff at the authority treated the American bicentennial of 1976 as a model for our 1988 celebrations. The symbols could be made to seem the same – the tall ships, for example – but the substance was totally different. In 1776, the Americans had taken up arms against the British and were celebrating two hundred years of independence. The Australian bicentennial was the reverse, celebrating the founding by Britain of the Australian colony in 1788. The misconception persists. In 2014, the Prime Minister, Tony Abbott, asked that the first governor of the British colony in Australia, Arthur Phillip, be seen as Australia's George Washington, commander-in-chief of the revolutionary army that fought the British and first president of the independent United States of America.

Australia did not begin life as an independent nation until 1901, when the Australian colonies united to become one nation, handed independence by the British without a shot being fired. The centenary of federation in 2001 turned out to be another occasion when, as an Australian, you felt at odds with the public presentation of history. It became, not a celebration of independence in Australia but a British gesture in London. A delegation of Australian prime ministers and state premiers, with a troop of soldiers to help guard Buckingham Palace, was sent to London to pay Australia's retrospective respect, while many Australians – and many of our neighbours, no doubt – had expected the occasion would be celebrated in Australia.

Occasionally, I was able to return to old interests. At a memorial for Macmahon Ball on 10 September 1987 I expressed the view that:

> in his struggle to maintain an Australian voice, he was perplexed, in the company of many others, by the Americans. He had worked out for himself in the wartime and early post-war years an Australian view in respect of the British, but the Americans, or more particularly the John Foster Dulles version of American foreign policy, had taken over in Asia. Mac's solution was Anzus-Yes, Seato-No. It led him quickly to condemn the commitment of Australian forces to Vietnam. It led him to welcome Whitlam's foreign policy initiatives, but not to appreciate, I suspect, its style, as he had not appreciated earlier the style of Dr Evatt.

In October 1987 I was invited by the Indian government to attend a conference in New Delhi to commemorate another conference held forty years earlier, in the year of India's independence. The architect of the first conference was India's first prime minister, Jawaharlal Nehru; the second conference was opened by his grandson, Rajiv Gandhi, also prime minister. The contemporary conference opened on 2 October, which was the birthday of Mahatma Gandhi. Such loaded symbolism invited the question in many minds, as we assembled, of the purpose of the conference. The organisers, India International Centre, had said in the letter of invitation "It is not intended to make this event a pure commemoration. The purpose of this conference is to look back to the conference of 1947, take stock of the situation in Asia four decades after the vision of a united and resurgent Asia was projected in 1947, analyse the extent to which we have been able to translate this vision into reality and, also, to look to the future." Yes, but what was the purpose behind the purpose?

Two theories were popular. One was that Rajiv, initially successful after he followed his assassinated mother as prime minister, had become overwhelmed by terrorism in the Punjab, political defections and the relentless scrutiny of the Indian media on scandals in his government. The conference was intended to project him in the image of his famous grandfather as host to foreign notables obeying the call of history. The other, which was not inconsistent with the first, was that India was concerned with signs of improving relations between China and the Soviet Union. The conference was intended to confirm India's independence of superpower pressure, whether from the Soviet Union, China or anyone else. The non-aligned movement had become so unwieldy and fissiparous that it no longer offered New Delhi an international role. The Commonwealth had lost its coordinating role under Margaret Thatcher. Asia, on the other hand, if it could be organised, even if loosely along the lines envisaged by Nehru, was a political and economic powerhouse of the future.

The Prime Minister's opening address gave support to both theories. He used language that his mother had liked and which he had dropped when he first took office. It suggested a present danger: "uninvited military presences in our area have grown and assumed increasingly dangerous proportions" The danger was not only military. It was easier to deal with direct threats to independence than to resist "temptations and blandishments … There are easy ways proffered by those who would suborn our freedom. Easy ways lead to debt traps, to the mortgaging of our interests, to domination of outside pressures."

Not being privy to the deeper thoughts behind these words, the delegates settled down for a couple of days to deal with the agenda, and it was soon evident that resistance to the notion of an "Asian" identity was strong. Delegates felt obliged to say that they valued more their national identity or their human identity or, if they did feel disposed to think regionally, preferred small regions, like South-east Asia or South Asia or West Asia (Turkey, Iran, Iraq and Egypt were represented). There were 258 delegates from twenty-five countries, with six observers (including Australia) and one of the difficulties was "Asia", the term itself. According to the organisers, the conference reached a conclusion in favour of pursuing an Asian identity but, if it did, the consensus was one of convenience, not conviction.

The Indian press sensed that the conference was getting nowhere and interested itself in a case of sati ("suttee" in English) or widow immolation. Roop Kanwar, 18, from the village of Deorala in Rajasthan, sacrificed herself on the tomb of her husband and a temple was to be built on the site to glorify her devotion. The resilience of old India, including caste, which I had learned to accept without nostalgia or melancholy, was a reminder of Nehru's brilliant idea of Indian culture as a palimpsest, a piece of parchment from which writing was partially erased to make way for a new text. Indians lived in several centuries at the same time. I was astonished, at a stop-over by Air India in Calcutta on this trip, when a child's incontinence in the seat behind me halted the aircraft's take-off. A cabin door was reopened, the mobile steps driven back to the aircraft and, in pelting rain, a black-bearded, barefooted figure in a yellow raincoat, carrying a bucket, ran across the tarmac. He burst into the plane, pointed by attendants to the seat in question. His unclean task completed, he left the plane, the door was closed, an attendant sprayed the air with deodorant and the reassuring inner world of international travel was resumed. Presumably, if an accident happened in flight, in international air, a crew member of high caste is allowed to clean up the mess.

In 1985 I received a letter from publishing consultant Frank Eyre about *The Australian Dilemma*, which had been published in 1983. I had developed in it an idea that I had been examining for some time, that our fear of being dominated by alien civilisations had created a need to prove our worth to a protector whose values we could share and who would not require us, as the price of that protection, to adapt our way of life to the region in which we lived. This, I argued, was holding back our development as a nation. "Australians have become intellectually and materially dependent on the power centres of the western world to protect them from Asia, thus inhibiting the growth of an Australian nation ... Until Australians seek for themselves a new form of western civilisation, their nationhood is crippled."

Following Arnold Toynbee's concept of challenge and response in the progress of civilisations, I suggested that the challenge of Asia to Australia was neither so much as to overwhelm nor so little as to be ignored, but about right for a positive response, if Australia could summon up the confidence to make it. I proposed a new form of western civilisation for Australia. It would be based on a different use of power, not on any special qualities of Australians. We had trapped ourselves. Alien to our region and environment, we sought powerful allies to protect us and we adopted their attitudes as our own, making us more alien. To break the vicious circle, we needed to become more nationalist first, in order to become more internationalist later. The paradox of nationalism as a step to internationalism was only seemingly paradoxical. Australians knew they could never be a great power. Nationalism meant co-existence and accommodation, not supremacy and aggression, and it was this that would distinguish Australian civilisation from the European, British and American versions that had gone before.

I was tackling the dilemma that has haunted Australians from the beginning. Australia was discovered and developed by the British entirely during the period of Western supremacy; since 1683, when the Turks were turned back at Vienna, the West held sway over the rest of the world. The wars were within the family; communism, as it sprang up in Russia in 1917, was a Western idea, Karl Marx and others presenting it as a further stage in the historical process of the West, feudalism conceding to capitalism, which would give way to socialism, then to communism.

For Australia, Western supremacy lost its inevitability with the Second World War. Japanese aircraft bombed the Australian mainland and, even in losing the war, Japan dislodged the Europeans from Asia, so that ancient Asian civilisations, dormant or suppressed for centuries, rose to the surface in our region. Since then, Australia's engagement with Asia became more urgent and more real. Asia became less a threat to European supremacy and more a test of Australia's own competence and intelligence.

Manning Clark had written a typically warm, complex letter. "I have just finished reading The Australian Dilemma which reached me here two days ago. It is such a wise, sensible, with disturbing undercurrents, book that I expect it will not be discussed properly in the media - that is I mean they will not discuss the book you wrote … some other book which they think ought to be written." He said the issue I had raised had begun in Australia in the 1840s and was never-ending. "You have been both a Mary and a Martha in the debate," he concluded mysteriously.

He was right about the media wanting to discuss "some other book". Some reviewers thought I wanted Australia to abandon its Western heritage and become "Asian". This was the opposite of what

I had intended (which was conveyed in the sub-title: *A New Kind of Western Society*) and Frank Eyre wanted to assure me that the critics were wrong. Not only that, it was "the best book of this sort ever written about Australia. I came time and again on phrases, sentences, whole paragraphs that seemed to me to encapsulate the causes and stages of Australia's development, its problems and possible solutions. Things I had never seen said before but which struck one instantly, in the way a good poem does, as being exactly right." He offered to write to the publishers with a proposal that they should reissue the book as a paperback, consisting mainly of the first and last two chapters, with a condensed version of the chapters between.

A phrase in his letter set me thinking. For many people expected to read the book, he wrote, it was "almost too good" – meaning too complex, carefully thought out and documented. It needed to be simplified, its evidence made more telling, its argument lifted and more boldly asserted. From the standpoint of a publisher's business model, this was good advice, but I was reluctant to take it. I had an affection for the book as it was. It had been written over a long period, every nook and cranny of it laboriously assessed and carefully placed. I knew that it would be unfamiliar territory for many readers, accustomed to a less demanding and more gratifying vision of Australian nationhood. I was also conscious that one reason why its message had been misinterpreted was that it fell tantalisingly short. I had presented a plausible thesis for Australia to become "a new kind of western society", but I had not said in sufficient, satisfying detail what kind of society that would be.

I decided to leave its message to be prized out by those prepared to exert as much labour as had been expended on writing it. And I started work on another attempt to discover what kind of country Australia was. *What Kind of Country?* was published in 1988.

*

To the house at 83 Grey Street, with the mean front door, we added a room at the back, with what the architect called a cathedral ceiling. But the house was still small for a growing family and increasingly busy professional parents, so we moved to a larger terrace house in East Melbourne (114 Hotham Street) that had once been occupied as an office by architects Evan Walker and Daryl Jackson.

I could still walk across Fitzroy Gardens to the city, but I longed for nature's space. Joan was a New Yorker who could manage well with urban parks and gardens. Some of our friends lived in semi-rural contentment in places like Eltham and Mount Eliza, and Melbourne had splendid suburbs reaching out as far as the eye could see, but she was pleased with East Melbourne. I convinced her I was not yearning for a return to farm life and she knew I was not drawn to hippy communes. We agreed eventually to buy land at Ferny Creek in the Dandenongs. Daryl Jackson sketched for us a house-in-the-trees, and we began visiting the site with the children for picnics, imagining what it would be like when we had our dacha in the hills. Then, in one of those periodic spasms of concern about bushfires in Victoria the land was resumed as a fire-break area and we were offered back what we had paid. We scanned the horizon around Melbourne for an alternative, with advice from Bill Purnell about the kinds of soils available. Since my arrival in Melbourne, when I was met at Spencer Street station by David Broughton and driven to his house at Shoreham, I had had a liking for the Mornington

Peninsula. Eventually, after much scrutiny of land in Flinders, Red Hill, Arthur's Seat and Balnarring, we found something we could afford, a sandy hill in a new development between Rye and St Andrews Beach. The block was large, you could imagine from the house a glimpse of the sea, and wells could be bored for water. However, Gunnamatta Beach was considered dangerous. Also, we were confronted by a snake in a beach cave and a huntsman spider in the parked car. My mother visited us from Perth and declared, astride the site, "You don't want to cut yourself off, dear." The family decided it was too desolate and we turned away.

We visited our daughter Johanna, who shared a house with friends in Lorne. Other friends had houses there – John Sumner, Prue Myer, Andrew and Andrea Farran. After the bushfires of 1983 we bought a block of land in Summerhills Avenue and Prue's son, Philip, who was a boat builder, built us a house. It was a simple house, perched on a hill, but for twenty years it served its purpose as a family retreat. We sold the terrace house in Hotham Street, East Melbourne, and moved to what was called "The Maisonette", the former residence of the local rabbi, at the back of an apartment block in Domain Street, South Yarra. With four bedrooms, it could accommodate two schoolboys and two working parents. From my point of view, the Lorne house had a singular attraction. Built on a slope, it had space underneath, which Philip turned into a head-high storage space for cartons of manuscripts and papers as well as a writing room for myself, with a window that looked out at the sea. I bought a second-hand desk and settled in quickly. My memory of houses is largely affected by whether I wrote well or badly in them. Lorne was productive. I wrote *The Budd Family* novel there, as well as essays and short stories.

The house had three bedrooms, one known as Betty's room (for Joan's mother, who had come from New York to live in Melbourne), which had its own bathroom, two other bedrooms, one large, one small on the other side of the house, sharing a bathroom. What was nice for a family was an open space in the middle over two levels. From the kitchen bench you could talk to people at the dining table and shout to others in either of the two living areas. You could also see across the roof of the house below, through the branches of the gum trees to a snaking road and breaking surf. Outside, a favoured spot was where the cream flowers of a jasmine climber at the back of the house fell so profusely that they had to be brushed aside to make way, and the perfume was so sweet that people lingered to fondle them and crush the petals to their noses. And there was a green love seat on rising ground at the back that gave you a panoramic view of the bay.

The garden became a floral mix that only fervent nationalists regarded as foreign – climbing roses, potted geraniums, pelargonium, hydrangeas, hyacinths, agapanthus, lavender, native trees and shrubs, especially wattle. A stone wall along the driveway was built by a local landscape gardener, who rode a horse to work along the beach and had a romantic disposition. I had not noticed a latent curve of the wall until he drew it to my attention, asking me to decide whether to let it go, or pull it back. Between the two options was a considerable difference of land. He wanted to let it go, and I agreed. When finished, it curved in a graceful arc above the driveway, which was also not straight, moving in the opposite direction, creating a satisfying balance when your eye brought the two levels together. "Good lines," he said approvingly. "Like Matisse."

A relationship grew between the house and nature that was satisfying. The house itself had a settled look from the outside and a calm, cool feeling inside. The cedar turned ruddy dark, the wood of the beams, floorboards and architraves around the doors and windows was a soft brown and the furniture and curtains were simple and subdued. The effect, with Japanese paper lanterns, was unobtrusive, a feeling of quiet and secure space. It might have seemed bare, were it not for the perpetual Australian green of trees and shrubs and creepers that could be glimpsed from every window. Some manna gums were removed when the house was built but enough remained for their heads to droop and toss between the house and the sky. Wattle, lining the steep driveway, created a blaze of yellow in early winter and a spectrum of green-blue leaves for the rest of the year.

I took up gardening, spreading horse and cow manure, bought from roadside stalls, to break the clay soil, which baked hard in summer and even in winter was inhospitable to tender roots. Beyond the brown and green of the house and its surroundings, which was satisfying enough, was the dramatic blue, or turquoise, or pea-green, or sometimes, in early morning on a hot day, flushed orange, or, in winter, grey and leaden, presence of the sea.

The sea could be seen, if not from every window, at least from three corners of the house, which was high enough to overhang the coast road and the rocky beach. You could see, through the gum trunks and above the roofs of the houses, the surf breaking and spreading over the sand like the lace of a quilt. People on the beach were mobile dots, with dogs like scurrying ants. Toy cars sped soundlessly on a road that, empty, looked like a black snake. You could see the blue bulk of the sea, the grey line of the horizon and the sky above, sometimes pale and shimmering, sometimes bright and busy with fluffy white clouds, sometimes heavy and motionless with dark and thunderous intent, sometimes in the mornings pink through the tree tops and, at sunset, streaked with red warnings.

One early winter morning I saw an astonishing sight: on my right, the white globe of a full moon setting through the trees and, on my left, a golden sun rising from the sea. Because of the intense mini-climate of Lorne, caused by the headland blocking the prevailing south-westerly winds, as well as the flippant southerlies that sprung up on a warm afternoon, the air was steadily moist and rainbows were frequent, often straddling land and sea, one leg in the forested hills, the other in the depths of the ocean, like a magically implanted beam of post-modern architecture.

The children liked to lie on a summer's day on one of the sofas in the living room and look up at the tree tops, gently moving in a breeze and through which you could see clouds drifting across the sky. It was like living in a tree house. Light aircraft buzzed past just above the height of the house, hugging the coast. Slow ships trailed the horizon like ghosts. Lorne could also be wet and windswept, when a south-easterly blew steadily, usually for a couple of days, so that the sky and the sea and the headland were flattened into a grey mass, the horizon and the coastline blurring into each other, the landmarks, like the pier and the radio mast and the old hotels and houses on the headland, obliterated by waves of rain. A swirling mist clung to ravines and crevices. But even on these days, it was a haven for human beings.

We stayed indoors, reading in bed, listening to the wind whistling and the boughs creaking and cracking, dreaming of wrecked ships and swollen rivers, drifting into the main room from time to time to find something to eat or to stoke the fire with red gum cuts or to help in the preparation of meals that became more extravagant as the weather blew harder. These were the days for lengthy contests of scrabble and computer games. There was usually a break in the late afternoon, when for an hour, the clouds in the west would part and the sun break through, bathing the stricken town in a perversely effulgent light. We would gather on the wind-protected side of the house for afternoon tea, ignoring the leaves and the broken twigs scattered over the decking, breathing the wet, fresh, bark-laden air. Or sometimes we would pile in the car and drive to the centre of the town to inspect the damage, like scouts of the State Emergency Services. The gloomy weather confirmed our opinion that nature and humankind must find a balance between their existential forces. When the south-easterly blew at Lorne, the only form of balance available to people was to retreat to the comfort of civilisation and let nature takes its course.

What stirred the imagination was that on that headland had been constructed human habitation without (as yet) disturbing nature, indeed without as yet making much of an impression on it. The Lorne headland jutted across the prevailing south-westerlies and southerlies, creating a sheltered climate of its own. The sea air and the tall eucalypts growing down to the water's edge combined in a potent ozone brew. We liked to sit on the green love seat with a high view over the roof of the house. From there you saw, through the slim upper boughs and swaying mop heads of gum leaves, the brilliant white surf and, beyond, the sharp line of the horizon, dividing dark green-blue sea from azure-blue sky. We could sit there to read, but more probably to gaze out to sea, a look of rapture on our faces.

My heart always lifted whenever we rounded a certain bend, saw the Lorne headland and began the climb through the forest on the Great Ocean Road. I knew that all the contending ideas and natural forces in and around me would reach a balance when I arrived.

11

MIDDLE POWER

When Gareth Evans became Minister for Foreign Affairs and Trade in the Hawke government in 1988, he asked me to work with him in Canberra as a "consultant". I did not bother to inquire what this inviting term meant. We had worked together on constitutional reform, and I was ready for another reason. As the Cold War was wobbling to a close, it might be possible to pick up some of the momentum in Australian foreign policy that had been promised by the short-lived Whitlam government. It proved to be so. We had a window of opportunity or, as Gareth remarked, a "dream run".

The Cold War formally ended on 19 November 1990, when the Conference on Security and Cooperation in Europe convened in Paris to declare that the NATO and Warsaw Pact states were no longer adversaries, or perhaps on 31 March 1991, when the military component of the Warsaw Pact was actually disbanded. But, for most people, it was over on 9 November 1989, when the Berlin Wall, erected in 1961 to prevent people in the east from mixing with people in the west, was breached at the Brandenburg Gate. No longer was there political will in the Soviet Union to hold the line, as there had been in Hungary in 1956 and Czechoslovakia in 1968.

Apart from assisting sometimes with the issues of the day, I was asked by the minister to undertake two tasks. The first was to investigate Indonesia's attitude to an upgrading of our cultural relations. We had established the Australia-Japan Foundation, the Australia-China Council and the Australia- New Zealand Foundation for that purpose. Why not something similar for Indonesia? Why not, indeed, an inter-active body, aimed not only at improving our knowledge and understanding of them but their knowledge and understanding of us. I went to Indonesia to gauge the level of interest.

The second task was to prepare a report on "preventive diplomacy", meaning diplomacy as a way of preventing military conflict rather than acting as a hand-maiden of security policy. For this I would need to visit the United Nations in New York, where hopefully I would be given evidence that the scourge of war was no longer rampant, and the State Department in Washington, where I would be given a lesson in the benefits of military power.

In Indonesia, I encountered immediately the imbalance in our relationship that I had known since writing my first book. The idea that Australia should establish a body that would give Indonesian culture equal billing with Japan and China was warmly endorsed. The idea that Indonesia should set up a counterpart body on the other side of the Arafura Sea to improve Indonesian understanding of Australian culture was received with puzzled frowns and, sometimes, amusement. Polite as always, whether in official positions or as writers, academics, journalists and business people, Indonesians struggled to find reasons why they should pay attention to Australian culture. They regarded it as a minor (indeed, barely visible) variant of Western culture, with which they were already thoroughly familiar, through established contacts with Europe and pervasive American popular culture. Their minds drifted north when they thought of Western culture and, while they were well-disposed to Australia (remembering that we had sided with them in their fight against the Dutch for independence), Australian culture was either unknown, or not distinctive enough to need their attention.

Sometimes, indeed, they confessed to finding Australians crude and boorish, friendly in superficial, practical ways but insensitive about inner feelings. When I pointed out that Herb Feith had developed an academic industry of sensitivity to Indonesian culture, and that I personally had several Indonesian friendships, they said that Herb was a rare human being and I was more like a "European gentleman" than an Australian. They probably meant this as a compliment, but I was on a mission representing an emerging new Australia, not an outpost of Europe, and I produced, with a show of indignation, my version of Australian Culture 101. Patrick White received a solemn nod, because he had been awarded a Nobel Prize, but it was hard to find anyone who responded to the others on my list.

Sport was popular with governments as a form of cultural exchange, but I could not strike up a useful conversation on sporting contests between Australia and Indonesia. Indonesians are not generally good at sport. There was no readily available sport, as there was with cricket in India, that could serve as cultural exchange, either for men or women. Any sport with body contact, like football, was considered an unequal contest. Indonesian men are slender physically. When I was writing *Indonesia*, I often had conversations with Indonesians about the colonial past in which big, blonde Dutchmen were shown to be no match for the wit and agility of their physically slight opponents, the freedom-fighters. Sometimes it was the delicacy of Indonesian women that unsettled the cumbersome overlord. Australian men were as big as the Dutch, if not as blonde, and their sporting prowess had given them a formidable reputation.

I examined the role of other foreign cultural organisations active in Jakarta, such as the British Council, Alliance Francaise, Erasmus House, the Goethe Institute and the Japan Foundation. The title "institute", which we eventually adopted, emerged from Indonesian language tests. In Indonesian a "council" could be a decision-making, political assembly, and a "foundation" could be a charitable organisation seeking funds. I had known Foreign Minister Ali Alatas from my earlier engagement in Indonesia and we were able to discuss the issues with relative frankness. The idea of reciprocity had his support in principle, but he added the ominous rider that it would need "thorough examination". Although the proposed organisation would be funded by the Australian government, it was intended to promote people-to-people contact and its main activities would be non-governmental. For Indonesia, to allow another government access to its people was a sensitive issue. In Australia's case, our long association with imperial Britain and our strategic partnership with the United States had given us the reputation with more nationalistic Indonesians of being a Trojan Horse of Western interests and influence.

There was some grumbling in Canberra about the one-sided traffic of Australia's cultural exchanges, when I reported back to the Minister. The Department of Foreign Affairs and Trade (DFAT) had to bear the cost and some officials, tired of dealing with the inscrutable charm and indifference of our neighbour, detected evidence of cultural cringe in our interest in their culture. But common sense prevailed: it was in Australia's interests to know more about important regional states like Japan, China and Indonesia, and we should not adopt a tit-for-tat response if they did not consider it necessary to pay similar attention to us. In due course, the Australia-Indonesia Institute was established, with a board from outside appointed by the Minister, and myself as chairman, accommodated in DFAT and funded by the government. The board met for the first time on 31 May, 1989, and for the next three years the earnest endeavours of its members and institute staff were an important part of my life.

The Australia-Indonesia Institute was generally welcomed in Indonesia. The *Jakarta Post* said: "The existence of the institute and its activities in Indonesia, of course, will not be a guarantee against irritations and crisis eruptions in Indonesian-Australian relations in the future. However ... the wider understanding that is created of each other's cultural heritage and traditions could at least provide a solid base to fall back on, that will prevent temporary misunderstandings and crises from causing a complete breakdown in the broad relations between the two countries." This turned out to be a wise summation. Among the irritations was Jakarta's habit of refusing visas to Australian journalists who had been critical of the Indonesian government, especially the president. When East Timor's future became an issue between Jakarta and Canberra, the Institute's hopeful program of journalist exchanges and transparent information had to wait for more favourable political weather.

Canberra officials were not as familiar then with public-private partnership arrangements as they are now. When Penguin Books applied for funds to reduce the price of a book it was publishing by my friend Pramoedya Ananta Toer, and we declined, welcoming the book but noting that the Institute did not wish to become involved in a commercial venture already underway, we were accused of banning the book in Australia because Pramoedya was banned in Indonesia. Automation Australia Pty Ltd interpreted our cultural mission broadly, applying for funds for a "motoring adventure rally" in Indonesia. The Australian embassy in Jakarta strongly objected, on the grounds that it was a commercial event capable of funding itself and, in any case, Indonesia's roads were narrow and crowded and the spectacle of racing cars using them was likely to have (in the mild language of our ambassador) a "negative impact". But these were teething troubles. The Institute gradually became more skilled at fostering contact and communication outside government circles between Australians and Indonesians.

There was a degree of urgency about its work. Australia and Indonesia are not just neighbours in a generic sense. We actually live next door to each other, and no two neighbours anywhere in the world are as different, in terms of history, culture, language and political and social traditions, as we are (although one would have to say the English and the French, divided by the English Channel, run close).

As flag-waver on "preventive diplomacy", I was received in official Washington like an emissary from another planet. The Minister may have had in mind something like the International Crisis Group, which was later established in Brussels as a global early-warning system, and of which he became president after leaving politics. My soundings in the universities and think-tanks confirmed, however, that Americans were relatively young and inexperienced in the world of diplomacy, still convinced that their model of nationhood was right for the rest of the world. If the rest of the world could not see that, American power would need to be used to bring them to their senses.

It was perhaps unfortunate that my interlocutor at the State Department was John Bolton, who was later to make a name for himself as ambassador to the United Nations with a hard-line defence of US interests. He was a believer in American "exceptionalism" and saw preventive diplomacy as a check on the freedom of the US to act in its own interests, which were, by his and true Americans' definition, the interests of humankind. Even among liberal Americans I encountered opposition to any strengthening of international law, which they reasonably assumed would be one of the consequences of preventive diplomacy. They pointed out that the British and the Dutch had established rules for the behaviour of ships at sea that benefited them as seafaring powers, and that the Europeans were now only interested in common markets and global rules because they had worn themselves out with conflict. They shared the patriotism of their conservative colleagues: the use of force by the United States was essential for the peace, stability and prosperity of the world.

Our ambassador at the UN, Peter Wilenski, arranged a lunch meeting with colleagues at which preventive diplomacy got a more sympathetic hearing, but with uncertainty about how, in practice, it might work. My discussions with UN officials also found support for the idea, but also exposed an awareness that sanctions and other forms of persuasion were cumbersome. Unfortunately, diplomacy was most effective when backed by the threat of the use of force. The UN had the capacity to broker deals, but not the capacity to enforce them. UN officials wanted to strengthen Chapter VII of the UN Charter, which gave the Security Council authority to intervene with military force.

Gareth Evans was not put off by faint hearts in New York or hard noses in Washington. The Cold War was ending and Australia was on the lookout for the "peace dividend". He decided that we should together write a book, in which some of the ideas that were being discussed in his office and department, especially the idea of Australia as a middle power, could be explored and explained. Writing *Australia's Foreign Relations*, which was published in 1991 and reissued the following year and in 1995, became a particularly subtle moment, explaining the theory of middle power diplomacy while actually doing its work.

According to myth, Albert Einstein, when asked how he thought up new ideas, said he had only had one. We were less modest. *Australia's Foreign Relations* had its origin in two ideas. Evans persuaded me – and set out to persuade his department – that being a "good international citizen" was in Australia's national interest. He had brought the idea to government from his background as an academic lawyer. It was new not only to me but to most senior people in his department, who had been raised in the realist school of international relations, where power determined outcomes, which could then be stabilised by diplomatic negotiation and international law, not the other way around. The Minister persisted. The department grumbled, but responded, sometimes productively.

I persuaded him that Paul Dibb's 1986 defence review and Kim Beazley's White Paper on defence the following year had "liberated" Australian foreign policy. By making the claim that, short of global war, Australia was capable of defending itself, foreign policy was relieved of the task of ensuring that we did nothing to upset our great and powerful friend, the United States. If we were confident that, short of global war, we could manage with our own security resources, we were free to undertake some foreign policy initiatives of our own, with or without the approval of the United States. From departmental responses to these two ideas, as well as from our own intellectual resources, and taking account of what was happening in the world, we developed in the book the notion of Australia as a middle power, indeed, in the Minister's telling of it, a "robust middle power", striving to be a good international citizen.

We were at pains to point out that being an active middle power did not mean abandoning care and prudence on issues of national security and economic benefit. First, there had to be careful identification of the opportunity for effective action. It was pointless to pursue ideas that were premature, over ambitious or for some reason unlikely to gather support. Then, a physical capability was needed to follow through, meaning resources, including budgets and personnel, and a network of diplomatic posts. Middle power activism needed to develop two tactical skills – niche diplomacy and coalition-building. The new phrases buzzed around the Department of Foreign Affairs and Trade building (known fondly as the Kremlin) in which I had an office. The Minister worked from his Parliamentary office.

The value of middle power diplomacy arose from a simple, yet contentious, presumption, which was that countries of middle rank had a more likely capacity than great powers to persuade others to collective action. When we looked at the issues that were piling up on the international agenda's To-Do list, we could see the need for innovation and imagination, as well as energy and goodwill. Great powers were wary of imagination, fearing it might undermine their authority, based on their power to coerce. Middle power diplomacy saw itself as interlocutor between states with resolute interests and those that were weak, incapacitated by internal strife or without the resources to devote to global diplomacy. Typically applied to a range of problems that involved the interests of not just a few, but many, nations, it relied on international law and convention and the practical exchange of ideas, people and goods.

I knew from my own experience that Australian diplomats had both the desire and the competence to think and act more independently, but they were hamstrung by the logic of power, which was compelling, and scared of seeming to be in sympathy with the Cold War adversaries of the US. I recalled what Marshall Green had told me in New Delhi, and what other Americans had said: Australia had good access to the White House, but when we got inside it we were only interested in discovering what was in the mind of its occupant, not in revealing what was in our mind.

Using a vogue term like "liberated", in relation to the United States, was politically risky. The case for the alliance had bipartisan support. By letting the United States do the work, Australia had kept its defence budget at enviously low levels during the long years of the Cold War. The political argument was also strong. A close relationship with a superpower, with the most extensive military and intelligence network in the world, made the public feel safe. The use of the alliance by conservatives for domestic political purposes had been largely successful. The kith-and-kin sentiment that used to underpin loyalty to the United Kingdom was no longer as strong, but in its place were the shared values of freedom and democracy represented by the United States. Australian governments who put this asset at risk, allowing even a shadow of doubt to trouble the certainty of the alliance, were likely to be punished in the media and at the ballot box.

My argument was not with the alliance as such but with Australia's grip on it, which I suggested should be flexible, not rigid (as, in cricket, the use of the top, against the bottom, hand of a batsman). At one point, I used the term "double-jointed", to which Gareth objected. For an alert politician, this was close to "two-faced". But, as political paranoia declined with the end of the Cold War, and we looked in detail at the issues facing Australia in our region, the general proposition that we should move under our own steam, seeking partners with whom to cooperate in achieving common ends, without having to look over our shoulder at the US, was both realistic and appealing.

Gareth became comfortable with the idea that foreign policy had been "liberated" and used the word in a speech or two, teasing some of his colleagues, especially Kim Beazley. Both Beazley and Hawke were strong supporters of the alliance with the United States and the implication in Dibb's report of a "denialist" strategic option for Australia had been corrected in the White Paper to assure everyone that Australia was still prepared to play its part in the region. New Zealand, under a Labor prime minister, David Lange, was pressing Australia to declare the ANZUS alliance to be non-nuclear, which meant, in effect, dissolving it. The response of DFAT and indeed the government, to New Zealand, was not to accept its invitation, but to rely on a fresh image of Australia as a more independently-minded alliance partner.

Co-authorship with a working minister of a book as comprehensive and as politically sensitive as this one was no easy task, especially when the minister was indefatigable. There are many stories about Gareth Evans' hyper-activism. My own is a mild version, reflecting my experience of working with a highly intelligent, sensitive man who had, like everyone, moments of irritability. We were dining together and I went to his office to pick him up. He was busy and I waited outside, reading magazines provided for waiting guests. He poked his head around the door, apologising for being late. Five minutes later, his head appeared again, this time to explain that he was waiting on an important telephone call and would come as soon as he was free. After another five minutes, he poked his head again around the door, observed me still languidly reading and exploded. "Why don't you … do something!"

It was difficult to marry our two styles – mine tending to be essayish and literary, employing light and shade in the service of argument, his logical and systematic, with words meaning only what they said, although, with a politician's knack of qualifying, inclined to adjectives, while I was fond of verbs. I wrote the first draft. He had the final say, as the book would be seen as government policy. In between was much to-ing and fro-ing. Sometimes I felt my prose had been run over by a steamroller and was reminded of what G.B. Shaw had said to Ellen Terry, when she had wanted a child with her looks and his brains. "But what if …?" Sometimes it was, as we say in the preface, a seamless mesh of two different approaches, but with the single objective of getting down on paper a framework for Australian foreign policy.

Behind the idea of a more active foreign policy were some general ideas about Australia. As a young state, we were more interested in the future than the past. We were modern in the sense that we sought fulfilment in social and economic progress rather than in ideology, tradition or destiny. We were competent and increasingly skilful. Our outlook was hopeful but sceptical, practical rather than dogmatic. Our aspirations were secular and humanist; we were wary of utopian or religious solutions. Except for our treatment of the Aboriginal people, we were respected internationally for what we had achieved in a short time. With a mixture of good luck and good management, we had produced a politically stable, economically vigorous and socially open society. In science, the arts and sport, we were making a mark in the world. Our small population and physical expanse limited the impact of our private sector, but with sufficient public resources and an economy around 12th largest in the world, we had room to move and to manoeuvre.

As the Cold War receded, the economic, political, cultural, religious and physical diversity of global humanity was exposed, especially in Australia's region, calling for interaction and cooperation rather than uniformity or enforced identity of interest. The region's essence was networks, not institutions, and the energy of these networks came from small and middle-size countries as well as powerful states. It embodied the pragmatic spirit of accommodation and consensus, ensuring compromise in the pursuit of better living conditions rather than a system of values. There was no equivalent of the North Atlantic Treaty Organisation (NATO). This suited Australia, which, although no longer the odd man out, was the odd man in. We had to acknowledge that our military history as a global terrier inclined some of our neighbours to be suspicious of us as a potential agent for intervention in their affairs by outside powers, especially the United States. We set out to convince them otherwise.

An active period in Australian foreign policy followed. On a peace settlement in Cambodia, we worked first with Indonesia, then all five permanent members of the Security Council, Vietnam and the factions within Cambodia. We were instrumental in the foundation of Asia Pacific Economic Cooperation (APEC) and ASEAN Regional Forum (ARF) and active in the Comprehensive Test Ban Treaty. Our military versatility showed in Cambodia, where we led the UN military contingent, and later in East Timor, where we led several coalitions of interested countries. We began the work that led eventually to the vote for the International Criminal Court, against the opposition of the United States. In creating the Cairns group, formed on the issue of fair trading in agricultural products, we worked with Argentina, Brazil, Canada, Chile, Colombia, Fiji, Hungary, Indonesia, Malaysia, New Zealand, Philippines, Singapore, Thailand and the United States. For Law of the Sea negotiations, our caucus was the so-called Group of Twelve, comprising mainly the smaller European democracies. On chemical weapons, we developed a close working relationship with Brazil, Egypt, Germany, India, Japan, the Netherlands, Norway, Sweden, the Soviet Union as it then was, and the United States. On oil drilling and mining in the Antarctic, we took the initiative first with France, then later Belgium and Italy, to swing the vote against.

What didn't happen was also important – the military failure in Vietnam had not caused dominoes to fall all over South-east Asia. There was a sense that, without the pressures of great power intervention, South-east Asia was settling down. New power alignments had not appeared. Australia, during the period of the Hawke-Keating governments, decided this was an opportunity to reduce, even eliminate, the threat of nuclear war, which had hung over the world for almost half a century. We became activists on the issues of disarmament and nuclear non-proliferation, hounding the French for testing in the Pacific.

A general estimate was that 50,000–60,000 nuclear warheads were then in existence, the vast bulk of them in the US and the then USSR. All five permanent members of the United Nations Security Council, possessing the important veto power, had nuclear weapons. Each of them had taken the fateful step for seemingly rational reasons of state: the United States, by dropping the first atomic bombs in 1945 in a race to end the Second World War; the

Soviet Union by beginning its own tests in 1949 to check the US in the Cold War; Britain, by continuing its own program in a bid to retain Western leadership; France determined not to allow the Anglo-Saxons to dominate, by detonating its first bomb in 1960; and China, uneasy with the Russians and faced with an alliance between Japan and the United States, by starting its own test series in 1964.

The Canberra Commission for the Elimination of Nuclear Weapons was established in 1996. Its members were political, military and diplomatic leaders with experience of the management of nuclear weapons during the Cold War and the strategic culture that arose from their possession. They had the advantage of later experience over earlier assessments, which tended to believe, based on the judgement of the International Court of Justice (that the use of nuclear weapons was legal if used in self-defence), that nuclear conflict could be limited. The commission's report presented three fundamental arguments against the possession of nuclear weapons.

The first was that their destructiveness was so great that they had no military utility against a comparably equipped opponent, other than that they might deter the opponent from using the same weapons. This was summarised in the acronym MAD (Mutually Assured Destruction). The second was that indefinite deployment of the weapons carried a high risk of their ultimate use through accident, miscalculation or inadvertence. The third was that possession of the weapons by some states stimulated others to acquire them, reducing the security of all. The commission noted: "The end of the Cold War has created a new climate for international action to eliminate nuclear weapons, a new opportunity. It must be exploited quickly or it will be lost. There has been no better opportunity since the beginning of the nuclear age. Permanent arsenals and proliferating nuclear powers will be the fate of the world if this opportunity is ignored."

Technically, the task of reducing and then eliminating nuclear weapons was laborious but not utopian. The commission presented a carefully detailed program of gradual elimination – take the weapons off alert, remove the warheads from delivery vehicles, end deployment of non-strategic weapons, end testing, reduce nuclear arsenals, reach agreement among all nuclear weapons states of "no first use" against each other and undertake not to use nuclear weapons against non-nuclear states. But the bomb continued to cast its mysterious spell. The twin-barrelled logic of threat and status played on the sovereign state's obsession that, to be really independent, it needed the ultimate in weaponry. India had become a nuclear weapons state because China was one, and, once India had the bomb, Pakistan followed. Israel, surrounded by angry neighbours, took the step for security reasons and Iran then considered the nuclear option because of Israel. North Korea claims the right to go nuclear out of a desperate sense of isolation, facing South Korea, which has a nuclear-armed ally.

A dilemma persists at the heart of the nuclear question, which is the human desire not to deny ourselves the fruits of our ingenuity. Splitting the atom was regarded as one of the great feats of science, and its application to human progress remains a challenge to our imagination, especially as nuclear is a cleaner source of power than fossil fuels in an era of climate change. The technical difference between splitting the atom for peace and splitting it for war is complex, detectable only by prolonged and intense scrutiny by the International Atomic Energy Agency. While incidents like Chernobyl, Three Mile Island and Fukushima have shown that security of nuclear reactors remains an issue, and the disposal of radioactive waste is a problem, countries are continuing to build nuclear power stations.

*

Joan spent an academic year in China, improving her Chinese language and teaching English at Shanghai International Studies University. I visited her in December 1988. She was in China during the Tiananmen Square rebellion in Beijing the following year and her experience of the tensions and turmoil in the student population of China is recorded in her book *Worm-eaten Hinges*, published in 1991.

In the aftermath of the Tiananmen Square incident, the Minister's office organised with Qantas an airlift for Australians who wanted to get out of China. Joan declined a passage; it was examination time and she wanted to stay to mark her students' papers. Some in the Minister's office regarded this as foolhardy, even a mark of ingratitude, but, although she did not seek my opinion, I agreed with her decision. It was the act of a teacher who valued a commitment to students above what the American writer Don DeLillo called "the perennial frenzy of the state".

It was at this time I declined for the second time what is described as an "honour".

When Lord Casey was Governor-General he had made what I took to be an offer of official recognition under the old honours system. "Isn't it time you had a gong," he said, in his brisk manner, as if offering a whisky and soda. I laughed his suggestion away. I was not able to take seriously the disposal of honours by people who had only a superficial understanding of what I was doing. Now I received a formal invitation under the new honours system established during the

Whitlam era and again declined. The timing – the Queen's birthday – reminded me that I was active in the republican movement for constitutional reform. The possessive attitude of Canberra's bureaucracy may have contributed. Also I had discovered the perverse Chinese essayist, Lu Xun. He wrote that over thousands of years Chinese civilisation had developed a subtle method of controlling people: "crush all those whom you can crush; as for others, put them on a pedestal." By putting them on a pedestal you also controlled them, whispering in their ears: "Do as I tell you, otherwise I shall bring you down".

Physically, Canberra was relaxing, like a large country town. The town planners who created it believed that humankind, having conquered nature, still had a soft spot for it, so they surrounded a central lake with pine plantations, remnants of forests and open spaces. But, unlike country towns, Canberra suffered from DeLillo's frenzy. Governments, with their plans and causes, came and went, ruffling briefly the surface of life in the national capital, but the state went on forever, and its secret intelligence agencies were also eternal. At the level of state and local government in Australia, official security is no more intrusive than in community and commercial life, but in the national capital, someone like myself, flying in from outside to work closely with a minister in a sensitive portfolio, could immediately feel the difference. The state and its mysterious agencies was – and still is – Canberra's industry. Parliament captures the headlines when it is sitting, but its roots are country-wide, out in the electorates.

The state in secular iconography is as mysterious as the Holy Ghost in Christian theology. For some it is an abstract idea lacking an actual presence; for others it is a dominant reality. For some it is the culmination of centuries of human progress; for others it is the source of tyranny. It is neither the government nor the nation, hovering over both of them, functionally a set of institutions, including the bureaucracy, the legal system and the forces of law and order. But to say it is a set of institutions does not convey its essence, its mysterious power. It is sovereignty, an inheritance from a distant past, that gives the state its peculiar status in law, its political potency and its obdurate sensitivity. *L'etat, c'est moi*, attributed to Louis XIV of France, provides the essence of the idea. The sovereign had personal authority as head of state, backed by the legal maxim that the Crown could do no wrong. The modern state emerged as a link in a chain of absolutism, as the more absolute a ruler became the more he or she depended on military, bureaucratic and legal support. The global system of states is based on this notion of inviolate sovereignty, and from it comes two stubborn pretensions: non-interference in its internal affairs and the right to do whatever is necessary to protect and promote its territory and its interests in the wider world. They are enshrined in the rhetoric of honour, duty, patriotism and the sacred earth of the father or mother land.

In the pursuit of what it calls "plausible deniability", the state infiltrates its own and other societies. It punishes secret and illegal activities undertaken by its own citizens within its own territory, but it mounts just such clandestine operations on its own behalf, which it piously declares it is entrusted neither to confirm nor deny. Justification, if or when it emerges, is clouded by mythology and the arbitrary and sometimes inexplicable fears and designs of *raison d'etat*. Two kinds of justifications usually emerge from the thicket behind which the secret state operates.

One relies on the anarchic nature of international politics. Espionage is justified in an imperfect world as a form of self-protection. The absence of an international society capable of establishing rules for everyone – the weakness of international law and the lack of agencies to enforce what law exists – makes it incumbent on the state to protect itself by all means at its disposal. The other justification rests on "time immemorial". The second oldest profession, like the first, has always been part of human society and always will be. Spying and prostitution are persistent themes in all civilisations and therefore of art and history. Both professions have a reputation for seedy excitement, which makes them attractive to journalists and novelists and keeps them in the public eye. The practitioners know that their societies are morally and often legally ambivalent about what they are doing but they can claim the human right of responding to need. There is a demand for the service, which creates the supply.

While these responses contain worldly wisdom, they do not meet the rising demand for governments to be more accountable for what they do in the name of the sovereign state. Using the powers of the state and acting on its behalf, agents are persistent violators of human rights. Much of the abuse (torture in particular) is carried out in secret. Sometimes, official activity that is shielded from scrutiny acts to safeguard a government, or leading members of it, not the state or the nation or the people. Even if action is genuinely in the national interest, there is a view that abusing human rights is injurious to both state and people. It injures the state because it is an inhuman and demeaning practice done in the name of the state. It injures the people because no one is safe from it: "the bell tolls for thee". Governments change, but the practices continue; new individuals and groups suffer.

In the case of Augusto Pinochet's Chile, or the apartheid regimes in South Africa, state policies against opponents could not have been carried out without the participation of the intelligence agencies in murder and torture. In the cases of several African heads of state and, notably, former president Marcos of the Philippines and former president Suharto of Indonesia, it is difficult to imagine how they could have accumulated so much private wealth and used the police and the military to destabilise their political opponents and stifle dissent without the active support of the intelligence agencies. A spectacular example of intrusion into the private lives of political opponents was revealed in 2000 in Peru, when 2300 video tapes were released by a disgruntled head of state security showing the elite of Peruvian society, especially politicians, business leaders, editors and military chiefs caught in extra-marital affairs and financial graft, visiting brothels and taking drugs. The tapes were used to blackmail the subjects into supporting the former president, Alberto Fujimori, who later resigned and fled to exile in Japan.

Espionage is pervasive, blurring the integrity of other work. Journalists are often suspected of espionage. In April 1999 two CARE Australia staff working in Kosovo were arrested. CARE Australia and the Australian government described official Yugoslav statements that they were spies as utterly without foundation, even "preposterous". The denial fell foul of the politically charged atmosphere in Belgrade as it mounted a campaign against NATO's bombing. The aid workers became pawns in a grim struggle, although they were eventually released. An account of their detention, beatings and the extraction of a false confession (Steve Pratt, *Duty of Care*, 2000) is a reminder of how, even when in a relatively mild mood, the secret state works. At the same time, the leader of an Australian aid team working from 1996 to February 1999 on water salination in East Timor said it had been made clear to him that he was expected to report on security matters to the Australian embassy in Jakarta. The Australian official response was that it was only natural that Australian aid workers in a foreign country should discuss security on the ground with the Australian embassy. So it is, and it is only natural that Indonesian intelligence should be suspicious of such communication.

Because its trade is secrets rather than thoughtful or reasoned analysis, espionage has more influence with policy makers than it deserves. As anyone who has worked in government knows, the value of secrecy is over-rated. In my work with Gareth Evans I had access to a daily digest of security information, much of it in classifications at the level of Top Secret and above. It rarely contained anything not already known from the public media, books and academic journals. A vast industry of fairly ordinary quality is given undue importance by being restricted in ever-decreasing circles to those few who are entitled to know.

The American scholar-diplomat George Kennan distinguished between intelligence and "clandestine operations" in foreign countries, the former being acceptable to him, the latter not. As one of those who, at the time, favoured the decision to set up such facilities, he wrote in the journal *Foreign Affairs*, in 1985: "The effort to conduct them involves dilemmas and situations of moral ambiguity in which the American statesman is deprived of principled guidance and loses a sense of what is fitting and what is not. Excessive secrecy, duplicity and clandestine skull duggery are simply not our dish – not only because we are incapable of keeping a secret anyway – but, more importantly, because such operations conflict with our own traditional standards and compromise our diplomacy in other areas."

In a private letter to Senator Patrick Moynihan in 1997 (quoted in D.P. Moynihan, *Secrecy: The American Experience*, 1988), Kennan said: "I would say that something upwards of 95 percent of what we need to know about foreign countries could be very well obtained by the careful and competent study of perfectly legitimate sources of information ... There may still be areas, very small areas really, in which there is a real need to penetrate someone else's curtain of secrecy. All right ... But ... maintain(ing) spies on the adversary's territory ... We easily become ourselves the sufferers from these methods of deception. For they inculcate in their authors, as well as their intended victims, unlimited cynicism, causing them to lose all realistic understanding of the relationship, in what they are doing, of ends and means."

Moynihan, my former colleague in New Delhi, created a wave of consternation in intelligence circles with the publication of his book calling for an end to the culture of secrecy in the United States government (and transferring the activities of the CIA to the State Department). As an anti-communist liberal and for eight years (1977–85) a member of the Senate Select Committee on Intelligence (the last four years as vice-chairman), his opinion could not be dismissed as ideological or uninformed. He did not call for an end to secret intelligence, only to the culture or cult of secrecy. His argument was robustly American. Secrecy was not in the United States national interest. It over-rated adversaries and protected inefficiency. Openness was an American comparative advantage, Americans were winners. Secrecy was for losers, for people who did not have the capacity to produce, and could not appreciate the importance of, real information.

Despite these seasoned and sensible opinions, the secret state becomes stronger. The Second World War ends but the secret state grows because of the Cold War. The Cold War ends, but the secret state is still needed, not now to organise the penetration of communist or anti-communist states and the theft of their secrets, but to obtain financial and other market data, information on drug trafficking, refugee flows, water resources, even environmental degradation and over-population – anything seen as a threat to the state. In some countries, the Internet has become a threat to the state. Then came 11 September 2001, undetected by the American intelligence agencies, who were rewarded with more money, more personnel and more power. In 2002 the Australian Parliament gave ASIO more powers to question people about suspected terrorist activity. And since then the activity and authority of Australia's secret agencies has grown.

State morality is different from individual morality. Individuals may sacrifice their interests, even their lives, for the greater good, but the state claims the moral imperative of survival and from this flows much that is immoral and inhuman. As human beings make the decisions on behalf of the state, how do they distinguish between morality that applies to them as individuals and morality that applies to them as servants of the state?

12

THE CONTEMPORARY WORLD

We are standing in a deserted street in a small village outside Knin in Croatia. An elderly man shuffles in eddies of dust along a side track. He is stooped, his legs are stiff, his broken boots are bound with twine. "I can't bear it," my companion says, and goes over to him, taking his elbow, helping him along. He leads us to a pillaged house, where a Canadian relative, who had arrived a few days earlier on a rescue mission, is preparing a meal. Only seven are left, she tells us, of a Serbian community of hundreds. She points across a creek to a trestle shaded by tarpaulin attached to a tree, then to shattered glass and a window repaired with newspapers and bandaids.

"They come there in the afternoon to drink. They all have guns. After a few noggins of courage, they shoot at anything that moves. If nothing moves, they shoot anyway. People say it's the Americans, who are supporting the Croatians. I think they're just young bloods who want to have fun." She shrugs her shoulders. She is too scared to go into the garden, which has fruit and vegetables but is exposed.

She takes us to other houses in the street. They have been ransacked, either by invaders or departing occupiers in a hurry. Floors are strewn with mattresses, curtains, broken furniture and rotting food. At each house, the old man breaks down in tears. He cannot take his eyes from my companion, Indonesian journalist Ratih Hardjono. His eyes follow her, his mouth slightly open, as if he needs air to cope with the excitement of an apparition. When we leave, he drops on one knee and raises his hands to her.

We drive down the coast road from Split to Dubrovnik, then back again, with a detour to Mostar, where I had wanted to see the bridge of medieval Turkish workmanship, a slender arch between two towers, as described by Rebecca West in her book *Black Lamb and Grey Falcon*, but we could not get near it. There were Muslim funeral processions everywhere, burials on the banks of the river. In any case, the bridge had been destroyed.

Mostar had come under artillery fire and the inner city was in ruins, people living among debris and girders, dogs scavenging empty cans. Make-shift shops sprang up everywhere, sometimes nothing more than a few packets of cigarettes or tinned food on an upturned box or some items of clothing and kitchen ware in the crevice of a building. The faces of the people are tight with despair and anger. It is like a scene from a black-and-white film, grainy and authentic. We drink plum wine and eat boiled eggs decorated with hundreds-and-thousands in the only surviving café.

We had started our journey in Salzburg, where Rebecca West had started and where Ratih was attending a seminar on the influence of international media. With some others from the seminar, we travelled by train to Vienna. In our compartment was a young Bulgarian woman who was studying at a private college in Vienna (fees $25,000 a year). She was tense, because she was going to be late for class, having missed an earlier train. She was particularly tense because she was convinced that children from wealthy Russian "mafioso" were queuing to get places at her college and would take her place if somehow she continued to fail to get an earlier train from Salzburg to Vienna on Monday mornings. She told scornful stories of the "nouveaux riches", dripping with jewellery and furs and other insignia of bad taste, clapping and cheering indiscriminately at the opera, buying up real estate and cars and generally making living in Vienna intolerably expensive.

To get to Belgrade from Croatia we had to travel by train through Hungary, with several stops for lengthy examinations of identity and travel documents. We arrived at the central railway station late at night and tired, to be surrounded by murky figures demanding foreign currency, offering to carry baggage and engage taxis. It was like a scene from Orwell's *1984*. In Belgrade, we met writers associated with the magazine *Vreme* who despised ethnic-cleansing but were powerless against the politicians who played the ethnic card and were popular for doing so. According to them, Milosevic and Tudjman were weak leaders seeking some way of maintaining power as the communist regime of the former Yugoslavia collapsed.

In old Belgrade, there is a high stone wall with one large black painted arrow pointing from the left and another large black painted arrow pointing from the right and in between, in small letters, "visas". Much of my time in Belgrade was spent on visits to the high stone wall, getting a Hungarian visa so that I could return to Zagreb. I had used my single entry visa getting to Belgrade.

You push a button in the wall and, if you listen intently, you can hear a bell ringing. No response. You push the button again. No response. Angrily, you push and push relentlessly and a door is suddenly opened. Inside is a small room crowded with people, most of them smoking. In the corner of the room is a grilled window with a red, velvet curtain, which is drawn at the end of each encounter.

When my turn comes, I discover on the other side of the curtain six people in a tiny space with microphones which they use to communicate with people in the outer room. On a desk with a strong lamp are piles of what are apparently visa application forms, of which I am given a handful.

"Fifty DM." I only had US dollars and was sent off to get local currency. One bank told me that because of economic sanctions they were not permitted to deal in foreign currency. Another would buy local currency but not sell it. The only way was the black market. When I returned to the high stone wall with the black arrows, I had prepared some thoughts on the quality of the sovereign Hungarian state for the young lady behind the grill with the velvet curtain, but they remained in my head. When the door was eventually opened in response to my persistent pressing of the bell, I was told the visa section of the embassy closed at 11 am.

Ratih was heading for Sarajevo, but it was under siege and she was held up waiting for a United Nations pass. We said goodbye in Zagreb's botanical gardens, with a taxi waiting to take me to the airport.

"Be careful. The snipers are still active. Stay indoors."

She, who was scared of violence on the screen, laughed away my fears. "I've been issued with a bullet proof vest. The television people asked for them. Makes them look brave. I won't need it."

We parted on a still, summery morning. As we walked away from each other, we turned every few metres and waved down a corridor of trees. She blew kisses. The night before we had talked about Sarajevo's role in the violence of the 20th century. I gave her a note I had written, based on Rebecca West's book. I felt, while writing the note, that the 20th century was coming to an end in much the same haphazard fashion it had begun.

See if the old town hall is still standing. By the time the Austrian Archduke, Franz Ferdinand, reached it, there had already been an assassination attempt. A bomb had been thrown at his entourage earlier that day, wounding his aide-de-camp. He seems to have been outraged by this, not frightened. He was described as "red and choking with rage" when he arrived at the town hall and he interrupted the welcoming speech, pointing out, in a threatening manner, that his reception so far had not been friendly. This was June 28, 1914, a day of holy mourning for the Serbs, combining the feast day of St Vitus and the anniversary of the battle of Kosovo in 1389, which the Serbs lost to the Turks, beginning five centuries under the Ottoman empire. West writes that Bosnia at the time was a seething mass of revolutionary and terrorist groups. Why Vienna chose that day above all for the visit remains a mystery, unless it was intended to mock the Serbs' new found freedom from Turkish rule. The Hapsburgs were reminding them by the archduke's visit that while they might have freed themselves from the Turks, they were still under Austria's control.

Anyway, at the town hall Ferdinand decided to visit the hospital where his aide had been taken. The royal party would follow the published route only for a few hundred yards along what West describes as 'the quay' (presumably running alongside a river – I do not know Sarajevo) to the second bridge, then instead of turning right to the main shopping centre, they would proceed directly along the quay to the hospital. But when they came to the second bridge, the lead car, containing the deputy mayor and other officials, turned right, because they had not been informed of the change of plan. The chauffeur of the royal car, who had been informed, was puzzled and momentarily halted the car in confusion. He did so right in front of a young Bosnian Serb, Gavrilo Princip, who was a member of the same group that had thrown the bomb earlier. He had failed to get a sighting on the archduke with his revolver on the earlier occasion and had come back for a second attempt! As the royal automobile came to a halt in front of him, he must have thought that the God of Orthodox Christians and Serbian nationalists was at last in command of the world. Anyway, he shot the archduke dead – and his wife, Sophia, accidentally, as well.

And so, as they say in the history books, began the First World War. According to West, you should be able to find a small black tablet on the spot (although, she says, it is placed so high above street-level that the casual passer-by might not notice it). It says "Here, in this historical place, Gavrilo Princip was the initiator of liberty, on the day of St Vitus, the 28th of June, 1914." A modest statement in the circumstances. I don't know what language is used – West quotes it in English. I wonder what the theme of your article will be. The contingency of history? Or the inevitability of fate? In any case, I hope this note will be of some help.

Later, at the Hotel Pera Palas in Istanbul, Ratih talked about Sarajevo, which she later recounted in a series of articles which were about neither the contingency of history nor the inevitability of fate. She built her account around a Muslim boy and a Christian girl who were forced apart by the war and the hostility of their families. They arranged a clandestine meeting on her side in a section of the divided city; he was killed crossing a disputed street.

Two weeks in Croatia, Bosnia and Serbia in 1992 was a disturbing experience. Although Yugoslavia had been an artificial creation, after a long experience of war and religious conflict, it seemed to be working. From 1918, it had brought together Serbs, Croats, Slovenes, Bosnians, Macedonians and sizeable populations of Germans, Hungarians, Albanians, Muslims and Jews. After 1948, when it was expelled by Moscow from the Cominform, it became known for the slogan of "national communism" and for industrial innovation, such as workers' councils, self-management and a constitutional tendency to decentralisation. It patched up its relations with Moscow and, non-aligned in the Cold War, established good relations with countries like India and Indonesia.

After Tito's death in 1980 (he was a Croatian), the Serbian communists and their new leader, Milosevic, began campaigning against the federal system and when the Cold War ended Yugoslavia was already in the middle of a constitutional crisis. Even so, the United Nations was ill-prepared to deal with the human crisis that rapidly developed. The UN declared Srebrenica to be a "safe haven" under its protection, but could not prevent Serbian forces under General Ratko Mladic from invading the besieged enclave and massacring some 6000 Muslim men and boys.

Because Ratih was Indonesian, we kept turning over the similarities and differences between the situations of Indonesia and Yugoslavia. Both had been non-aligned in the Cold War, emerging intact. Now, Yugoslavia, once a federation of six republics, was disintegrating. One reason was that its neighbours, led by Germany, were quick to give formal recognition to seceding republics. Yugoslavia had successfully maintained its hard-won neutrality during the Cold War, but at the cost of developing a regional network. Indonesia had been active in establishing the Association of South-East Asian Nations (ASEAN), which provided a cushioning effect on outside intervention. Indonesia might have thought that ASEAN, and a close security relationship with Australia, would keep East Timor safe, which proved to be wrong, because the Indonesian military and, after the independence vote of 1999, the pro-Indonesian militia backed by the Indonesian military, in East Timor were reckless and brutal. East Timor, as a colony of Portugal, not the Netherlands, was always a special case.

But ASEAN had been useful to Indonesia in containing independence movements in Aceh and West Irian (Papua). If Indonesia had neighbours prepared to meddle in these volatile and resource-rich provinces by recognising breakaway regimes, its dismemberment would have been as likely as Yugoslavia's. With thousands of islands and straddling the Pacific and Indian oceans, it was even a more likely prospect. Or, if Yugoslavia had had an ASEAN-type arrangement with its neighbours, its bloody break up would not have occurred or, at least, would not have run its full course.

In 1994, Ratih was spending a year at Harvard and, on a visit to the US, I joined her on a trip to Cuba. We went as tourists to see the emerald sea, the Spanish terraces of old Havana, Hemingway's house and haunts and for a glimpse of the ordinary Cuban people. We put politics aside, talked to no officials, gathered no statistics. Yet history is so strong in Cuba and the people you meet in the ordinary way so self-aware that you cannot stop thinking politically. I used this visit to Cuba as material for a short story, which was published in *Quadrant*.

You stroll down promenades like Paseo de Marti in the shade of its bountiful trees, stay at the Inglaterra Hotel, with its coloured glass windows, tiled walls and floors, high, decorated ceilings, eat at the La Bodeguita del Medio, the Café Paris and in somewhat isolated splendour on the ninth floor of the Hotel Seville, swim in the startlingly light blue sea at Veradero, and all the time in your mind is a question: can Castro hold on and provide an alternative to the all-American model of free market capitalism and multi-party electoral democracy?

It would seem impossible for this small island to continue to defy the will of the great United States – and not just the will of the US but the mood of the rest of the Americas. The US has won the Cold War. Cuba's great protector and provider, the Soviet Union, is in ruins.

You visit churches and former convents, now being restored by UNESCO (as is much of old Havana, piece by piece), the museum of the revolution, with the original yacht *Granma* on which Castro sailed from Mexico to begin his military campaign against Batista, and an aircraft used to quell the US invasion at the Bay of Pigs, and you wonder how long it will take for the US to see Cuba the way the rest of the world sees Cuba.

The behaviour of neither side inspires confidence in reconciliation. Castro has an instinct for bravado. When he took over in 1959, he was treated at first like a hero in the US, but he declared he had been a secret communist (was this true and, if so, why declare it?), provoked the Cuban missile crisis (did he provoke Khrushchev or the other way around?), put Cuban troops into Angola in a display of solidarity with the Russians, giving the impression that Cuba had lost all sense of perspective.

On the US side, victory in the Cold War had confirmed the view that a communist state in Central and South America was doomed. And there was an additional problem for any US president, like Clinton, who might like to remove the embargo on economic activity with Cuba – the wealthy and politically influential Cuban exiles in Florida. Also, there was little incentive for US business in Cuba. The place was so run down, the infrastructure so poor, that investment was unappealing. The US was therefore likely to wait to see the end of Castro until a reformer, a Cuban Gorbachev or Deng Xiaopeng, emerged, with whom they could deal.

So we resumed our encounter with the ordinary people of Cuba. We decided that they were what made Cuba seem different. You felt physically safe in Cuba. You were pestered by children asking for money and by prostitutes, some of whom were little more than children themselves, but nothing compared with what you experienced in many poor countries, or even Moscow. What you had in Cuba was rare in today's turbulent world – an orderly, community-conscious, hard-working and patriotic people. Cubans were old-fashioned, down at heel but dignified, not screaming for revenge, not killing themselves with drugs or AIDS or gambling or guns, believers in progress but not messianic, a bit cynical about government, fed up with rationing and hostile to the United States, sad about the collapse of the Soviet Union, but still part of that stream of human purpose that believed there was more to life than the commercial bottom line.

We went together to South Africa for a meeting of the Truth and Reconciliation Commission. In Port Elizabeth, after a day at hearings, we visited the police station where Steve Biko had died in custody, walked along a grassy embankment overlooking a sports ground, where Australia's Test cricketers had played. We stayed at a bed-and-breakfast, with white-quilted beds and egg-and-bacon breakfasts and were like students, endlessly discussing the pros and cons of the truth and reconciliation process.

She liked its honesty: if your motive for the crime was political and you confessed, you were given amnesty. The decks were cleared, terrible wrongs were acknowledged, the relatives of those tortured and killed now knew what had happened and could grieve realistically, the state was exposed as torturer and murderer, which was a salutary reminder of what it could become in unscrupulous hands. In the judicial process, by contrast, guilt was more often than not denied, the truth rarely established to everyone's satisfaction, the state protected by claims of confidentiality and security, friends and family of victims often left in emotional limbo. And in time – a couple of years, a decade, half a century – the guilty become martyrs.

I tested her. Yes, truth was important and the adversarial legal process rarely uncovered it. But justice was as important as truth, less profound perhaps but socially powerful. Truth might set you free, but people wanted order as much as they wanted freedom, perhaps more. They did not associate order with truth, but they did associate it with justice. Punishing wrong-doers satisfied a public need for moral standards and orderly behaviour. It also met a human desire for revenge – not a virtue, true – but deeply felt.

I argued that the South African situation was unique, because the society was undergoing a revolution, in which both sides still believed they were right. If Indonesia had a truth and reconciliation commission, would not the guilty remain untouched? The military, government ministers and senior bureaucrats, the president and his family, business leaders – they didn't do the dirty work. They paid someone to do it. You would never be able to trace a command to any of the real culprits. The deeds were by underlings, the word was by mouth, the money was in cash, delivered in brown paper bags by couriers who half the time did not know what was in the bags or why they were delivering them. Obedience to authority and a reluctance to accept responsibility were such ingrained attributes that the truth and reconciliation process would not make a dent.

She listened in silence. Indonesia was her country, not mine, and she wanted something that would set her people free. She brushed aside quibbles about truth and justice and liberty and order. What about poverty? So many people all around the world were poor, yet some countries, like the United States and Australia, had more than enough for their own people. In fact, Americans were consuming themselves to death. They were over-weight and they drove everywhere in gas-guzzling cars, polluting the global atmosphere. Why was poverty allowed to continue? She stamped a foot and glared, hands on hips, as if I were deliberately concealing the answer, or was myself the reason.

*

The Department of Foreign Affairs and Trade decided that the world was changing so profoundly that it needed to subject its diplomats to a kind of intellectual boot camp to prepare them for it. A newly formed school of government at Monash University won the tender for a master's degree in diplomacy covering politics, economics and law and for three years from 1995 I was in a team that flew each week from Melbourne to Canberra to teach a class comprised of the annual DFAT intake and young diplomats from neighbouring countries, funded by Australia's foreign aid agency, AusAID. A board of studies, representing DFAT and Monash, was established to run the course and I became chairman. When, on the grounds of cost, the course was terminated in Canberra and transferred to Melbourne, I continued teaching at Monash in the department of management in the faculty of business and economics.

The world we sought to explain to these young diplomats was changing before our eyes. Through the 20th century, the state had grown stronger. Two world wars, the Great Depression and a Cold War that had occupied what was left of the 20th century had concentrated power in the executive arm of the state. Legislative and judicial functions were subjected to the principle that, in the national interest, the executive had primacy. Now, an economic phenomenon known as "globalisation" swept the world, transplanting the capitalist system and contesting the power of the state. The communist model was discredited, the social-democratic model was by-passed and the capitalist model was in vogue everywhere.

A boisterous private sector, trade and commerce, drugs and arms trafficking, refugee flows and a revival of human rights combined in a heady brew to undermine the authority of governments. Some states lost control. The Soviet Union contracted, becoming the Russian Federation, and Yugoslavia broke up. A new phenomenon, the "failed state", arrived. During the Cold War, states were not allowed to fail; they were propped up by their patrons or wedged between contending forces. States were now downsizing like corporations and were sometimes described as "virtual states". Weak governments that were also powerful – weak because they failed to provide leadership to their people but powerful because of their command of police and military forces – were the most unstable.

The Cold War in retrospect seemed reassuringly stable. The two superpowers, the US and the USSR, had developed a rational response to the threat of nuclear war, which both accepted would be catastrophic. In a departure from the military dictum that surprise was an advantage, they told each other what they were doing and developed together what were called "confidence building measures". Now, global power was fragmented and diffused. Terms like hegemony, primacy, sphere of influence and balance-of-power were no longer useful. Power did not behave according to the models with which the world had become familiar since the 1648 Westphalia treaties. The US emerged from the Cold War head and shoulders above the pack, the sole surviving superpower, yet seemed unable in the confusion to confirm its supremacy. Nor did other states combine to balance it in the manner central to realist theory. Not surprisingly, these changes unsettled governments. Power had shaped the political world. Now it seemed to have lost confidence.

Two staples of the West, democracy and capitalism, spread. Democracy was now practised in a majority of the countries of the world and by a majority of the world's people. Its attributes, freedom of speech, religion and association, became part of the emerging contemporary world. Capitalism was even more widespread. Economic competence, backed by new technology, became more highly rated than military power. Countries like China and Vietnam, which did not adopt democracy, accepted capitalism, even if their version retained strong state control.

Human rights, always in the background since the Universal Declaration of Human Rights and in the wings after the Helsinki Accords of 1975, were now thrust to centre stage. The secretary general of the United Nations, Kofi Annan, announced to the General Assembly in September 1999 that the world had now to deal with two forms of sovereignty – the sovereignty of the state and the sovereignty of the individual. In a thoughtful address, he tackled the need to redefine not just "sovereignty", but "national interest", "vital interest" and "common interest", terms that had been used glibly, as if we all understood what they meant.

State sovereignty needed to be redefined, he said: "States are now widely understood to be instruments at the service of their people, and not vice versa." Individual sovereignty, by which he meant the fundamental freedom of each person, was at the core of the UN charter and subsequent international treaties. "When we read the charter today, we are more than ever conscious that its aim is to protect individual human beings, not to protect those who abuse them."

The world – and therefore the UN – could not stand aside when gross and systematic violations of human rights were taking place and the task now was to see that intervention was based on legitimate and universal principles.

The secretary general was foreshadowing the first New World Order of the 21st century. It has a long journey ahead of it on a booby-trapped road, but it is significant that an official of the United Nations, in which the sovereignty of states and the principle of non-intervention in the internal affairs of those states has been strong, should make such a statement. The idea of two sovereignties, individual and state, underlines an important assumption, which is that the relationship of the individual with the state and the relationship of the state with the international system are connected. It is not too extravagant to predict that the ability of the governments and peoples of the world to reconcile these two sovereignties will determine the course of the 21st century.

Interest in human rights revived international humanitarian and criminal law. A campaign developed for a court that could try individuals, not just states (as in the International Court of Justice). The International Criminal Court was established at The Hague in 2002 (with bipartisan support in Australia). Political leaders, once arguably immune as servants of the state, were now prosecuted for war crimes. A new doctrine – "responsibility to protect" – arose, to be applied when a state failed to protect its citizens internally against mass atrocities. Technology was also a game-changer. The internet and its progeny undermined the power of the state, especially the secret state, while, at the same time, the doctrine of dual sovereignty highlighted the difference between state morality and individual morality.

The course we conducted in Canberra and continued later in Melbourne managed to make sense of a confusing world because it had three sturdy staples – government, economics and law – combinations of which offered alternatives to the traditional, state-centred model of foreign policy and also to the utopian, one-world model that remained like a dream in many minds and emerged when wars ended and peace was declared. The course accepted the realities of the nation-state and the profit motive, but not that war was the inevitable outcome of rivalry and competition. The students, young Australian and foreign diplomats, sensed that this was not merely a training course in diplomatic skills; they were being given an opportunity to both understand and change the world into which they would shortly venture. They were a pleasure to teach. The engagement was mutual; teachers gained insight from the instinctive responses of the foreign students in particular. The titles of final research papers in one year gives an indication of the range of work undertaken: 'Redefining the Thin Blue Line: the Political and Legal Evolution of Humanitarian Intervention'; 'The UN Convention on the Rights of the Child and its Application to Bangladesh'; 'The International Criminal Court – Dead in the Water?'; 'Swiss Neutrality'; 'NATO's attack on Kosovo: Assessing its Legality'; 'The New Mercenaries: Private Security Companies'; 'Japan's Northern Islands or Russia's Southern Kuriles?'; 'Will Trade Liberalisation Benefit the South Pacific Region?'; 'The Impact of Confucianism on South Korea's New Economy'; 'After Suharto – Media Relations Between Indonesia and Australia'; 'Public Diplomacy'; 'Globalisation: the Case of Mozambique'; 'Enhancing the UN's Capacity in the Maintenance of International Security'; 'China and the Balance of Power in Asia'; 'A Question of Sovereignty: China's "Push" to the Spratley

Islands'; 'Is Terrorism Justifiable?'; 'Challenges Facing South Africa's Development'; 'The Implications of the Case against Augusto Pinochet'; 'The Proliferation and Control of Biological Weapons'; 'Middle Powers'; 'Australia and Disarmament'; 'The Impact of Islam on International Relations'.

Politicians from both major parties, as well as senior diplomats, were persuaded to address the students. Ratih Hardjono had developed an interest in mercenaries, or private armies, in her work as international correspondent for the Indonesian newspaper *Kompas*; they were finding a role for themselves in a world of failed and lawless states. She gave a talk on the topic. She was also close to the Indonesian Muslim leader, Abdurrahman Wahid, who was to become a presidential candidate (and eventually the Indonesian President) and I was able through her to arrange for him to address the students on a visit to Australia.

I attended the trial of Slobodan Milosevic at The Hague. On one side of the court was the prosecution. Here is a body. Who killed this person? Here are three women who have been raped. Who raped them? Here are hundreds of Moslem men and boys in mass graves. Who shot and buried them? And so on. On the other side of the court was Milosevic, fervent in defence: I was the president; I had to save my country from Muslim terrorists; not just my country but its culture; not just our culture, but civilisation; it was war; in war people get killed, property is destroyed; and so on.

Two different worlds. The world of forensic evidence about the death of a particular person and who should be held responsible. The world of a political leader who uses the power of the state to repel its enemies. The world of human rights and the world of statecraft. It seemed to me, sitting in a room that was more like an office or a television studio than a court, and whose proceedings laboured under the title International Tribunal for the Prosecution of Persons Responsible for Serious Violations of International Humanitarian Law Committed in the Territory of the Former Yugoslavia since 1991, that the task of reconciling these two worlds was going to be a long haul.

Milosevic seemed to be having a good time. I wrote later:

> Surely he cannot be enjoying himself. He has been incarcerated at The Hague for a year already, betrayed by a puppet government at home and is facing, whatever the verdict in his case, a gloomy future. Surely, he must be thinking, make war in haste, repent at leisure. But the energy of politics, especially the politics of revenge, is powerful. He is not fighting for his life (there is no death penalty at The Hague), but he is fighting for himself (and Serbia) as a victim of history. For him, Kosovo is the cradle of Serbian culture, threatened when he was president by terrorists no less dangerous than those who later destroyed the twin towers in New York.

A tram ride away (for a Melburnian, The Hague's trams were a sign of civilisation) is the city square of Delft, with a statue of Hugo Grotius. I paid my respects to the father of international law and wondered if some time in the future a statue would be erected in Melbourne to celebrate a successor. Grotius was, after all, an improbable figure, leading a small, flat piece of European land, locked in battle with the North Sea, to corner the international legal market. In 17th century Holland, his liberal Protestantism was in disfavour. He was imprisoned and made a celebrated escape (in a chest of books), spending most of his life in exile. He was at one time appointed Swedish ambassador to Paris. Grotius believed that social and economic intercourse, especially trade, were the essential ingredients of a sustainable international society, not religion, military power or national identity. Further, it was the regulation by law of the activities of states that would best keep international peace and maintain order. His ideas survived centuries of war and evangelism. In 1899, the first international court to deal with disputes between states was established, the Court of Arbitration, followed by the International Court of Justice in 1913. They are housed in a building in The Hague, portentously described as the Peace Palace, which looks like a cross between a medieval palace and a Harvard college, and was originally financed by the American tycoon Andrew Carnegie. While I was visiting, preparations were under way to accommodate the latest addition to international law, the International Criminal Court.

After visiting Moscow and parts of the old Soviet Union (to test its recovery from defeat in the Cold War), I wanted to visit the home of Anton Chekhov, another toiler in the field of human kindness and goodwill. In Yalta, the warm, moist air reminded me of Lorne. I had found the air of Samarkand and Tashkent dry and enervating. I became thirsty and irritable, unable to write, while in Yalta I immediately drafted the first chapter of a novel. Yalta was considered "aristocratic" before the revolution. It lacked industry and farming and only the rich could escape to such a distant and idyllic place. Intourist had opened it up with new hotels and group bus tours. My impression, strolling on the promenade beside pebbled beach and milky blue water, was that most of the visitors were foreign. German was the most common language.

I went to Chekhov's house, a white dacha in the old part of the town, without a sea view. Was Chekhov, who went to Yalta for health reasons, politically conservative, part of the elite? If he had lived after the revolution, whose side would he have been on? I decided he would have agreed with opening up Yalta but might not have liked the Intourist invasion. He was a medical doctor, forced to acknowledge the game of life and death. His plays and stories appeal to us because they do not take ideology seriously. The rules of ideology, like the rules of organised religion, were too rigid for the game of life and death. In his garden he personally planted trees for every season, but his treatment of the land owner in *The Cherry Orchard* suggested to me that he was not an environmentalist. He would have supported reform, but of the Gorbachev brand, not that of Boris Yeltsin, who was proclaiming that the fight for freedom in the 21st century was being carried out in Russia!

Back in Australia, I had by chance on a visit to Government House in St Georges Terrace, Perth, come across details of the Audrey Jacobs case. In 1925 Ms Jacobs had, in front of hundreds of dancing couples in the ballroom of Government House, shot her former lover and killed him. I had grown up with this case – and another murder, the jigger button case – and it had always intrigued, even excited me that, in a city as staid as Perth, someone as romantic and decisive as Audrey Jacobs had lived. So in *The Budd Family* Little Joanie does an Audrey Jacobs, although, following the more modest homicidal impulse of Lara in *Dr Zhivago*, I allowed her hand to tremble and she only wings her lover. When Geraldine Doogue, who was born in Perth, launched the book in Sydney, I sensed that she identified somewhat with little Joanie – not, I hasten to add, because of her trigger finger but because of her style and her desire to shake the social foundations of the Perth establishment.

I was able to write without interruption for almost three years. In *The Budd Family*, published in 1995, I was responding to a need to return to basics, reacting perhaps to the frantic, open-ended world that seemed to be emerging from the Cold War. In that sense only is the novel autobiographical. Australia was being reinvented almost daily, so I wanted to confirm for myself its abiding quality. I went back to Western Australia because it was where I was born and grew up and because the marginal quality of political life in the west and its resentment of the eastern states seemed to me to represent an element of the Australian story. I went back to the years of depression and war because of their impact on Australia and the world.

The politics of the Budd family reflected vaguely the politics of my own family. The head of the family, Tom Budd, who owns an import-export and trucking business (like the Cadd family), is anti-Labor, but also anti-British and a republican. Clarice, of German background, identifies with the Aborigines and the natural wonder of Australia. Colin, the first child, who is killed in Crete, probably votes Country Party, as it then was. Max, the second son and a teacher, momentarily joins the Communist party. Little Joanie votes Labor.

But the politics of the Budd story was merely incidental. What I wanted to show was a family affected by the depression and then war, both of which had created the Australia we now knew. In the political debate about "family values", not enough thought was given to the effect of the great destroyer of families, war. Old Tom never recovered from the experience of the First World War. Colin's death left a widow Marianne and a young son Joshua. Max and his wife, Lilly, a Jewish refugee from Europe, learned how to kill and now to wonder whether they should have a family.

It was the first book I wrote using a laptop. The others had all been written in longhand or typewritten. I enjoyed using a computer. It made writing physically much easier. Also, it helped concentration.

There was something compelling about the throbbing little screen. You could not take your eyes off it. But I wondered whether that affected the quality of the writing. It was so easy to produce the words, store and transpose them. The first manuscript of *The Budd Family* was 200,000 words, and had to be substantially cut.

I began work on *A Furious Hunger: America in the 21st Century*, an attempt to explain America to myself, and therefore to Australians. I chose the title from Thomas Wolfe's *Of Time and the River*, which seemed to catch the great, pulsating reality of the United States and the big questions that people like me were asking when we contemplated its power. "All we know is that having everything we yet hold nothing, that feeling the wild song of this great earth upwelling in us we have no word to give it utterance. All we know is that here the passionate enigma of our lives is so bitterly expressed, the furious hunger that so hurts and haunts Americans so desperately felt – that being rich, we are all yet poor, and having an incalculable wealth we have found no way of spending it, that feeling illimitable power we have yet found no way of using it."

I also wrote a third edition of *Indonesia*, which had been first published thirty years before. *Indonesia* was a young man's book, seeing the world as if for the first time. It was difficult to seem to be seeing the subject of it again for the first time. I knew a lot more about Indonesia than when I wrote the first edition. The publishers, Melbourne University Press, suggested, however, that as much as possible of the old book should remain, and this was sensible, both from an intellectual and a marketing point of view. It meant that the Sukarno era, the past that the Suharto successor-regime had been trying to remove from the minds of the public, was still there and that the brash and critical tone of the book would remain, although the author had become more mature.

I received a note from art activist, bookseller and now obituarist Philip Jones, after one of our lunches. "I have been ruminating about what you were saying about various aspects of your life coming together, and linking this to my contention that Australian writers almost ignore a literature which explores what it *feels like* to be an Australian. What our society is in a *personal* sense. You, of course, have written *The Budd Family* on the one hand and also marvellous books on the Australian identity, our place in the world etc. But, although you talk of writing a book about America, you don't mention an autobiography. In Europe or America, a man of your sensibility and achievement would *assume* (as would his friends and intellectual colleagues) it essential to write his autobiography. It would be unthinkable not to do so. Why are we, you, other eminent Australians, so shy about our lives?"

I don't know how I answered Philip, but I had never thought of autobiography. My life always seemed in progress and I had not stopped to think where it was progressing. Who was I to claim attention to myself when so much of importance to us all was happening in the public sphere, especially in the world? His question touched an intellectual issue that is at last being resolved as I write these memoirs. I have tried to deal with this by putting my personal feelings, sometimes disguised, in fiction, but until recently the duty to understand, and even manage, public affairs has had the upper hand. This has allowed me to bypass moments in life that the mind readers in Vienna had described as the male "midlife crisis". I was always too attentive to my country's midlife crisis to be aware of any of my own. The short answer to Philip was that I had been too busy to contemplate my own life.

The wonder world of the internet and digital technology created turmoil in the traditional forms of publishing and journalism. The proliferation of the so-called social media, as well as internet advertising and retailing, put my disagreement with Graham Perkin over his interpretation of "independence" into the perspective of history. Independent commentators, often fresh and incisive, were everywhere, although Walter Lippmann's strictures on "straw men" and the calm logic of John Stuart Mill were blown away in a torrent of brash opinion, fancy speculation and personal abuse.

In Australia, this distilled into a debate about ownership, reflecting Australia's small portion of the global English-language market. Rupert Murdoch had become an American citizen to secure the dominance of News International in that market, while maintaining 70 percent ownership of print media in Australia. For some, quality journalism was a product of diverse ownership, but others thought that journalism could only be of high quality, in the sense of being committed to the public interest rather than the interest of media owners, if journalists were protected by guarantees of editorial independence. Owners, as dominant share-holders, could dominate boards of directors, it was argued, and were entitled to decide senior management appointments, such as chief executive, who in turn could appoint an editor or editor-in-chief, but, from then on, the editorial process should be free of management and divorced from corporate objectives.

This formula followed the general direction established by schools of journalism, especially those associated with universities, which sought to underpin journalism with professional ethics, as other professionals, such as lawyers and doctors, were obliged to accept. It was anathema to old fashioned owners, including Murdoch, the grand master of what he liked to call "disruptive" journalism; business-minded entrepreneurs scoffed at its implications. They argued that diversity was more likely to come from diverse owners pushing their diverse interests than from professionally minded journalists all pursuing the same, politically correct value system.

When the Fairfax group, including the *Sydney Morning Herald*, *The Age* and *The Financial Review*, announced in June 2012 a major restructuring, the debate took a sharp turn because Gina Rinehart, mining billionaire and the largest shareholder in Fairfax, demanded a seat (or several) on the board, but refused to accept a "charter of editorial independence" that had been in place at *The Age* since 1988 and in Fairfax generally since 1992. As the value of Fairfax shares had been declining steadily, it was assumed Mrs Rinehart was buying them in order to enlist Fairfax to protect and promote her mining interests.

*

As a production or demonstration effect, which is often said to be the purpose of terrorism, the spectacular terrorist attack on the United States on 11 September 2001 was brilliant, especially the destruction of the twin towers of the World Trade Centre in New York. Imagery is important; even if we discount intention (it would be surprising if those who planned the event expected that there would be television cameras nearby to catch every moment, or had studied the engineering of the building to know that it would collapse on itself in the way it did, prolonging the agony of the imagery). The event was quickly established by the media as a defining moment in the contemporary world.

It certainly simplified American politics. For the first time since the British sacked Washington DC in 1814, Americans had been attacked on their own soil. Hawaii was legally American when the Japanese attacked in 1941, but it was a distant island in the Pacific, not part of the homeland. Modern Americans, having established supremacy in their hemisphere and having been successful in two hot world wars and a cold one, could have been forgiven for believing they were invulnerable to attack. The president had to act. If he had not seized the moment, he would have been pilloried by the media and possibly impeached by Congress. George W. Bush chose punitive military action in Afghanistan, and in consequence rose from being a controversially elected president without a mandate to being the most popular ever after a year in office, followed by an historic victory for his party in the mid-term elections a year later.

He carried most of the world in varying degrees with him, creating a new dynamic in global politics. The United States took the lead in a series of actions, including a follow-up United Nations rescue mission to revive Afghanistan as a failed state, and a campaign, both within countries and internationally, to deprive terrorists of support, especially financial resources.

All the major powers, and most of the minor ones as well, declared themselves against terrorism. Countries like Russia, China, India and Israel took the hint, declaring that they also needed to respond to terrorist attacks. So the "war against terror" had a positive global response, even though it was obvious that terrorism took many forms, not just the al Qaeda variety masterminded by Osama bin Laden. We need only to think of Ireland, Basque separatism, Palestine, West Papua,

Kashmir, the Kurd minorities in four adjacent countries, the Uighurs in China as well as the Tibetans, to appreciate the range of activity and the political complexities involved. Spectacular events like the Sarin nerve gas attack in the Tokyo subway by the Aum Shinriyko sect in 1995, the destruction of the Oklahoma federal government building with home-made bombs in 1995 and the bombing of the US embassies in Kenya and Tanzania in 1998 indicate the extent and depth of terrorism long before the twin towers were demolished. Shortly after 11 September, Americans were terrified by a series of anthrax attacks, sent in envelopes through the post. There was also cyber terrorism, which could be highly disruptive but not necessarily violent. There was random terrorism which was violent, but without a political objective.

A rise in militant terrorism had occurred after the end of the Cold War – messianic Zionists, underground Christian sects in the United States, radical Hindu and Sikh groups in India, millenarian cults in Europe, North America and Japan. Wanton acts of death and destruction in the pursuit of "evil" – apostates, demons of disorder and other opponents of holy causes – increased. Weapon stocks left over from the Cold War were a factor. A wide range of weaponry became available – not just rifles and machine guns, but land mines, rocket-propelled grenades and shoulder-launched surface to air missiles. Some areas, such as South Asia, were awash with arms after the withdrawal of Russia from Afghanistan. Parts of southern Africa, Cambodia, Russia and eastern Europe were active trading regions. Arms exports to sub-Saharan Africa nearly doubled in 1999 and military expenditure in the region increased 14 percent (while its economic growth rose by less than one percent). The question was seriously raised whether terrorists might resort to weapons of mass destruction. Chemical and biological agents were more easily available, nuclear smuggling from Russia was a persistent concern and the technical expertise was available on the internet or from Russian experts desperate to supplement their incomes.

The focus on Islam stirred evangelical yearnings, recalling the Crusades. Islam's great days had been in feudal times, with its hierarchical political structures and powerful military. Since capitalism defined our modern era, Muslim states, unlike Confucian states, had not prospered. Some were rich, because of natural resources, but their societies were brittle. A high birth rate filled the streets with youth, mostly young men, without prospects. There was a violent quality about the resurgence of Islam, conveyed not just in the destruction of twin towers in New York but in an increase in evangelical Islam, caught in another arresting image, the demolition by the Taliban of the giant 2000-year old Buddha statues in Bamiyan, Afghanistan.

During the Cold War, the non-aligned bloc, including many Arab states, played one side off against the other, keeping the fundamentalists reasonably satisfied or at least wrong-footed. With the end of the Cold War, the Communist bloc ceased to offer an alternative. The West was supreme. And with the surge of capitalism as a global phenomenon, Muslims who were already concerned about the influence of the West became alarmed. With no power model they could manipulate, they decided that the only way to resist the influence of the West was to do it themselves.

To some in the United States, it was the start of another Cold War. But there was an important difference, which is why 11 September 2001, on more careful examination, did not stand as a "defining moment". Terrorism did not have a great power fountainhead. It had cells and mysterious leaders, as communism had, but George

Kennan's idea of containing the Soviet Union – a long slow haul as much moral as military – could not be reproduced, because there was no great power to contain. Then President Bush, under pressure from a group of advisers who regarded containment as too passive a policy for the civilising mission of the United States, made a fatal mistake. He took pre-emptive action, based on false intelligence, to invade Iraq.

His "war on terror", coupled with his "axis of evil" – Iraq, Iran and North Korea – ignored lessons learned from the history of terrorism. Terrorism is a weapon of the weak. Terrorists exist because they are powerless to right some wrong they wish, however improbably, to correct. Terrorism is a clumsy weapon, reached for in desperation. Its strategy is to unbalance its stronger opponent, not to fight but to scare.

Terrorists cannot win, but they can fray the spirit of a society, wear it down. So the history of counter-terrorism has a clear message. Deny terrorists oxygen. Don't give them publicity.

Turning a weak opponent into a fearsome enemy runs contrary to this. Even with advances in technology, the core strategy of terrorism is unchanged. It avoids confrontation, relying on dramatic effect, known as "propaganda of the deed". Adopting a war footing to deal with it, throwing budgets dangerously into deficit, hampering trade and commerce, tampering with long established legal rights, turning fugitive terrorists into ghostly celebrities was counter-productive.

John Howard said during the 2008 US presidential election that al Qaeda was praying that Barack Obama would win, because he was not firmly behind the military commitments in Afghanistan and Iraq. This was a mistake, not just of crude politics but of strategic thinking. The presence of American soldiers in those countries, with the consequent daily incidents and abrasions, was the evidence al Qaeda needed of the evil of American power.

The Australian prime minister happened to be in Washington at the time of the terrorist attack, and he was quick to respond in sympathy with the United States. The political effect bore fruit in elections on 10 November 2001 and in the response to the Bali massacre on 12 October 2002. Most Australians understood the need to respond in Afghanistan, where the attack of 11 September had been planned and the terrorists trained. But when Australia joined the United States to invade Iraq in 2003, the past rose before our startled eyes like an avenging angel. Iraq had nothing to do with 11 September.

It was a war of choice that was costly in money, men and morale and undermined the effort in Afghanistan. After the Australian foreign policy initiatives of the 1990s, it was a return to the old policy of follow the leader, no matter how mistaken the endeavour. I had once playfully described Australia's role, thinking that it had ended, as "spear carrier to the chief". Now we were playing it again, with trumpets sounding.

Iraq became one of those issues, like Vietnam, that haunted anyone who took an interest in foreign policy and defence. It wouldn't go away and it got worse. Like Vietnam, Iraq was an election-winner when the troops first went in. Anyone who opposed the commitment was soft on terror or anti-American, or both. The invasion of Iraq was linked with the invasion of Europe on D Day. The free trade agreement with the US was called the economic equivalent of ANZUS. Condoleeza Rice's alarming metaphor that if we took more time looking for a smoking gun we could find ourselves looking at a mushroom cloud, was repeated as gospel. We were asked to associate the sacrifice of the soldiers sent to Iraq with what their grandfathers and fathers did in Gallipoli, Dunkirk and Kokoda. But we were not ourselves at war. There was no sense of shared sacrifice. Profits soared, stock markets surged, taxes were reduced, unions campaigned for better living conditions, libertarians (indeed liberals) fought for civil liberties, young people worried about education, jobs and getting their foot in the door of real estate.

It provided background for *Fatal Attraction: Reflections on the Alliance with the United States*, written in 2004. I argued: "A combination of American hubris and Australian loyalty has exposed a weakness in our alliance. The Americans under George W. Bush are too entranced with their exceptional virtues and global military reach to pay attention to the voice of a marginal player, and we under John Howard are too concerned with our need for American protection to raise our voice …" The book was launched in Melbourne by the former Liberal Prime Minister, Malcom Fraser, and in Sydney by the former New South Wales Premier, Bob Carr.

In Indonesia next door, a different and more successful form of counter-terrorism was taking place. The Bali bombings in 2002 were of special significance for Australia. Less spectacular than the terrorist attacks on the United States the year before, the symbolism was nevertheless the same. They were both attacks by militant Muslims on emblems of Western power and privilege, in one case the heartland of American capitalism and military supremacy and in the other the affluent tourist who treated the undeveloped world as a playground. Yet our response to Bali was quite different from our response to September 11. The response to Bali was civil, not military. The Indonesian police, with assistance from Australia, brought to court those they suspected of having carried out the bombings, and a lengthy trial followed.

The explosives that ripped apart the Sari Club and nearby Paddy's Bar killed 202 people, including 88 Australians, and wounded 320 others. The Australians killed were mostly pleasure-loving young Australians who had, over a couple of decades, turned the beautifully fragile Hindu-Buddhist island into an extension of their version of the pursuit of happiness. The fact that, when there, they ignored the ancient local culture and romped in bars filled with people like themselves, may say volumes about trans-Arafura Sea understanding, but the circumstances of their deaths brought their families and indeed the Australian people into communion for a moment with the people of Bali. Each day at the court in Denpasar, members of the bereaved Australian families, assisted by the Australian government, came to watch the proceedings.

This was not kill-or-be-killed frontier justice, as in Afghanistan and Iraq, where the crimes of those sought were deemed already to be established. The men accused of the Bali bombing were subjected to the normal procedures of Indonesian law. The Indonesian legal system does not have an international, nor, indeed, domestic reputation for resisting political influence, so it was surprising to find in Bali a hopeful sign of integrity and calm in the counter-terrorist frenzy of what seemed like the rest of the world. Moreover, the Bali trial was only one of several taking place in Indonesia, including that of Abu Bakar Bashir, the leader of the regional terrorist network, Jamaah Islamiah.

It was the police forces of Australia and Indonesia, not the intelligence agencies and the military, that combined resources to sift through the horror of Bali. They worked effectively and with greater transparency than in the past and the result was an increase in confidence between two quite different civil societies.

13

FAMILY AND FRIENDS

In 2012, our daughter Johanna died, after a battle with cancer. Her son and friends spoke about her lovingly at the funeral service. A poem by David was printed in the funeral order of service.

Lorne Beach
At last,
the sea lies calm,
under a lowly,
grey-lit sky.
no longer crashing
with futility
against the shore.
All is melancholy.
The waves still ebb and flow,
addressing sand,
wave-wiped clean.
What one was,
is no more.
And sadness,
like a forgotten ache
when touched,

returns.
Remembering
is all now
No longer to see your cheeky
smile,
your impish charm,
and grace,
except in mind.
So, sister-
Rest.
Rest well.
And
well loved,
know you're missed,
by us.
And we will see you hence –
glimpsed in a crowd,
on a grandchild's face
in the smell of sunlight on line-
dried sheets,
high on the wind,
swooping low and free,
and in the crisp, dry taste of
Chardonnay.
In each,
our own sweet tribute –
a yearning;

to return to you
and you to us.
And standing,
with the water gently lapping at our
feet,
We say goodbye.
Darling girl,
Farewell.

I made the following remarks at a reception afterwards.

It's my privilege to add a few more words to what has been said about Johanna. I will not summarise or editorialise. I can hear her mocking laughter. Rather I have selected some glimpses of her, which you can add to your own collection.

But first, some thank-yous. To those who sent me personal messages, suggesting that of all bereavements that of parent for child is the worst, because of the sense of disorder in the death of a child preceding that of its parents. I thank you for your kindness. I was not myself sensitive to any sequential disorder, however, partly because Johanna's illness had been long and troubling but also because I did not associate her with order. She was, in some ways, timid, and she was conventionally stylish, but she was not especially respectful of the established order. So declining to die according to the natural order was, you might say, in character.

I would like to thank you all for coming here to celebrate her life, especially those friends and family members who spoke at the service. I thank our family, for pulling together at a time of sorrow. Mip, Stacey, Polly, Jack, Jaems, Georgina, Alice, Campbell, David, Anita, Natasha, Lucinda, Susan, Benjamin and Joan. We are what might be called an "open mike" family, in which views and feelings are freely expressed, but we have also learned how to work together.

I was on holiday at Airey's Inlet with David's family when the news came. I stayed on holiday, in a sense, while everyone got to work. The church, the funeral director, the eulogies and readings, the music, the photographs, the order of service, the pall-bearers, flowers and greetings, food and drink. Everyone was engaged. But I'm sure no one will be upset if I single out Susan, whose dedication to her sister throughout a ghastly illness, affecting her throat, tonsils, voice box and tongue, which made it difficult for her both to swallow and to communicate, was magnificent.

I would like to thank John Button's family for making available the house at Sorrento. Jo loved it there, inviting her friends down and spending time on the beach. Last Easter, we rented another house at Sorrento and she cooked an elaborate lamb dinner for the entire family, although she couldn't eat any of it.

Thanks also to Stacey, for producing seemingly without effort and just in time, a grand daughter for Johanna, a great grand daughter for Joan and me. The sight of tiny Polly, dressed up as Father Christmas, giving out our presents, warmed all our hearts, not just Jo's.

Thanks to the Alfred Hospital and, particularly surgeon Peter Thomson for medical attention of a high order. And to the Catholic hospice Bethlehem for their comforting care of Jo in her last hours. And to Christ Church South Yarra for sensitivity in responding to the needs of a religiously challenged family.

Most of all thanks to Johanna herself. She left detailed instructions of what she wanted to happen today. She was never short of an action plan, and it was a great help to those she left behind to have one. We have done our best to follow her instructions to the letter.

And now three glimpses of the "darling girl" of David's poem.

1. From a letter I wrote when Jo was seven and we were living in Hawthorn Grove. I had asked the children to clean up the back lawn.

> Johanna loafed around with the kitten out of sight behind the hedge. The other two piled into the work and when they had finished Jo came sauntering in as if she had done it all herself. I scolded her enough to make her break into tears. Later I got a letter, delivered to me very seriously by James.
>
> "Dear Daddy, You are awful and so is Sue and James. I am going away to the North Pole and I am taking the cat. Johanna."

I commented in the letter. "It all blew over in a few minutes. The other two enjoy Jo when she plays up. They stand back admiringly, as much as to say: What will she do next?"

2. From Patricia Harewood. In her Melbourne days, she and son Michael Shmith, and the three children and me, played in the back garden at Hawthorn, in the Botanic Gardens and on various beaches, especially Red Bluff.

> I loved Johanna dearly, as you know, and, even though I had not seen her for years, she was, and will remain, one of the brightest stars in my memory. All those happy hours Michael and I spent with those three lively children come racing back as I think of her and also the few days she spent with George and me here at Harewood when she and I sat up late into the night talking about those distant days and her life since.
>
> ... the sheer fun we used to have. They swam, dug, climbed (and often fought) with the innocent passion and abandon of childhood and gave me some of the happiest days of my life.

3. And last, from Johanna herself. Just a week or so before she died, I asked her if she would be interested in assisting me with research on letters and family papers for work that I was doing for this book. I sent her A Country Boy.

Morning Dad,

Finished reading Country Boy and thoroughly enjoyed it, even though it took two days to get through it. Could I read more please?

I'd love to help out and do some research/sorting/filing for you (especially those airmail letters) but I can't do anything at present. My energy/health situation is fairly dire, I can barely maintain the strength needed to complete very basic day to day tasks and I seem to have a doc/palliative care/ENT or GP appointment every day.

I'm really sorry Dad as I feel if I were able it would be a very rewarding and interesting time for me. I only wish I was back at Sorrento and feeling as I did.

It looks like Sue and I may move over to Brighton … and stay while you are all in Airey's – I'm looking to get a night nurse in to give Sue a break (two nights with no sleep) and we will have a bit more room.

I want to say you gave me (well all of us) a real gift in Sue – she has been so patient/considerate and determined in her care for me in what has, without any exaggeration, turned out to be the hardest time of our lives.

I'll drop the papers in soon.

Come and visit us.

Love, Jo.

Johanna was responsible for two brown corduroy sofa beds that had arrived at my place under her direction from Morry Schwartz's apartment in Spring Street, which he was vacating.

Morry had established the book publishing company Black Inc. and was a courageous newcomer in the seemingly doomed print media market, about to join Frank Lowy, the Myer family and other

Jewish business philanthropists in the Australian story of capitalism's good works. *The Quarterly Essay* quickly demonstrated that enough Australians had an appetite for detailed analysis of serious issues in the public arena, followed by *The Monthly,* which had intellectual leanings in a magazine format, and, later, *The Saturday Paper,* a one-off, left-wing, non-newspaper commentary that, at the time of writing this memoir, was still finding its feet. Based in Melbourne, his engagement, combined with the activity of The Wheeler Centre, has given Melbourne an intellectual edge over the dominant media city, Sydney.

Georges and Mirka Mora were friends from their salon days at the Paris end of Collins Street, through the controversial issues of the Vietnam War, domestic upheavals and opening of the Tolarno restaurants in East Melbourne and St Kilda. More than anyone, they introduced simple people like me to the stylish intricacies of bohemia. I launched an exhibition of Mirka's work and have several of her drawings. She wrote me letters in charmingly stilted English. Georges had serious political interests, as shown in this letter written while on a holiday in Noumea in 1984.

> *Voila, I have been (at last) reading your The Australian Dilemma ...What I like best is your optimistic and positive attitude about our country's possibilities and future. Yes, indeed, Australia could become a kind of small lighthouse among the nations of the world. A nation intolerant of racial or religious or ideological wars. But tolerant and understanding of its own citizens' beliefs and traditions. It could become a prestigious peace delegate by keeping a self-conscious neutrality and independence. (Have we not talked a lot about this during the Vietnam war?) There is no doubt in my mind that Australia could win enormous prestige and worldwide*

> *admiration if we can succeed to achieve a true multicultural society on this continent – very much as you describe in your book.*

Always sensitive to the interests of business, he added: "All nations (and Australia is no exception) are dependent economically on other nations. But this does not mean we have to take sides with other ideologies and other political systems." And ended with his usual flourish … "Yes, Bruce, let us believe in your unique proposition. Let us call it The Australian Chance!"

Joan's mother Betty eventually came to live with us in Melbourne. At her funeral I offered the following appreciation.

> Some are born great, some achieve greatness and some live in New York. That was the Betty I encountered.
>
> Betty was first and foremost an American. She never quite came to terms with Australia and I feel guilty now, on this occasion, for having been the reason she came here. At a pinch, she might have accepted French citizenship. She liked the French language, and she loved Paris. But she was essentially, quintessentially, an American.
>
> She was born almost at the beginning of the century that was to become the American century. Just a little over half way through it, she lost Sam, her husband and the great love of her life. Then she lost, in a manner of speaking, her two daughters and she ended up transported to the fatal shore.
>
> She reflected the confidence of an America that was modern and financially and industrially powerful and had not yet taken on the mantle of western leadership, with all its ambiguities and sensitivities. She was a product of the melting pot. You went into the pot as a Pole, a Russian or a Swede and you came out an American. You never looked wistfully back. You perhaps kept your religion, but in a form appropriate to being modern and American, someone who drank cocktails and danced the Charleston.

Her house was entirely American, labor-saving devices, maple wood furniture, soft couches, her sporty Chrysler alongside Sam's Cadillac in the driveway. Joan's apartment in Greenwich Village was multicultural by contrast.

She made several trips to Australia before deciding to stay, always flying first class. They knew how to mix drinks in first class.

You would not say Betty was a person of character. She was a person of spirit.

Australia was for her at first a kind of Peter Pan never-never land, full of pirates and mysterious bush creatures. She never quite got the language. It was some years before she fully understood what people were saying.

And the dollar! There was only one greenback. Her eyes would narrow, as if she detected something not quite right when confronted with an Australian dollar.

She was financially independent, which was a relief to her family as she grew older. She was financially independent partly because of Sam but also because, after he died, she worked in the office of another doctor and received from capitalist US each month a social security check which was enough to pay the rent.

In Australia, Betty became a solitary person, creating demands on others, especially Joan, but she was not hard to please. A visit, a drive, a film and especially a meal would bring her quickly to life. As recently as Christmas Day, she was in good spirits, enjoying a lunch of oysters and prawns, fruit salad and ice cream.

She enjoyed her family. She would say, when we drove back from a family occasion: "You have a very nice family." She would emphasise "nice". It was meant as a compliment and I accepted it as such.

I am sorry, Betty, that your final years in Australia were not as fulfilling as your earlier years at the heart of the American century. But you brought something to us which we will not forget. You brought your own style, your own memory and history, and, in your dying, exquisite timing, a reminder that human will power can manage something even as determining as death.

That's not nothing, as they were wont to say in your neck of the woods.

On your 25th wedding anniversary, Sam wrote: "Stick with me, kid, and you'll have this in gold on your 50th."

And so we say farewell to Betty, with words that he no doubt used many times.

"You were quite something, kid."

Philip Jones was an old friend who had moved in and out of my life since the 1950s. He dedicated his memoirs *Art and Life*, published in 2004, to Joan and me "both separately and together", a reference to the fact that we were living apart while still, in a sense, together and, for a while, Philip, who had a flat in St Kilda Road, was equidistant between us. He became an obituarist, contributing regularly to newspapers in Australia and abroad, late in life, after a start as an actor and years of engagement with the modern art movement, arising from his friendship with John and Sunday Reed, who lived at Heidi and founded the art gallery there. A homosexual, he had a warm and generous circle of friends that included many women and conventionally married couples. He had several dogs in his later life, always called Charlie, until the last, Gusto. When he moved from St Kilda Road to a small apartment in the city, you always knew in which bar or café he was by the presence in the doorway of an amiable Labrador.

Philip had not only a remarkable capacity for friendship but a gift of what might be described as "encounter". He gave a lot to his friends, but he also demanded that they explained themselves to him – your feelings, your motives, your understanding of politics and history. He was always "there", like the Charlies on the doorsteps.

It did not surprise me that when my mother-in-law broke her hip on the driveway at Lorne, he was there to call an ambulance. Or that when he was on his way to visit us in Washington, he should happen to meet in a café Joan's sister Margot, then a pianist serving as a waitress. If he were not actually "there", he would need to know about it. When Joan was stricken in Melbourne with meningococcal infection, I rang to tell him, and he records in *Art and Life* that five minutes later, John Button also rang.

Philip died at night in his Melbourne flat on 24 August, 2006. He asked me, in his will, to write his obituary for *The Australian*, which I did.

The Subtle Gifts of Friendship

To write the obituary of a master obituarist is a daunting task and I would not be doing it had he not, in his will, asked me. Philip Douglas Ellerton Jones was born on 14 March 1932 in a Victorian country town, Kerang. He died in his Melbourne flat during the night of 24 August 2006. In between was a life that was always dramatic, always productive and, for his friends, a poignant source of anxiety and delight.

He chuckled over his role as "chronicler of the lives of the recently departed", but it suited him. He had a nose for gossip, a good turn of phrase, a sense of history and the political culture in which people sought achievement and satisfaction. In 2002 he wrote his own obituary in his anecdote-studded memoir "Art & Life". He concluded that he was an affectionate and sentimental man, who lacked "vulgar ambition". He observed shrewdly that this enabled him to grasp opportunities when they presented themselves in a life lacking direction,

One such opportunity was the death in 1995 of Barrett Reid, his lover of 27 years. Philip's obituary of Barrie, his first, was a test of character and skill and he rose to the occasion, displaying the insight and compassion that became his signature as he reinvented himself as an obituarist for the *Australian* and the *Age* and, in London, for the *Times*, *Guardian* and *Telegraph*.

His obituaries were exceptional because he had experienced and learned to appreciate the subtle demands of social and personal responsibility, including friendship. "It can be fairly said that he tried to give more to the world than he took," he wrote of himself. His earlier life had been charmed with good fortune. Through Barrie, then a young poet, he entered the exciting world of Heide, the now famous garden property of John and Sunday Reed in which life and art imitated each other with such audacity, heartache and abundance.

Heide became his spiritual home, John and Sunday his surrogate parents. He was fiercely protective. His nonchalant, worldly manner disguised a serious person whose values, although defiantly godless, were quite traditional, like his boisterous leftwing politics. Part of him remained a boy from the bush with his heart on his sleeve. He was upset ("hopping mad" was his term) at the image of Heide as a hotbed of promiscuity. It was for him a crucible of integrity, both of friendship and of art, and these became the staples of his personal moral code. His public spat with Barry Humphries was partly because he thought Humphries had spurned those who nurtured his early talent and had become a "dreaded expat" and celebrity showman, but also because, like Sidney Nolan, Barry had rejected John ("the broken Reed").

Philip never finished school at Trinity Grammar, leaving for London to become an actor, which he did with some success on stage and radio. Back in Melbourne, he worked as proof-reader, publisher's representative and book-seller. He became part of a lively Melbourne arts scene. He was not, as he said himself, creative, and Heide was not the only show in town, but it was the most influential and he was a worker at the coalface of its version of modernity. He became assistant director of John Reed's failed venture, the Museum of Modern Art and, with assistance from Sunday, established with Neil Hudson the Eastend bookshop, which became a hive of literary activity. He travelled widely at this time both within Australia and internationally, importing books for the first time directly from the United States.

In later years the support system he inherited from his Heide life subsided. His hand-to-mouth existence depressed him. He was in any case prone to panic and anxiety. Disappointments (like the loss to developers of his roomy apartment in St Kilda Road, the theft of Gusto, his much-loved Labrador, the sale of my family house at Lorne, where he had liked to work, and the collapse of a proposed biography of Nolan) weakened him. But his journalism kept him busy. His friendships, many of which he had acquired through others, remained and, as his life narrowed, were now his own. He treasured them and was treasured in return. I do not know of anyone who had more real friends. A few days after his death we discussed how many there might be. We thought more than one hundred, perhaps two hundred. Friends, not acquaintances.

Philip had many loves, but essentially he was in love with life. He learned that the more you embraced it, the more sadness it brought, but if you remained in love with it, the sadness could be managed.

One of his oldest friends discovered his body. I arrived shortly after the police. Philip was reclining in his red velvet Queen Anne chair. His eyes were closed; he might have been sleeping. On a table was a light, elegant meal, barely touched, and a half glass of red wine. In front of him was an untidy kitchen. Behind him, the walls of his small flat were covered with books and paintings.

It was death as still life, a scene waiting to be caught, life imitating art again.[1]

William Ernest (Bill) Purnell died in 2008, after a lifetime devoted to science. He had been a member of the Australian scientific

---

1 Grant, Bruce. 'The Subtle Gifts of Friendship', *The Australian*, 2006. This work has been licensed by Copyright Agency Limited (CAL). Except as permitted by the Copyright Act, you must not re-use this work without the permission of the copyright owner or CAL.

and technical mission to Germany and Austria at the end of the Second World War, which was intended to transfer useful technical knowledge to the allies. In 1946 he was appointed head of science cooperation in the natural sciences department of the United Nations Educational, Scientific and Cultural Organisation in Paris. In 1950 he went to Cairo, covering the area for UNESCO from Turkey to Pakistan, and in 1955 to Jakarta, responsible for South-east Asia. Returning to Australia in 1957, he became head of the newly established Science and Technology Careers Bureau and in 1961 the first executive secretary of the Royal Australian Chemical Institute.

At a memorial service in Melbourne, I mentioned some of his personal traits. He always called me "young fella", even as the difference in our ages narrowed as we grew older. He and Kathryn had a small farm at Dean's Marsh, inland from Lorne, and we were often invited to "stretch your legs." On parting, he always said "Oo-roo", a variation of the old Australian farewell "Toodle-oo".

Bill was knowledgeable in many ways that I was not. He could explain in simple language the difference between the processes of fusion and fission in making a nuclear weapon. He also had an instinctive understanding of international politics, not shaped by the usual indices of power but national characteristics. He was especially confident of the "thought processes" of the Chinese. He liked to contrast the secular and scientific nature of Chinese thinking with the religiosity of Indians and lack of intellectual rigor in Indonesia.

His Australian identity overlapped with his sense of the right way to live. It was from an older Australia that Bill had learned the principles that guided him. Essential to his value system was the "deferred good". It meant living within your means and taking the long view. Living on credit to sustain conspicuous consumption was not the good life he envisaged for himself nor his recipe for a strong Australia. Another inheritance from old Australia was his belief in education as the great social escalator. "He examined the quality of schooling on offer around Melbourne with the same care that he examined the soil," I said. "He gave me advice, tailored for what he thought were the attributes of each child, for every member of my family."

What I admired about Bill was that, as he aged, he remained thoughtful of others and optimistic about human progress. He did not slump in despair, or jump on the apocalyptic bandwagon, proclaiming only the past to have been worthwhile. His life became more and more restricted, especially after Kath died two years earlier, yet he stayed cheerful. The food was always good. The flor fino sherry and blue cheese never lost its taste. The company was always interesting. He was sweet tempered to the end.

When Gough Whitlam died on 20 October 2014, the *Indian Express* asked for a comment. I wrote that, although he had been prime minister for only three years, Whitlam was being celebrated in Australia with an emotion that, in India, would place him somewhere between Jawaharlal Nehru and Mohandas Gandhi. This was unprecedented in Australian political history, owing something to circumstance and something to the man himself.

The circumstance was that Australia had become a nation in slow motion, without the drama of India's struggle against (or America's war with) the British. Independence being handed to us partly explains why we felt it had yet to be won. Outpourings of grief and affection on the Indian or American scale had been reserved for war heroes and sporting celebrities. Political leaders in Australia went to their final resting place hobbled by the suspicions of a partisan political community. The acclaim of one side of politics was often regarded by the other side as evidence of shortcoming: he or she was not one of us.

The man himself was also remarkable. His social background and style seemed to his opponents to suit him for their side of the political divide, but he was proudly partisan: "Australia's conservatives are the Bourbons, if not the Romanoffs, of our time." His self-confidence was legendary, but there was something grand and uplifting in who he was and what he did, so that even his political enemies were impressed.

Whitlam's importance in Australia's search for identity as a nation continued after his death. One reason for the unusual display of feeling was martyrdom. The Dismissal reverberated in Australia's political culture. Perhaps the most powerful piece of oratory in Australian history took place at the memorial service in Sydney Town Hall on 5 November, when Aboriginal leader Noel Pearson paid a soaring tribute. Three short years were enough, he said, for reforms that were unprecedented and unlikely ever to be repeated: "I don't know why someone with this old man's middle class background could carry such a burning conviction that the barriers of class and race of the Australia of his upbringing should be torn down and replaced with the unapologetic principle of equality ... it could be said without a shadow of doubt that he harboured not a bone of racial, ethnic nor gender bias in his entire body".

Others spoke of the Whitlam era as a turning point in their lives, because of changes in education, health, foreign policy and the arts, and also of a more general or personal nature. Whitlam represented a new confidence in Australians. As his speechwriter Graham

Freudenberg reminded those at the memorial service, he wanted to replace the habits and fears of the past with hopes and demands of the future. Only a person of great personal confidence could expect to achieve this, but those who were there knew that it made a difference to the way they saw their own lives. Australia was changed by him and while some conservative leaders tried to return Australia to what it was before Whitlam, they found that time and the Australian temperament had found another future.

*

Joan (dutiful Jewish daughter from New York) and I (boy from the Australian bush) had a long, strong relationship. We were devoted to our family yet demanded from each of us the freedom to live separate lives. We were both dedicated to the virtues of fortitude and social cohesion, staples of the conservative commitment to marriage, but we also valued innovation, individual initiative and personal liberty.

Work, a moral imperative I had adsorbed as a country boy, was always a priority. Whatever the season or the weather, your state of health or mind, there was always work to be done. I had developed the hard core of this experience into a more sophisticated outlook that valued competence and excellence of performance, but accepted leisure and pleasure as mitigation and opportunity for further learning. The other priority was that children were entitled to both material and emotional security.

Before we had our own children, Joan accepted the responsibility of a family with enthusiasm and devotion; her thoughtful and warm attention to every member of the family was a staple of its resilience and unity. For my part, I made it a condition of terms of employment during the years I lived abroad that arrangements were made for the children to be with me as much as possible. Joan endorsed both priorities, although our relationship was essentially an intellectual commitment to reforming the world. It took several years for us to marry. There was no pressure from her to do so. We lived together as foreigners in emotionally neutral Singapore, but, when I was about to return to Australia, Joan had to decide whether to come with me or return to the United States, which is what her mother wanted. If we married, it would be easier to coax her mother to come to Australia. Also, she was now in her thirties and the question of children hovered.

She adopted an Australian perspective, as shown in these poems.

I have noted conversation,
Growing rife within the nation
On Australian coinage names, which we now lack.
I should like to be emphatic:
If we are not astigmatic
We will cast our vote for deener, quid and zack.
For a currency is current
Though some snobs would wish it weren't,
So at this suggestion no-one ought to sneeze.
As we never shall be rid
Of the unit called the quid,
Though we name our money anything we please.
But a more important thought
Which geography has brought
Since I've left Australia, travelling our Near North,

Is that if we're to be Asian
This would be a good occasion
For some new financial sounds to issue forth.
In the East the choice is wide,
Kip, yen, rupee side by side
And the coinages with startling tones abound:
So the Asians may be keener
On the sound of zack and deener
Than the old imperialistic pence and pound.
And the dollar will not do;
Hong Kong has it, Taiwan too
Not to mention our old friend, United States:
And the very sound of dollar,
Might well prove a canine collar
Even if we give the most appealing rates.
But we won't be in a pickle
If we join the bath and tical,
For a currency without old ties is cleaner.
If an Asian role we play,
Then the schilling has to say:
"You're a better coin than I am, Gunga Deener."

Or, more personally, on my birthday, 1963:

In this strange country which you've brought me to
My alien eyes see shapes through different light
Than they have known before. Trees I thought grew
In dreams grow here; the stars I knew at night

No longer shine, and southern winds blow cold.
Sheep graze like shadows on fleece-coloured land
Whose blunted folds are haunted eons old;
In glades where ferns furl taller than I stand
The bell-birds beat their quivering silver gongs
And from the limbs of ghostly flaming gums
Whip-birds cry "crack!" like feathered leather thongs.
But slowly now a cryptic land becomes
Translated as your lips and arms reveal
That this is love's landscape, dreamlike yet real.
Happy Birthday, darling.

Later, Joan was affected by the need to renounce her American citizenship formally in order to be the wife of the Australian High Commissioner in India, but she was a conscientious diplomatic wife, even if depressed at times by the combination of sterility and authority in official life. Our marriage was always shadowed by her self-esteem as a professional woman, which I accepted. It was up to her, in the particular circumstances of her own life and, indeed, of life as she found it in India or later in China, to decide what was appropriate and what was not.

I had met Ratih Hardjono at a conference on Indonesia when Joan was spending an academic year in China. When Joan returned, it became a triangular friendship. Ratih intrigued us both. Her father was a Javanese mystic and her Australian mother, an academic, was Catholic. As a child, she seemed to have been brought up by the family servant, which accounted for some of her favourite sayings, such as "The best place in the entire world is your own bed" and "A plate of rice never did anyone any harm" and "If you've got to wring a chicken's neck, do it quickly." Spiritually and emotionally, she followed her father, not her mother: "You know, spirits in the stones and trees," she would say. Each year she made a pilgrimage with him to Pacitan, a small town on the south coast of Java. At night, they slept by the graves of their ancestors. (Later, they took me with them, but I acknowledged the singularity of their mission by sleeping in a motel). She would watch for the effect the telling of this had on you. "Otherwise I'm just a regular Sydney girl."

At times, when Joan went to Indonesia with Ratih for her sister's wedding, and when they were working together on Ratih's book on Australia, *The White Tribe of Asia*, I felt like a third party. I had no idea how much they told each other about me and was inclined to a sort of fatalistic detachment.

From a letter from Joan to Ratih, written from Lorne:

> *Dear, Thoughtful Ratih,*
>
> *Just a note to tell you how much I appreciated your Valentine phone call … In one sense, Valentine's Day is a vulgar, commercialised "holiday" … in another, it's a formalised and ancient European occasion for expressing affection, acceptable often even to those too shy or constrained to do so otherwise. Unlike pragmatic Australians, I was brought up in the latter tradition and have many early memories of the warmth, opportunities and mysteries of the day. As with many special Indonesian days for you, I imagine, it's important for one's individuality or "soul" or links with one's origins and memories to observe, even if only internally, such occasions. And how satisfying to have someone close to you to share them … Please don't think I'm going "over the top" … This setting and solitude give me the spiritual security to acknowledge your particular emotional delicacy on this, and other, occasions. It*

truly is life enhancing to know you and I draw strength from all our meetings, because you know about life and feelings.

A huge thunderstorm in the middle of last night, with the usual power failure, noted when I tried to see the time. I wondered what to do if the house were struck by lightning and caught fire. But today it's all sunny innocence.

Love, Joan.

At times, Ratih behaved like a street-smart Sydney girl, or, as she occasionally said, a "ratbag feminist", but it became apparent that she wanted her ambiguous relationship with me to be formalised in marriage. She was sensitive to her standing in Indonesia as the daughter of an Australian mother. In the darker recesses of Indonesian identity, she believed, she was not really Indonesian. An affair with an Australian was possible, but she wanted children and the security of marriage for them. I was not interested in marriage. I had worked out a way of life for myself by the time I met Ratih that did not include what was called "falling in love".

Joan created a minor crisis by confiding in Ratih details of an affair she had had while we were in India. Her intention may have been to show that such things can happen without disturbing an established relationship, but it had the opposite effect, fracturing their friendship and making Ratih more determined. Even so, it took years for matters to come to a head. Joan and I had many terse, inconclusive conversations until, on 7 May 1994, she wrote a lengthy note, setting out her position, with rhetorical flair and in honest detail, concluding as follows:

I have been struggling against changing my view of (Ratih), which was as a fascinating and lovely person, full of warmth, energy, creativity and generosity, and interested in me as a person, and perhaps as a kind of friend, or at any rate an aunty for whom she felt affection. I suggested living together; I suggested that you marry her; I have told her that if you have a child and anything happens I would always care for it as a sibling of the other children; I have assured her, at her request, that if anything serious happened to you I would inform her immediately, no matter where she was. The attitude behind these offers (I leave aside the emotional obstacles which I had to overcome to make such offers and mean them) has not been reciprocated. Further, I have discovered, through things you have inadvertently said, that things I have told her in confidence have been repeated to you. And of course I know that anything I say to you is repeated to her. In other words, put crudely, it is a duet vs a solo, certainly not a trio, and I feel, quite reasonably, it seems to me, isolated.

So there it is. I find myself in a situation which is emotionally and physically intolerable. As I said to you, I do not want to live in an environment in which I feel it is the wrong thing to answer my own telephone, or to have my name mentioned. I have to tell you that I will not become invisible, or fade away through grief, or kill myself. I feel a little sorry for you, because I feel you are caught between on the one hand some residual fondness or respect for me, or perhaps just for my relations with the children, which you do not dare express or reveal, partly because you are afraid that I will then sobbingly fling myself on you with unmeetable demands for human affection and support, and partly because of Ratih's reaction; and on the other you need to do whatever Ratih requires of you because of the preciousness of your relationship with her. The problem is, it seems to me, that Ratih wants it all ways: she doesn't want to live with you (yet?), but she also doesn't want me to remain in your environment. I suggested that she put in a separate phone line; perhaps I should go further: shall we sell South Yarra and each get a flat in Melbourne?

In fact, what happened was a version of her final sentence. We had a lengthy discussion, in which Joan said I had to choose, and I accepted, offering to spend the weekend alone at Lorne to make the decision. It was a perfect test of our two personalities. I wanted the freedom to think out for myself how to tell Ratih that her need for marriage and children would have to be met elsewhere. Joan said she didn't intend to "hang around while you make up your mind," and that same day went flat-hunting, discovering an apartment that she liked in St Kilda Road, which she still occupies.

On 3 December 1991 our son David wrote the following letter.

> *Dear Dad,*
>
> *This letter has taken a long time to compose. I've chosen to write to you to let you know how I feel … I have not had the benefit of knowing Ratih long, or well, unlike other members of the family and, perhaps because of this, the discovery has been a little difficult.*
>
> *When Mum told me about your relationship with Ratih, I was very upset. I was upset because something inviolate had been shattered. I felt uncertain about how this left the family, in a way that I never thought I could, or would. I felt, and still do, very sad for Mum, and I cannot express my sincere respect and admiration for what she has done for you, and for the family.*
>
> *I'm also disappointed that you did not share this with us earlier. I understand that you were afraid, and uncertain, of our reaction but, as you have taught me in word and deed, the easiest route is often not the right one.*
>
> *Having said all that, however, there is much that I do understand, not the least of which is the love of an intelligent, beautiful woman. We are, of course, both men and both human.*

I am scared about what this will all mean – to you, to me, our relationship, our friendship. There are many things I want to ask and discuss and I hope we can do this soon.

Please understand that this is difficult for me and I will need some time to digest the change. But please understand that I know it is not a decision you would take lightly and I will therefore assume that you think it to be the right one.

I ask only one favour. Please care for and respect Mum, knowing that she has only spoken the best of you, and asked me to understand.

I love you unreservedly, Dad, although you may doubt it, and I forgive you. Know that I feel for you and wish you well. Would that there were another way, but know that I will support you regardless.

Please call me to talk – dinner, the cricket, whatever.

Dave

I was wary of Ratih's frolicsome personality, which made it difficult for me to know when she wanted to be taken seriously. In addition, we were both so busy and our lives so embedded in rival family obligations (hers in Sydney and Jakarta, mine in Melbourne) that contemplating something as substantial as marriage seemed a formidable undertaking.

Eventually, we reached a three point agreement, two of hers (marriage and children), one of mine (living in Melbourne, where my family was settled). I also agreed to her wish to be married on the first day of spring. Our marriage was, however, short-lived. With my blessing, she left to take part in the Indonesian elections in 1999 to work with the presidential candidate Abdurrahman Wahid. I visited Jakarta during the campaign. We looked at land in Puncak to buy and an architect friend of her father's was to draw up plans for a house. I assumed that when the election was over and if there were a change of government, I would spend half the year in Jakarta. When I came back to Australia I began discussions on whether a think-tank on the cultural, political and religious implications of globalisation might have one leg in Melbourne and one in Jakarta. Then, a month after my visit, she informed me by e-mail that she wished to marry a co-worker on Wahid's campaign and had decided to become a Muslim. I was so surprised that I thought at first it was a clumsy prank. She often used fanciful ideas and extravagant language to stir a response; her favourite words were "stunning" and "gorgeous". But re-reading confirmed a serious and steady tone and content, almost as if written by another hand. I concluded that the intense world of Indonesian politics had created an identity crisis for her, in which I was a liability.

I could not take seriously her intention to convert, if that is the right word, to Islam. Following her father, she was contemptuous of the "Mussies" (and ironical about her mother's Catholicism) and it was her devotion to the old religion of Java, with its worship of nature and spirits, that had fitted sweetly with my secular humanism. I visited Jakarta, hoping that, at least, she might have had second thoughts about Islam. As she often said: "You know me. I get caught up in something and say things I don't mean."

We met on neutral ground, the Hotel Indonesia. The lunch was, as they say in diplomatic circles, a frank exchange of views. She presented her case across the table as if she had been briefed by a lawyer. Her language was studded with "rights" and "interests". Once among the most open-hearted people I had known, who would break into tears at the sight of something beautiful or sad, she was now as emotional as a matrix, as tearless as an empty glass. She was icily determined that her future was with a new man and the Muslim fraternity.

Moreover, her rediscovery of Indonesia could no longer accommodate affection for Australia. She disliked everything Australian, including, apparently, me. She was marginal in Australia, she now said, whereas in Indonesia she was at the centre. As long as I had known her, she had proclaimed the opposite. Australia had allowed her to discover herself as a real person.

I had an emotional meeting with the Indonesian president and his daughter Yenny at the Mandarin hotel. I had met Gus Dur, as he was known affectionately, through Ratih. We had visited him in hospital when he was still thinking about running for the presidency. He told us, and anyone else who was listening, of his difficulties with the presiding mullahs of his Muslim party, who were worried by his political friendship with Sukarno's daughter Megawati. She was Balinese and believed in Hindu-Buddhist deities, like the Sea Goddess. He roared with laughter at the enormity of their concerns, then confided, like a little boy caught in the act, how he had privately placated the Sea Goddess to Megawati's satisfaction.

We became friends. We both had an instinctive understanding of the limits of politics, while sharing a fondness for its democratic delights and obsessions. During the election campaign, he was as insouciant as ever, telling all comers that his chief of staff was the wife of an Australian writer and diplomat, as if this demonstrated what a many-splendoured institution the Indonesian presidency could be. But the independence of East Timor had revived suspicion of Australia. Even Wahid entertained the fancy that Australian interception facilities would be relocated to Timor from the Australian mainland, ribbing me about Australia's "splendid technology". Later, his political opponents in the parliamentary foreign affairs and defence committee seized on Ratih's Australian connections, accusing her of being an Australian spy, bringing about her resignation.

I told him in the Mandarin Hotel that if Ratih really wanted to be a true Muslim she could regard our marriage in a registry office in Sydney as null and void. Gus Dur was sympathetic, but noted shrewdly that he did not wish to be associated with the campaign to introduce sharia law into Indonesia. Back in Australia, I received eventually the following letter from him.

Dear Bruce,

I write this letter on the eve of the Presidential election, which I hope to win. It looks that my opponent would be Megawati Sukarnoputri. It is a very difficult task, since I like her very much as a person. If I beat her in the race, I would like to offer her the job of an opposition leader, since a good democracy needs a good government as well as good opposition leaders.

I don't know when this letter reaches you, since the current situation tends to make my letters late in reaching their destinations. Because of that, if it reaches you late, I would like you to understand the reasons for it.

I was moved very much by our farewell in hotel Mandarin two days ago, and I am moved by the personal tragedy inflicted on you by life at this late time. I know how you do feel about it; and believe me, the same feeling I also felt in the past because of the same reason: something wrong has been done to me. However, life has to continue and we have to accept the sadness in our hearts and accordingly have to rewrite the whole concept of life, except that our life should be dedicated to reach its final dedication: to help other people to reach another phase in life. This means a great deal of sacrifice on our side, but our lives become more satisfactory, and, accordingly, enrich us.

Because of this, I would like to suggest that you part from Ratih in an amicable way, and let her find a new life, happily or not, with Fajrul Falaakh. This thought I share with you and with nobody else (except my daughter Alissa who type this letter). Please don't share this with another person so that I would be able to be satisfied with what I do: to be your friend.

May God bless us together in finding our different targets in life although with the same aim: to make other people happy while we, ourselves, are suffering. Maybe this constitutes spiritually it will be satisfactory, the more so if you can do that alone without anybody else knows about it.

May God bless us and we can meet together in the future in a better understanding about life.

Regards,

Abdurahman Wahid

A strange experience followed when Ratih came to Melbourne to collect her things and supposedly to "talk it over". She spent most of her time in her bedroom reading the Koran and on the telephone to Jakarta, unrecognisable, not only to me, but to some of her Australian friends, one of whom later gave a graphic description of the change. "It was as if she had been captured by a gang and brainwashed."

Ratih returned to live in Indonesia, Joan established a relationship with the former Labor minister, John Button, and the family re-grouped around Joan and me in Melbourne. Our experience is a rebuttal of Tolstoy's remark that all happy families are alike; while every unhappy family is unhappy in its own fashion. Our family has been happy in its own fashion, sustained by two principles, one liberal, one conservative. The first was that, if you love someone, you must trust them to deal with life according to their own resources and values, not yours. Each of us had to find his or her own way in life. The children were encouraged to think for themselves and, as they matured, to plan their own futures.

A small but striking example was the decision by James to change his name to Jaems. He made the decision in his early twenties after he had been studying photography under Paul Cox and was setting off on a career. We all assumed that he wanted a more distinctive name for professional reasons, but I discovered, when I inquired later, that the reason was more personal. He had read an article in *The Age* about an actress who mixed up certain letters in her scripts and could not spell some words unless she closed her eyes and imagined the words in the sky. "I was like that," Jaems told me. When he thought of his name in the sky, it came up as Jaems. So he changed it.

The conservative principle was that, whatever were the needs of adults, the emotional and material security of children came first. This required planning and negotiation to fit in school holidays with my itinerary abroad. Sometimes it was emotionally dramatic. When James was living with us in Washington, he was bitten on the leg by a dog in a park. He mentioned it casually to Joan on returning to our home nearby, but, as an American doctor's daughter, brought up in fear of rabies, she asked the local police to find the dog's owner to check whether it was rabid. She also received medical advice that anti-rabies injections were necessary immediately to be effective.

So James had two painful injections in his stomach before it was discovered that the dog was not rabid.

Now, as this memoir moves toward conclusion, Joan and I live apart, yet thoughtful and attentive to each other and cooperative in the management of a loving, blended family. We enjoy the freedom of living alone and from time to time congratulate ourselves for having worked out a way of life that suits our personalities and meets our needs. There are obvious problems with living alone as age progresses and memories and limbs lose elasticity and authority. When Joan was struck with meningococcal infection, the family was thankful that John Button discovered her quickly.

It was remarkable that our blended family, children, grandchildren and great grandchildren, were all living in, not just Australia, but the same city, Melbourne, which had become not only the world's most liveable city, but also international, appealing to all members of a large family with diverse interests. While my generation had often deserted Australia for more stimulating locations, I was always drawn back, calling Australia home. The children have followed suit, enjoying the reality of the contemporary maxim that local is global. Sue, who seemed to have been born with the instinct to care for others, became a nurse and social worker, including through a stint in Cambodia, and now is roustabout and provider for the entire family. Benjamin seemed at one time to be spending his life abroad as an actor with French-Canadian Robert Lepage's company Ex Machina, but is finding more engagements now in Melbourne as a man of the theatre. Jaems is settled with a family in Melbourne, with frequent travel abroad as director of photography on documentaries. David is busy as partner in a Melbourne law firm, almost daily updater of his Facebook status, and occasional family poet, as with his Father's Day note on the "companionable silence" of a walk we took, with purpose-shaped sticks, retracing my steps to Karlgarin school.

> Shortly,
> Perhaps,
> A thought prevails –
> Articulate and clear.
> Or not.
> It matters little
> On this day in the West
> As son imbibes his Father's time
> Breathes his Father's air,
> And walks his Father's walk
> When he was him.

And to the list of friends, I would add students, research assistants and professional colleagues who became friends after the exigencies of our initial contact had gone: Julie Asker, Khali Challis, Pera Wells, Luci Zhang, Andrew Farran, John Helmer, Geoff Miller and Peter Varghese.

*

I am in a Tai Chi class of ten senior citizens, performing on the lawn beneath a large tree in Fawkner Park under the instruction of Master Han Jin Song. Ten years earlier, staying at the Peace Hotel in Shanghai, I had noticed each morning a similar Tai Chi group on the waterfront and, one morning, a surprising intrusion nearby of a group of elderly Chinese dancing in pairs, male and female, to gramophone music of Viennese waltzes. What might have seemed graceful and old-fashioned was, by contrast with the slow, intricate movements of Tai Chi, dashing and lively, even brash. Such is the indelible signature of culture. The Viennese waltz reflected the end of an empire and was therefore both nostalgic and upbeat (the oom-pa-pa beat, the nostalgia of "After The Ball"). Tai Chi reflects the stability and ordinariness of Chinese civilisation, associated with health, physical survival and well-being. It has gentle reminders of the martial arts.

I have joined the group because, working at home and desk-bound, I have noticed with age joint stiffness and problems of balance. Friends and family recommend pilates and gym and swimming, but Tai Chi presented itself because the classes are held just a few minutes walking distance from where I live and work. Following a heart attack in 1987, I walk regularly on doctor's orders in the Royal Botanic Gardens, also a short walk away, but walking, while good for the heart muscle – and other muscles – does not have the satisfactions of Tai Chi, which are, you realise after a while, mental and emotional as well as physical. It is not strenuous. No equipment is used. The movements have come down to you through thousands of years of trial and error and that is itself reassuring. Learning the movements is a test of memory and performing them is a test of balance and mobility, so mind and body are linked.

When *Who's Who* ask for recreational habits, I say "walking and thinking".

Walking to school prepared me for a lifetime of wondering what was hidden in the landscape as it unfolded. Whenever I moved to another country or another city I tried to find a place near somewhere to walk. I still sometimes find myself walking as if the world around me is revealing itself for the first time. Walking is the right height and pace to keep one both curious and humble.

The staff of Melbourne's Royal Botanic Gardens have got to know me and we sometimes chat. I learned from them where the eels and black swans go when the Ornamental Lake loses water. The resident harpist, Michael Johnson, has played at family birthdays. Occasionally, I encounter a governor, taking a break from duties in the Italianate mansion over the fence, copied from Queen Victoria's residence on the Isle of Wight. One explained that Melbourne's gardens were good for exercise, compared with the flat landscape of Kew gardens in London and others he knew in Europe. He drew my attention to Conan Doyle's description of the undulating landscape of the Melbourne gardens: "I do not know what genius laid them out, but the effect is a succession of the most lovely vistas …"

If you keep your wits about you, a stroll in the botanic gardens can be educational. For a start, it is the *Royal* Botanic Gardens. For republicans, that's the first reality check. You have to accept its vice-regal status as part of our history. You could be forgiven for thinking that every Royal who made a visit to Melbourne planted a tree in the gardens. If you examine the name tags on the shrubs and trees, you realise that the world is a vast nursery, that more annuals and perennials seem to have originated in China than anywhere else and that Latin is still the botanical lingua franca. You realise how lucky Melbourne was to have, from its beginning, two individuals of singular talent, a scientist, Ferdinand von Mueller, and a landscape artist, William Guilfoyle. From their joint contribution, the dual quality of the gardens evolved – a botanical laboratory and a beautiful place.

If you stand on one of the sloping lawns you can witness a turning point in Melbourne's skyline – the Eureka building on Southbank rises above the turret of Government House; the commercial city of concrete and glass, not the imposing mansion in the Italianate style, is dominant. But the gardens remain inviolate. The elders and burghers of Melbourne over the years steadfastly resisted the sticky fingers of commerce, determined to maintain their gardens as public spaces, not only beautiful but free. No admission charge. No extra charge for specials, as when the roses are blooming or the autumn colours are out. Free.

Those who came to the colony of Victoria did their best to make it habitable. They came to a strange land on the other side of the world and, confident that they knew what civilisation was, recreated it on the spot. This is a church. This is a bank. This is a small house and this is a big house. This is a parliament. And this is a public garden. Free and beautiful, at all times of the year.

Of course, what they thought was civilisation was a British, especially English, form of it. Dr Ferdinand (later Baron) von Mueller had differences with Government House and the social elite of Melbourne. They gave scant treatment to the Australian bush that had existed for thousands, maybe millions of years, and the Aboriginal civilisation that had learned to live in it. Still, with all their mistakes and vanities, they left us with something great and precious, and the people of Melbourne have accepted the gift and treasured it.

All these matters come to the surface as I walk in the gardens. And there are other questions. What is valuable in life? Jane Sullivan, *The Age* literary critic, wrote of *The Governor's Moment*, a novella (with illustrations by Diane Masters) I set in the gardens: "(It) poses once more the great philosophical question: how are we to live? It confronts an issue in a world of post-modernism, deconstruction, temporary relationships and suicide bombers: what is now worth dying for?"

Melbourne's botanic garden is both a maze and a labyrinth. You can get lost in it but you can also follow a preordained path from entry to exit. It is a secular space, but its air is spiritual. People adopt a code of behaviour in the gardens that may not be as reverent as in church, synagogue, mosque, temple, museum, art gallery or library, but is markedly different from their behaviour on the beach or at the football or at Federation Square, in the Rod Laver arena or the Myer Music Bowl. They jog and power walk on the tan around the gardens but inside they stroll, pausing to admire (and take photographs of themselves with) a scene or a plant. They don't play games. They don't play loud music. They sometimes sunbathe, in a partial display of flesh, but mostly they sit on the grass or on a bench, read and meditate, look over the waters of the lake, observe the swans, listen to the bellbirds, peer over the side of bridges at eels in the water, or photograph themselves against flowers or vistas. There are certain rules – no bike-riding and roller-skating – but there's very little supervision of public behaviour. You can spread a rug on the grass and have a picnic lunch with a bottle of wine. There's no security staff searching eskies. I have never seen drunkenness in the gardens. There's some cuddling in its recesses and arms encircling waists on its walks, but I have never seen a case of what my grandmother would call "immodest behaviour". Is this because not many people go to the gardens and those who do know the unwritten rules? Or is it that people go to the gardens not just to express themselves but in search of something - the beauty and the solitude that the gardens provide.

I struggled with the ending of *The Governor's Moment*. I had known several governors and some diplomats of my acquaintance had become governors at the end of their careers, as an alternative to appointments in academia or the corporate business world. My governor was an Australian of the old school, practical, patriotic, conventional but not religious, who had discovered, when he stood before a class of young soldiers, that the world had become a confusing place. When it came to the point of reminding them of their legal and moral right to kill, he could not find the words. The profusion of human rights, international humanitarian law and non-state belligerence had robbed the state of its impeccable credentials. I could not leave my governor in limbo, so I turned him into a reluctant hero, affirming the morality of action to save life rather than to take it. That is the effect the gardens have on you. They give you hope as well as pleasure.

I wrote *The Governor's Moment* at first as a short story. I wangled both Conan Doyle and an ex-governor into the story. A former soldier, the governor revisits the gardens and, reviewing his life, wonders why he took the job. He knows that when he dies the obituaries will lead with his period as a governor, yet he regards it now as the least important appointment of his life. But I knew, from my thinking walks, there must be more to tell from anyone who almost lived in the gardens.

So our governor, facing up to the simple question why he had taken the strange job in the big house, has not only to deal with the state of the world, in particular the role of the soldier in maintaining law and order, peace and stability, and with Victorian premiers who wonder why he took the job and whether he will try to do the "Kerr-thing", but also to wonder whether his fellow Melburnians realised how remarkable the gardens were. Of course, they knew: but did they *appreciate* what they knew.

I imagined the fears and desires of four young people to represent our contemporary world. Chloe is a Polish Catholic, with looks and style that are attractive to men. Jason is an idealistic Jewish lawyer who is frustrated by the legal system's obsession with evidence and neglect of the truth. Elizabeth is "old money", contemptuous of, yet fascinated by, the social upheaval created by "new money". Patrick is a theatre director, who yearns for an original Australian culture bridging Europe and Asia, yet gloomily sees himself as an old man, "thin legs in puckered Shakespearian hose, hovering on the fringes of Melbourne's theatre, bowing and scraping to an audience so lethargic that it can barely raise its hands to clap".

I had noticed a gap between generations. Young people were so enthralled with the new technology that they had stopped asking the How and Why questions. They asked instead what used to be called inside-dope questions: What's going on? What's the latest? Everyone was on the lookout for sensation. What kind of political system, including social and economic priorities, law and order, defence and security, might come from a desire for sensation? I wondered how to bridge the divide; history showed that if you don't ask the How and Why questions you are likely to become fodder for those who do – fodder for the battlefield or fodder for the market.

I almost chose a black swan for the cover. The swans are a presence in the gardens, sauntering on the lawns, paddling sedately, landing like parachutists on the lake, accosting young persons their own height. And there's the tantalising lines of Australia's immortal, non-existent poet Ern Malley: "I am still/The black swan of trespass on alien waters". I chose a green sprig instead, although a single bird, looking very relaxed and comfortable, is still there in one of Diane Masters' illustrations.

Ern Malley was a fake, yet something about the black swan of trespass, and other lines from the concocted poems, has entered the literary imagination and will not go away. In 1943, two young Australian poets, James McAuley and Harold Stewart, put together his poems from scraps of paper and inconsequential thoughts, so as to discredit the modern art movement. They invented a sister Ethel (at 40 Dalmar Street Croydon, a Sydney suburb) who nursed the dying Ern and then released his poems to the world. Sidney Nolan was inspired by "The Arabian Tree" to paint his work with the same title. Ern Malley does not exist, but the poems do. Such is the power of art.

I composed an essay "In Defence of Small History" in which the Separation Tree, the William Tell Rest House and Magnet House feature as examples of inconsequential icons which Melbourne's Royal Botanic Gardens has nevertheless striven to preserve. I realised when writing that I was also thinking about Australia, which is as inconsequential now in the world as was the Separation Tree, the William Tell Rest House and Magnet House in their time. But their creators did not think so and the curators of the gardens have preserved that spirit, reminding us that history is a delicate flower, needing constant attention.

While writing the essay, I noticed that the Royal Botanic Gardens had become an ersatz cemetery for garden-lovers, or just lovers. You are not supposed to scatter your ashes there (although it is hard to stop family or friends, if they are secretive about it), but you or they can donate a bench, with a brass plaque on which can be inscribed personal details and simple sentiments. These benches, with their homely grief and wisdom, and flagrant plagiarism, are scattered all over the gardens. One inscription I did not mention in the essay. I preferred to sit on the bench and wonder at the circumstances of the death of Mark Alistair Steenson, at the age of 36. Why had someone, anonymous but presumably the person or persons who donated the bench, chosen the botanical gardens for his memorial? And why did they remember him in such painfully stark prose? He, she or they wrote: "You Were Lost We Could Not Find You," then a second line, "You Were Found But You Had Gone," and a third line, "Love and Peace."

14

STILL ROLLING

The title of this Scene is from *The Myth of Sisyphus* quotation in the foreword: "a blind man eager to see, who knows that the night has no end, he is still on the go. The rock is still rolling." As the writer, like Albert Camus, contemplates his mortal end, the Australian nation, which is also the subject of this memoir, is merely beginning.

There has been a subtle change in perspective from earlier Scenes. What had seemed to be Sisyphean, in the sense of an endless task of getting Australians to accept some responsibility for what happens in the world, especially our part of it, has become merely Herculean, still formidable but no longer futile. The virtues of being responsible have slipped into the consciousness of Australians, while the pleasures of being a lucky outpost of peace and prosperity secured by others, although still the default position of some, has lost authority.

We can trace this evolving sense of nationhood from letters D.H. Lawrence wrote in 1922 from Australia, in which he detected a "rather fascinating indifference, a *physical* indifference, to what we call soul or spirit ... The country has an extraordinary hoary, weird attraction. As you get used to it, it seems so *old*, as if it had missed all this Semite-Egyptian-Indo-European vast era of history, and was coal age, the age of great ferns and mosses. It hasn't got a consciousness – just none – too far back." And: "But for the remains of a fighting

Conscience, I would stay. It is rather like falling out of a picture and finding yourself on the floor, with all the gods and men left behind in the picture."

A year later, in his novel *Kangaroo*, he roamed the Australian bush as poet Richard Lovatt Somers, observing weird dead trees, almost phosphorescent in the moonlight, sensing the "hollow distance" of the Australian outback, wondering at the "night sky that makes a man feel so lonely, alien: with Orion standing on his head in the west, and his sword-belt upside down … and with the Southern Cross insignificantly mixed in with other stars, democratically inconspicuous." Scared and anxious, because everything was so different, Somers ponders the philosophical implications of Nothingness, but, convinced there must be Something, he conjures up for the Australian continent a "terrible ageless watchfulness, waiting for a far-off end."

Somers has an English fear of anarchy and instinct for authority. In Australia, there was neither anarchy nor authority. No one was in charge. No one was in open rebellion. "Demos was here his own master, undisputed, and therefore quite calm about it." Lawrence tries to understand how Australians communicate with each other. "Each one known in silence, reciprocates in silence, and the talk just babbles on, on the surface … Each individual seems to feel himself pledged to put himself aside, to keep himself at least half out of count … But the continual holding of most of himself aside, out of count, makes a man go blank in his withheld self."

Self-conscious Australians have struggled with the identity of the withheld self, glimpsed in narrowed eyes, a flat, nasal accent, riding in the front seat of taxis, grudging service in shops and refusal to tip waiters, resentment of tall poppies and cultivation of a low-life philosophy, "If you can get away with it, give it a go". Artists, writers and aspiring politicians detected nascent nationalism, but their efforts had a dash of bluster. Australia when Lawrence visited was a nation publicly devoted to the institutions, and even the values and manners, of imperial Britain.

Frank Fox (knighted in 1926) celebrated Australia's place in the British empire in his book *Australia* (1910), dismissing talk that it might "fall into the arms of the United States" or "drift into the hazy 'internationalism' of some European countries". The radical, egalitarian Australian style should not be misread as a desire to "cut away from the great privileges of Imperial citizenship". The population was exclusively Anglo-Saxon or (in deference to the Irish) Anglo-Celtic. There was no "servile coloured race, no raw and indigestible mass of foreign immigrants". As though by design, he concluded, there was an opportunity for the "founding of a new all-British nation, destined one day to rival in material prosperity the Motherland whose shrine is at Westminster".

Fox undervalued the nationalist sentiment of the bush ballads and popular culture, as they had no effect on foreign and defence policies. In 1923, Labor brought on a debate in the House of Representatives, moving an amendment to the Address-in-Reply, during which Frank Anstey put the case for a self-reliant Australian defence capacity, arguing that if the Boers in South Africa could defend themselves against the British empire for two years, Australia should be able to do at least as well. The Prime Minister (Stanley Melbourne Bruce) put the traditional view: Australia could not defend itself, the best strategy was to have a voice in London where overall imperial policy was decided. Until Singapore fell in 1942, a succession of Australian prime ministers spoke from the same script. Even later, as the Australian government's support of the British during the Suez crisis in 1956 showed, what the most successful Australian political leader of the time, Robert Gordon Menzies, called the "high instincts" of the imperial connection, prevailed.

Vance and Nettie Palmer were both active in the years between the two world wars imagining a national literature that would express Australia's character. In 1932, in an essay "Talking It Over", Nettie refers to two letters by writers (not named) she was re-reading. Both letters dealt with Australian life as a subject for literature and the point of her essay was to reconcile them. One, from a foreigner who had written stories set in Australia, complained that Australian life was not exciting:

> In this country, the picturesque is lacking: there is no terror, no mystery; the people themselves are not picturesque. A Mexican, an Argentine gaucho, an Arab, each takes a little pride in his saddle or bridle, or in his clothes. Here, the man on his old saddle has nothing photogenic – his trousers pulled half-way up his legs, his socks (if he has any) falling down over his half-laced shoes, never giving him the look of a real horseman. One could make a comparison between the American authors and the Australians who have described the same life of the plains, the bush and the gold-mines. In America the settings are more grandiose, their mountains, forests, rivers; their Redskins are replaced here by a race that, having no history, is interesting from the ethnographic point of view alone. We have not so much as the rifle and the revolver, which for them make by no means negligible accessories ... What I miss in Australian authors is a pathos, an emotion, something to make the heart beat a little faster, something exciting.

Nettie comments: "The writer deplored, in one breath, our life and our expression of it: our life was uninteresting and our books, unfortunately, were sincere enough to express it as it was. If only our life were romantic, or, failing that, if only our novelists were able and willing to apply some cosmetics to its sallow face!"

The other letter expressed a sentiment shared by Australian nationalists, suspicious of imported concepts of drama and romance:

> It seems to me that a story, to be truer than reality (that mirage effected by grouping and selection) should follow natural contours and rhythms. A pulse artificially accelerated, or extraneous outlines because of spurious conventions as to what is really 'action', must be eschewed. The desultory style of pioneer settlements themselves should be suggested, growing up unpretentiously as they did to meet immediate need ... The old pioneer yarns, 'yarned' by the old bush granddads (with, as like as not, a grandma contemptuous of their inconsequences and deviations from original versions) rubbing their tobacco in their palms, and holding up the climax (there mustn't be too much climax) to light and draw, have a charm as characteristic as their environment.

Nettie resolved the differences between the two letters, at least to her own satisfaction: "For all its dissatisfaction with our life and our literature, that letter finding fault with our literature *because* it succeeded, up to a point, in expressing our life, seemed to me a basis of satisfaction, and not the reverse. Everything points the same way, to the assurance that our best way of writing is the quiet, the unemphatic, the simple and sincere."

But a restless world challenged unemphatic Australia. The First World War slid via the Great Depression into the Second World War, which brought about the end of European (including British) colonialism and the beginning of the Cold War. Australia was thrust into an industrial society, turning away from the simplicities of frontier life. A new generation of Australians began to grapple with the mystery of what was lacking in a country that was on the move but seemed uncertain where it was going.

In 1963, in *The Australian Ugliness*, architect and social critic Robin Boyd put it bluntly: "The Australian ugliness begins with fear of reality, denial of the need for the everyday environment to reflect the heart of the human problem, satisfaction with veneer and cosmetic effects. It ends in betrayal of the element of love and a chill near the root of national self-respect." He coined the word "Austerica" to describe a feverish aping of the latest in America and railed against taking bits that caught our eye from the hard-won, creative work of others, which he called Featurism.

Donald Horne in *The Lucky Country* of 1964, and Geoffrey Blainey in *The Tyranny of Distance,* first published in 1966, drew attention to awkward contingencies of history and geography that consigned Australia to the margin. A.A. Phillips discovered a "cultural cringe". The popularity of Horne's book made it especially influential. The first sentence of the last chapter was repeated, in one form or another, by anyone wishing to enter the cultural debate. "Australia is a lucky country run mainly by second-rate people who share its luck."

The magnet of exile was powerful. Australians escaped to London to develop their stifled talents. Later, they went to New York. Some lived creatively in Italy, France, the Greek islands, Japan or Indonesia, but those who succeeded in London or New York were paid particular attention. The English language created quick and understandable connections with these two countries, and political culture, reflected in the media, was also a factor. There was a sense that success in London and New York was more convincing than success anywhere else because those cities represented the authority of Western civilisation. Military power and culture reinforced each other. Our association with Britain had been with the greatest of the European colonial powers. Our association with the United States was with the world's leading superpower.

The men and women who went to London in the 1950s and 60s were aware that the Americans, not the British, had come to our defence when the Japanese threatened, but they still thought of London as the cultural centre of the world. Those who went to New York or to Hollywood later saw themselves not only as escaping from Australia but also from fading British traditions, including the monarchy. They were hard-edged, less sentimental; indeed more like Americans. Americans believed in themselves; whingers were un-American. The Australian businesswoman Jill Ker Conway, in her memoir *Road from Coorain* (1989), was exhilarated by this, which she contrasted with Australian fault-finding and nay-saying.

The expatriates were sometimes brilliant and funny and even at times endearing, but they lacked the daily reminder of living and working in Australia, where it had become emotionally testing for those who stayed behind. Australians were being asked to accept a new protector, who had somewhat the same language but whose inner soul was dark and anguished, lacking the languid finesse of the British. The American model of authority rested, not on a benign constitutional monarchy, trusted forms of parliamentary democracy and the ageless rationalities of class, but on the aspirations of a restless, strident society devoted to commercial success and military power. At the same time, a new generation of Australians were demanding that local creativity and understanding of Asian cultures and histories be the key to Australia's future. The shafts of expatriates, ensconced in other cultures, caught us in poses and disguises that were at times telling, providing uncomplimentary images of us for the rest of the world. Yet we sensed they were caricatures, lacking the authenticity of life as we were now living it. We knew we were not like that, even if we were not yet sure what we were like. This is the way adolescents feel. They don't know who they are but they are sure they are not what their elders and betters say they are.

In 1973, in his study of the "creative spirit" in Australia, Geoffrey Serle detected a faint coming of age, taking his title *From Deserts the Prophets Come* from the last lines of A.D. Hope's poem …

> Hoping, if still from deserts the prophets come,
> Such savage and scarlet as no green hills dare
> Springs in that waste …

Serle agreed there had not yet been much "savage and scarlet", but rejected the idea of a cultural desert, ignoring Hope's biting earlier lines:

> And her five cities, like five teeming sores,
> Each drains her: a vast parasitic robber-state
> Where second-hand Europeans pullulate
> Timidly on the edge of alien shores[2]

I was part of Serle's home-grown "coming of age". For me, the Australian story contained a persistent contradiction: we had underdog values at home and topdog values abroad. We resisted British cultural mythology at home, with dreams of mateship and a republic, but we accepted an imperial view of the world. When Britain's power declined and was replaced for us by that of the United States, we

---

2 Hope, A.D. 'Australia', *Collected Poems, 1930–1970*, Sydney: Angus and Robertson, 1975. By Arrangement with the Licensor, The A.D. Hope Estate, c/- Curtis Brown (Aust) Pty Ltd.

accepted an American world view, turning for local comfort to Judith Wright's reformulation of Australian mateship: "Where the American dream made use of the competitive individualistic element in life, the freedom of any man to become richer and better than his fellows by hard work and emulation, the Australian dream emphasises man's duty to his brother, and man's basic equality, the mutual trust which is the force that makes society cohere."

Whenever I came back to Australia I fell in love again with Judith Wright's version of the Australian dream, but I had spent enough time in the world to know that mutual trust was not the normal condition of relations between states. The world remained blissfully unaware of the Australian dream. It responded to events, as it always had, with the exercise of power, sometimes soft, sometimes hard, including the use of military force. So I set out to fashion an independent foreign policy for Australia based on a resilient defence capability. These needs were briefly addressed during the Whitlam phenomenon and sporadically afterwards but remain largely unmet.

The Australian Dilemma ends with a carefully balanced proposal, anticipating an end to the Cold War.

> Australia must therefore begin the process of adapting to life in its own part of the world in the 21st century. A modest nation, humane, sceptical in the face of ideology, a trading nation committed to rising living standards, a nation devoted to innovation in science and the arts, uninterested in acquisition but devoted unsparingly to its own protection, would have a contribution to make.

The post-Cold War world seemed at first to confirm this, by not behaving according to accepted "realist" principles of statecraft. As noted earlier, the US was head and shoulders above the pack, with as much military power as the other major states combined. A combination of states should have emerged to check its supremacy but global power was diffused, even confused. Economic globalisation transplanted the capitalist system world-wide, followed more doggedly by democracy.

The failures of international peacekeeping in Rwanda, Somalia and Bosnia stimulated fresh thinking on human rights and international law. The International Criminal Court, established at The Hague in 2002, could try individuals, not just states (as in the International Court of Justice), so political leaders could now be prosecuted for war crimes. Technology was another transforming factor. The internet and its progeny undermined the power of the state, especially the secret state. Radical Islam, deprived of the leverage it had on the major Cold War blocs, became assertive, threatening the stability of regimes in the Middle East and northern Africa, and creating a counter-terrorism consensus among the major states.

The global financial crisis of 2008 added to uncertainty, spooking markets and governments, whether left or right, and scaring people around the world. It drained the world's states of their capacity to deal effectively with other challenges, such as climate change. In particular, it weakened leading industrial economies, including the United States and European states. However, states like Russia, China, India, or a combination of them with other rising global players, were still not eager to test US dominance by combining against it. China's growing economic and military power was seen by some analysts as a challenge to the United States, but China did not itself see it that way. Russia behaved at times like a traditional great power, but so far only in respect of recovering territory lost in the Cold War, like Crimea and Ukraine. That new global groupings were not emerging to check the United States was a sign that we may be in transition from one form of global order to another.

Australia was well placed in this exceptional situation. Our economy emerged from the global financial crisis relatively strong and we were not physically threatened. While we shared the values of Western industrial societies, we were also under-developed and shared some of the interests of developing countries. We had, after a baptism of false starts, found a place for ourselves in a diverse and productive region and, as the American imperium faltered and the Asian giants, China and India, rose in our neighbourhood, we had, for the first time in our history, a seat at the top table, through the G20.

The management of global economic power had been entrusted to the G8 (America, Britain, Canada, France, Germany, Italy, Japan and Russia), all industrial states in the northern hemisphere. The G20 brought to the table states from the developing world and the southern hemisphere (Argentina, Australia, China, Brazil, India, Indonesia, Mexico, Saudi Arabia, South Africa, South Korea and Turkey). It was politically and economically diverse and covered the world's major religions. It had both scope and legitimacy, representing 60 percent of the world's population and 80 percent of global GDP, while its membership was small enough to focus on practical outcomes.

Our strong vote in 2012 for a two-year seat on the United Nations Security Council showed a potential for an honest broker role in global diplomacy. We were no longer the fox terrier of British authority, chasing the imperial tail all over the world, nor the cheerleader of American values and military power. We were seen rather as a multi-cultural society, peace-keeper rather than warrior, supporter of international law and human rights, stalwart of nuclear weapons disarmament, defender of everyone's right, especially women and girls, to health and education, active on climate change and racial discrimination.

A withheld self that D.H. Lawrence could not have foreseen, even imagined, was peeping out at the world.

*

I nodded in sympathy at Bob Carr's engagement with the world, thrust into the role of foreign minister in the dying days of the Gillard-Rudd governments, providing in the following a glimpse of basic Australian values.

> On one occasion my advisers and I were being bustled through the VIP section of Singapore Airport and I saw two blue-collar staff – may have been cleaners, may have worked with ground transport – bundle themselves out of the way of this VIP party. For a split second I saw the dark eyes of one of the staffers – an Indian, maybe a migrant worker from the subcontinent – flash with trepidation and deference. I wished there had been a way to get a message to him. It would read: no one in this little delegation being escorted to their first class seats deserves your deference. The Australian Foreign Minister in his navy-blue tailored suit and his Hermes tie – he grew up in a fibro house on a sandhill where bare feet wore out old lino and fried eggs on fried bread would pass as Saturday night dinner. The Minister for Foreign Affairs of the Commonwealth of Australia is like all his ilk: making it up as he goes along, improvising and thinking out loud and hoping it all hangs together.

But what kind of foreign and defence policies might we expect from an egalitarian society, with its hints of inclusion and community, so different from British imperialism and American exceptionalism and, indeed, the dominant realist tradition in international relations.

When Kofi Annan announced the doctrine of "two sovereignties" he was thinking of the clash of human rights with the principle of state sovereignty, which had been the core of realist statecraft for centuries. States were now required to be servants of their people, he said, not the reverse. Whether or not consciously, he was suggesting a different state morality from that which had traditionally proclaimed survival (by hook or by crook in the vernacular) as the state's first duty. As the state is run by human beings who do not, at least publicly, admit to amorality in dealings with their fellow citizens, there is inherent in the management of defence and foreign policy a subtle moment of some intensity.

Australians are both beneficiaries and victims of an uneventful history. Australians clutch at straws like Gallipoli and the Eureka Stockade but we avoided revolution and wars of national liberation. The mundane fact is we got nationhood by a stroke of the pen.

The challenge today is whether this peaceful and privileged origin can be the launch pad of a mission of 21st century statecraft, using the unique quality of our region to establish a model for global peace and, in Australia, harmony between domestic and foreign policies. Our region is increasingly important economically and politically, but its most tantalising promise is that, unlike other regions of the world, it does not have a dominant culture. Unlike Europe (Christian except for Turkey), or the American hemisphere (Christian except, perhaps, for Cuba), or the Middle East (Muslim except for Israel), or Africa (Christian south and Muslim north), there is no common religion. Islam, Christianity, Hinduism and Buddhism are all present, as well as Shintoism, Confucianism and Communism, with capitalism, the engine of globalism, and democracy, the electoral system most sensitive to human rights.

Whether the region is called Asia or Asia-Pacific or Indo-Pacific, it is a fusion of values and customs. It is also physically spacious, its components separated by stretches of sea, with many small island states with their own local customs. It contains Japan, China and ten South-east Asian states, including Malaysia, the Philippines, Vietnam and Indonesia, as well as (in another definition) the United States, Canada and Chile and (in another) India and Russia. Because of diversity and diffusion, uniformity and identity of interest do not occur naturally. There is no equivalent of the North Atlantic Treaty Organisation (NATO). The region's essence is networks, not institutions, and the energy of these networks comes from small and middle-size countries as well as big and powerful states. There are unresolved issues of history and disputed territory, but also a pragmatic spirit of accommodation and compromise in the pursuit of better living conditions rather than protecting or projecting values or interests. This suits Australia. We have shown, in a short span as a nation state, an unusual sympathy with the practicalities of ordinary life.

The challenge is not just to plug ourselves into the current Asian ascendancy for obvious material benefits, although we should do that, but to take the next step and use the opportunity of our region to establish a new model of global power. Our geo-political identity, long considered to be our nemesis, has become an asset. We are sited in a region that is increasingly powerful but not culturally defined. This also suits Australia. Once the odd man out, now the odd man in, we are uniquely placed to be an agent of peaceful change in our region.

Should we not get our own house in order before we start bothering others? Australia is unevenly developed. It has a population of only 24 million, occupying territory about the size of Brazil, which has a population of 180 million, or greater than India, which has over a billion people. The population is clustered in the eastern states and is highly urbanised, copying the model of developed, industrialised societies, and is as far as possible from the people of our neighbourhood, with the exception of New Zealand. The empty spaces between our cities and our neighbours were once seen as a form of defence. They now glare at us as a case of lop-sided development. Western Australia is physically the size of Queensland, New South Wales and Victoria combined. The Northern Territory, with Darwin offering itself as the gateway to south-east Asia, is not yet a State. The convicts and soldiers, who were the modern nation's first settlers, treated the local inhabitants, who had been here for 40,000 years, perhaps longer, with a mix of neglect and contempt, for which an apology has only recently been given. And we have a constitution that says we are governed by a vice-regal system, whose head lives in London, and which does not even mention the prime minister and cabinet.

In short, Australia as a nation-state is immature. But time and place have combined to present us with an opportunity for a singular role, that if successful could provide us with the energy, enthusiasm and direction for our own nation-building.

The world we face is unsettling and fractious, but not yet dangerous. Radical Islam is disruptive but it has no powerful state as its ally. Terrorism, while disturbing, is not a threat to the Australian state. It is another element, however, in the climate of uncertainty and fear that people and governments all over the world are facing and which the media feeds on – extreme weather, nervous investors and job seekers, unregulated refugee flows, drug-addicted social behaviour, sexual abuse of children, domestic violence and political rivalry without civility, not to mention traffic accidents and murders. Governments know how to impose discipline and cohesion in time of war but they are less confident in establishing an orderly peace.

The challenge for Australia is to take a conscious decision, through the political process, to become active in our region, working with other states to establish attitudes and patterns of behaviour that aim to avoid serious conflict. If our region can be peaceful and productive the world will likely be peaceful and productive. How this is done will depend on circumstances and opportunities. If the prospect arises of a concert of powers, like that which gave Europe a relatively peaceful hundred years from 1815, we should do what we can to encourage it, but it is more likely that an informal consensus will develop from a series of discrete agreements. For example, as an interested party without territorial claims we are in a strong position to take a diplomatic initiative on managing access to the South China Sea.

The objective would not be a blueprint for a legal association, like the European Union, but a loose concept of "community" or "shared enterprise". This is the suggestion of Henry Kissinger, from an American perspective, in his book *On China*, in which he discusses confidence-building measures and shared development in a Pacific community similar to the Atlantic community between Europe and the United States, as a way of avoiding conflict between China and the United States. "It would enable other major countries such as Japan, Indonesia, Vietnam, India and Australia to participate in the construction of a system perceived as joint rather than polarised between Chinese and American blocs". Other prominent Americans, in addition to Barack Obama, are beginning to accept that the 21st century will not be an American century in the way the 20th century was. In a speech by Bill Clinton at Yale University in 2003, the former president suggested that the US should be looking to new "rules and partnerships and habits of behaviour that we would like to live in" when the US was no longer the world's primary military and economic power.

For the first time in history a global society is possible, but the rules of engagement are still being worked out. The authority of the state, which has been at the centre of international politics for centuries, is being tested. Global tendencies are strong in trade and investment, communications, sport, education, law and non-government organisations and institutions. On the other hand are signs of withdrawal, a turning inward to local identity, ethnicity, religion, culture and history. In the absence of effective global force projection by the UN, where the Security Council is restricted by the veto power given to five of its members – America, Britain, China, France and Russia, because they won the Second World War – there has been an increase in low-level violence. Most conflict is not between states but within them. Increasingly the victims of conflict are civilian, not military.

A first step in civilising the state will be to reduce its paranoia. Its belief in the existence of enemies is well-founded because the international system in which it operates is still based on the power, ultimately the military power, it claims for itself and is wielded by other sovereign states, who also believe their integrity and their interests are threatened. It engenders suspicion of foreigners in order to justify its own values.

Internationalising the state, by encouraging open collaboration with other states, rather than privatising it, would reduce its paranoia. The state has been privatised enough recently and in many countries, especially those in early stages of industrial development, the state is the only national agent able to undertake the foundation work. This was the case in early Australia, where the national infrastructure of transport, power and water, post and telegraph was pioneered by the state.

The nation-state's flaws are well known. It is harsh and acquisitive, paranoid and defensive. But the alternatives are not appealing. From time to time, we yearn hopelessly for global government to quell the clamour of nationalism and religion but, in reality, global government would be a bureaucratic nightmare. There are some two hundred states in today's world, responsible for seven billion people at every conceivable stage of development. A borderless world, sometimes presented as a desirable future, would likely be run by criminal syndicates and big corporations.

The state has shown itself to be capable of inspiring loyalty and of organising efficiently people with a wide range of social and economic aspirations and moral convictions. It has proved to be durable, withstanding utopian and sectarian assaults from within and without. It has shown that it can create conditions for social and economic wealth and well being, establish law and order and at the same time protect human rights. As a laboratory of democracy, the state can also be a vital ingredient of restless and evolving contemporary life. It is the instigator of civic values, which elevate public service above the battleground of the market place and provide different interests and communities within the nation with a common standard. In the current clamour and contention of religious and ethnic rivalry, celebrity notoriety, extravagant wealth and leisure, the maintenance of civic virtue is an important contribution the state can make to the quality of life in the 21st century.

Shortly before he died, I had a conversation with Malcolm Fraser about his position that, if Australia wished to have a useful role as a middle power in our region, we would need to scrap the military alliance with the United States. He had launched my book *Fatal Attraction* in 2004 and we occasionally exchanged views on the state of the world. We agreed on many policy options, but not on my insistence that Australia did not have to reject the alliance in order to take independent initiatives in our region.

I presented as evidence the range of new policies pursued by Gareth Evans during the Hawke-Keating governments (and also, in the case of APEC, by Hawke himself) without consulting Washington. We had runs on the board as a middle power and a professional preference, established over years of different governments, for a rules-based rather than a power-based international order. Fraser shook his head in his customary lofty manner, despatching me to the world of dreams. "Gareth was lucky. The Cold War had ended in victory and Washington was basking in the collapse of the Soviet Union. Now, China is threatening to take over from the US as No.1 global economic power. You wouldn't get away with it now."

His point warrants consideration. The United States has a lot to learn from the rest of the world, including an understanding of the rise and fall of great powers. Its rise as a great power was based on its prosperity, which was in turn based on its workers being highly paid – so that, as Henry Ford famously explained, they could afford to buy the cars they were making. The rise of industrial Asia, especially but not only China, threatens the potency of the American business model. Another staple in American empire-building was the Monroe Doctrine, which in 1823 warned off great powers from America's patch, the Western Hemisphere. China has no such doctrine but "overseas Chinese" have long been an irritant to local nationalism in South-east Asia and China is building a proprietary presence in the disputed South China Sea.

The US developed from a country that wanted to stand apart in order to hold its own values to one that wants its values to be accepted by the rest of the world and, having become powerful, is tempted to impose those values. It is rare for armed forces to be stationed in another country, but the US has its forces in about sixty countries and if "deployment" and "prepositioning" is taken into account, the number is greater. Its air force and navy patrol the globe and it has the most advanced satellite technology for gathering intelligence. Moreover, it has more nuclear weapons than anyone else and is the only state to have used them.

A combination of military power, commercial primacy and religious conviction makes American political leadership impatient with the slow processes of multilateral diplomacy. The list of abstinence or resistance by the US on global issues is lengthy. In these circumstances, the most valuable service Australia can provide as a friend of the United States is to persuade it to accept a non-dominant leadership role in our region, urging it to use its currently strong position to help build a security regime, so that when it is no longer as powerful as it is now, its people and territory will still prosper and be safe.

I suspect that my differences with Malcolm Fraser were emotional as much as strategic. He had a low opinion of the Australian public, which he believed was trapped in a culture of entitlement and contentment, defying his admonition that "life was not meant to be easy." I believed that Australia, by the fortune of both history and geography, was unique, and its people, neither better nor worse than any other, had no choice except to respond to the existential challenge of where they lived. Responding to the contemporary opportunity would bring out the best in us.

It will not be easy (vale Malcolm). Political leaders will need to develop skills that enable them to keep the support of their own people while at the same time collaborating openly with other people and other states. The state has shown itself able to act as go-between its people and international agencies, organisations and institutions, but the process is complex. The individual, the state and global governance work together, as they do already in trade, investment and in sport, for example, as individual athletes and as members of national teams, accepting international rules laid down by a variety of appointed, elected and co-opted bodies.

Weaning the state from the military, and the military from the state, will be difficult, even in democracies where political supremacy has been established. The state is vulnerable to the armed forces. At its crudest, this is because they are armed. Where civil society is weak, the state is potentially captive to disgruntled military elements. When anarchy rules outside, the armed forces are seen as guardians of the state's integrity and, in a literal sense, protectors of the people. While the soldier-state monkey grip is losing its hold, old emotions persist. International policing does not have heroic symbolism, patriotic resonance or sacrificial mysticism. It also lacks the allowances, psychological and emotional, that are made for men and women who have been trained to kill. Peace-making with diplomacy and peace-keeping with armed forces are, in warrior terms, for wimps. Soldiers need to be crude and violent, it is argued, to do their job properly …

Most people are not crude and violent, but don't face the likelihood of having to confront an enemy whose only quality worth considering at a given moment is his determination to kill you.

A glance through the political leadership of the 20th century shows how the state has been hostage to military conflict. The dreaded charge of appeasement hovers over Neville Chamberlain and the images of wartime leadership linger: courage and ruthlessness (Churchill and Stalin), freedom (de Gaulle), supremacy (Hitler) anxiety (Curtin), passion and vision (Mao), bravery (Willy Brandt, when mayor of Berlin), disillusionment (Nehru, after the border war with China), grace under pressure (a reflective John F Kennedy in the Oval Office during the Cuban missile crisis), catch the public's imagination. They are powerful images, not to be underestimated.

Even the most liberal and law-abiding states cling to the protection of secrecy, in particular the secret universe of the intelligence agencies. Governments treat it delicately because they know it can be turned against them. Also, the state, like any big institution or organisation, has to protect itself against disclosure of information provided to it in confidence. The blanket response of neither confirming nor denying the existence of secret activities is the state's classic response, but, of course, it does not answer the questions raised. It may be unrealistic to expect states to stop spying on each other, when the system expects each to defend itself, but it is one thing to be prudent and well-informed, another to be propelled by alarming intelligence into an arms race and strategic decisions that lead to war. For every piece of intelligence that reveals a lack of trust or a propensity to aggression, there will be evidence that the interests of states can be served by measures that are cooperative and consultative.

There are some signs of Australia's willingness to embrace change.

The death penalty has not been used in Australia since 1967, putting us with the majority of states. On race and culture, we inherited Britain's insular attitude to foreigners. It served the sceptred isle and ruler of the seas well enough but did not transplant to an ancient continent on the other side of the world. "White Australia" was an affront not only to the original inhabitants but to all our neighbours. When the United States replaced the United Kingdom as the guarantor of our security, we adapted White Australia to a populate-or-perish program of assisted immigration from Europe. But the reality of the racial diversity of our region eventually had to be acknowledged. White Australia and Melting Pot Australia were dropped by the 1970s in a politically bipartisan acceptance of Multicultural Australia.

In 2002 the International Criminal Court received bipartisan political support in Australia, despite powerful opposition from the United States. Australia's foreign ministers then (Alexander Downer) and now (Julie Bishop) both supported the new court, against criticism in their party, and Bishop wrote the foreword to the final report of Parliament's treaties committee. She wrote: "The 20th century will be remembered for its unprecedented social and economic progress and astounding advances in science and technology. It was also a century marred by armed conflicts so unprecedented in their scale and intensity that it may well be remembered as the most violent and bloody century in recorded history. At the beginning of the 21st century, the international community is prepared to take a significant step forward in pursuit of international peace and security." This could have been written by Gareth Evans and its sentiments reflect a consensus among Australian foreign policy professionals that the nation's interests are best served by a global system based on rules rather than power.

Our martial history, which once seemed to disqualify us for any other role than spear carrier to the chief, has helped us to develop global attitudes and aptitudes. It seemed dishonest, even immoral, to build our security on a strategy of fighting wars in other people's territory rather than meeting the first responsibility of nationhood, which was to defend yourself. The danger of such a strategy was that it invited provocative, pre-emptive action. Some of Australia's neighbours thought so and were suspicious. But the experience has produced adaptable military skills, associated with a diplomatic style that has been as much concerned with global issues of war and peace as with Australia's national interests. We have been captive to the conflict model of international life like everyone else, but we have retained, even in our most military moments, a sense of the futility of war that nations more engaged in their survival have not had the freedom to do. Our most celebrated engagement, Gallipoli, was a military failure and, if my father's stories are believable, a source of more anti-British sentiment and affection for the enemy than a military instructor would like.

We have avoided the impossible dream of trying to be invulnerable. We toyed with the nuclear option but discarded it. We looked to self reliance after Vietnam but kept in mind also the need to contribute to regional and international security. On the west flank of the Shrine war memorial in Melbourne is a garden dedicated to those who have served in recent actions many Australians might have difficulty identifying: Cambodia 1991–93; Somalia 1991; Rwanda 1994–96; Namibia 1989–90; Iraq 2003–; Afghanistan 2001–; Balkans 1992–97; Kuwait 1991; East Timor 1999–2003. Some of these were more like police actions, lacking the drama of old-style heroic war. Australians who served as UN peace-keepers are now included in the annual Anzac Day march.

As a young state, we are more interested in the future than the past. We are modern in the sense that we seek fulfilment in social and economic progress rather than in ideology or destiny. Our aspirations are secular and humanist; we are wary of utopian solutions. We are competent and increasingly skilful. In science, the arts and sport we have made a mark in the world. Our outlook is hopeful, imaginative rather than dogmatic. We are internationally respected for what we have achieved in a short time. We have runs on the board to show there can be cooperation between the state and civil society in establishing civilised rules of behaviour. With a mixture of good luck and good management, we have produced a politically stable, economically healthy and socially open society.

Above all, we know that we can never be a great power. And we have learned from bitter experience to avoid heartfelt rhetoric of our minor status, like Harold Holt's "All the way with LBJ" and John Howard's declaration that we were "deputy sheriff" to the Americans in our region. That is why the role of middle power is so suitable for Australia. By their nature, middle powers lack the capacity to get their own way in the world, so they have an interest in a rules-based system which they have a say in establishing. Their manner is cooperative rather than assertive. They have "an ability to see a way through impasses and to lead, if not by force of authority, then at least by force of ideas," as we say in *Australia's Foreign Relations*. In other words, middle powers have to be imaginative, which great powers are reluctant to be. To do so would suggest that they do not value enough their prime possession, which is power. Middle powers, on the other hand, especially when, as in most cases, they have no hope of becoming great powers, rely on the appeal of ideas in statecraft. Ideas are not enough; the resources and the energy to implement them in a practical way are also needed. An active middle power needs a competent diplomatic service, as well as discretionary funds. But, as the old ideas of statecraft fail to work in the contemporary world, imagination is an essential starting point.

The core of an imaginative outlook is a belief that a peaceful world is desirable and possible and that war is not only economically costly and humanly brutal, but an uncivilised way of settling differences. After the most violent and bloody century in recorded history, we may be in the mood to reconsider Immanuel Kant's famous "hesitation" – that if the people are given the authority to decide whether or not to go to war, they will "think long before they will begin such an evil game". His reasoning was simple. Unlike the rulers of his time, whose lives were relatively undisturbed by war, the people suffered many deprivations: having to fight, having to repair painfully the devastation left behind by war and, to top it all, having to carry the burden of debts which can never be paid off because of the approach of new wars.

The great task of 21st century diplomacy is to create the conditions where the necessary use of force to establish order is exercised internationally with the same consensus that backs the use of force domestically in law-abiding countries. It's a tall order and a long haul, requiring stamina as well as imagination, but it's an alternative to war. The sovereign state in international politics, like the individual in domestic society, has to learn how to live with others. It would be a game-changer if this happened, changing not only relations between states, but the nature of history and even of the human race.

*

While writing this book, the political airwaves were blue with anger and abuse, raising questions about the calibre of Australia's political culture. On the surface, Australia is a peaceful and stable society, lacking the kind of religious, ideological and social violence that marks the history of other countries. Underneath, there is a state of psychological uncertainty about the value of belief and the validity of action.

The challenge of possessing and developing a large island continent in the southern hemisphere, far away from the power centres of the world and the heroes and legends of history, made us a sceptical, practical people. We did not confront the British and had little inclination for civil war, partly because of a pervasive stoicism, even fatalism, about the prospect of action in a continent as vast and dispersed as Australia, but also a fear that conflict would endanger the security of an already vulnerable country. Unresolved differences simmer on the political surface as dislike and distrust, below boiling point but creating tension and anxiety, with a streak of sympathy for the rebel, fear as well as dislike of authority, a gambler's temperament, a bourgeois desire for stability and comfort, a sense of entitlement and respect for honest labour, each at times convinced that its particular kind of Australia is threatened by the others. Without a long, deep-rooted culture of our own, we are inclined to grasp at best practice and new thinking from elsewhere. Add the so-called social media and an anxious conventional media and you had a political brew that made Lippmann's advice against "straw men" in argument sound like a lament from the Age of Enlightenment.

A new political paradigm from the 2010 elections was created by Labor's alliance with two rural independents and the Australian Greens. It could have produced a national perspective, sensitive to the needs of the whole continent, not just the populous suburbs in the big cities. It would be a progressive alliance, balancing the coalition of Liberals and Nationals, which also sought to combine the interests of rural and urban constituencies. What happened, however, was that the temptation of a quick result on the floor of the House of Representatives tempted the conservative Opposition into a campaign of provocative and personal politicking, which reduced public debate to its lowest level in living memory.

Labor in office tossed and turned like a sleepless dreamer, between two leadership candidates, Kevin Rudd and Julia Gillard. The two sides of Australian politics, unable to reach agreement on how to deal with big issues, like climate change and a global financial crisis, instead combined to create a local crisis of their own, turning the magnet of Australia to refugees fleeing oppression and disruption into a threat to national security. Faced with a revival of the "war on terror", in response to the campaign by the Islamic State of Iraq and Levant (ISIL) to establish itself as a caliphate in succession to the 7th century Muslim prophet Muhammad, Australian political leaders shared a sense of panicky uncertainty, struggling to find a balance between social and economic priorities and combating terrorism. "Stopping the Boats" became a three-word magician's trick, ignoring the complex reality of distressed and oppressed people on the move.

When the Coalition won a majority in the House of Representatives at elections in September 2013, installing Tony Abbott as Prime Minister, Australian politics slipped into low gear, with inquiries and exposure of cabinet documents intended to embarrass political opponents, a pugnacious style abroad and restoration of the titles Knight and Dame. One could only wonder at just how thin was the veneer of Australia's political culture when the outgoing Labor-appointed Governor-General, Quentin Bryce, who only shortly before had declared herself to be a republican, became the first woman to accept the revived title. Then, after only two years of Abbott, the Liberal Party brought back its earlier leader, Malcolm Turnbull.

Australia had had five changes of prime minister in five years. Indeed, at one stage there were eight former prime ministers on the loose – Whitlam, Fraser, Hawke, Keating, Howard, Rudd, Gillard and Abbott. We had for the first time as prime minister a Mandarin-speaker, a woman, a monarchist who trained as a Catholic priest and, currently, representing the conservative side of politics, a republican who was not sceptical about climate change and was in favour of same-sex marriage. His lieutenants in the war-making portfolios of defence and foreign affairs were both (each for the first time) women. In addition, the Senate, always inviting to small parties because of proportional representation, now had to accommodate non-party individuals, who, although able to attract only small numbers of primary votes, were elected by trading hidden preferences.

Something was happening in the land of coal, ferns and mosses, but no-one seemed sure what it was. A group of worthy citizens bearing the banner Accountability Round Table, under the chairmanship of former Supreme Court judge Tim Smith, met regularly at the former rabbi's residence in South Yarra, where I still lived, to discuss issues of public accountability, trust and corruption. At each meeting the agenda grew longer.

When the Turnbull government, with the support of the Greens, reduced the Senate to something like normality and called a double dissolution election for 2 July 2016, the polls were showing the two major parties evenly balanced. At the start of a long election campaign, there was confusion about how it would be conducted. Not just the size and complexity of ballot papers and the mysterious destination of preference votes, but the relationship between politicians and their constituents, sometimes called the people.

The style of political discourse used to be debate or discussion, implying a degree of knowledge and partiality by participants that was or was not capable of resolution. It was also the style of serious media commentary. The new style of political discourse was what was called "conversation". By chance, I have been long familiar with the new style, having first encountered it in Chile in the 1970s, when Claudio Veliz used it as the organising principle of a conference on the Pacific. He later brought it with him to Australia as an academic and it continues under the title The Melbourne Conversazioni, of which I am a committee member.

The ideal conversation is explained by the English philosopher Michael Oakeshott. "A conversation ... has no predetermined course, we do not ask what it is 'for', and we do not judge its excellence by its conclusions; it has no conclusion, but is always put by for another day. Its integration is not superimposed but springs from the quality of the voices which speak, and its value lies in the relics it leaves behind in the minds of those who participate ..."

This doesn't sound like an Australian, or any other, election. In the rough and tumble of politics, it sounds more like a device of political leaders who are not sure what policies to adopt and are playing safe by testing the waters. In today's political world, with blogs and conglomerate websites, having a conversation is like shouting, egged on by friends, at an excessively large and rowdy party.

In the 2016 defence white paper, Australia plans to spend $450 billion on defence in the next decade. It is a very large amount, lifting the defence budget from $32 billion this year to $59 billion in 2025–26. In his pre-budget announcement of defence expenditure of $50 billion on submarines, the Prime Minister spoke with excitement of jobs and growth that would flow from it, apparently lost in admiration of the military-industrial complex that Dwight Eisenhower, an army general, had warned us about in 1961, in his farewell speech as president of the United States. Today analysts call it the "deep state", noting that the military is a major human and industrial component of state power. And, of course, when you spend generously on weapons of war, there is a predisposition to demonstrate how useful they are.

For advocates of resilient defence like myself the burst of defence spending at a time of supposed budget stringency was unnerving. Are we preparing for conflict? Have we, in the excitement of being alive at this moment, forgotten that we have been through this before. The industrial revolution was as life-changing as anything we are now experiencing. And it led to the 20th century, with two world wars and a cold war that lasted for half a century. We are barely into a new century but seem to have lost sight of the peace dividend that was supposed to have accompanied the end of the Cold War.

Standing back from current events, I sought to see Australia and its region in a context of imagined reality, with three novels on the theme "Love in the Asian Century", published as e-books.

The central characters in *A Young Woman from China* (2014) are an Australian professor, negotiating middle age as a bachelor, and a Chinese girl student, negotiating the hazards of freedom in Australia. A tender, thoughtful, unfulfilled relationship is set against a background of China's rising power and Australia's struggle to find a response, while remaining an ally of the United States, all played out in and around a class of international and local students in a Melbourne university.

In *The Last Kiss* (2014), a dramatic meeting at night in a garden in New Delhi is the beginning of a tragic affair between an Australian archaeologist, Annie, and an Indian poet, Gopala. Love poems of a 14th century Indian poet – Vidyapati – are used as a leitmotiv. Eventually, Annie says the three words that lovers down the ages have said to each other. It is too late, but Gopala hears the words and acknowledges them. A moment in life becomes eternal; because she said "I love you", death has lost its sting. Annie returns to Australia, determined that her experience in India will change her life.

In *Crossing the Arafura Sea* (2015), he is an Australian businessman with a secret hope that Australia will count for something important in its region and the world, she is the daughter of an Indonesian mystic whose secret hope is that she will become the country's president. She wants marriage and children. He believes that free love, like free markets, will find its own way. As a compromise, they marry in a secular ceremony in Prague and become crusaders for a liberal, democratic new world order. But Indonesian and Australian politics – and the Goddess of the Arafura Sea – conspire against them.

The three novels are hopeful in tone and neighbourly in disposition, but, in recognition of reality, none has a happy ending. The rock is still rolling.

INDEX

INDEX